I lay back down and cringed as the tender flesh of my back touched the sweat-dampened sheet. I was relieved to know that I hadn't missed Mom and Dad. I still had no idea what I would say to my exhausted parents.

God, please give me something to say to them. Please . . . something . . . Before I had time to listen for an answer, the door slowly opened. Two pale, worried faces peeked in. Cautiously, they advanced toward the bed.

Not even knowing what I would say, I began, "Mom . . . Dad . . ." We paused and stared at each other with anticipation. I blurted, "God is going to use this so I can help other hurting people."

Those few words broke all the tension. Tears rolled down their cheeks and they quickly approached the bed. We all knew it was true . . . How, I didn't really know. God would show me in time . . .

In the Shadow of His Wings

IN THE SHADOW OF HIS WINGS

CAROL SCHULLER

JOVE BOOKS, NEW YORK

This Jove book contains the complete text of the original hardcover edition. It has been completely reset in a typeface designed for easy reading, and was printed from new film.

IN THE SHADOW OF HIS WINGS

A Jove Book / published by arrangement with
Thomas Nelson Publishers

PRINTING HISTORY
Thomas Nelson Publishers edition published 1986
Jove edition / November 1988

Contents

Be merciful to me, O God,
  be merciful to me!
For my soul trusts in You;
And in the shadow of Your wings
  I will make my refuge,
Until these calamities have passed by.

Psalm 57:1

1

The Race Is On

I LOVE YOU, LORD, and I lift my voice to worship You. O my soul, rejoice!

Quietly, with eyes closed, I sat in the newly fallen snow. The truth was, I was nervous. I really wasn't appreciating the stunning sight of the snow-covered mountains. All I could see was the treacherous downhill course that lay before me.

I lacked experience in this race. I was skiing against other women who had national and even international reputations. However, the downhill was still my favorite, and this was one event in the 1984 Handicapped Nationals that I had a chance at winning.

I always enjoy the exhilarating feeling of speed. The snow is a blur as it rushes beneath me. My muscles fight to hold every inch of body in a tightly formed tuck; mustering all my strength to keep from being jolted out of control; holding myself together with trained strength of mind and body; never knowing what tiny flaw in the unpredictable surface may challenge my remaining strength.

The downhill is a battle over the mind. A spirit of fear constantly seeks to overpower strength and skill. Often, the key to a good run is replacing fear with excitement. An indescribably fascinating feeling overtakes you when sheer excitement snatches your breath away.

Still, the fearful questions invaded my mind as I waited on the Colorado mountaintop: *What if I fail? What if I fall and don't even make it to the finish line? What if I disqualify?*

I turned again to my constant source of comfort.

Take joy, my King, in what You hear.
Make me a sweet, sweet sound in Your ear.

My reverie was broken by a shout: "Number 105, line up!"

The long-awaited time had arrived, and my anticipation intensified. My heart quickened its pace rapidly as my mind rushed with multiple thoughts. Determinedly pushing them aside, I stripped away thickly padded warmups to reveal the sleek, red downhill suit. From the blinding white snow beside me, I gathered the remainder of my equipment: helmet, gloves, outriggers, and goggles along with one technically tuned, 215-centimeter downhill ski.

As insecurity began to overwhelm me anew, I slowly pushed my way past the silent competitors toward the restricted starting area. My coach approached to give last-minute instructions along with the usual prerace rubdown.

"You have five more girls ahead of you," he said briefly as the vigorous movement of his strong hands loosened my tight calf muscles. My thighs burned with the heat of friction. He continued the rubdown in silence. The stillness at the top of that mountain was almost haunting. It seemed like hours before his reassuring voice continued.

"Well, do you feel ready?"

I nodded as he bent down to tighten a boot buckle. "Okay, then. Take a deep breath, relax, and have fun." He finished the conversation with an uplifting smile.

The last racer before me made her way out the starting gate, and I took her place with a ready stance. *If I could only see that my God is the only spectator who matters . . . that would cure these sickening nerves.*

"Racer ready?" the official inquired. At my reassuring glance and accompanying nod, he continued, "Ten seconds . . . five, four, three . . ." Triggering the starting wand with the full force of my body, I exchanged nerves for energy and went out for the win.

Adrenalin kicked in as I set up to make the first turn nice and early. Then, passing the first gate I took a second, then a third. I began to pick up the wanted speed. The excitement built to such a degree that I had difficulty keeping the necessary control. The snow became a blur beneath me. It made me dizzy to look at it.

I continued to ski as planned. *How can anyone have more fun on any course other than the downhill?* I just couldn't understand the girls who yearned for the slalom or the giant slalom. But then, they didn't understand my preferring the downhill.

My red Atomic ski ran fast and smooth upon the firmly packed snow. The whiteness almost hypnotized me, as my mind ran fast. I became so caught in the oneness of body and ski that the course seemed to disappear from sight. I had all the freedom in the world, nothing to hold me back—no course, no care, no fear. I was reminded of a feeling somewhere away in my past: the wind passing me swiftly, as if that were what I raced. The helmet compressed about my skull. Trees whizzed by. Concrete instead of snow. Motorcycle replaced ski. Two persons instead of one riding against the air. Evening instead of morning. Summer instead of winter. Loss instead of gain.

2

Never to Be the Same

BLOND STRANDS OF HAIR escaped my helmet as the wind rushed in a whistle past my ears. We flew by the open plains with thrilling speed. The black concrete below us hissed in response to the churning wheels. A chill pierced my body through my lightweight jacket.

The summer evening of July 7, 1978, was cool as my cousin Mark and I traveled along. The large, handsome machine beneath us moved smoothly on the surface. This expensive, fully equipped motorcycle was Uncle Norm's pride and joy. Great trust had been placed in Mark when Uncle Norm offered him the key. Of course, Mark had earned that trust by driving it responsibly many times before.

"Have fun!" Uncle Norm had called, as he and Aunt Margene left for a night out.

We rode quickly and quietly along the deserted

country roads of Iowa. The distant horizon was unfolding a beautiful setting sun. I looked respectfully on the peaceful scene. A soft breeze was gently stirring the unharvested fields.

With joy and satisfaction, I thought back over the last two weeks. I had had a pleasant time visiting seldom-seen relatives. Since Iowa is my parents' native state, nearly all of their siblings still lived there. So, Iowa was a natural place to be while my father and mother, Robert and Arvella Schuller, were in Korea speaking at a friend's church.

My little sister Gretchen and I had stayed with various family members, but we always spent most of our time on the farm where our father was born and raised. His brother and sister-in-law, Uncle Henry and Aunt Alberta, now owned the picturesque farm. They had no children, so Gretchen and I had long ago adopted them as part-time parents. We had many beautiful memories to file away from there.

The last week, however, we had been staying with Aunt Margene and Uncle Norm. They had five children who always insured entertainment beyond our highest expectations. Mark at nineteen was the oldest.

We traveled in silence behind a car on the darkening road. I continued to drink in the God-given scenery as I huddled for warmth in my jacket. Out of the corner of my eye, I noticed oncoming headlights from a lone car ahead. Everything was so perfect. The sun was nearly set on our last night there. We would soon be back at the house, and it would be time to pack. Gretchen and I were to leave bright and early the next day for California. I would be glad to be home and to see Mom and Dad.

Suddenly, the car ahead stopped, and I was jolted back to reality.

We can't stop in time! I screamed to myself.

Mark whipped into the opposite lane.

Oh no! The oncoming car is too close!

The two headlights became one, as Mark yelled, "Hang on!" I couldn't hang on. My body was torn forcibly from the big, black engine and tossed like a leaf in a mighty wind. Car horns blared furiously. Everything went round and round as headlights seemed to penetrate me. I hit the earth, face down.

Suddenly, everything was still, like the quiet after a storm. Time seemed to stop before the scenario moved on. Tears blurred my vision. I fought for strength. Questions began cluttering my mind: What happened? Where am I? Where is Mom? Where is Dad? *I want my Mom and Dad! The plane leaves tomorrow for California. What will Gretchen say? I want to go home.*

The thoughts tripped over each other as if fighting their way to be heard. My body throbbed from swollen head to bruised toe. People were running about me, yelling questions right and left. *They sound so far away!* But I didn't care. A new fear seized me. *Where's Mark? Can anyone see Mark?* "Mark, where are you? Mark! Mark! Mark, where are you?" The attempted yell was merely a hoarse whisper, but he heard me.

"I'm here! I'm over here, Carol!" He sounded scared. "Carol, are you all right?"

Talking was so hard. My mouth felt like it was full of cotton. "I think so. My leg's broken."

"Yeah, mine too." Through the pain in his voice I could tell he was doing his best to reassure me.

"Mark, was anyone else hurt? What happened?"

A woman beside me answered. "Everyone is fine. I was in one of the cars and everyone is fine. Just be still."

My whole face hurt. My lips hurt, my head hurt, my chin hurt. Tears filled my gritty, swollen eyes, but I wouldn't let them escape. They stung my cheeks when they did and only made the pain worse.

We lay in silence, awaiting medical attention, unaware of our bloody surroundings. I knew nothing of my mutilated left leg. I lay on my belly with it hidden from view. *It's only a simple fracture,* I told myself firmly, when in reality the leg was torn apart.

I lay in a daze: ten minutes, twenty minutes, thirty minutes went by, and still there were no sirens. Yet in the midst of the pain and waiting, a calm began to overtake me. All thoughts were silenced. One lone voice filled my head. "Though I walk through the valley of the shadow of death, I will fear no evil: for thou art with me; they rod and thy staff, they comfort me." Through the memorized psalm, strength was whispered in my ear.

I'm not in the shadow of death, I told myself and discharged the thought. *Sure, I'm hurt. My leg's broken and I have a lot of pain in a lot of places, but I'm not dying! What will Mom say when she hears about this? I've ruined my best jacket!*

Finally I heard it. Far in the distance, faintly, came the screaming sound I had expected. The siren drew closer and closer until the noise and the light filled my head. Doors slammed; feet scattered. Voices again filled the night as the crowed stirred around the ambulance attendants. I heard the murmurings: "They're so young . . . It's a shame."

One of the attendants knelt beside me, and with gentleness in his eyes, he began the necessary procedures. A shot of pain bolted through my limbs as he turned me onto the cold, hard stretcher.

"What's your name?" he asked.

"Carol."

"Carol, how old are you?"

"Thirteen."

"Well, we're going to take care of you now, okay?"

"Okay."

The stretcher was hoisted and placed in the back of the ambulance, next to Mark. It hurt so much to talk that we said little. We were helpless to do anything but wait: wait for the arrival at the clinic and wait for the diagnosis of the doctor.

Through the windows I could see that it was completely dark now. Nighttime had set in on the countryside, and a full moon made the cornstalks merely shadows. An occasional cloud skirting by created an eerie, total darkness.

"Excuse me." I tried to draw the ambulance attendant's eye. "Could I have some painkiller?"

"I'm sorry. We can't give you any. We're almost there." His voice was solemn.

Why can't I have anything? I didn't understand. I hurt so bad; I needed something. Again, my quiet, raspy voice—so distant from my body—tried to be heard.

"Why can't I have any?"

"I'm sorry." He paused helplessly. "We can't give you anything without the doctor's permission. It could make you worse. Just try to be quiet; it will hurt less."

I turned my head to the side and waited. Moonlight

filtered through the dirty windows in silent contrast to
the continual shriek of sirens.

Abruptly we pulled into the driveway of the small,
county clinic. As we drew near the emergency
entrance, the hustle and bustle started again. The
doors flew open, and people darted quickly about as if
the drill had been practiced many times before. I was
lifted out first, wheeled through the waiting area and
into the examination room. Doctors and nurses were
everywhere.

Aunt Margene and Uncle Norm came to my side,
their faces distorted with worry.

"Carol, are you all right? We're right here." Aunt
Margene's voice trembled with panic. "Do you know
who we are? It's Aunt Margene and Uncle Norm." As
I was wheeled away I caught a last glimpse of their
horrified expressions.

The examination room was white everywhere. The
smell of disinfectant filled my senses. I was rolled into
a small, clean cubicle with a curtain immediately
drawn around my bed for privacy.

As I wondered where they were going to take
Mark, Aunt Margene's scared voice announced his
arrival. He was wheeled next to me. I heard him
talking and asking about me, but no one would tell
him anything. They were saying that *he* was going to
be just fine.

"Carol, I'm the doctor. How are you feeling?"

"It hurts. Could I have some pain medicine?"

"It's too dangerous. If we give you some, you
could go into a deep shock. Try to stick it out for
another hour, okay?" He smiled kindly and continued. "We're going to have to send you to another
hospital in Sioux City. It's about an hour's drive, and

then you can have some. Your leg is hurt very badly, and this clinic is too small to take proper care of you. Your cousin will also be going with you."

"Can he ride in the same car with me?"

"Well, you'll have to go in an ambluance; but yes, he'll be riding with you."

As the doctor was speaking, my aunt and uncle's pastor came into view. He smiled down at me and gently took hold of my aching hand. How nice to see someone who had treated me so kindly in the past two weeks.

I focused back on the doctor.

"Carol, listen to me now. Are you listening?" He looked me squarely in the eye.

"Yes," I replied.

"Carol, what I have to tell you is terribly important." He paused hesitantly. "Carol, they won't be able to save your leg."

What! What did he say?

"What do you mean?" I asked frantically.

"They'll have to amputate."

The words echoed in my brain as I tried to comprehend. *Amputate! What did he mean? Cut it off?*

"You've got to be kidding!"

His face was somber. "I don't kid about a thing like this."

My insides churned. Disbelief filled my head, and I forgot all pain. Suddenly anger and panic seized me. "Let me see it!" I cried, and fought with all my might to try to see what these strangers wanted to take away from me. But the doctor and nurse held me down.

Why won't you let me see it? I shrieked inwardly as I wrestled. *It's my leg, and I want to see what's been done to it! It can't be that bad! It can't! It's just broken!*

"Let me see it!"

Exhaustion overtook me, and I fell back on the bed. The doctor and nurse stepped back, and the prayers of the loving pastor surrounded me. I remembered the pain. I remembered how tired I was, how weak I was. I gave up the fight.

"I don't care. Just get me to that hospital. I want this pain to leave."

The doctor nodded sympathetically, and I was sorry I had caused him the extra stress.

Once again they wheeled me into the now-familiar ambulance. Side by side, Mark and I were ready to go. The same, caring men attended us, which eased my mind. The vehicle began its race through the night. The darkness outside was bringing sleep to my weary eyes. Maybe I could just forget the pain if I succumbed to the darkness.

A stern voice broke the serenity.

"Carol! Don't go to sleep!" It was the attendant.

"Why?"

"Because you'll go into shock. You must try to stay awake. I know it's hard, but you must."

He continued to speak to me throughout the journey. He talked of various things. Sometimes I'd listen; other times I'd begin to drift. Then the voice would take a higher and louder pitch. He asked me questions of home, questions about my family. Mark joined in and encouraged my fight.

"You can make it, Carol. Come on, stay awake."

I repeated, "I must stay awake. I must stay awake. I must stay awake. I must stay awake." My voice became softer and softer. The lonely night seemed endless, like a light forever away at the end of a long, black tunnel. The once-booming talk around me became distant, their warnings less threatening. Peace enveloped my body. The taunting throbs diminished. A woozy warmth came over me. I was drifting away, high on a cloud. *Sleep, finally sleep.* Tremendous shock imprisoned me, as I gave way to a dangerous peace. Panic filled the ambulance. It would be a race against time.

Finally, the driver spotted the lights of Sioux City. Through the city streets, cars made way for the racing vehicle, but the time seemed endless to the attendant and to Mark. It was a long, long way to the hospital drive.

My sleep was undisturbed as I was prepared for life-changing surgery. Scrubbed and sterilized, my young body entered the operating room, never to be the same again.

3

Cradled by the Shepherd

SATURDAY MORNING THE SUN DAWNED brightly, the long night put behind. I awoke to a clean, white-bandaged stump. I stared at the sheets without emotion. A supernatural peace, along with the mood-altering drugs, allowed me to accept my loss. There was no depression; sleep was all I cared about. As the yellow rays of the sun spilled into the room and across my face, my eyelids closed and sleep again came heavy on me.

Meanwhile, my family was flying in from all parts of the world: my oldest sister, Sheila, and her fiancé, Jim, from California; my sister Jeanne, twenty, from Wheaton College; Mom and Dad from Korea. My brother, Bob, was in London on his way back from leading a tour to the Holy Land, but the news had reached him and he, too, was making the difficult arrangements to return.

Even as the family traveled, they left behind many friends supportive in prayer. Dr. Cho in Seoul, Korea, summoned all the prayer warriors to start interceding for the young life in Sioux City, Iowa. Korean after Korean made their way to Prayer Mountain, a mountain infiltrated with caves designated strictly for prayer. The praises and worship coming from their lips as these faithful hearts sought God were unexpected sounds amidst a people reared in Buddhist surroundings. Yet the trust and love they had for Jesus and the powerful signs they witnessed in their lives overrode any previous ancestral ties. Their faithfulness has been continually blessed by the power of God, as they have upheld brothers and sisters in prayer. Once again they approached the throne of their King, and over and over again could be heard the name "Carol."

Deep in their spirits, my weary parents could sense the prayers of their brothers and sisters in the Korean caves. As they flew to Hawaii, then on to Los Angeles and Sioux City, God continually rained peace on them. Each flight, they saw a sunrise, and each time the words of praise for God from Psalm 57 rang in their hearts: "Let us greet the dawn with song! . . . Your kindness and love are as vast as the heavens. Your faithfulness is higher than the skies" (Psalm 57:8,10 TLB).

Although I could not hear those prayers from Korea, I, too, could feel them. In the core of my soul I was bound with my spiritual family by our mutual source of life, Jesus Christ.

When I awoke some hours later, a familiar face sat

in silence next to me. Jeanne greeted me with pain in her eyes.

"Good morning, Carol." Her voice was soft and gentle. "Mom and Dad are on the plane now. It's a long ride, so they won't be here until early tomorrow morning. How are you feeling?"

"Fine." My voice was barely audible.

"Gretchen came in earlier to see you. She fainted when she saw the blood transfusions. She'll be fine, but she wanted me to explain why she isn't here."

"Okay," I responded. "How long have you been here? . . . Oh, Jeanne, I'm *so* glad you're here."

"I know . . . me, too, Carol." Her voice began to tremble.

"Jeanne, I haven't heard anything about Mark. How is he?"

"He'll be all right, Carol. His leg is broken, so he'll be in the hospital for a few months while it mends, but he'll be fine. He asks about you constantly."

"Can I talk to him?"

"You'd better wait a little while. Give yourself some time to rest."

I knew my sister's strength. *I can rely on hers for a little while,* I thought and was comforted. I wanted so desperately to reach out and touch her, but the slightest movement brought a surge of pain. I lay quietly. Much was felt and shared in our mutual silence. I turned my head, touching my cheek to the soft pillow, and returned to the beauty of sleep.

Morning passed into afternoon. I experienced a new kind of pain that was a haunting from my past. It started at the tips of my missing left toes and shot up to the top of my head. Nausea gripped me as my head spun. They were phantom pains, a dreaded part of being a new amputee. They came every few minutes, despite the massive doses of morphine. My weary mind, not yet adjusted to the missing limb, continued to send messages to the nerve endings, as if the mangled leg was still intact.

Jeanne cringed at each little shriek that escaped my lips. Sleep came and went. The wait for Mom and Dad seemed endless. *What will they say to their little girl who has looked death in the face?* I knew they would be exhausted when they arrived, so I tried desperately to accumulate some inner strength that I could pass on to them. *I must say something first,* I thought to myself. What that something was I didn't know, but I would think of something—I had to!

This race I was running alone with my God. Although prayers from around the world supported me, the fight was ultimately mine, a spiritual battle between darkness and light. The result would be life or death, sanity or insanity.

"Jeanne?" I turned my head toward the woman beside me.

"Hi, Carol, it's Sheila. Jim and I are here now. Jeanne went for a rest."

Oh, I was so glad to see her! My oldest sister, twenty-six, had always been a source of security to me. With each family member who arrived, I felt the growing strength of the fortress around me.

"Is anyone else here, Sheila?"

"No, Mom and Dad should be here soon. But Bob and Linda won't be here for a couple of days."

I nodded and closed my eyes.

Sheila and Jim had arrived in the early morning, and Sheila relieved Jeanne from the heart-rending task of staying by my side. My sisters had to hear and bear it all: the nightmares, the phantom pains, the fear. Whether they bottled up their emotions inside or expressed them later, I never knew. I felt only their strength.

Pain wracked my body and my mind. Nevertheless, I focused intently on the seven hours which separated my parents from me. The wait seemed like forever. Eventually my concentration was broken by physical weakness, and I again drifted into troubled sleep.

Five hours later, I bolted awake in panic. Surely I had missed Mom and Dad's arrival. Who was holding my hand? I opened my eyes. It was Sheila.

"Shhh . . . It's okay, Carol. Mom and Dad aren't here yet, but they should be any minute. You're awake just in time."

I lay back down and cringed as the tender flesh of my back touched the sweat-dampened sheet. I was relieved to know that I hadn't missed Mom and Dad. I still had no idea what I would say to my exhausted parents.

God, please give me something to say to them. Please . . . something . . . Before I had time to listen for an answer, the door slowly opened. Two pale, worried faces peeked in. Cautiously, they advanced toward the bed.

Not even knowing what I would say, I began, "Mom . . . Dad . . ." We paused and stared at each other with anticipation. I blurted. "God is going to use this so I can help other hurting people."

Those few words broke all the tension. Tears rolled down their cheeks and they quickly approached the bed. We all knew it was true. God would use this destructive plan from the enemy for His purpose.

How, I didn't really know. God would show me in time.

My mother did what all mothers do when their children are hurt—she hugged me. But I cried out in pain! Mother jerked back, her apologies stumbling over each other. But the joy of being near Mom and Dad soon overshadowed the uneasiness.

Everything was going to be okay. Mom was sitting by my bed, singing softly. My father was sitting on the other side, rubbing the only place on my body that didn't hurt, the toes on my good right leg. Again, I drifted into deep sleep. This time it was one of peace—Mom and Dad were here.

Once my parents saw that I was sleeping soundly, they were overwhelmed by their own fatigue. A nurse showed Mom to a private room to rest. Dad, however, could not leave my side just yet. Looking over the cold, plastic oxygen mask strapped about my face and the many tubes coming and going everywhere, he thought, *Why did I have to be so far away? Why couldn't I have been there when it happened? Maybe I could've helped in some way.* His thoughts carried no guilt, only sadness and helplessness. How grateful he was that his little girl had a faith in Christ of her own. *At least the strong Shepherd was there to hold her and love her in that lonely, dark ditch.*

His musings were interrupted by a slight tap on the shoulder. It was the nurse.

"Dr. Schuller, there's a young girl on the phone, calling from California. She's asking for Carol. I told her I would get you."

"Do you know who it is?" my father inquired.

"She says her name is Angie and that she's a good friend of Carol's."

"I know who it is. I'd better talk with her. Thank you." My father smiled at the nurse and made his way to the phone.

As he walked to the nurse's station, he recalled the pretty little girl who was frequently at our house. He remembered softball games we had played together, the giggles he had overheard about boyfriends.

I wonder how she heard about the accident? he worried. *I don't know of anyone who would have called her.*

He reached the phone and brought the receiver to his ear.

"Angie? This is Mr. Schuller."

The voice on the other end burst out, "Mr. Schuller! It isn't Carol, is it? Please tell me it's a mistake!" Angie gasped between sobs of fear. "Please, tell me it's not true! It isn't true, it isn't! Is it really true?"

My father's heart broke. "Yes, Angie, I'm sorry to say it is."

"No, I won't believe it! It's not true!"

After speaking with her for several minutes, the gentleness in my father's voice finally calmed Angie's hysteria. Then he asked cautiously, "Angie, tell me. How did you hear about it?"

"Well," she answered between sobs, "I read it in the newspaper. My dad showed it to me, wondering if it was the same Carol. I didn't know what to do! I knew it was her, but I just couldn't believe it!"

"I know, Angie, none of us can. But it is true. All we can do is pray for her. Her life seems to be out of danger at this point, but the doctors don't know about the rest of her leg yet. So keep praying, okay?"

"Oh, Mr. Schuller, I will! Thank you for everything. I don't mean to cut this short, but I'd better go. This is going to be expensive."

"All right, Angie. Bye."

"Good-bye, and please say 'Hi' to Carol for me."

"I will. Good-bye."

My father hung up the receiver. The newspaper! He couldn't even imagine hearing about the accident in such a dreadful way. He wondered how many others would have to hear of it in just such a fashion. Again he returned to my bedside. As he listened to the rhythmical, deep breathing, his head gradually relaxed backward in sleep.

With a jerk he awoke to a scream of pain. "Are you all right, Carol?" he questioned frantically.

With a deep sigh, I answered, "Yes, I am now." I sighed again. "It was just a phantom pain. Sorry I woke you, Dad."

"My goodness, Carol, that's perfectly all right. I shouldn't have been asleep anyhow."

I had been receiving many messages from friends back home and from unknown friends around the world who were upholding me in prayer. It was such a blessing to hear their encouraging words. "Dad, has anybody else called?"

"Yes, Angie," he answered.

"Really?" Excitement and curiosity sparked my weak voice. "What did she say? How did she hear about it all? Do you think I could call her back?"

"Well, I think we should wait until you're a little stronger before we let you start talking on the phone again. You know how you talk, Carol Schuller, and you'll wear yourself out!" We both smiled at the truth of his statement.

I questioned again, "How did she hear about the accident? Did someone call her?"

"No, Carol." Dad hesitated. "She read it in the newspaper."

"The newspaper?" I cried in surprise. "You mean I'm a star? Wow!"

A little twinkle formed in my eyes. Little girls with their big dreams. I had never really desired fame; rather, I dreamed of being a "David Wilkerson" working with street gangs. I had read every one of his books on street life. I had always loved those people and had always seen them as victims. How I longed to see them set free! I dreamed of moving to the Bronx and being David's sidekick. However, for now, I'd settle for a little stardom.

Then, I thought back to Angie. "Poor Angie. It must have been awful to read such a thing in the newspaper."

"Yes," my father agreed.

I breathed another great sigh. "Dad, could you please ask the nurse to give me another pain shot?"

"Yes, I will. It's about that time. I'll be right back."

"Dad," I called as he moved away from my side, "thank you, and I love you!" Deep sincerity filled my heart, as the oft-said words were repeated.

Tears filled his eyes anew. "I love you, too, darling." *Darling—he calls me that often. I like it when he calls me that.* The word was always accompanied by the same, familiar, soft tone.

The door closed behind him gently.

It was my mother who re-entered the room as guard and comforter.

"I ran into your dad down the hall and persuaded him to get some sleep. The hospital has provided a nice room with a shower and a bed for us to use as long as we need it. I feel really refreshed after a shower and a nap. And I asked your nurse to bring you another shot." When the nurse arrived, she checked my vital signs and gave me the welcome shot of relief. My temperature had been rising slowly over the past hours, and a small frown crossed the nurse's brow. Urging me to get some more sleep, she left. Mom and I looked at each other in silence. We both knew that a high temperature probably meant infection. The doctor had warned us of that possibility due to the germs my thigh had picked up in that ditch, but we pushed our speculations aside.

"Mom," I said in a tired voice, "I'm chilly. Could you tuck my covers around me?"

"Sure." She approached my bed in caution, for she had learned the hard way that even the slightest jolt caused me pain. Gently she pulled the covers up and tucked them about my shoulders. Then, tenderly stroking my hair from my forehead, she placed a kiss on my temple. Her concern grew as she felt the heat radiating from my body.

To keep her fears from running rampant, Mom opened up the journal she'd been keeping since this whole unexpected adventure began. Tears spilled onto the blank pages as she wrote:

Nine A.M. It's morning again and all is quiet. In the distance I hear church bells ringing. It's Sunday morning, and I am alone with Carol, except for the nurse who comes every so often. Carol's white-bandaged short limb is hanging in traction in mid-air. The toes of her other foot, with its beautifully manicured nails, are touching the bottom of the

bed. Tubes seem to be coming from all parts of her
body. Above her head, the heart monitor displays a
regular pattern, but everywhere I look there are
black and blue bruises and abrasions. Her body
and face are so swollen. She continues to awaken
and sleep, as I sit beside her. Her temperature has
risen steadily over the past hours. If it doesn't go
down, it could mean infection. They might want to
amputate more of her leg. I'm worried about her.

Mom paused. "God, please don't let that happen!
Don't let my little girl lose any more!" she whispered
fervently. "You saved her life, and I praise You for
that, but please, now save her leg. I want to trust You,
Lord, but it's hard sometimes. Please build up my
trust in You. Help me to remember that she's more
Your child than she is mine."

She remembered the story in Mark 9 of the father of
the demoniac boy. He had cried out loudly to Jesus
concerning his son, "I believe; help my unbelief!"
She knew her request would be gladly fulfilled.

She turned back to her writing until I awoke once
again. A sudden question had formed in my mind with
such desperation for an answer that it had invaded my
sleep. I had to find the answer.

"Mom, I have a question." I paused a few seconds,
then blurted it out. "What did they do with my leg? I
mean the part they cut off."

Taken aback, Mother quickly tried to regain her
composure. Finally she answered, "Well, I signed a
paper yesterday to have it buried."

A strange sense of relief filled me. I was thankful
that it had been buried like the rest of my body would
be some day. Even though it was gone, it had been a

part of me, and I cared what happened to it. I had hoped it wasn't just thrown in the trash, and I was glad to hear it hadn't been. "Good, I sure am glad they didn't give it to me to take home in a jar like an appendix!"

Mom gulped, and her face turned green. Valiantly she tried to be amused with my typical wit. In all the anxiety over the past days, she had forgotten my spunk.

The hours wore on until weariness pressed strongly on Mom again. As if on cue, Dad walked in.

"Arvella, how are you doing?" Dad looked at her worriedly.

"I'm tired. I need some rest again."

"Well," my father replied, "I'm feeling good now. You do need some more rest, but the doctor has asked to speak with us."

"Do you know what he wants?" Mom asked in concern.

"No, Arvella. I'm sorry, I don't. Let's go see."

My father held out his hand, and together they stepped into the hall where the doctor waited patiently.

"Hello, Mrs. Schuller, Mr. Schuller. I'm one of the doctors who operated on Carol. How are you both doing? Is the room we've supplied for you meeting your needs well enough?"

"Oh, yes, it's an answer to prayer!" Mom exclaimed, and my father agreed.

"Good. I know how tired you both must be. We'll try in any way we can to make this a little easier for you. Please let us know if there's anything you need." Sympathy filled the man's voice. "I'm afraid I have some bad news. It looks like Carol has osteomyelitis, a bone infection in her thigh. It's very serious, and untreated, it can be fatal. The chances of its being fatal are slim because we do plan on taking care of it, one way or another. There are a couple of different ways we can deal with it. The method determined will depend on the severity of the infection."

Mother simply sighed and dropped her head on my father's shoulder. His strong arm wrapped tightly around her for support. The doctor went on.

"The result of the infection could very well mean amputation of her thigh. We won't know until tomorrow. We'll have to take her back into surgery and see what's going on inside that leg of hers. I can't say it looks good. The chance of further amputation is very high, but it could save her life. I'll have to have you sign a release in order for us to remove more of her leg. The nurse can help you with the form." He paused and sighed heavily. "Mr. and Mrs. Schuller, I am sorry! We're trying our best to help your daughter, but sometimes we have nothing more to do. We haven't given up on her knee yet, but we might have to soon. In the meantime, we'll keep pumping antibiotics into her and praying."

Regret filled the doctor's eyes as he saw the pain in my parents' faces. They thanked the doctor and proceeded to fill out the necessary papers with assistance from another nurse. Dad reluctantly signed his name and looked at Mother with tears in his eyes.

"I feel as if I lack faith," he said. "I've got to pray this through. I want so badly to believe that the doctor will say after the surgery, 'It wasn't necessary.'"

Mother nodded in agreement. Dad walked her to their room, then kissed her and made his way back to me. Alone, Mom slipped numbly between the cold sheets and cried herself to sleep.

I was awake when Dad returned to my beside, and I greeted him with a weary smile. Though my voice was extremely weak and muffled by the oxygen mask, I insisted on talking. "Dad, look at my traction bar. See those numbers? Forty-eight and eighteen?"

Dad searched around the mass of metal and finally spotted what I was referring to. He nodded. I proceeded. "Forty-eight, I'm going to be great! Eighteen? I'm going to be keen!" A small smile creased my swollen cheeks. "I'm getting as good at those little sayings as you are, Dad. Do you think I could be famous now, too?" If I could have elbowed him in the side, I would've done so, but he caught the joke and smiled reassuringly.

"Yes, I suppose you could, Carol." He chuckled lightly, then turned sober. "Carol, I need to talk with you." I could hear the urgency in his tone, and my lighthearted mood quickly subsided.

"Your mother and I had a talk with your doctor," he continued. "It looks like you could have a serious infection in your leg. There will be more surgery tomorrow, and they may have to take more of your leg."

The dull nausea I was already fighting became acute as I thought of all the vain prayers and hopes I had offered up for keeping my knee. Fear and defeat began to well up inside me as I thought of losing the hard-fought battle. I wanted to keep my knee so badly! But I knew what the result could be if the infection wasn't taken care of.

My father, seeing the first sign of despair in me since the accident, became alarmed. I had been doing so well with my attitude. Silently he pleaded, *Don't give in now, Carol. Please, don't give in! Oh, God,*

*don't let her become bitter or depressed. Protect her
from the fear and the attitudes that will destroy her.
God! Fight for her! She's so tired!*

The positive strength, the surprisingly uplifting
times we had been enjoying were suddenly gone. The
doctor's words had burst our fragile bubble. Wearily, I
slept, and as I did, despair crept silently into the
room. Devastation was all about my father. Gone was
our hope. Slumped in his chair, he watched the nurse
who had come in for the routine check of vital signs.
This was her territory, and she knew it well.

*Likewise, there is another watchman working confi-
dently on call,* thought Dad. *He is the Great Physi-
cian, and His protection is settled heavily upon Carol.*

"As this nurse watches over her territory, so I watch
over mine," Dad seemed to hear Him say. "Carol is
My territory. I fear no invader. I fear no enemy. I walk
boldly about My territory as a mother lion about her
cub."

I know God is watching over her, Dad reminded
himself. *He has kept her alive, and He will carry us
through the intense times that lie ahead.*

After the nurse completed her well-memorized
procedures, she whispered to my father that he had a
phone call down the hall. On the line was his friend
Cory SerVaas, medical doctor and editor of the
Saturday Evening Post.

"Bob, I heard about Carol. I'm very sorry," Cory
began in sympathy. Her next words were underlined
with urgency. "You have to get Carol back to
California! Don't let them take any more of her leg! I
know they're doing the best they can there, but there
are places that have much more advanced equipment.
If we can fly her out within twenty-four hours, we

may be able to save her knee. I've already talked with Carol's doctor, and he gave us the okay. The only thing we need is yours and Arvella's approval and an ambulance jet."

Dad was stunned. The emotions that had been running inside him like a yoyo—hope, despair, hope, despair—suddenly turned upward again.

"So what do you think?" Cory demanded.

"Oh, Cory, that's a lot to answer!" Dad gasped. "I need to talk to Arvella and Carol. How long can I have?"

"I'm afraid we'll have to know within a few hours. I'm sorry, Bob, but many arrangements have to be made, and the longer we wait, the slimmer the chances for success will be."

"But Cory, can Carol even be moved?"

"Yes. It will be painful for her, but she will have a specially equipped jet and a nurse, and the doctor there can give her heavier sedation. Bob, I really think you should do this. Talk to Arvella and Carol, and call me back."

"All right. Thank you very much, Cory! This could be an answer to prayer! Good-bye."

Dad slowly hung up the receiver. Shock mixed with anxiety and excitement covered his face, but there was new hope. He could hope once again! Quickly he headed down the hall, praying all the way.

"Arvella! I have news! I think it's good!" he shouted, bursting in on my sleeping mother. Wide-eyed, Mom listened to Dad's account of the phone call. She was silent as he finished, and then she knelt beside the bed. "Let's pray about it," she said, and together they offered up tears of fear and confusion, wonder, and finally, peace. They knew what had to be done. Now it was time to ask me.

A gentle shake slowly brought me out of a deep sleep. Patiently my parents waited for me to regain full awareness. After a few minutes I asked, "What's the matter?"

"Carol, there's nothing to be afraid about." Mom took hold of my hand and stroked it softly. "There are just some decisions we need to make as soon as possible."

As they relayed the details to me, fresh hope kindled inside of me.

"Well," I replied carefully, "if it's going to save my knee, I want to go. Anyhow, it sure would be nice to be home where my friends could come and visit me." Then I remembered, *It hurts so much when they just touch me here. What will it be like to fly me to California?*

But in my heart, the decision had been made. I wanted to save my knee, and I had a feeling it wouldn't be saved unless I went.

"Let's go home!" I finally said to my parents, and looking into their eyes I was reassured I had made the right decision.

Within hours, the arrangements were made. Mom and the family would fly directly with me to Orange County. As each minute passed, the excitement for home built inside me. But as the day wore on, the unusual activity and the mounting infection took their toll, making me weaker than ever, and I slept almost constantly.

At eleven P.M. I awakened with a start. In my dreams I could feel many people looking at me, and when I opened my eyes, I was surrounded by five strangers all dressed in white. As I recognized my floor nurse, I relaxed slightly. They were here to help prepare me for the upcoming flight, only an hour away.

"Where are Mom and Dad?" I asked childishly. "I don't like all these people around without them here."

The nurse's answer was soothing. "Your parents are packing their things. They'll be back any minute. I'm sorry about all these people. I know it's a little scary, but we need their help. In a few minutes we'll be putting a large splint on your leg to keep it steady, and then we'll put you on a gurney and take you to the ambulance."

"Okay." I trusted her, for she had taken such good care of me here. "Will you ride with me to the plane?"

She nodded as my mother and father appeared, the relief of the decision plain on their faces. Gingerly they each planted a kiss on my swollen cheek.

"All right, Carol. Are you ready to go?" The doctor had entered, too. "It's time to put your splint on."

Fear began to fill me as I saw the two men behind him with the four-foot-long, blue splint. I took a deep breath, stared once more at the dreaded splint, and nodded my approval.

"Mom, will you come hold my hand while they put it on?" The fear could be heard clearly in the quivering of my voice. To think of their touching, let alone moving, my thigh sent chills down my back, but it had to be done. Mom held my limp hand firmly in her.

They set the splint on the bed beside my leg. Then the two men lifted my leg, while the others slipped the splint beneath.

Unbearable pain gripped me, as a flash of heat shot to the top of my leg. Tears welled up in my eyes, and I clenched Mother's hand with all the strength in me. Then the nausea took over.

The job finished, the immense throbbing in my leg diminished slowly to a slight pulse until an uncomfortable tingling was all that remained. I was thankful the nurse had given me an extra-heavy pain shot a half-hour previously as prescribed.

Then, without warning, I was lifted onto the gurney. Again, I burst out with a cry of pain. How much more could I take? Yet, as before, the pain eased and we were ready to go.

The clear sky shone brightly with a fluorescent, full moon as the ambulance sped us to the airport. Tips of cornstalks whizzed by the windows as Jeanne, the nurse, and I endured the hour's drive. The pain that had been intermittent began to throb steadily.

Once we reached the airport, Jeanne would fly straight to the Holy Land for a long-planned study program, and this was her last chance to spend some time with me. I knew she had been looking forward to this trip for a long time, but her expression, as we rode through the night, showed concern and hesitation.

"I'm *glad* I'm going home. Everything will be great!" I burst out. "I hope the family won't be too disappointed if I spend a lot of time with my friends. I haven't seen any of them for a while, and I have a lot to talk to them about."

Jeanne lifted her head and smiled. My excited words seemed to comfort her slightly. Silence again filled the ambulance as we sped out of the city.

The lights of the sleeping airport gave off an eerie welcome to the parade of cars that arrived with our ambulance.

The pain was almost unbearable as they transported me to the silent jet, but nothing could diminish my excitement. Photographs were being taken and hands were waving frantically as if these were the last good-byes ever to be stated.

Jeanne looked softly into my eyes. "Carol, I'll miss you. I'll be home again soon, and I'll bring you something, okay?" Tears were forming in her deep brown eyes. "I love you! I'll be praying for you!"

Many close relatives, including Aunt Margene and Uncle Norm, watched as I disappeared into the plane. What they were thinking was hard to tell, but the dominating emotion I felt was one of peace as I recalled my beloved home. The lights of Sioux City, Iowa, were left behind, blending with the glow of the stars.

Mom sat close beside me, holding my hand. She looked at me with obvious satisfaction in her eyes. "Well, Carol, we're going home and how grateful I am." A smile of relief crossed her face as her weary, still-sparkling eyes caught mine. No response was needed; she spoke for everyone.

Throughout the flight, the pain gradually intensified. A sickening stench escaped from the bandages, and worry settled over all the passengers except me. I drifted in and out of an almost euphoric state. My attention was aroused only when someone walked near my unstable, temporary bed. The terror of being bumped was often uncontrollable.

Each time, just when I thought I could stand no more, I felt my Shepherd gently pick me up and cradle me in His strong arms. He was the only one who could touch me in those times, and how I cherished the moments He did.

4

Sirens in the Night

LIGHTS FROM NEARBY STREETLAMPS became a blur as the ambulance raced through Orange, California. No more cornstalks, no more alfalfa fields, no more farmland. Only buildings, freeways, and an occasional spread of grass in a nearby park could be seen from the ambulance windows. The sirens screamed loudly despite the emptiness of the streets. Dawn was barely visible in the eastern sky as the ambulance pulled into the entrance to Children's Hospital.

I lay close to hysteria with pain and fever by the time I reached the examining room. The stench was so overpowering no testing or probing was needed. My orthopedic surgeon, Dr. William McMasters, spoke first. "Get these bandages off immediately and prep her for surgery. We have to go in and see what's happening."

I was wheeled quickly away from the small gathering of medical experts. No introductions had been made, but a sense of trust filled me. I could feel their care and concern, and I knew they desired to save my knee as much as I did.

Meanwhile, my mother and father received the disappointing news that, in spite of having made the trip, the leg might have to be removed. Once again they experienced the agonizing process of signing release forms.

Dr. McMasters explained. "Mr. and Mrs. Schuller, I wish desperately that I could give you more hope, but creating false wishes is not my style. There is still a small chance, but it's slim. I want you to know that. The doctors in Iowa did a remarkable job of keeping Carol alive. They deserve high admiration for performing their jobs so well."

Mom and Dad nodded, but they knew in their hearts the One who in reality had kept me alive. They owed a deep gratitude to the doctors, but they knew God deserved the praises, not man. Only God could save the remainder of my leg.

The doctor left for surgery, and my parents collapsed on a waiting room couch in exhaustion and frustration. Alone in the darkened room, they held each other and sobbed until their emotions were thoroughly emptied.

One hour, two hours, three hours passed. Mom and Dad had fallen asleep, still holding to each other for security. The light of a new day pierced the darkness of the room and wrapped itself warmly about them. The hospital slowly came to life, but the two were left undisturbed. Nurses changed shifts, and doctors wiped exhaustion from their eyes as they headed home.

A strong ray of sun awakened Mom and Dad as Dr. McMasters entered the waiting room.

"Well, I have some good news to start off your day!" A smile spread over the young, deeply tanned face. "Carol's leg is going to be okay for now. We still have a long, hard fight ahead, but for now, she has her knee."

Praise leaped in the hearts of my parents, as once again they exalted their faithful God. Once again the words of the beloved Psalm filled their hearts: "Let us greet the dawn with a song! Your kindness and love are as vast as the heavens. Your faithfulness is higher than the skies." Nothing could shake God's faithfulness. If I had lost my knee or even my life, God's faithfulness as a Shepherd could never be altered by this world's destruction.

Upstairs in the white, sanitized, post-op room, I slowly came back to reality after the surgery. My mind swam as I became aware of my surroundings. Nurses scurried all around me as they tended the other surgery patients, most of them still unconscious. My eyesight blurred from the anesthesia, I attempted to focus on the white bandage about my stump. The length of my leg had not changed. *I have my knee!* Ecstatic happiness leaped inside me. *I still have my knee! I still have my knee!*

Then as quickly as the joy had come, the dizziness returned. Chills began to grip me, and the impersonal surroundings slowly wrapped fear and loneliness about me. The nurse, realizing I was awake, briskly approached.

"Hello, Carol. How are you feeling?" Her face was fuzzy and I tried to concentrate.

I answered in a slur. "Fine. I'm cold, though. When do I get to see Mom and Dad?"

"Soon. You'll have to wait a few more minutes, so we can make sure you're ready. Would you like another blanket?"

I nodded. She gently wrapped the extra blanket about me, and I dozed off to sleep.

After what seemed like hours, I woke again, still dizzy and drugged, but more in control of my thoughts.

"Carol." It was the nurse. "Are you ready to go back to your room now?"

Relief filled me as I thought of leaving this cold, unpleasant room. Being surrounded by strangers was making me more and more anxious. How I longed to see Mom and Dad!

Quickly they rolled me out, down the hall and through a set of large double doors. Then, finally, the door to my room appeared. Comfort washed over me as I caught sight of Mom and Dad. I was transferred to the bed, painfully, before greetings could be exchanged. Once I was situated and the violent throbbing in my body calmed, I received their tender kisses and careful hugs.

"Carol?" Mom's gentle voice broke the silence. "How do you feel? Are you in a lot of pain?" She seemed worried, despite the recent victory we'd just experienced.

"Yes," I responded hesitantly. I did not wish to deepen her concern, but trying to disguise the weakness in my voice was impossible. She smiled dubiously.

My father undespairingly encouraged, "You kept your knee! Half the battle's over, Carol! We're going to make it! God is so faithful!" His eyes sparkled with a mounting flame of hope.

A smile spread across my feverish face. My eyes closed peacefully as my thirsty heart absorbed his powerful words. To rest in God's faithfulness is to rest in peace. I would learn to do so.

The anesthesia brought more sleep, and Mom and Dad watched me prayerfully. Although my knee had been saved, the wounds in the leg remained open, and the threat of infection hovered in the silent, unknown future. The need for miracles was not over. Night settled outside the hospital room window. I stirred in my sleep often as the nightmares set in again. Mom and Dad exchanged glances, wondering what was taking place in my sleeping imagination. The now-familiar weariness huddled about them and multiplied with every passing minute.

My mother looked drowsily at my father. "Bob, I think you should head home. It's getting late, and you need a good night of sleep. You don't want to be sick for Sunday. You still have to preach." Mother paused a moment, then continued, "I'll stay with Carol, and I can sleep a little if I stretch out between two chairs."

Dad sighed in deep hesitation. Mother continued her attempt at persuasion.

"Besides, Bob, you can't really help Carol as much as I can. You'll have to call the nurse every time Carol needs the bedpan or needs to have her back massaged. I can be of more assistance. You can come and have breakfast with me in the morning and then take over while I go home and get some sleep. I can't give her the bath. Her wound is too sensitive; the nurse will have to do that, so I won't be needed as badly then. Carol can be alone for a few minutes by then, too."

Dad was thinking intently. He had forgotten I wasn't a little girl anymore, but desperately he wanted to be of more help.

"Arvella!" His voice choked with tears. "I feel unneeded—as if I can't do anything."

Mom interrupted before he could speak another word. "Bob, the prayer and support and encouraging words you give Carol and me are vital! You may not be able to help her so much physically now, but her mental health and spiritual health are just as important, if not more so."

Tears fell freely from his eyes. Mother quietly approached him, placed a gentle kiss on his forehead, and said, "Go home, Bob, and be with God. Intercede for us, and get some rest so you can hear God clearly tomorrow when He gives you words to speak to your hurting daughter."

Still Dad sat in reluctance to go, until a slight knock came at the closed door. Mom and Dad pulled away from each other to see who it was. A white-haired man peeked in carefully. The well-known uniform of his black suit could not be mistaken. He stood trim and tall, and the white clerical collar set off his tanned, weathered complexion. As he entered, he glanced at my sleeping form and compassion filled his eyes. He walked toward my parents.

Charm and gentleness filled his voice. "Hello, my name is Father MacNamara. 'Father Mac' for short." His reassuring smile lit the entire room. "I would like to put my blessing upon Carol. Would you mind?"

My parents nodded in approval as they sensed a love being planted in their hearts for this stranger.

As he turned to me, I awoke. Pleasant surprise registered on his face.

"Carol, I'm Father MacNamara—'Father Mac' for short. I wish to leave my blessing with you."

I was unsure of what he was suggesting because of my lack of acquaintance with Catholicism. Yet I felt secure with him, as if a bond of some sort existed between us. I agreed.

Gently, he lifted my pale hand in his tanned one and stroked it softly. I closed my eyes. He spoke briefly but effectively.

"Carol, I bless you now with the peace and comfort of God in your sleep and for your days to come." He again lightly stroked my hand, then replaced it on the bed. He nodded graciously to everyone as he whispered, "Ciao." Then he left. Deep appreciation filled our hearts for this servant of God. Peace indeed lingered on in the room.

Dad interrupted the stillness. "Carol, I am very tired, and I need some sleep. I'm going home now. I need to preach Sunday, and I mustn't get sick. Your mother will be staying with you. Is that all right?" I was hesitant to say good-bye to my father, but I knew he needed to go home.

"No, I don't mind." The disappointment in my voice increased his reluctance.

"I'll come early tomorrow morning, while your mother goes home for a rest," he insisted.

I replied with a satisfied nod, and we all were happy with the decision. My father quietly rose and drew near my bed to place a kiss on my hot cheek.

"Dad?" He paused at the door and looked back. "Will you ask my nurse to bring my pain shot?" He could not quite hear my words, so he returned to the bed, bent down, and put his ear toward my mouth. I repeated the request with a slight increase in strength, and he smiled in satisfaction. He was useful!

Soon, the shot had been administered by one of my new nurses. I fell into a heavy sleep. Mom sank in her chair, sleeping also as exhaustion overtook her.

Silence muffled the room. A clock on the wall opposite my bed ticked softly. The heart monitor and I.V. machine beeped in unison, and the only human sound to be heard was heavy breathing. Suddenly, a scream pierced the air. "No!" Mom and I jolted instantly awake, but then I fell back on the bed in pain and moaned in despair. Mom leaped to my side.

"Carol." Her voice was frantic. "Are you all right? Should I get the nurse?"

I could only whimper painfully, for the sudden movement had left me in a tremor of pain. Finally, I was able to speak. "I had a dream! A car hit us, and I was flying through the air." I cowered in my bed like a wounded puppy.

Gently, carefully, Mom drew me near. Stroking my cheek, she crooned over and over again. "Shhh . . . It's okay now"—just as she had when I was a little girl. "Just start saying the name *Jesus,* Carol. Jesus . . . Jesus . . . Jesus." She gently whispered that precious, powerful name. "Jesus . . . Jesus." Surely a calm settled about me, and stillness began its descent again. Mom kept on murmuring, "That's it. Jesus . . . Jesus."

I began to repeat the name that meant so much to me. "Jesus . . . Jesus." Tears trickled from my bloodshot eyes.

Jesus, Jesus, Jesus
There's just something about that Name
Master, Savior, Jesus
Like the fragrance after the rain.

The words of the familiar song ran softly through my responding heart, and soon I was asleep again.

My mother's watchful eyes guarded over me, as if to keep the terror from returning. She thought of the horror that must have come, and would continue to come, with the memories. She shut her eyes tightly, trying to keep her imagination from consuming her. She, too, whispered the powerful name for her own comfort. As her fear subsided, reluctantly she pulled away from my side. Giving the watch over to God, she repositioned herself in the chair and slept. Throughout the night the nurse crept in to check my vital signs. Other times I woke needing a pain shot. The pain seemed worse at night than during the day, as if the eerie blackness of the room somehow added to the discomfort.

Morning finally came, and the sun shone brightly through my window. When I awoke, sitting content-edly beside me was Dad.

"Good morning, Carol," he said pleasantly. His eyes were renewed with energy, but his voice remained soft. "Did you sleep well last night?"

He took hold of my hand and held it firmly in his. Slowly he drew my small hand to his cheek, held it briefly, kissed it, then reset it on the bed. "Your mother and I have already eaten breakfast, and she's gone home. Are you hungry?"

I shook my head no and continued to lie quietly, concentrating on absorbing the security my father supplied. But despite my lack of hunger, a breakfast tray arrived, delivered cheerily by another new nurse.

"Good morning, Carol," she said kindly. "My name is Beverly. Are you hungry?"

Again, I gave a negative response, but the tray was

placed in front of me anyway. I hadn't eaten since the accident. I was getting glucose from the I.V., but that wouldn't sustain me much longer. Obviously, everyone else was getting worried.

The smell of the bacon and eggs suddenly hit me, and a wave of nausea swept over me. I turned my face away from the tray.

Beverly, sensing the problem, placed the food farther away. "I'll leave it here in case you change your mind." She smiled and proceeded to take my temperature.

She was a young, beautiful woman. Her brown hair curled away from her face, setting off shining, deep-brown eyes.

"Carol, we'll have to give you a bath in a little while. Is there some soap you might want to use from home? Something that smells real pretty?"

Dad was standing at the foot of the bed and answered for me. "I brought some this morning." It was my favorite, a Christmas gift from last year. I loved the soft, slightly flowery scent. In the midst of the smell of disinfectant, it would be a pleasant change.

"That sounds nice."

Setting the tube on the nearby nightstand, Dad smiled and left Beverly and me in private.

I looked forward to the feel of the warm water and being clean again, even if it was to be only a sponge bath in bed. But as soon as Beverly began, I realized the procedure wouldn't be as pleasant as I had hoped. The pain kicked up again as I moved a little here and a little there, and by the end of the washing, my entire body throbbed violently.

Frustration filled me. I did feel refreshed, but when

would I ever again be able to do anything without pain? I turned my face away from Beverly, and a few tears of despair rolled slowly down my cheeks to the white pillow. When would this world of pain be destroyed? When?

5

The Eye of the Storm

HAD I KNOWN how long the pain would continue, had I known that my visit to the hospital would stretch into nearly a year's stay, had I known that nurses and doctors would become an integral part of my life, I would have never believed it. Day after day, week after week, month after month: the monotony would have been unbearable, had it not been for the many people who cared. Here are only a few of the people who brought sunshine into my dreary hospital stay.

DODGERS VS. GIANTS

Baseball season was drawing to an end, and with it, 1978 play-off time. As my strength slowly increased, I began focusing more of my attention on one of the sports I loved—baseball. As usual, rivalry was flaring between the L.A. Dodgers and the San Francisco Giants, and, needless to say, I was a faithful Dodgers fan.

One day I was lying silently in my bed, awaiting the upcoming game on TV to cheer on the Dodgers. The rays of midmorning sun danced around the flowers in my room in what seemed a playful game of their own. My mother sat nearby.

Ring . . . ring. . . . The telephone sounded loudly, interrupting the quietness. Ring . . . ring. . . . Annoyance filled me at the sound.

Mom picked it up quickly to silence the racket.

"Carol," she said enthusiastically, "it's for you. I think you'd better take this one. It's someone very special."

I'd been avoiding most calls, but from Mom's tone, I could tell I should speak with whoever was on the other end. I put aside my disgust at this intrusion on peace and tried to stop the pounding in my head.

"Hello?" Unsuccessfully I tried to bolster my scratchy voice with strength.

"Hello, Carol? This is Tommy and Steve."

Tommy and Steve! A wide smile spread across my face. I almost whooped as I recognized the familiar voices of Tommy Lasorda and Steve Garvey—my two favorites in the sport of baseball. I had met them earlier in the season when Dad and I visited outside the team locker room.

Concern broke through Tommy's gruff New York accent. "We're in Missouri, ready to go play, but we wanted to call you and tell you we were praying for you."

In the joy of talking to him, I forgot my weariness.

After a few minutes, Steve got on the line. "Carol," he started, and then paused, not quite knowing how to continue, "are you feeling okay?" Worry and regret overshadowed his voice.

"Yes," I said, with deeply felt gratitude for the care they were showing.

"I hear you're really hanging in there. Are you going to watch our game today?"

"Oh, yes," I answered confidently. I wanted to talk so bad, but what little strength I had was fading quickly. They both realized it and cut the conversation short.

"We'll play today's game for you if you just keep hanging on," Steve promised.

"Okay!" I responded excitedly and said good-bye.

I couldn't believe it! They had called me from Missouri. My spirits were so high from their show of love.

As I hung up the receiver, Dr. McMasters entered.

Before he could begin his usual questions, I started to boast with a wide smile. "Dr. McMasters, you'll never guess who just called me!" I had heard from the nurses and interns how much a fan Dr. McMasters was of the Giants.

"Who?" he asked absently, looking down at my chart.

"Tommy Lasorda and Steve Garvey. They're going to play today's game for me."

He looked at me quickly in surprise. "Who?" he repeated.

"Tommy Lasorda and Steve Garvey!"

Grinning slyly, he said with fake sarcasm, "Well, it's really too bad that they're going to lose."

"You just wait, Dr. McMasters, you just wait."

Finally, it was time. The game was exciting, and by the ninth inning, the score was almost tied. The Dodgers were ahead by one run.

I lay quietly, barely aware of the soft buzz coming from the television. As much as I tried, I couldn't stay awake for the whole game. The lights of the TV flickered softly on my bed, and energetic screams from the baseball crowds were muffled by the low volume. Mom sat close by, thinking I was asleep.

Suddenly, the announcer's voice rose in excitement. I opened my eyes as he exclaimed, "Steve Garvey has done it again! What a beautiful hit! Right over the board! Another home run!"

Mom looked at me quickly to see if I had heard. My eyes sparkled as I raised my thumb in approval of my favorite baseball player. Mom smiled in return, knowing I had seen Steve's winning run.

I did not see Dr. McMasters again until the following morning. He walked in casually and avoided any mention of the game, but there was no way I would allow that.

"Dr. McMasters," I teased in a singsong tone, "did you watch the game last night?"

"Carol," he answered, "we have not time to discuss baseball. Let's get down to business."

I pursued the subject nonetheless. "Did you see Steve's hit? It sure was a beauty!"

"Well, they weren't playing the Giants, were they?" he challenged boyishly. "You just wait until they're destroyed by my team. You won't be bragging about victories then!"

The jesting began to take place often during his visits and made the hard times a little more enjoyable. Many others around the hospital joined in the fun as well.

When the week of the play-offs arrived, the teams involved were, of course, none other than the Giants and the Dodgers. A competitive atmosphere filled my hospital room and spilled over to nurses, interns, friends, and family.

It was the morning of the second game. On the first game the day before, Dr. McMasters and I had made a bet. If the Giants won, I had to buy him a six-pack of root beer. (I was too young to buy real beer like he wanted, and I refused to ask my father. What would people think if they saw a dignified, well-known pastor buying beer?) If the Dodgers won, my reward would also be root beer.

Now, on the morning after, I was suffering the consequences. My team had lost, much to my dismay, and I didn't know how to make the payoff.

I would have to ask Mom or Dad to bring back a six-pack when they went home for dinner, but my pride was deep. I couldn't just go down without some kind of revenge. Dad pitched in, and we worked together on a plan.

One hour passed, two hours passed, then finally we heard the sound of familiar voices in the hall. Dr. McMasters, along with two other specialists, neared the door, and suddenly we heard a burst of laughter.

They were reading our revenge—a tailormade warning just for the doctor. The sign read:

> PRO-GIANT, ANTI-DODGER STATEMENTS
> ARE KNOWN TO BE DANGEROUS TO PATIENT
> HEREIN. IRRITATION TO FATAL INFECTION
> COULD BE RESULT. PLEASE KEEP ALL SUCH STATEMENTS
> TO YOURSELF.
> SIGNED,
> CONCERNED PARTIES

Dr. McMasters laughed about it for days. As the play-offs continued, the Dodgers were the final victors. My team reigned—at least in the National League.

WITH LOVE FROM EDDIE

Day after day my body weight was dropping. My once slightly plump form was becoming grotesquely skinny. Everyone urged me to eat, but the pain made me too sick to try. My leg was not healing well, and the intravenous feedings could not support me much longer. I knew how vital it was that I start eating, but I couldn't force the food down.

Mom began bringing all kinds of home-cooked goodies, but I could manage only a few bites at a time. My five-foot-seven frame now carried only eighty-five pounds.

Finally, a dear family friend and wonderful cook came to visit one day while Mom and Dad were there. Eddie Balestero, six-foot-two, two hundred pounds plus, and Italian, walked quietly through the door carrying a huge pot. The green isolation robe pulled tightly about his jolly belly, and a cap covered his thick, black hair. All visitors had to wear the isolation garb to guard me against further infection.

As Eddie walked closer, homemade chicken soup spilled over the edges of the kettle onto his robe. I could see the worry in his eyes as he set the pot on a nearby nightstand and bent down to kiss my brow.

"Carol, they tell me you haven't been eating. Why do you give these nice nurses and doctors so much trouble, eh?" He followed the scolding with a smile. "You eat Eddie's soup, do you hear me? I made it, and you've always loved my cooking, so you eat it."

The room brightened with his love. The delicious aroma of the soup filled the room, but my appetite remained unchanged.

I answered as cheerfully as possible. I was so glad he was there. "Hi, Eddie. I sure am glad you came to see me, and thank you for the soup. I'll try my hardest to eat as much as I can."

"I know you will. You're such a good girl." He patted my head.

As our visit was proceeding, Beverly arrived to make another dressing change. This procedure, done four times a day, caused me excruciating pain and nausea.

"Eddie," I asked plaintively, "they're just getting ready for my dressing changes. Will you stay and hold my hand?" My gaze held his. My requests could never be denied by the softhearted man.

"Sure I will. All I have to do is hold your hand?"

"Yes."

Mom, quietly watching from the corner of the room, exchanged glances with Dad. *Poor Eddie*, they both thought. *He'll never make it through this*. They knew how sensitive he was and how this could hurt him, but they kept still.

His large, pudgy hand took hold of mine, and the nurses began. As I screamed in pain, tears streamed from his big eyes and trailed down his fattened cheeks. His lower lip began to quiver, and both hands clenched my own. His eyes widened as he caught sight of the open wounds packed with soaked and stiffened gauze.

Soon it was over, and quickly he wiped away the wetness from his face. As I began to relax again, he carefully wiped the sweat from my forehead.

After a few minutes had passed, he said softly, "Carol, I must go now. You must get more rest, and I must get back to my restaurant. When you wake, you eat my soup, eh?"

I nodded in return, and he slipped out.

Soon after his visit, I received a big, old-fashioned, red gumball machine, filled with colorful gumballs, and a four-foot-tall Winnie the Pooh. The card read, "With love, from Eddie." But more than these, I cherished the love, the concern, the strong hand that had held mine. I'll never forget the gifts of tender care that came with love, from Eddie.

MOM'S BIRTHDAY

A brightly colored present sat on my nightstand table. The green paper set off the bright red bow, which held the card to Mom. I had been in the hospital for about a month, but it was Mom's birthday, and permission had been given for a family party in my room. Soon the celebration would begin. I had worked secretly on her present for days, and now the time was near for the unveiling of the gift I had so proudly prepared.

Red, green, blue, and yellow balloons decorated the plain white room, along with my many flower arrangements. The recreation coordinator, who had also become a dear friend, had helped to make a big "Happy Birthday" sign, and excitement was in the air. The party atmosphere was perfect.

The nurses shampooed and combed my hair. I picked out the nightie that I knew was Mom's favorite and wore it joyfully. In minutes, the family began to arrive with presents and laughter. Almost everyone was there. A nearby table held all the beautiful packages they brought. I didn't know what they all contained, but I knew that mine was the best. Mom loved homemade gifts, and mine had turned out so well. I couldn't wait to give it to her, but first, we were to eat the birthday cupcakes that Gretchen had made.

Mom came to my bedside and greeted me with a sparkle in her eye. "Carol! You look so pretty!"

"I know!" I replied. "I knew you loved this nightie, and my hair's all clean, and I even put a little makeup on." *How wonderful to have an occasion to look nice again!*

Jokes were told, and more laughter filled the room. Chocolate left its residue on more than a few faces, as we quickly devoured the cupcakes and ice cream. Finally Mom interrupted the confusion. "Okay," she announced loudly. "It's time to open presents. I want to see what's in all these boxes!" She sat near my bed as usual, and a huge grin broke across my face at her words. "Let's see. Which one should I open first?"

I responded quickly. "Open mine, Mom. I can't wait any longer for you to see. Open mine first, please?"

She smiled at my enthusiasm and gladly picked the package I indicated. Everyone was silent as she carefully began untying the ribbon and then removed the paper. My heart beat loudly, and I nervously wondered if she would like it as much as I'd hoped.

Now she held the box in her hands. Slowly she lifted the lid, pulled away the white tissue paper, and stared down at the contents.

Before anyone else could see the gift, tears began spilling over the rims of her beautiful hazel eyes.

Confusion gripped me. *Are they tears of sadness, or are they tears of joy?*

She took from the box a mirror in a frame. I had scratched the silver off the back of the mirror so that an oval patch of clear glass allowed a picture of me to show through. My blond hair fell from beneath a softball cap, and the white uniform I wore emphasized my tan, muscular legs. I held a bat and smiled properly for the individual softball photo. I knelt on my right leg with my healthy left leg securely positioned in front. It was the last picture taken of me before my accident.

Was it really a good idea to give her such a picture? The stance, by contrast, freely exposed the nakedness of my now-missing leg. *I never thought how hurtful it could be to her.* She slowly rose from her chair and planted a wet, gentle kiss on my forehead. Then carefully laying the picture down, she said softly, "It's beautiful, Carol, just beautiful. I will always cherish it."

And cherish it she has, despite the bittersweetness of the gift.

FAITHFUL FRIEND

A summer in California for teens means beach parties, surfing, and tans, and for teen-aged girls it means teen-aged boys. It was late summer, school was still out, and all my friends were having the traditional California summer vacation. However, mine was slightly different. There would be no tan for me this summer, no boyfriend, and no beach parties. I often felt lonely, frustrated, and left out as my friends jumped headlong into summer activities. *I want to go, too,* I often moaned to myself. *When will I be able to get out?*

One day when I was feeling particularly blue, the door slowly opened and the familiar face of my friend, Lori, peeked in. "Hi, Carol. Can I come in?" she chirped. Her brown hair was streaked blond from the sun and fell loosely across her face.

"Yeah," I said quietly. "Come on in." Mom sat beside me, but as Lori entered, she excused herself to go to lunch.

Lori's shorts emphasized the deep tan of her legs. She walked toward me and slid into the chair my mother had left.

"Here—I made chocolate chip cookies," she said and handed me a small tin container. Chocolate chip cookies were our favorite, and we had made them together many times previous to the accident.

"I don't want any right now, but thanks," I replied, setting the tin on my table. "I'll have some later."

"Okay, but I'm going to have a couple first."

"Okay."

She retrieved the tin and placed it on her lap, reaching for one of the treats.

"Carol," she sighed in between bites. "When do you think you'll be getting out?"

"I don't know, but soon, I hope."

"Yeah, me too." She paused as she drew another cookie out. "I can't wait until we can go to the movies, and you can meet these new foxes that have started coming to youth night." As she chatted, crumbs fell loosely in her lap. "One of them has blond hair and blue eyes. He's a total surfer, and all the girls are fighting over him. His friends are babes, too."

"Well," I said coolly, "I can stop the girls from fighting. Just bring him to me. I'll take him."

We laughed and continued our teen talk with fun and teasing as Lori kept munching cookies.

"Lori!" I exclaimed. "The cookies! You ate them all."

"Oops," she said, as we peered into the empty container and broke into laughter.

"I'm sorry! I'll make you some more. I promise!" she said between giggles.

We spent tender times together as well, listening to Amy Grant and B. J. Thomas. But most of our time was taken up with gossip from the youth group: who had a crush on who, and why so-and-so wasn't talking to so-and-so, and on and on. My isolation from my friends was greatly minimized as faithful Lori brought me a taste of their world outside. The more I tasted, the more I once again desired to be part of my friends and their lives.

SPECIAL MEDICINE

Even with Lori's encouragement, I battled new fears as summer wore on. Would I ever get out of the hospital? Would I ever be active with my friends again? What would I look like in a bathing suit? Would I even be able to keep up with them while they ran on the beach, or would I always be left behind? My knee was giving me a lot of trouble: the doctors said my thigh muscles had become bound tightly to the bone with scar tissue. I only had from five to ten degrees of mobility in my knee, in spite of the strenuous physical therapy. After fighting so hard to save it, I faced the possibility that my knee could be useless.

Again, surgery was planned, to go into the side of my leg and lift the muscle from the femur to give it the needed freedom. However, fear was kindled afresh in my family and me as Dr. McMasters told us the infection might reawaken.

The risk was taken, and the fear became reality, as the osteomyelitis returned with new fury and violence. New antibiotics were tried again and again, and we prayed for the death of the stubborn invader.

The August heat outside my window became a world far separated from the frigid, feverish one in which I now lived. As people lingered along the sweltering sidewalks, I shivered in chills upon my bed. My temperature hit 105 degrees in spite of the desperate battle by nurses and aides to bring it down. My naked body was packed in ice in the air-conditioned room, and I had to force myself to drink cold, icy water, which multiplied the already over-powering chills.

My arms lay limply on the bed, black and blue from my fingernails to my elbows as the I.V.'s full of antibiotics were changed again and again. Nothing was working. The nurses searched continually for new, unused veins, but their effort took longer and longer and were finally unsuccessful. The I.V.'s would last only a few hours before the veins would go bad.

One night the nurses poked twelve different places unsuccessfully. Finally, Dr. McMasters ordered a rest for my arms. My veins had given up their fight, and the I.V.'s were removed. Nothing could tame the anger of the infection.

The morning after the I.V.'s were removed, I was relieved to have my arms finally free of tubes. However, the sickness in me hindered any possible celebration.

Mom was sitting beside me, praying with intensity for my health to return. Dad entered the room with two cups of coffee. The steam lifted in swirls from the dark liquid. They both drank long and slow.

"Mom?" I interrupted the silence. "Could you read me a scripture pill?" My sister, Sheila, had taken an old prescription bottle, found some plastic capsules, and filled them with strips of colorful paper with Bible verses on them. Each day I was to take a pill out of the bottle, open the capsule, pull out the Bible verse, and read it. The bottle was nearly empty since my stay had lasted many days.

Mom reached for the bottle as she looked at my feverish body. She was scared. I looked worse than ever. She thought to herself, *Maybe this is all too much for Carol. Maybe we should just take her knee, and get all this over with. What if this infection kills my little girl?* She fought off tears of hopelessness and began to read:

> *I have created you and cared for you since you were born. I will be your God through all your lifetime, yes, even when your hair is white with age. I made you and I will care for you. I will carry you along and be your Savior. (Isa. 46:3–4, TLB)*

A few tears spilled from my eyes as I repeated quietly, "He will carry me along and be my Savior." Mom was calmed by the powerful, tender words, as was I.

The surgery on my thigh muscles was a time of trusting for everyone. We had all thought I was so close to recovery, when again, I seemed on the edge of death. To hear the promises of God meant nothing. To trust in them meant everything!

CORRIE

The threat of death was now past, but victory was still a far distance from view. No visitors were allowed during this time, with one exception—Corrie ten Boom.

That first visit, she sat next to the head of my bed with an air of spiritual authority and strength about her. A green isolation cap framed her beautiful, elderly face. She knew the subject of suffering well, having been confined in a German concentration camp during World War II and having observed the deaths of several of her own family. By a true miracle of grace, God had spared her life, as He had mine, from the enemy of death.

She held a different attitude about her from most. Instead of fear and worry, she seemed to expect me at that moment to be raised in health. She gazed at me with a strange look of confidence in her eyes, as if she knew harm would not prevail. Her soft, wrinkled hands shook slightly from age as they held my own, but her voice was strong and commanding as she spoke. "Jesus is victor, Carol! Do not forget it!"

I could not answer her but only listened to the mighty words she spoke. As she continued, I was awestruck. Finally, I interrupted timidly. "Corrie, sometimes I feel like I can barely make it. I wonder if

it's worth all the pain and hard work to keep my knee.
I want it so badly, but sometimes, I just don't know if I
can keep fighting.''

She was silent, but her countenance was strong
with unwavering hope.

"Carol, let me tell you a story about when I was a
little girl," she answered.

"I used to go to my father and crawl on his lap in
his old clock shop in Haarlem. 'Papa,' I would say, 'I
don't know what I would ever do if you died. I think I
would die, too.' Gently he would say back to me,
'Corrie, the Lord will provide.'

"'But Papa!' I would exclaim, 'I really don't think
I could live without you!'

"Then he would say, 'Corrie, when it is time, the
Lord will provide. When you need to go to the store to
buy something, I give you the money. I don't give it to
you way in advance, because you'd lose it; but at the
time you need it, I give it to you, don't I?'

"'Yes, Papa.'

"He would pause to let me think on those words,
and then complete his lesson with, 'Corrie, the Lord
will provide.'"

When she finished her story, the wise words sank
deep into my heart. In the security that her words
brought, I found rest. She came to visit more than
once and freely gave me the strength of her faith.

During my days in the hospital, I received many
phone calls, flowers, cards, and telegrams. Some
were from very well-known names and faces as well:
John Wayne, Frank Sinatra, President Carter.

I deeply appreciated the time they took to think of
me, more than I can ever say. The attention they

showered on me, the glamour many of them repre-
sented, was exciting. Yet none brought the peace,
none brought the encouragement and hope, none
brought the excitement that Jesus gave. He was my
hero, and He alone. He was my strength, and He
alone. He was my joy, and He alone. He was my God,
and He alone.

6

Homeward-bound Christmas

MY STAY IN THE HOSPITAL had been a long one; one of
pain, yet one of joy; one of loss, yet one of gain. I had
gained life from the hand of God and from His people.
I had fought long and hard the battle put before me so
unexpectedly. A new antibiotic finally put to rest the
infection that had so devastated my recovery, and I
was able to come home three days before Christmas. I
had begged Dr. McMasters, and he reluctantly agreed
to my discharge. Home! What a joy to my heart.

Now, learning to live again brought new challenges
and new goals to my life. Learning to walk was a big
one. I wanted to walk down the aisle in Sheila's
wedding in February, and now that I was attending
therapy six days a week, I hoped to achieve that
dream.

The only fake leg I had was one for looks, not for

use. I wore it when I sat in my wheelchair, so that people wouldn't stare at me out in public. I couldn't handle the fear in people's faces as they noticed my missing limb; when they stared in horror I would burst into tears as soon as I was out of their sight. The fake leg helped, but I wanted to walk.

Every day in therapy I took bedadine baths in the whirlpool to keep my still-open wounds clean, followed by a variety of exercises to build my strength for crutches and to gain better mobility in my knee. I learned how to fall so I wouldn't hurt myself and how to get up. I realized most of the therapy focused on getting me ready for crutches, not a leg. I wasn't ready to walk yet because of the tenderness of my stump. But February was nearing, and I was determined to have a leg—and a useful one.

The Christmas season was in full swing, and everyone was busy. However, my activities were restricted by the wheelchair in which I now lived. I was still very weak and couldn't even wheel myself about. Moving around our Country French house, which was decorated beautifully with Christmas wreaths and lights, depended completely on the help of others. The Christmas spirit was strong and joy was in the air due to the fact that I could be a part of the celebration. Gratitude to God filled the hearts of us all that Christmas as the restoration of the once-wounded soldier was evidently underway.

One day Christmas shopping was on the agenda for Mom and me. I couldn't wait to see the decorations, the bustle of people, and the expressions on the children's faces as they looked in toy store windows.

My anticipation grew as we began to get ready. We had to start early because getting ready took a lot of time these days. Just washing my hair required a complex orchestration of maneuvers to get my hair clean and rinsed without drenching me, Mom, and the room in the process. Mom lifted me from my wheelchair and then lowered me, with what little help I could offer, into my beanbag chair next to her sunken bathtub.

I couldn't sit in front of a sink to wash my hair, because the wheelchair was too low, and sitting in any other chair was too painful. I couldn't stand at the sink because I was too weak. We had tried letting me sit in the wheelchair outside the shower, while I stuck my head in, and that didn't work. Finally, after much thought, Mom had come up with the beanbag chair.

After I was in position, lying on my back with my head lowered, Mom took the hand nozzle and began wetting my shoulder-length hair. Once in a while, a shot of water would spray past my head and strike the surrounding mirrors, or land in a puddle on the carpet or in my lap.

My hair clean, Mom put a towel over my head and began helping me back to the wheelchair. As I struggled to stand, I knocked Mom off balance, and we both went down in a crash on the floor. My leg hit hard beneath me, and I cried out in pain. Frustration filled my mother. She burst into tears and cried along with me, until suddenly she was laughing. I looked at her in surprise.

"What's so funny, Mom?" I whined in self-pity. "It hurts!"

"I know, honey, but just look at us!" She bellowed in a new fit of laughter.

Looking at our tangled mess, I forgot about my pain and laughed as well. We laughed and laughed until all the frustration, hurt, and anxiety had disappeared.

I finished dressing, and soon we were in the car and ready to go to therapy. The beauty of the Christmas decorations along the streets intensified the holiday spirit.

As we neared the hospital drive, it became clear that everyone at the hospital was also wrapped in the contagious Christmas atmosphere. The windows with their artificial frost painted about the edges brought a small taste of white Christmas, however warm the California temperature. On other windows, reindeer danced with a sleigh behind holding the charming Old St. Nick. The lobby held a tall tree with colorful balls and ornaments dangling from the green branches.

Mom wheeled me past my many nurse friends, and we exchanged cheerful greetings. The joy that hung so freely in the air erased all residue of the morning's frustrations.

Soon we entered the therapy room. I was ready to work hard so we could have time for shopping. The first step of my therapy was my bedadine bath. I enjoyed that part. Once we were in the privacy of the small room, Mom locked the door behind us.

"Carol, here's your bathing suit," she said as she handed me the red-and-white-striped one-piece. I took it from her hands and waited for her help to change. As usual, any movement sent shooting pains through my leg, but soon I was dressed and ready for the therapist.

Minutes later I sat deep in the warm swirls of water while the red soap lathered about me. It felt so good to be surrounded by water again. I was not allowed to bathe or shower at home; all cleaning was done with a sponge. Because the wounds were still open, my leg had to be watched and treated very carefully. Osteomyelitis never totally leaves a person once it harbors itself in the bone. The infection sleeps quietly—for how long, no one knows—but if disturbed by some violent intrusion (such as surgery) or any other kind of break in the bone, the terror can return.

As I lolled in the water, boredom set in. The Jacuzzi was no longer exciting, and the forty-five-minute bathing time seemed to go on and on.

Finally, I was lifted out, changed, and ready for the real work. They wheeled me into the white gym room as a mixture of anticipation and reluctance crowded my thoughts. Working my knee back and forth was always very painful, and trying to stand upright with the parallel bars was even harder. My head spun rapidly, and my stomach turned round and round. I forced myself to think again of Sheila's wedding day. Everyone would watch me as I walked down the long aisle. I wanted them to comment on how beautiful I looked—my hair, my dress, and most of all, the way I walked—graciously and elegantly. I had to be careful, though; I couldn't upstage the bride!

"You're looking good, Carol," My daydreaming ended abruptly. The comments of the therapist were soothing and fed my hope. But I could have done without his next words: "Okay. Time for the exercises."

He brought his large hands to my bare stump and placed them gently about the kneecap. He looked up at me kindly, his eyebrows raised. "Are you ready?"

I said nothing but looked down at my scarred leg as the kneading began. His strong hands moved the kneecap back and forth. I ground my teeth together, causing grating in my inner ears, like the sound of someone running his nails down a chalkboard. The sound drove me nuts and caused headaches, but it distracted me from the pain I dreaded even more. As my knee was worked up and down to increase the mobility, the muscles which had bound themselves to the thigh bone resisted fiercely. They screamed out with piercing pain, sending fire from fiber to fiber.

Next, I did some exercises to build my arms for crutches and some leg lifts to regain the strength I'd lost in my good leg. All of the workouts were difficult and tiring, and on my bad days, I fussed up a storm, but most of the time it felt good to have the muscles active again.

We were at the last exercise for the day. I had to try to stand for one minute. They wheeled my chair between the parallel bars and helped me up. I clutched the bars quickly, determination throbbing inside my frail frame. To stand for a minute was my goal. I had made forty-five seconds yesterday, but today I was going for a whole minute. I set my jaw and pressed my lips together until they turned purple. Thirty seconds . . . forty seconds . . . fifty seconds . . . fifty-five seconds . . . fifty-six . . . fifty-seven . . . fifty-eight . . . fifty-nine . . . sixty! The arms of the therapist caught me as I collapsed into my chair. Pride welled inside me and I wore it like a crown for everyone to see.

Soon I will be running around, not on crutches, but on two legs! I thought excitedly to myself. *I'll be walking everywhere! I won't need any help! So what if one leg is wood, I will have again two workable legs.*

Reality set in and soon dissipated my success when

I thought how far I still had to go. However, I pushed these thoughts aside, for the fun I had been looking forward to all day had come. I was tired from therapy, but my energy began to come back as I thought excitedly about going to the mall.

On the radio Bing Crosby sang, "I'm Dreaming of a White Christmas." His voice was low and mellow and made me think of how beautiful a white Christmas would be. I'd never had one, despite my love for mountains and snow and despite the fact we owned a family cabin in the local San Bernardino Mountains.

"Mom." I interrupted the quiet mood about us as we drove. "Could we go to the mountains for Christmas? That would be so fun! We've never had a white Christmas, and the whole family could go and we could all take our presents up there. Could we?" I waited hopefully.

"Carol, I'm sorry. You know we can't do that. Daddy has to preach at seven services Christmas Eve. Besides, there's no way you'd be able to go. There's a lot of snow up there now, and we wouldn't be able to get you around. It's just too much for you."

She's right, I thought to myself. *There's no way I'd make it.* I knew how Mom and Dad had disliked the snow—especially since the time Dad had had to get out in a storm and put chains on the car with four girls and no boys to help him. It had taken him nearly two hours to set the chains, then another four to get down the mountain because the visibility was so bad.

I spoke aloud. "No, I think you're right. We'd better stay home. I love you, Mom! We sure are going to have a good Christmas, aren't we?"

"We sure are, Carol, now that you're home." She smiled, and the love we had for each other relayed back and forth from heart to heart.

As we pulled onto the freeway, the car picked up speed. I looked quietly out the window. The pavement beneath us rushed past faster and faster. As I looked down at the black blur, my heart began to pound wildly. Suddenly, the accident flashed before me. I gripped the dashboard frantically.

Mom watched the terror creep into my face. She knew the reason well. This fear had clung to me since I had come home from the hospital. I had quickly grown accustomed to riding at slow speeds again, but going fast still frightened me terribly.

"It's all right, Carol. I'm only going fifty. We're almost there. Hold on just a little longer."

The nightmares continued to haunt me. I remembered the sunset on that bloody night, the chill air, the corn fields, and the wind—that mighty wind that rushed in a whistle past my cold ears. I remembered the cars, the horns, the screams. When would my life be free of the Iowa memory? When would it leave me alone? Would I always be so afraid of speed, of the swift wind rushing past me? Would I ever again be able to enjoy a fast ride at Disneyland, or a movie about a race horse, or riding my quarterhorse that now waited for me in her stall at home? And when? I had always loved going fast, and now it was a deathly fear.

The answer I longed for would be found sooner than I thought, in ways I had never imagined to be possible. Had I known what my future held, I would have probably laughed in disbelief. But soon I was to be living in a world far different from any I had ever known, a world where the obsession to go faster and faster would become my life.

We slowed to exit the freeway, and the fear subsided. Shortly we pulled into the mall parking lot and began searching for a parking place. There was none. Mom and I had been told over and over again, by nurses and doctors alike, that amputees qualified for disabled parking places. Therefore, we parked in a space right at the entrance to the mall, labeled HANDICAP. Mom looked at me with a smile. "Well," she said deviously, "isn't this nice?"

"Yes. At least there is one nice thing about being an 'amp."

Mom got out the wheelchair, helped me out of the car, and off we went, with excitement again bubbling in us at the joys of Christmas.

We entered the crowded doors to a mob scene of people scurrying to and fro, bumping into each other in their frantic pace. Many hurried from one store to the next, calling rude remarks to people who got in their way. They grabbed angrily for the last toy or a certain blouse before someone else could take it. I looked at them in sorrow, knowing the joy and peace they lacked in their lives. Christmas was the day the Prince of Peace had come to earth to bring rest to men, and as I watched the crowds, I thought about how few actually knew the peace our Prince represents.

We walked on. Mom and I spoke of the delicious menu that was planned for our table in three short days. In the middle of the mall we passed a Santa Claus taking children to his lap and listening to their hopeful requests. Elves and reindeer filled the windows. A mechanical Rudolph shone his bright nose at the many people passing by.

Mom pushed my chair slowly as we took in the

activity and decorations around us. My stump had been too sore to wear my cosmetic leg that day, and people stared at my missing limb with shocked expressions. Many of them could not bear the sight of such a young girl without a leg. Children ran and played and laughed until they noticed me; then they looked at me with fear in their eyes before they ran and hid behind their mothers. That was what always hurt most. I loved children so much, and to have them afraid of me made my heart ache.

"Look, Carol," Mom said and spun my chair around. A sporting goods store window was filled with new ski outfits, skis, and boots, for the skiers' Christmas. Pictures of mountains and posters of skiers framed the display. One large poster in particular caught my eye. World-famous downhiller Franz Klammer, in his white Austrian downhill suit, raced through the treacherous course. The caption beneath stated the location: *Wengen, Switzerland*.

As my eyes took in the display, Mom continued. "Do you remember that letter you got in the hospital about amputee skiing?"

My eyebrows shot up as I recalled the words from the Colorado resident. She had written of a program in Winter Park, Colorado, led by Hal O'Leary. He had taught many people how to ski on one leg and through his teaching had put together a racing program that now reached nationwide. To the ones who were interested and good enough, he taught special racing techniques and began taking them to other countries to race against the best amputee racers in the world. Few were that good, but the ones who were stood right up there with the nonhandicapped racers.

I had paid little attention to the letter at the time. I

had been very sick, and the last thing on my mind had been learning to ski. However, now that I looked at the huge, beautiful photo of Franz Klammer, my curiosity stirred. The snow behind him blurred from his speed, and his thighs looked like tree trunks as they held his body in position for a long, left-hand turn.

I wondered if I could really be on skis again. *Even if I didn't really like it, or I weren't any good, at least I wouldn't be left behind when my friends went.*

I looked up at Mom. There were questions in her eyes as she waited for a response. "You know, Carol," she said, "we could fly you up to Winter Park with a friend at Thanksgiving vacation next year. You're still too weak to go now, but you could make that another goal."

I stared back at the poster. I wondered, *Do I really want to risk it? I've only skied a few times before and it was fun, but my leg is so sensitive. I'm afraid it would hurt so much to fall? Do I really want to risk looking like a fool if I fail?* Everything within me cried *Yes!* I was always one for adventure and new excitement, and the challenges these new ideas created in my heart had to be searched out. Yes, I had to try.

Finally I responded. "Mom, I think that would be great! I want to learn how to ski."

Mom smiled. "Well," she asked. "where do you want to go now?"

"I know we haven't got much shopping done, but I'm getting really tired, and I'd kind of like to go home if you don't mind."

I knew inside that she wouldn't mind at all. She was always so tired herself nowadays, despite her denials.

I could see the fatigue in her eyes and in the way she walked. Taking care of me was hard work, lifting me all the time and having to lift the wheelchair in and out of the car. Her role as nurse had been added to that of homemaker. As she tried to fulfill both occupations successfully, as well as be a pastor's wife, a spirit of weariness hung constantly about her. She never complained and seldom allowed others to take my care off her shoulders. Besides, I was hurting and very selfish with my mother's time.

Christmas came and went with love, peace, and joy surrounding the Schuller clan. Therapy continued, and I learned slowly how to support myself on crutches. I gained more strength each day. The wedding drew near, and I began to wonder about reaching my goal. I still had no leg I could walk on, although Mom and I went from prosthetist to prosthetist, trying to find someone who could make a leg that would work well for children. I don't know why we had such problems finding a leg that worked, but time ticked on as we continued our search.

I was becoming better all the time at maneuvering my crutches, and I now walked nearly everywhere on them. I had started using underarm crutches and put up a tremendous fight with the therapists when they tried to change me to forearm crutches. They made me look more disabled, and everyone stared at me twice as badly. However, my stubbornness gave way when I saw the extra mobility I could have on them.

While we searched for a new prosthesis, I was not wearing one at all. The cosmetic one I had was too heavy to wear while I was on crutches, and it hurt my stump. It stood in the corner of my closet, untouched and unused.

As I hobbled around, restlessness began to boil inside me. The desire for athletic activity was coming to a head.

One month before the wedding I received a letter from my father's office relaying a message sent from a man in Baltimore. In an interview on my father's program, I had talked about my love for horses and my love of riding. I had not ridden since the accident. My horse, Lady, stayed in our backyard, getting fat on carrots and apple treats. I was afraid to ride. The thought of my thigh rubbing against her side sent chills of imagined pain up my spine. Besides, the doctors had cautioned me not to get any kind of dirt inside my bandages. Riding just seemed very unwise.

But this one letter cut through all my doubts and fears. I was alone the morning I read it, in the corner of our small kitchen by the glass kitchen table which only seated two people. The bright January sun shone through our sliding-glass door, warming the back of my neck. Outside, hummingbirds buzzed about a tree of hibiscus. The rays of sun hit the stove top nearby, with a piercing reflection. The day was picturesque in its freshness. I forgot the beauty outside, however, as I reread the letter in astonishment.

Dear Carol,

My name is Doug Griffith. I have an Arabian horse farm here in Baltimore. It is a beautiful farm, and we have many excellent national show horses. I have heard the news of your love for horses, and I know your father is coming out this way for a speaking engagement in a week and a half. Would you possibly be able to join him, and the two of you come spend some time on my farm? I would love to

*show you our beautiful horses and help get you in a
saddle again. Please let me know of your thoughts.*

> *Sincerely,*
> *Doug Griffith*
> *Imperial Horse Farm*

My heart leaped with excitement. *Arabians! I've
always wanted to ride an Arabian!* I loved Lady, my
faithful quarterhorse, but she was getting old, and
there wasn't much spirit in her. I had been getting
bored with riding her, but I loved her so much I
couldn't bear to sell her. *But Arabians! Wow!* They
were known for their spirit.

Then, suddenly, I remembered my leg. *How can I
handle an Arabian with my leg? I'm afraid to ride
even Lady now! And what about what the doctor said?*
Disappointment rose in my heart.

As I sat with the letter drooping in my right hand,
head hung low, Dad walked into the sunny room.

"Carol?" His unexpected presence startled me, so
that I had no time to wipe my face. My makeup was
streaked with tears and my nose was red, I was sure.

"Darling, what's wrong?" he asked as he knelt in
front of me and hugged me.

"Daddy, I'm so frustrated! When am I going to be
able to *do* things again? The wedding is only a month
away, and it's obvious I'll have to walk down the aisle
on crutches. I won't be able to learn to ski until next
winter, if I can even then, and now I have the chance
to go to an Arabian horse farm and learn to ride again,
and I'm afraid that the doctors won't let me, or that it
will hurt my leg!"

"Wait, wait, wait! What's this? What are you

talking about? An Arabian horse farm? Where?" He looked at me in puzzlement.

"In Baltimore. This man, Doug Griffith, sent a letter to your office. He knew you were going to Washington, D.C., and he lives nearby in Maryland. It's only about an hour away. He wants me to go with you and the two of us come over to see his horses, and then he wants to teach me to ride! It's a big horse farm with national show horses! I've always wanted to ride an Arab, Dad! Always!"

"I know, Carol. I know."

I cried on my father's shoulder, and the tears soaked into his shirt.

"Carol." He took hold of my shoulders to look me in the face. "I know you'll have to walk down the aisle on crutches; no one can get a leg made for you by then. But you know what? That's okay. It's amazing that you'll even be able to do that! It's a long aisle, and just two months ago, you couldn't even wheel your own wheelchair! And as far this visit to the Arab farm goes—well, why don't we just talk to the doctors and see what they have to say? Even if you can't ride, it would be a delight for me to have you as company in Washington. We can drive down and spend a day at the farm, and you can see all the horses. We'll have a great time! Just you and me! You tutor can give you assignments in advance for you to do before you leave. How about it? And one more thing—guess who's going to be at the conference singing? B.J. Thomas!"

"B.J. Thomas?" I asked quietly between sobs. His music had helped so much in the hospital. When the situation got so bad that nothing helped, when my prayers seemed distant and the words from my family brought little comfort, I had always put on B.J.'s tape, "Home Where I Belong." His mellow voice would quiet my anxious heart as he sang of the love we both carried for our God. Somehow, to hear again the truths of the goodness and mercies of God the Father would rekindle the flame in my heart and make it burn with passion.

"B.J. Thomas?" I repeated. "He's going to sing? Really?"

"Yes," my father answered in satisfaction, as he saw the sparkle of joy and anticipation return to my eyes.

"Dad, are you sure it wouldn't cause a problem to take me with you? Wouldn't it cost a lot of extra money?"

"Don't worry, Carol. The people who ask me to come take care of that, and they always make arrangements for two people."

The dreams that moments ago had seemed so far away now seemed to be in reaching distance. Maybe I wouldn't be able to walk down the aisle, but at least I could go to the horse farm, and I could learn to ski the following year, and I just *knew* I'd be walking soon, too. *And to hear B.J. sing! Oh, how great!* The music would remind me of all the times God had rained His peace and grace on me. Of these mercies would I hear again, and of new ones for the future would a hope be sparked, in a journey that would bring both past and future together in beauty.

7

On the Mount Again

THE TIME HAD COME FOR MY LIFE TO BEGIN AGAIN in earnest. No longer did the consequences of tragedy rule my life. I was on crutches, not in a wheelchair. No longer was I confined to hospital or home. I was my own person again, able to walk when I wanted to walk, able to do what I wanted to do. I no longer depended on nurses or my parents. Here I was on an airplane again, but *this* time sitting in a passenger seat instead of lying on a stretcher fighting for my life. I would soon be in Washington, D.C.—no therapy, no school, no tutor; just me and my Dad!

The sky outside the 747 was streaked with splashes of red and violet as the sun set on the horizon. I lost sight of its glory, however, when the plane began its descent. We broke through the clouds momentarily, then the peaceful blanket of white closed behind us and the setting sun again displayed its beauty.

Dad sat next to me, sleeping soundly. I reached over and fastened his seat belt, then secured mine as well. My stomach could barely contain the butterflies as we made our approach. My excitement hit its peak as the plane hovered only thirty feet from the runway beneath. Then the plane hit the ground with a thud, and my father jolted awake.

"We're here!" he said, smoothing his hair back to its proper place.

"Boy, Dad, you were out like a light," I teased. "You would have thought you hadn't slept for days. And your snores were so loud they kept the rest of the plane from getting any rest!"

I laughed and he responded by tickling me. "You just leave me alone, you smart aleck."

We continued to laugh while we reached for our carryon baggage beneath the seats. The plane pulled to a halt, and we prepared to disembark. After we said our good-byes to the hospitable flight attendants, we headed for the baggage claim and a taxi stand.

From the taxi, Washington spread before us with the first few twinkles of light as the sky darkened with the coming of night. Trees passed quickly by, then more buildings, their lights ablaze. The city was clothing itself for its beautiful nighttime spectacle.

Abruptly the yellow taxi pulled curbside at the front of our hotel. Bellboys hurried to relay the bags to our rooms.

Tonight we had a scheduled meeting where my father would speak and B. J. Thomas would sing. I hoped, deep inside, that the songs he performed would be my favorites. Tomorrow we were scheduled to see as much of the city as possible before I was too tired. Luncheon invitations had been extended for the

Senators Dining Room with a tour of the White House afterwards. The following day would be the visit to the horse farm. I couldn't wait! The doctor had given his permission for me to ride if I was careful not to ride too hard. I promised gladly, and fearful excitement welled inside me as I anticipated that first mount.

The whole week's plans were beginning to run over and over in my mind, but it was time to put them aside and dress for dinner. I had only an hour before we would be picked up. Emptying my suitcase, I headed for the bathroom with shampoo and creme rinse in hand. Suddenly, I stopped in my tracks. *How am I going to shower?* Stunned that I would have forgotten all my previous troubles with cleaning my body and hair, I frantically tried to think of something. Last week, I had showered at home for the first time. I still wasn't allowed to bathe, because the doctors didn't want me soaking when my leg was still draining. Mom had gone to the store and found a shower seat, but we had never thought about what I would use here! I had no idea what to do. I couldn't stand in the shower; I didn't have good enough balance or strength to stand that long without crutches. What would I do?

I knocked loudly on the door adjoining Dad's and my rooms. He opened it quickly. "Yes, darling. What can I do for you?"

"Dad, I don't know how I'm going to take a shower! I never thought about it, but I have to figure something out! Is there anything I could sit on?" The thought of going around Washington for three days without showering horrified me.

"Well, just calm down, Carol. We'll think of something. Now, let's see." He lifted his hand to his chin, as deep thought consumed him, then looked around and around the room for the solution. "Well," he continued, "we can't use the desk chair: it would be ruined. Hmmmm . . ." We continued to search.

"Hey! How about the waste basket?" He beamed at me with pride at his suggestion.

I didn't return his enthusiasm. "It will be too low. It's too small."

"Well, now," he said defensively, "just wait a minute." He ran from room to room collecting baskets. "How about this?" He stacked one inside the other. Four waste baskets high, and there he held in his hand the definite solution.

"It's perfect!" I exclaimed as he set it in the shower. "I think it's going to work."

"Well, we'll soon find out, won't we?" He smiled and winked as he left the room and closed the door behind him.

The plan worked. The plastic baskets were a bit wobbly, but the shower was done within fifteen minutes. I was nervous getting in and out by myself, but I had taken one more step toward independence. The freedom felt better and better with every step.

At last I stood before the mirror, my hair curled, makeup in place, my dress soft and flowing. I felt so pretty! And the "high" continued as my father proudly escorted me to the banquet. Oh, I was having so much fun! It had been so long since I'd gone to something like this. I didn't care about the people who looked curiously at my leg. Tonight, I really didn't care.

We rode down in the elevator and waited at the front door for our car. When the driver arrived, my father asked, "How much of a walk is it to where we're going? My daughter is still quite weak, and she tires quickly."

"Well, Dr. Schuller," he answered respectfully, "I'm afraid once we get to the dinner hall it will be quite a walk. Do you have any kind of wheelchair with you?"

"I was afraid this might happen, so we brought one from home. We knew we wanted to tour tomorrow, too. Carol prefers the crutches if it's not too far, but I'll run up and get it, just in case."

I looked at Dad and nodded in agreement.

We had forgotten about the shower, but it was a good thing we had brought the wheelchair. The walk at the airport had been long as well, and I would have never made it without my chair despite my desire to be rid of it. I didn't mind so long as I only had to use it for long walks. The rest of the time I insisted on crutches.

That night was wonderful. The dinner was a feast: stuffed chicken, potatoes and gravy, salad, broccoli, and apple pie à la mode. The people were extremely friendly as they welcomed us with sincerity. During their conversation with Dad, I wasted no time gobbling down my pie, along with half of his. My eyes were constantly alert, in search of B.J. I was hoping for a chance to meet him, but he was nowhere to be seen.

"Where's B.J.?" I whispered in my father's ear when the conversation quieted for a few minutes.

"His airplane arrived a half hour ago. He should be here any minute," he said encouragingly.

"Dad, do you think I might be able to meet him?"

"Well, we'll have to wait and see. I don't know how tired he'll be, but let's just see what happens. We'll try."

That answer was good enough for me. I would be excited just hearing B.J. sing, whether I met him or not, but I also knew what my father meant when he said he would try. He would do everything in his power to bring the meeting about.

Dinner was over and the program about to begin. As the lights lowered, a dark shadow ducked in through the side door and slipped quickly on stage. Just as the master of ceremonies began to make excuses for B.J.'s late arrival, the handsome singer appeared at his side. The microphone was presented to him as the introductions were completed.

I waited in anticipation for the music to begin.

His voice sang out "Home Where I Belong," reaching the high notes with ease. His clear blue eyes shone with love as he sang those precious words. Warmth filled me as I remembered the peace the mellow tones had brought me over and over again in that often-dreary hospital room. After the song was finished, B.J. spoke of the way God had saved him. He spoke of his drug addiction and how its power over him had been broken. The night he decided to give up drugs, B.J. had sat up and waited for the withdrawal symptoms to come. As he was waiting, he fell asleep. Miraculously, he had never experienced any withdrawal symptoms.

The background music started again, and he began to sing.

> *Hallelujah!*
> *You have made us what we are,*
> *By Your blood and by Your scars.*
> *We want to praise You in ever way we can.*

The words washed soothingly over my soul, as I thought tenderly of my God. He sang on:

> *Words are so empty, and time is so short,*
> *To show You how much we love You.*
> *Hallelujah!*

Darkness circled him, until the single spotlight focused on his face. Head tilted back, his heart sang out to his newfound Jesus. I felt as if we in the audience were intruding upon his intimacy with God.

The last note resounded with strength and concluded his brief concert. He was brought back to the present by the applause of the audience. It was clear how much these people appreciated his heartfelt songs and triumphant story.

Now it was Dad's turn. My father got up quietly from his chair and walked to the stage while the master of ceremonies skillfully switched the people's attention from B.J. to Dad. The audience graciously welcomed him as he approached the lectern. His well-known message, "Turn Your Scars into Stars," brought hope to those in the audience who had lost hope and inspiration to those who had lost their dreams. He spoke of me and my accident, and I blushed at the mention of my name.

The night was soon over, and Dad stood by my side meeting the other guests. Many shook his hand, some crying and some laughing, but all thanking him for his words of encouragement. B.J. stood nearby, receiving similar words of love. Then, as the last of the people filtered through the doors on their way home, B.J. and Dad met and shook hands warmly.

"B.J., let me introduce you to my daughter, Carol."

I heard my name and stepped forward, my crutches clanking as I did so.

The kindness in his eyes overpowered all other emotions as he placed his hand warmly on my shoulder. "Carol," he said easily, as if speaking to an old friend, "it's a delight to meet you. I've heard a lot about you."

"Well," I said excitedly, "I can't begin to tell you how happy I am to meet you. You were such a help in the hospital to me. So many times I would get fed up with everything. Mom would put in your tape, and I would calm right down. Your songs 'Hallelujah!' and 'Home Where I Belong' were my favorites. It was so neat that they were the ones you sang tonight! I had to fight back the tears."

He looked at me with tears in his eyes and smiled. "Carol, they're selling my albums and tapes outside; let's go and get you one."

We walked out together. He took his new album *Happy Man* and signed it before handing it to me. "I hope this one brings you as much joy as the last."

"I'm sure it will," I answered excitedly. "Thank you."

Our friendship has grown since that first meeting. I see him very seldom now, but his tape *Amazing Grace* is heard often in my truck as I drive to my many destinations.

> *Amazing grace—how sweet the sound,*
> *That saved a wretch like me!*
> *I once was lost, but now am found,*
> *Was blind but now I see.*

I think of the way a man named Jesus touched two totally different lives in the same powerful way.

Sleep came easily that night, but morning came all too quickly, peering through a small slit in the drapes. Dad and I eagerly dressed and breakfasted, then spent the day seeing Washington—the White House, the Pentagon, and the Washington Monument. After having lunch in the Senators' Dining Room with Senator Strom Thurmond, I was exhausted. The hotel was a pleasant place, and I decided to take the rest of the day easy. Tomorrow, the biggest day of all, would come quickly.

And so it did. The next morning I stretched in bed, trying to fight off the last vestiges of sleep, and looked at the bedside clock. Five A.M.. My eyes squeezed shut as I yawned heavily. Suddenly I remembered the day's plans, and a burst of energy shot through me. Reaching for my crutches, I proceeded through my routine of showering, which I now had down pat, and joined my father for breakfast.

By seven A.M. we were riding in the car that Doug Griffith had sent, with his horse trainer, Randy, at the wheel. My brown cords covered my bandaged left leg but failed to hide the deformity. The swelling combined with the thick padding of bandages made the stump look twice the size of my right leg. Today, however, was a day to dwell on the future, not the past, and no one seemed to take notice of the handicap.

An hour went quickly by as we passed through the beautiful countryside. The brisk air outside fogged our windows, and I cleared them again and again with my hand so I could see the rolling green hills and bright sun. The winter had been short, and spring already seemed to be near.

We were definitely in horse country. White, wooden

fences stretched for miles near the roadside, and grazing mares with their nursing foals dotted the hillsides.

"The farm on the right is ours," Randy said. The land seemed endless where his finger pointed. The only border signs were the familiar, white fences. After following the acreage for what seemed forever, we turned onto a long gravel driveway and through a large, white gateway with a sign identifying the ranch.

We pulled to a halt in front of a lovely home, where a distinguished, white-haired man dressed in a sport coat was waiting to welcome his visitors. Doug Griffith smiled with delight as his guests stepped out of the car.

"Hello!" he said warmly. "I'm Doug. Dr. Schuller, Carol, it's so nice to meet you!"

Dad took hold of his offered hand and smiled. We immediately liked the man. Mr. Griffith's eyes went quickly from my father to me, and from that point on, most of his attention was focused on me. I saw the delight in Dad's eyes as my excitement mounted, asking question after question.

A delicious brunch awaited us in the house, but I could think only of the many horses I wanted to see. As Mr. and Mrs. Griffith and Dad lingered over coffee, I fought my rising impatience. The minutes went by so slowly! I wandered around the large home, studying the many bronze horse statues and the oil paintings of beautiful Arabians in desert scenes.

Finally, they called from the dining area.

"Carol, we'd better leave for the barns now. It's a long walk and the car is leaving. Come now!"

No urging was necessary on Mr. Griffith's part. I went as fast as my crutches would allow.

We all piled into the car and drove down the long road to the main barn, where all the indoor training facilities were. My heart beat faster and faster in anticipation. I thought of seeing the area and the horses more than anything, even more than riding. I hoped we could watch some of the training take place.

A large, white barn loomed before us, trimmed neatly in blue along the edges. The grounds were full of activity, with many riders leading their horses to and fro. Some groomed, some washed, some saddled. Since the farm was privately owned, Doug and Randy did much of the work themselves, with only about twenty other riders. But this was the time of day to begin, and the full staff was preparing for the day's work.

Doug guided us into the building, explaining. "What we'll do is go to the indoor arena. Randy will bring out some horses so you don't have to go to the stalls. You can't get a very good look at them in their paddocks, anyway. Is that all right with you, Carol?"

"Yes. That's great!"

"All right, then. He'll bring out our best horses and ride them for you, then show you some training techniques and what we look for in a good horse. He'll also show you some of our prize foals that will hopefully be champions one day."

He led us through the arena and up some stairs to a room with windows which overlooked the arena. The room was beautifully decorated, complete with couch, chairs, and television. Here they displayed all the trophies and ribbons they had won. Dad found this new spot especially inviting, since he wasn't crazy about being around horses. However, I preferred to be out in the barn with Randy.

"Doug?" I looked away from the windows. "Could I go down with Randy? I'd really rather be with the horses—if you don't mind," I asked politely, with fingers crossed.

"Of course, I don't mind! I understand totally. I was actually thinking of your father." We smiled together and looked at Dad. Although he had been a farm boy and around many cows and chickens in his day, he was obviously no horseman and had little desire to become one now.

Dad chuckled in return. "This *is* more comfortable, but this is your day, Carol. I want to be with you. Let's all go down!"

Randy was bringing in the first of the horses. He led it inside the arena near where I stood. The fence that separated us was a low one, so that reaching over to pet the muscular animal was easy.

He explained the qualities that are sought in an Arabian horse: a dipped nose, small head, a level back, and certain forms in the legs. Then he mounted for a ride. As he rode around and around, from walk to jog to canter, Doug showed me the head position of the horse and the proper seat the rider should take with each gait.

The horsemanship was beautiful. I had learned all my riding on my own, so I knew nothing of showing horses—Western-style or English. I almost always rode bareback. Occasionally I used a Western saddle, but I had never even sat in an English saddle, which was what this farm used. I listened curiously to the explanations and threw in many questions as well. After Randy was finished, he brought the horse back to me.

"Well, Carol, how about it? You want to mount up?"

I looked at them in surprise. I knew I was going to try to ride, but this one? It was so beautiful! Were they serious? One of their best horses?

"Well?" he repeated.

Dad nudged me. I walked to the small gate and entered the arena. My crutches pushed away the sawdust as I approached what weeks ago had seemed to be but a fantasy.

My stomach was tied in knots as I came closer and closer. I reached out to the beautiful arched head before me and stroked its velvet muzzle. Randy handed me the reins.

"Carol, meet Hossni. Hossni, meet Carol." The horse let out a gentle neigh and turned its large, dark eyes on me. The fire I expected to see was not evident in this animal—only a gentle but energetic twinkle.

It took a bit of thinking out loud with Randy and Doug before we figured out a way for me to mount without hurting my leg, but soon it was done and I sat high on the sixteen-hand horse. The Egyptian Arab was too big for his breed, and his muscles surged beneath me as Randy led him in a walk. I held the reins in hand but allowed Randy the control, before I found my confidence again on horseback. The unfamiliar English saddle felt strange. Deep inside, I longed for the bareness of the horse beneath me rather than the leather separating us. I knew there was no way I could manage bareback—not yet, anyway.

Randy loosed the lead to me, and I continued to get a feel for my mount. As my confidence grew, I relaxed a little. My leg throbbed slightly and I still felt terribly awkward. Balancing was difficult, and I kept slipping slightly to the right, where my good leg hung.

Little by little, I let the horse have more rein. Randy walked close by, coaching me how to sit in an English saddle. Obviously, I knew nothing of being a proper English horsewoman, but no one seemed to mind. At Randy's orders, I brought Hossni to a jog and circled the arena as his smooth stride lengthened beneath me. My body jostled as I fought for comfort. I still felt insecure and my leg began to hurt more, but I said nothing.

I clucked quietly, and Hossni broke into an even canter. Dad clapped out of joy as he watched me guide the obedient horse. After one round I slowed the creature down and returned to a walk. Randy ran to me.

"Well, how did it feel?"

I looked down at him. "Okay. I feel really unsteady, and I know I look unsteady. It feels really weird with just one leg. I guess I just have to get used to it."

We were standing away from the others, so I continued to speak honestly. "Randy, my leg really hurts. I don't think I should ride any longer. Don't tell Dad or Doug—they'll feel really bad, and I don't want them to. But I do think I should quit for the day. Thank you *so* much. Even though it hurt, I would do it all over again. It was all worth it, really." We smiled, and he ran to get my crutches.

We rejoined Dad and Doug, and I told them what a beautiful horse Hossni was to ride.

"Doug, I'm sorry I couldn't do your horse justice as a rider. I wish I could've ridden him a year ago."

"You know, Carol, you can come back as you begin to heal up a little more. You're a good rider. I know it's got to be hard to adjust, but I can see it in you. You're an athlete, and you could be a *very* good rider if you would put the time into it. I'd love to have you come and stay with us next summer if you're interested. I could give you a job here, and you could live with us. Randy could see how you do. Maybe we can make a real rider out of you."

I was shocked. What was he saying? Stay at this farm for the whole summer?

"Well, Mr. Griffith, that's some offer!"

"I mean it," he replied. Randy looked at me curiously. I could read the approval in his eyes. Dad spoke up.

"Carol, that's a rare opportunity. I would think about it strongly if I were you."

I looked back at Doug. I couldn't believe what he was suggesting! "Well, I thank you sincerely. But I would really have to take some time. Can I let you know next year? I have to adjust back at school, and I just don't know how that's going to go."

Doug smiled. "Of course, Carol. Don't rush yourself. I want you to know that the offer is there. Now, let's bring out the foals."

The subject was closed, and I was relieved. The prospect was too much to think of now. I said my farewells to the beautiful horse, with a kiss on his nose to keep as a thank-you, and Randy hastily took Hossni back to the barn.

In minutes, Randy had returned to the arena with three young foals. After closing the gate behind him, he snapped the lead ropes from their halters and let them go.

Doug instructed us to step behind the gate so we wouldn't get in the way. The foals' heads stood high as spirit filled their small, three-month-old bodies. Realizing their freedom, they ran and ran and kicked high. Their friskiness was contagious. I laughed, and in my spirit I played right along with them. They sped by and I caught a glimpse of the fiery eyes I had always dreamed of in an Arab. I stared in awe at their beauty.

"Carol?" Doug interrupted my dreams. "Tell me which one is the best. Remember what I told you to look for."

I studied their little forms carefully. After scrutinizing the specific areas I had been instructed about earlier, I pointed to the jet black one with white star and socks. "That one."

"That's right!" he said enthusiastically. "Randy, bring her here."

The filly was caught and brought before us. "We just bought this one. Isn't she beautiful?"

I nodded as I reached for the velvet head. I stroked it quietly, but she jerked away with fury. Excitement filled me at the sign of spirit.

Doug continued. "Guess how much we purchased her for."

I looked at him. "I have no idea. Maybe five thousand dollars?"

He shook his head. "Forty thousand."

The words stupefied me. "Forty thousand dollars! Are you kidding?"

My father's face was blank with shock as we stared at the beautiful animal. Randy led her away while the other two foals continued playing.

"Okay, Carol, which is the next best one? One is worth about fifteen thousand dollars and the other about ten thousand."

My mind still reeled from the price of the first one. The filly was gorgeous, but what made her worth so much, I couldn't tell. I put my questions aside and studied the remaining two. I pointed to a dark brown one. "Him."

"Right again. That's Hossni's boy. His name is Hosstar. He's a beauty, isn't he?"

Randy led him over as well. I reached out again, and Hosstar rested his head gently beneath my hand. As I stroked him, he pushed his head deeper beneath my arm and nuzzled me. But in seconds he lifted his head again, the fire returned, and he was ready to return to play. Randy let him go. The four of us stood and watched.

"You like him, don't you, Carol?"

"Yes," I said, admiring the treasured animals.

"He sure took to you."

I glanced at him, smiled, then returned my attention to Hosstar.

"How would you like to take him home with you?"

My head swiveled sharply. This man was remarkable! What else did he have up that sleeve of his?

"Mr. Griffith, I'm afraid we can't afford that. I'm sorry. He's beautiful and I would give anything to—"

My remark was interrupted. "No, no, no! You don't understand. He would be a gift from me."

"What?" I couldn't hide my amazement. This man had said it all. "What did you say?"

He repeated himself, adding that he would fly Hosstar to California. We wouldn't have to pay a penny. There were no strings attached. I threw my arms around his neck and shook my head in disbelief.

With permission from my astounded father, the incredible gift was accepted and arrangements were made. After reluctant good-byes to Hosstar and our friends, we headed back for Washington. The vacation had drawn to a close, but a door had been opened to my future that held more surprises and adventure than any fourteen-year-old girl could ever dream of. How was I ever going to handle an Arabian colt? I didn't even want to think about that. Instead, I decided to leave reality behind for a little while and become engulfed in my dream.

8

A New Discovery

THE ALARM RANG LOUDLY, waking me from sleep. It was February 24, 1979. The morning of the wedding had arrived. I tried to snuggle down for a few more precious minutes of slumber, but one sunbeam pierced the shutters of my window and caught my eye sharply, pushing the remainder of sleep from me.

Across my room hung the beautiful, burgundy taffeta bridesmaid's dress, all pressed and ready for my walk down the aisle. A perfect day had dawned in answer to many prayers. The rainstorms of winter which had hovered over us for weeks were abruptly interrupted this morning for the important occasion.

I sat up slowly and hung my leg off the side of the bed. Reaching over to the shutters, I opened them wide to let the flood of light illuminate the darkness of my room. As sure as the dawning of the morning, there was Hosstar waiting to see me. His nose rested on the pane of glass that separated us.

"Hi, Hoss!" I said loudly, trying to project my voice through the glass. I knew all he heard was muffled noises, so I tapped lightly. The young colt threw his head back in joy. He had become a cherished friend in the few weeks he had been with us.

I dressed quickly in blue jeans and T-shirt, then hurried outside to feed him. There was much to be done before the morning wedding, and I had little time to complete it all. I brought a carrot with me, left a kiss with him, and then raced back to the house to get ready for the big day.

Inside, I was greeted by many of my relatives from Iowa. They had flown out for Sheila's wedding, and the past few days had been filled with reminiscing and relishing the many baked items they brought with them. Rhubarb shortcake continually threw its heavenly scent from the kitchen, enticing me to indulge, but I was careful not to gain weight. I wanted to look as pretty as I possibly could for this day. I had worked hard in therapy in order to meet the goal of walking down the aisle. Even though I would be on crutches, I had gained enough strength and independence to make it on my own.

"Good morning, Carol!" everyone sounded in turn.

Mom called from the dining room, "Come, everyone, we have breakfast on the table. Good morning, Carol. Eat some breakfast, then you should start getting ready." She appeared in the sunny kitchen as she finished speaking. No sign of nervousness could be seen in the mother of the bride. She hid it well. "Carol, just put on a clean pair of jeans after you

shower. We'll all change at church so our dresses
don't get wrinkled."

"Okay."

Mom walked over and kissed me cheerfully. "Go
sit down and eat some breakfast now." I joined the
others and ate quickly. My aunts were nervous and
urged everyone to eat. The uncles kicked back
leisurely, shrugging off the nuisance of noise. The
house had been a web of chatter ever since the family
arrived.

I drank the last swallow of milk and excused
myself. Showering quickly, I took a half hour more
than usual to fix my makeup and hair. I wanted to look
perfect.

Soon I was ready and joined the others in the
kitchen. We waited for the rest of the aunts and began
car-pooling to the church. Dad was already there,
preparing for the big day and going over the special
things he would say to make the most of the day for
my sister. Mom had also left earlier to help Sheila.
Everyone piled into the cars, taking care not to
wrinkle the dresses and tuxedos.

The tall cross on the church tower was surrounded
by billowy, white clouds, as rays of sunshine broke
through, giving a look of glory to the cross. The
flowers in the entrance showed their many colors
proudly as we drove past to the parking area in back.

Jeanne led the way, with Gretchen and me in tow, to
the bride's dressing room. The room was alive with
excitement, giggling girls, and rustling taffeta as the
bridesmaids slipped on their lovely dresses. Sheila
stood dressed on the opposite side of the room. She
was beautiful! Mom was helping her fasten her veil in
place.

We dressed quickly. The photographer was due in only a few minutes. The plaid bows were tied at our waists and baby's breath tucked in our hair. All the maids held bouquets in hand, except me. Mine was tied to the handle of my crutch. That way I wouldn't have to carry it but could still give the illusion that I was holding it. We posed for pictures for the bridal scrapbook and then watched as Mom, Dad, and Sheila posed for theirs.

The time of the procession drew nearer and nearer, and we headed for the sanctuary. I was having trouble walking because the long, taffeta folds fought my crutches and threatened to entangle them. I prayed I wouldn't trip. The church was filled, which in this case meant approximately a thousand people. Everyone knew about my goal, and I knew I would be receiving nearly as much attention as my sister, the bride. *Oh, please! Let me make it!* I prayed. I would be so humiliated if I did something wrong.

All the bridesmaids lined up in their assigned order and waited for the procession to begin. Behind us stood Sheila in her long, flowing gown, talking quietly and lovingly to Dad. He was in his minister's robe so that he would be ready to complete the ceremony after giving her away. What a tender moment, watching those two! Dad's eyes were teary, and Sheila wore a nervous grin. Affectionate words were obviously being exchanged.

I heard the organ, but mostly I was aware of the butterflies in my stomach. I stood patiently with the others for what seemed to be hours; in actuality, a mere two or three minutes. Jim Coleman, the handsome groom, and his groomsmen waited near the altar for their partners to proceed. Finally the organ music gave its cue, and Jeanne, the maid of honor, started down the carpeted aisle. Just a few seconds later, another girl followed. I was next. I waited nervously as I looked at the many people watching. I prayed silently, *Oh, God, please let me do okay. Please don't let me fall or stumble.*

The time came. No hesitation could be permitted. I began the walk. The people murmured with joy as they watched me, for many had upheld me in prayer over the past devastating year. Behind me followed eleven-year-old Gretchen. Each step I took I held my breath, hoping to make the next stride safely. I looked straight ahead, holding my chin high as I looked neither right nor left, nor down where I was stepping.

I reached the front, took my place, and breathed a sigh of relief. The traditional wedding march blared loudly, commanding the people to rise for the giving of the bride. Sheila's innocence clothed her with splendor. Her white gown hung elegantly about her slim, tall figure. The old-fashioned collar drew high on her neck, and the extravagantly beaded material gave her a look of royalty. My eyes filled with tears.

What a day of complete and holy joy! Watching the union of two children of God as they committed their lives to each other and again to Him was a sacred, blessed time. The ceremony passed quickly and ended with a kiss. This was a relationship that God had planned and placed His hand upon from the beginning of time, and as I watched it fulfilled in marriage, I dreamed of when I would have such joy.

The magical day drew to a close. The groom and bride left for their honeymoon, and the guests departed. Tomorrow, all the family would begin the task of cleaning up. I slipped out of the house to see

Hosstar. He was anxious to be free of his pen, and during a break in cleanup, I harnessed him to grant his desire. The little horse was so spunky, he was a delight to be around. He bit playfully at my clothes and turned quickly away, then repeated the little game.

"Hosstar, you cut that out!" I laughed, trying to settle him down. As I led him from the stall, he danced about excitedly. His mood altered, and he became more nervous than playful. I looked at him quizzically. "Hosstar, what is the matter with you today? One day without exercise, and you go nuts! Quit being so hyper!"

I could sense he was going to be very unpredictable today, and frankly, that idea made me a little restless as well. I led him near our back gate where there was plenty of room to exercise him. I had learned to lunge him on his lead rope around and around in a circle while I pivoted in the middle on my leg. Maintaining my balance wasn't easy, for I had to hold Hoss with one hand and support myself on a crutch with the other.

Slowly he began jogging around me. He picked up a pace, then settled into it. His jitters began to dissipate as he circled me.

"Good boy, Hoss!" I encouraged his improved behavior. "Good boy!"

I clucked, and he went into a slow, controlled canter. I ordered him to stop. Amazingly, he obeyed. He was doing great! I began to relax.

"Okay, now, let's walk." He followed my coaxing and began to circle me again. I had led him to a jog, when a car sped noisily past the gate and blared its horn. Before I knew what happened, Hosstar jolted to one side in terror and the lead rope was torn from my hand. I fell to the ground as Hosstar ran wildly from me.

"Hosstar!" I cried after him, but he ran on. The lead rope trailed behind him and entangled itself around his back legs. He became even more frantic as he fought for freedom from the binding rope. He loosed himself and sped away.

"Dang it!" I murmured. There was no way that I, a one-legged, fourteen-year-old could catch this high-spirited, frightened colt. I decided to go find Uncle Henry, a farmer who fortunately had come for the wedding. *Poor Hoss, he's been around such few cars, and that stupid smart aleck just had to harass him.*

I was quickly making my way to the house for help when I heard the crash of splintering glass. Horror gripped me, and I screamed. "Hosstar!"

I couldn't see the sight, but I knew what had happened. I ran as fast as I could on crutches, tears blurring my vision. I had to stop a few times to keep from tripping over pebbles that caught my crutch tips.

I reached the house puffing with exhaustion, my leg burning from the stress of the big hill, and simply stared at the shattered, sliding-glass door. I couldn't move for fear of seeing my baby horse. I fully expected a terrible, bloody sight. In panic I burst into tears, thinking of my dream and the treasured friend I was sure had been destroyed like the plate of glass.

My uncle ran to me. "Carol, he's all right. Come on!"

He motioned me into the house, and we passed through the now-empty door frame.

"Where is he, Uncle Henry?"

"Well, the last I saw, he was running through the kitchen. I don't know where he is now!"

Squeals and screams came from the south side of our house, where my bedroom was. We ran toward the ruckus.

In the kitchen we stopped to see what was going on. The room was full of excited women, some frightened as they pointed down the hall. Others were laughing and plugging their noses as they pointed to a large pile of steaming horse manure sitting on my mother's tile floor.

I ran ahead of Uncle Henry, ignoring their laughter, and picked my way carefully down the steps that led to my room. At the far end, my closet stood open, with the rear end of my colt sticking out. I approached him easily. "Hosstar, come here."

He lifted his head but refused to retreat from the darkness of the closet. He had found his security.

After joining him in the small space and reestablishing his trust in me, I guided him back outside with Uncle Henry's help.

We carefully checked his trembling body for cuts and damage. Uncle Henry had owned a horse for many years on the farm, as well as many other animals, and he knew a little about nursing them to health. We found only one cut on Hosstar's back left leg.

"It doesn't look too bad," Uncle Henry said as he studied the bloody area. "But we should still call the vet, just to be on the safe side. You don't want it to get infected."

The cut turned out to be minor, but I had to give Hosstar shots every day to keep infection from setting in and new bandages to keep it clean.

Hosstar brought a whirlwind of excitement to the

Schuller household for many months. Soon after he ran through the house, he again spooked and pulled away from me. This time he landed in our swimming pool. Fortunately, he found the stairs and was out in a matter of minutes.

We were relieved there was no damage to him or the pool, especially considering the fact that only weeks before a friend of mine had had a horse do the same thing. Hers had panicked while trying to escape. He had ruined the swimming pool and hurt himself badly in the process.

Hosstar was nearly a year old, but as I waited for him to grow old enough to ride, I became restless. I recalled over and over again the brief feeling of freedom and joy I'd felt back in Baltimore when I rode Hosstar's sire. Even while I looked at the brochure I'd been given about skiing, I dreamed of the day I would fly on the back of Hosstar. The desire for that freedom and speed brewed inside me. I knew I couldn't wait until Hosstar was broken; I wanted that feeling now! I grew more and more anxious for Thanksgiving, when I would learn to ski. Maybe, that would hold me over until I could ride Hoss.

The flight to Denver from Los Angeles had been short and beautiful as we flew over the Rocky Mountains on the 747. Debbie Harmes, my best friend from church, had gladly accepted my invitation to accompany me on this exciting trip—just the two of us alone. It was an adventure we barely ever dreamed of taking.

The drive to Winter Park from Denver took two hours by bus, and the whole way we chattered excitedly about the week that lay ahead. We snuggled deep into our California coats, which provided little shelter outside against the biting wind. Two feet of snow had fallen just days before our arrival, and Colorado was in store for a white Thanksgiving. The tall, rugged peaks loomed above us magnificently as we weaved through the mountainous roads. The side of the road dropped hundreds of feet out of sight as we crossed Berthoud Pass. The view was spectacular! My heart pounded uncontrollably at our surroundings.

Upon arrival, Debbie and I soon settled in at our cozy, homey lodge and were quickly befriended by the generous hosts. Despite our excitement, we were both exhausted. We were given a quick bite to eat before retiring to our room. Tomorrow we would have our first skiing lesson, and I wanted to be ready.

I soon heard Debbie's deep breath coming from the twin bed beside me; however, sleep escaped me. I couldn't believe how excited I was. I seemed to be even more excited than when I had learned to ride again. Somehow I knew I would love everything about skiing. The mountains and the snow stirred something within me. The majestic masses of rock that reached high into the heavens awakened in me the awareness of the untameable awesomeness and power of God. The blankets of snow only magnified their beauty.

Morning came, but not soon enough. I awakened before dawn with the same excited anticipation I had gone to sleep with the night before.

After Debbie woke, we showered and dressed for the ski slopes, and, of course, we curled our hair to perfection for the many teen-aged boys we hoped to meet. Breakfast was provided by the lodge, and then we were driven along with other guests to the ski area.

Driving through town, we took in the many sights

we had missed because of our late arrival the evening before. We neared the slopes and waited our turn in line for drop-off. The lodge owner showed us where the office for handicapped skiers was, and arrangements were made to pick us up that afternoon around five. We found the office despite the holiday crowds and were welcomed warmly.

The small office overflowed with people who had all kinds of handicaps, as well as people without handicaps at all. Artificial legs lay everywhere, piled in every corner of the room. At first I was shocked, but then I laughed to myself as I took in the sight. I'd never seen anything like it. We were escorted to an office and introduced to Hal O'Leary, the young tan-faced founder of the special program.

"Carol, what a pleasure to meet you," he said, extending his hand graciously. "Who's your friend?"

"This is Debbie."

"Hello, Debbie." He smiled warmly, then continued. "Let's talk a little and get to know each other, shall we? Take a seat, and make yourselves comfortable. I'll tell you what we will do to get you on skis, but first, I want to know a little more about you."

"Well," I said easily, "what do you want to know?"

"Have you ever skied before, Carol?"

"A little, before my accident, but not much."

"How did your accident happen?"

"Motorcycle. My cousin and I were crushed between two cars."

He winced. "Yeah, we have a lot of motorcycle victims here. Cancer is a biggie around here, too. How old are both of you?"

"Fourteen," Debbie answered.

"Fourteen!" He raised his eyebrows. He repeated to himself in surprise. "Fourteen! I thought you were both eighteen!"

Of course we loved it! He couldn't have said a nicer thing, but we managed to keep our appreciation of the compliment hidden. Getting excited over something like that wouldn't be very mature! Actually, ever since our arrival in Colorado, we had been mistaken over and over again for being older than we actually were. Our height (five foot eight) probably contributed heavily to the miscalculations.

As we continued talking, three college-aged fellows hobbled into the outer office. Two of them had only one leg each; the other appeared to be normal. Their raccoon faces gave away the fact that they were frequent skiers.

Hal interrupted our conversation and pointed toward them. "They're part of the Handicapped National team that's going to Norway in February to race in the World Cup."

The fellows came closer. Each of the two who had only one leg didn't walk on crutches but on outriggers. I had seen those "ski crutches" in pictures from the Handicapped Ski Association. The crutch-like device snapped to the forearm, just like forearm crutches. A handle to grasp for control protruded about seven inches below the cuff. The outrigger shaft then extended to a short ski, approximately eight inches long, that glided on the snow to give the amputee support. However, the outriggers used in the pictures looked much longer. The ones these guys had were so short; they bent away over to walk. How could they use them for balance? They looked so terribly awkward!

"Hal, are their outriggers always that short?"

"Yes."

"How do they use them to balance when they ski?"

"They don't. They really just use their ski. They wear the outriggers just in case they catch an edge or something happens to throw them off. Then they can put the outriggers down and catch themselves so they don't fall and continue on without interruption. One of our girls uses poles when she skiis, but a lot of people don't like to take a chance on blowing a race, so they use outriggers."

Seeing my puzzlement at his explanation, he added sympathetically, "Don't worry. You'll learn what I'm talking about as you ski more and hang around."

"Will mine be that short?" I was beginning to get a little nervous.

"Oh, no! They're racers and very good skiers. You're just learning. Most of our skiers don't ski like they do. They're the exception." His words were comforting, but they also built awe in me. I wished I could watch them ski. "Hal, did you teach them to ski?"

"Yes, they were some of my first students."

The threesome walked into the office and began jabbering at Hal until he interrupted.

"Chris, Ri, Bill, this is Carol and Debbie. Carol's taking her first lesson today."

They all greeted us, then they continued their chatter. I couldn't understand a thing they were talking about, and by the look on Debbie's face, I knew she couldn't either. They were telling Hal about their day of training.

Chris was blond with gold-rimmed glasses and looked like John Denver. Ri was Cambodian, with a big, conniving smile, and Bill was over six feet tall with dark hair and an easygoing look about him. Chris and Ri each had one leg.

After a few minutes, Hal interrupted them again. "I have to start Carol on her lesson now, you guys. We'll talk later."

"Nice meetin' you," they said and left.

"Hal," I asked, after the three were gone, "what's wrong with Bill? Why is he on the team?"

"He's an amputee. His leg is off below the knee, so he skis with his prosthesis on. If you ever get your mobility back, you can do that, but your knee will have to work well in order for you to ski that way."

"Does he compete against those guys?"

"No, he's in a different class."

"Does he use outriggers, too?"

"No, he uses poles. If you saw him on the mountain, you'd never know he was a 'gimp.' One of our guys, who skis the same way as Bill, taught as a ski instructor for 'normies' at another ski area for a couple of years before they even knew he had an artificial leg. That's how good they look. Come on, let's go get you equipped."

"Hal?"

He stopped and looked at me. "Yes, Carol?"

I paused, wondering if the question I wished to ask was foolish. "What are 'gimps' and 'normies'?"

Hal laughed. "Sorry! We forget many people don't know what we mean when we say that. A 'gimp' is a person with one bad leg and 'normie' is short for us normal people."

"Oh!" Debbie and I nodded in understanding.

We followed him closely and tried to take in everything we were experiencing. This was all so overwhelming! Hal fit me carefully with the necessary equipment and then led us to the mountain, carrying my one ski and outriggers along with his single ski and outriggers. He was not handicapped, but he, too, skied with one ski and outriggers when he taught, so he could demonstrate for the student. I followed behind on crutches, picking my way carefully across the foreign terrain. My crutches sank deep into the snow, and the boot I wore made my steps uneasy.

Hal stopped and dropped my ski in the snow, and with a lot of his help and support, my boot clicked soundly into the binding. He put his ski on and then showed me how I was to use my outriggers to push myself around on the flats. Debbie waited and watched curiously.

With little coordination, I learned how to sidestep up a hill with one leg, using my outriggers. I placed my ski sideways, then put my outriggers farther up the hill than my ski. Then putting my weight on the outriggers, I dragged my ski up to where they were centered. That was my sidestep, and as I got stronger and the outriggers became more a part of me, I would be able to do it quickly and easily. For now, the steps were mere shuffles.

Next, Hal brought me to a bunny hill, where all the small children were learning to ski. The run was only about twenty feet long, and I felt foolish skiing on such a hill. I was determined to learn fast so I could leave.

At the top of the tiny slope, Hal showed me how to use my outriggers for balance and demonstrated a stop for me. Following his instructions, I glided straight down the hill, wobbling from side to side but upright. When I turned my ski to the left for a stop, I tipped over.

"That's all right, Carol. You'll get the hang of it. I can tell you're going to learn fast."

We sidestepped up again. Hal demonstrated again for me how to hold my outriggers and then skied down to a stop. Again, I tried to follow his instructions. I placed my outriggers in front of me, letting them rest on the ground. I pushed my weight forward and began moving. I dug the metal claws on the back of the outriggers into the snow to help brake myself, then as I turned my ski to the left, I brought myself to a halt—a standing halt.

"Good girl!" Hal encouraged.

After repeating the maneuver a few more times, it was obvious I had caught on.

"Okay. Now you need to learn how to turn and how to stay stable for a longer period of time. We have to move to another hill. It will still be a beginners' slope, only longer. We'll get a snowmobile to take you up so you don't have to get on a chair yet. You two wait here, and I'll go round one up for us."

In minutes he was back with a snowmobile and a driver.

"Carol, this is Bob. You sit on the back, hold onto his waist with one hand, and hold onto your ski with the other. I'll take your outriggers, and Debbie and I will ride up on the chair and meet you at the top. Now Carol, don't worry. It's not steep at the top, but if you get up there and you don't like it, we can always put you back on the snowmobile and he can bring you down."

I handed my outriggers to Hal and with Bob's help settled myself on the back of the snowmobile. I fought to get my boot out of the binding. Hal helped me.

"Hal, don't worry about me. I'm tough!" I called

as the snowmobile zoomed off toward the top of the mountain. My excitement intensified, along with my fears, the higher we went. We drove on the side of the slopes, past all the skiers. Bob tapped me and pointed to our right. There was a one-legged skier.

He leaned his head back and yelled, "That's one of the team members: Ri Armstrong."

My heart jumped as I watched him bound to and fro with ease and grace. His dark face showed the ecstasy he felt as he completed the run. Determination flared violently within me. I wanted to ski like *that*. I wanted to have total freedom with my ski, just like that! The mountain no longer intimidated me.

At the top of the hill, we waited only minutes before Hal and Debbie joined us. The two were laughing as they skied to our side. I was glad to see that Debbie was having fun as well.

"Are you ready?" Hal asked enthusiastically. He took my hand and helped me to stand. I put my ski on the snow and took the outriggers from him. The area where we stood was flat but before us lay a long, gentle slope. My nervousness returned, but it looked like so much fun! I couldn't wait. Hal put his arms around my waist and helped me keep my balance while I jiggled my foot around, trying to get my boot in the binding. We tried again and again, but I couldn't get it. I was embarrassed. *How stupid, not even able to get my own ski on!* But I knew it would come with time. Bob got off the snowmobile to help. He got down in front of me and directed my foot carefully, until it clicked tightly in place.

Hal continued to hold me steady with one arm around my waist, while I slipped my arms into the outriggers. After I had gained my balance, he let go. I leaned on my outriggers and listened as he gave instructions.

"Now, remember, put your outriggers about a half a foot in front of you. What you're going to do is go a little ways, and then make a stop, just like you did on the bunny slope. Like this."

He skied twenty feet and stopped, just like before. Again, I pushed my weight forward a little. I had trouble getting my ski to point downhill, so Bob helped again, then I was off. I skied right near Hal and stopped.

"Good!" He "skated," or walked on skis, to me. "Now, this time, do the same thing, only instead of turning your ski so far up the hill for a stop, turn it just a little so you're still skiing downhill. Then turn it the other way, and stop. Watch me."

He was so smooth he made it look easy. "Okay, Carol. Come on! Just do exactly what I did."

I shuffled my ski until it faced downhill and began sliding. I leaned heavily for support on the outriggers and glided down slowly through the powdered snow. What a beautiful day! The sun shone brightly, and the clouds were wispy and few. The scenery that spread before us was spectacular, complete with a village nestled in the distance. But as beautiful as the scene was, my concentration was focused on that one ski. I began to turn it as if I was going to stop, but before it was too far up the hill, I shuffled it back to point downhill again, just like Hal said. I went a little ways, holding my breath and hoping for success. I turned it the other way and stopped.

"I did it," I whispered to myself.

"You did it! Good girl!" Hal came to me and gave me a hug. "You're doing great. Let's go some more."

It wasn't much longer, however, before I tired. I could only ski a little way before I had to stop and sit in the snow for a rest.

As the week went on, I became more and more confident with my ski and began adventuring with Debbie on other runs. Hal took me out a few more times and was overjoyed at my progress. Every word he spoke I cherished like gold, and I practiced what he showed me over and over and over again, until I was too tired to go on. Chris, Ri, and Bill quickly befriended Debbie and me, and nearly all our free time off the hill—as well as a little time on the hill— was spent with them. I questioned them again and again about skiing and how I could be better. I'm sure I nearly drove them nuts!

Chris talked with me about the Handicapped Nationals at Winter Park in March and encouraged us to come back for them. "Carol," he said, trying to convince me, "you should really ski in them. They divide the skiers into three classes: A, B, and C. The skiers you know are all in the A class, and you wouldn't be able to ski in those races, but you could go in the qualifications race and get into the C class. There they'll start teaching you how to race. The experience would be really good for you, and then you could watch *us* race and get more of a feeling of what it's all about."

"I don't know, Chris," I responded. "First of all, I just learned how to ski this week! I wouldn't know the first thing about going through those poles."

"They're called *gates*, Carol," he interrupted.

"Oh, excuse me! *Gates*. Second, my parents probably wouldn't go for it. It sounds like a blast; but I just don't think I could."

"Well, think about it anyway."

"Okay."

When the week drew to a close, I had learned more than I could have dreamed of. Chris and Ri were a big help, and I think I learned twice as much as I would have if I had not had the privilege of their attention. I wanted to be able to ski like them so badly, yet I had other things to do: Hosstar, school, church, friends. . . . But I hadn't seen the skiers actually race, and I now began thinking seriously of going out to watch them in the Nationals. I had no idea that watching a simple race would catch me—hook, line, and sinker.

9

Choosing a Course

THE HOLIDAY PASSED quickly after my return home. February rains flooded California, giving the local San Bernardino Mountains snow beyond measure. As the date for the Nationals in Winter Park came closer, I became excited and grateful about going. But despite my yearning to ski, my free time was still focused on my darling Hosstar. I visited the nearby mountains only twice before leaving for the national races in March.

The sun was bright on the first day of the races, and the snow which spread across the mass of mountains glittered as it caught glimpses of the intense rays. March in the Rockies raised hopes of warm weather and pleasant spring skiing, and as usual both expectations were met.

Registration had been hectic and confusing for a

novice like me, and I was glad when the races were
ready to begin. High encouragement was showered on
me as I prepared my equipment for use. I had no clue
about what I was doing, but I tried with little success
to copy what I saw the others doing around me.

I'm crazy! I said to myself, watching all the people
scurrying about getting ready to go to the top of the
mountain. *I have no idea how to go through the
"gates"! I don't even know how to wax my ski! I'll
probably fall on my butt if my ski is waxed anyhow!
What am I doing here? Why did I listen to those guys!*
Even as my nervousness multiplied, I gathered the
remainder of my equipment and headed for the
chairlift.

This was the day of the qualification race where
officials would determine by our times what classes
we would compete in. I knew I would be in class C,
the beginners' class, and although no one had to
qualify for that particular class, Chris and Hal talked
me into running the qualification race anyhow.

As I walked out into the bright daylight, I squinted
my eyes for protection from the rays, then pulled my
glasses in place. Debbie walked close beside me
carrying my ski and outriggers. She had made such a
wonderful traveling companion on the Thanksgiving
trip, and her company was more than welcome again.
Besides, she also wanted to see our friends on the race
team.

I walked carefully on the treacherous terrain of
slush, shaking my head back and forth. "Debbie, I
don't know why I'm doing this. I'm going to feel so
stupid," I said.

"Well, Carol," she said with sarcastic overtones,
"you sure learned your father's teachings well. Posi-

tive thinking, huh? Maybe like father, like son, but for sure it's not like father, like daughter!" Then she added encouragingly, "Just have fun, Carol. Who cares what anyone thinks of you? They might not all be that good themselves. Who knows? You haven't seen them ski! The important thing to remember is you're just doing it to have a good time."

"I know, Debbie, but it is a race, and naturally a person wants to win. But you're right. I do want to have fun."

I tried to make myself believe my own words and the words Chris had said to me earlier in private. "Carol, you could make the B class. You've learned fast, and the people in B class don't train all the time, like the team does. Race the qualification run. After all, what can you lose?"

Something inside me hoped that what he said was true.

We stopped near the chairlift, and Debbie dropped my ski before me and handed me my outriggers. I sat in the cool snow and put my ski on. As I tried to tie my boot strap about my ankle, my fingers fumbled clumsily. Finally, I was set. I worked my way up from the ground to a standing position. Debbie and I slipped to the handicap entrance to cut past the long lines of people. We were put immediately on the chair and soon watched the many waiting skiers disappear from view.

The small ski town, nestled beneath the clear blue sky, grew smaller and smaller as we continued our ride to the summit. Mountains loomed about us in splendor. *God,* I whispered in my head, *this is all so beautiful!* Peace broke through my preoccupation with the race, but only for a moment, until we glided over the course that awaited me. It was a simple one to a racer's eyes, but to me, it was a maze of "bamboo." (Bamboo is a term used by skiers to refer to gates.)

The chairlift ride drew to an end. We stopped briefly to check our equipment.

"Well, Debbie, I guess we'd better get to the top of the course." I hesitated.

"Come on, Carol, quit stalling. It really will be fun, and it doesn't look hard at all! You're just nervous."

As we skied closer and closer to the course, I realized the truth in her words. From the air, the bamboo poles seemed to jumble together, but now in proper perspective, the course really didn't look all that hard. I just hoped I could turn when I wanted to turn. I had been skiing for such a short time and hardly at all since Thanksgiving. I was not confident about the basics, much less having the control to turn on demand. I tended to take time between turns, so having these poles set before me made me nervous. What if I crashed into one? I pictured myself taking down a couple of gates and laughed at the thought.

Skiers sat at the top of the course waiting for the race to begin, but we knew no one there. Since the team members didn't have to qualify (they automatically were put in A class), Chris, Ri, and Bill waited at the bottom of the course to hear the results. Everyone else, however, had to qualify for A, so I would be racing against many A class racers in this qualification run.

Debbie helped me fasten my race bib. Silence fell between us. Finally after a few minutes, I broke the irritating quiet. "Debbie, talk or something! This silence is driving me nuts!"

The picture I gave Mom for her birthday. It was the last one taken of me before the accident.

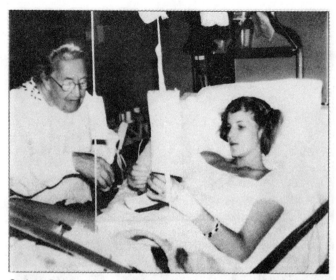

Corrie ten Boom somehow knew I was going to be well again.

Lori was a faithful visitor during my hospital stay.

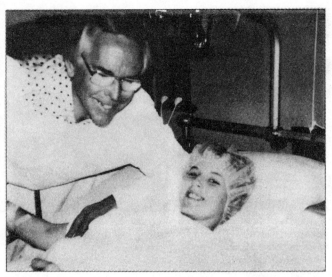

"God is faithful," Dad said when I recovered from my second surgery. No truer words were ever spoken.

Mom hands me my cake on my fourteenth birthday—a holiday away from the hospital.

It was a thrill to meet B.J. Thomas after listening to many hours of his inspiring music.

I still enjoy my beautiful Arabian horse, Hosstar.

Several months after the accident, I was determined to walk down the aisle in Sheila's wedding. Jeanne is to the left of Sheila and Gretchen is on the far right.

My first time on skis after the accident and three years later with Mom and Dad, who came to see me in the 1983 U.S. Nationals.

A good tuck...

...and a fast turn...

can take seconds off your time.

Fundraising for the National Handicapped Ski Association with Hal O'Leary.

Relaxing between speed runs. I never expected to ski fifty-five miles per hour.

Carrying the 1984 Olympic torch made me feel at one with the athletes.

"What do you want me to say? Why don't you talk!"

"Just say something."

Before she could reply, the starter began calling off the numbers of the first racers. They lined up and then one by one began leaving the starting gate. The next racer in the gate stretched his outriggers in front of him, the tips turned outward. The starter ordered him out, and the racer pushed hard, shooting himself out the gate.

"Debbie, how am I supposed to start? I don't know how to put my outriggers like that!"

"Not that many are starting like that guy did," Debbie answered. "Most of them are just letting their skis slide out. Just do that."

"Yeah." I still didn't know what I was doing here.

The starter called out, "Number 25, line up!"

I was looking again at the beautiful scenery surrounding us, hoping to ease some tension. Debbie nudged me.

"Carol, they called your number, go up there."

"Oh, I didn't even hear him."

I got up unstably and eased my way over. Everyone watched me approach the starting gate. I accidentally poked a girl who was sitting in the snow with the tip of my ski. "Sorry," I said. I nearly fell trying to get by someone else lying around waiting for his start and then hit someone else's ski. Everyone just watched me. I was so embarrassed. *Well, Carol,* I thought, *you've always liked sticking out in a crowd. Now you've got it! Oh well, who cares what anybody thinks!* I pushed the feelings aside and entered the gate as I'd seen the previous racers do.

As I approached the timing wand, I began to lose

my balance and my ski slid forward. The starter wasn't ready for me to start, but apparently my ski was. My heart beat furiously as I fought for composure. The starter quickly pulled me back. I tried again. The same thing happened three times. Finally another official got down and held my ski from going over the starting mound. He said with a friendly smile, "As soon as the starter gets to three seconds, I'll let your ski go, okay?"

"Yes, that will be fine. Thank you."

He was bigger help than he realized. Chris had told me it was legal to start leaving the gate at two seconds. "Don't leave before three though, or you'll be disqualified." His words rang loud and clear. I fought to keep my head clear from confusion.

The starter began, "Racer ready?"

I nodded yes.

He continued, "Ten seconds, . . . five, four, three, two . . ." My ski slid easily from the small mound. The first set of gates came up quickly. I skied through or around them as if they were just an obstacle in the way that I had to avoid. I did the same thing with the next set, the next, and the next. It was actually a simple course. There were no really tricky parts in it. Everything became self-explanatory as I proceeded. I went faster and faster. I tried hard to ski the way I'd seen Ri and Chris ski on the mountain at Thanksgiving. I could feel that I wasn't even close, but at least I was making it down okay.

Finally the last turn was completed, and I glided across the finish line. Hal and Chris met me as I stopped.

"Good girl!" Hal said as he hugged me. "Good girl!" he repeated.

Chris's voice was excited. "I told you you could do it. That wasn't so hard, was it? You did so well! You really looked good! You really did!"

Hal interrupted. "Carol, I can't believe how good you looked for the first time on a course! I just can't believe it! You've only been skiing a couple of times. I'm so proud of you!" He put his arm around my shoulders and shook me proudly. Their compliments were put aside at the sound of the announcer.

"The time for Carol Schuller: 48:62." Hal and Chris sounded together, "All right Carol, that's a good time. You've made the B class, no doubt about it!"

I had no clue as to what was a good time and what was a bad time. I just took their word for it. They seemed to be pretty excited, so I thought they were sincere.

"I'll go doublecheck for you, Carol." Hal ran to find out the results. He was soon back. "Yep, you're in the B class. That means you have two more races to run, a slalom, and a G.S. The slalom will be tomorrow, and the G.S. on Wednesday."

I looked at him in bewilderment.

Chris explained. "The slalom race is the shorter of the two. It has smaller and quicker turns and will probably be the hardest one for you. When you're in a more competitive slalom, they throw some trick gates in, and you have to be careful to inspect the course before running it so you don't go through a trick gate backwards and get out of line for the next turn. But your race won't have anything like that. You'll just have to turn quicker and more often than you did in this one. The G.S. is the giant slalom. It will be a lot like the one you ran today, only a little longer."

I nodded as I listened to my short lesson.

He went on. "The A class has a slalom race, a giant slalom race, and a downhill race. All our races are over on 'Hughes run.' They're a lot steeper, faster, and much more difficult. Your races will be at different times from ours, so you can come watch us. Now that you've run a course, you should be able to learn more by watching us. I'll explain more as you have questions, okay? Just ask me if you don't understand."

"Thanks, Chris."

By the end of the week, I found Chris to be right in just about everything he'd said. The slalom was hard for me. I fell. I was more disappointed than I had thought, but I made up for it in the G.S. when I took second. To say the least, Hal, Chris, Debbie, and especially me, were incredibly surprised. I had loved every minute of that race. I only wished it had been a little more straight and a lot faster.

After experiencing racing firsthand, I learned a tremendous amount watching the team members race. I was in awe of their speed in the downhill. My heart pounded furiously as I watched their skis hold long, fast turns. I wished with all my heart to ski like that at those speeds. The slalom and G.S. were incredible to watch as well, but skiing the downhill became my dream that day. I had to make the A class to race the downhill.

Someday, I told myself, *I will run that race; that is my race. I want to be a downhiller!* I remembered vividly the picture I'd seen in the store window at Christmas the year before. "Franz Klammer: World Downhiller." I remembered the blur of snow behind him and the muscular legs as they strained to hold the long tedious turn. I dreamed a lot to myself but said nothing to others. I was afraid of being a foolish dreamer. It was a big dream and probably an unrealistic one, but what else are dreams for?

Life resumed its normal pace of school, youth group, and Hosstar. Despite all my activities, my mind remained captivated by my new, big dream—*racing*. I called Chris often as questions came to mind. I asked him about skis and why he had four or five pairs. I asked him about training and what it involved. I asked him anything I could think of, and he answered everything patiently and efficiently.

One night while I racked up my parents' phone bill talking with him, he remarked, "Carol, if you're so interested in racing, you should move to Winter Park. This is about the only place where a handicapped skier can get good training. Maybe you could come out here for college in a few years and then train on the weekends. You should think about it."

"Chris!" I answered in frustration, "I don't want to wait that long! Why shouldn't I start training now? Couldn't I train at a local mountain next season?"

"Well, I don't know if you could find any good coaching. There are some good coaches out that way, but not for the handicapped. We ski so differently. I'm afraid they might teach you a technique that could screw you up. I suppose the best thing for you to do next season is just ski as often as you possibly can. Try to remember how Ri and I looked, and try to do that. You need to gain confidence on your ski before you do anything. Just ski as often as you can."

I made up my mind to do just that. I knew I could get free tickets at the local mountain, and in December I would be getting my driver's license so I could drive up myself at least once a week! Maybe I could even go more! A two-hour drive wouldn't be too bad!

All summer I waited anxiously for the winter snows to begin. Mom and Dad were highly supportive, and they, too, were eager to see me reach success. Meanwhile Hosstar continued to grow. He was developing rapidly and needed more advanced training than I could give him. I didn't know how to break in a horse, and it was that time.

Finally one day I received a letter from a family up in northern California who had seen me interviewed on my father's television program. They owned an Arabian farm and had experience in teaching handicapped children to ride, as well as in training horses for the handicapped. Their desire to help in any way they could resulted in my sending Hosstar to them so he could be broken for riding. I hated saying good-bye to him, but they had offered their services freely and I knew he had to be trained. I would just have to keep myself busy with skiing.

All the following winter, I spent one to three days a week skiing on the local mountains. I missed some weeks, but most of the time I stuck with what I had set out to do. I used almost all my free days off school except Sundays, and my parents even gave me permission to skip school some days for "training." I didn't know how to begin to teach myself to race, so I just started at the top of the mountain and, clocking myself, skied as fast as I could to the bottom. I would try to ski each run faster than the last.

The Nationals that spring were a disappointment for me. Even after putting so much of myself into training, I remained in the B class and watched the others race the beautiful, exciting downhill. However,

I took home a gold in the G.S. and a silver in the slalom *after* falling. Slalom was quickly becoming a jinx to me. I yearned to ski the downhill, yet I kept my dreams a secret.

I continued to talk on the phone with Chris frequently and finally decided to ask my parents if I could move to Colorado that year. In my heart I knew I had to make the A class at the next Nationals. Training there was the only way to do it. Chris thought I was crazy to ask them. I hadn't graduated from high school and wouldn't for another year.

"Do you really think your parents are going to let you leave school, Carol? You're nuts!"

"Who said anything about leaving school? I could go to school up there or take correspondence courses where you go to school by mail!"

"I don't know, Carol. I don't think they're gonna go for it."

"They're my parents. You let me worry about that. If I come out, will you help coach me?"

"Sure, I'll try, but I may be accepted into a journalism school, and I'm getting a little tired of racing. I've been doing it for a long time, and I do have other things in life to do, like earn a living. I really can't promise anything, but I'll try."

"I could still learn a lot, even if you didn't help me—right?"

"Oh sure! Just being around all the good racers and coaches will help incredibly. Also, you'll have a chance to race a lot more than if you were in California."

My decision was made. Now I only had to get my parents to go for it. I knew they would do anything in their power to help me, but moving to Colorado! I wasn't so sure they'd agree to it, but I had to try.

Before going to my parents I asked questions of my school counselor. She responded positively to my idea and told me good things about the correspondence courses. She said I could go to school in Colorado, but I could get a diploma by correspondence as well. The next issue I explored before going to my parents was finding a place to live. I decided I could put an ad in the local Colorado paper for a Christian family with rooms where I could board. After I had gathered all information to support my plan, I went to Mom and Dad.

Their first reaction was silence. I waited nervously for a response. After minutes of thought, they asked the questions I was expecting.

"What about school?" Mom asked.

"Well, I could either go to school there or take correspondence studies from U.C. at Berkeley. I can get a diploma from them."

"Where would you live?" Dad asked.

"Well, I thought I could put an ad in the paper and see if there is a Christian family who would let me live with them."

"That's a good idea, Carol," Dad answered. Mom glared at him. She was much more uncertain than he was.

She asked, "You couldn't get any training down here?"

"Mom, I already tried that! I'll be seventeen in December. That's almost eighteen, and I'm mature for my age. Could we just think about it? I know you would miss me; I would miss you, too! But I also know that you trust me and that you want me to do my best in skiing. Hosstar's up in northern California, and they won't be finished training him for at least another year. Mom, I know I can be good! I just know it, as long as I can really work hard for it!

"They're picking another national team in '84 to go to Austria for the Olympics, and maybe I could make it! I know it's a long shot, but at least I could realistically shoot for the '86 World Cup team! This would be the only way to do it, and if I don't start now, I know I won't make it and I don't want to wait until '88. That's just too far away!"

"Arvella," my father interrupted, "I think it's worth looking into. Maybe there's even some kind of boarding school she could go to. I think we should really think about it."

She looked down at the floor in silence. "Well, I guess you're right. We should think about it, but I don't know if I like the idea of your being away from home. I'll miss you more than anything, and you know how much I worry." She looked at me with a light smile parting her lips.

"I know, Mom, and I would miss you, too, but I could wait to leave until after Christmas, so I could be here for the holidays and my birthday, too, and the season ends in March, so really that's not too long!"

She just nodded her head and looked at me. I would miss her most of all. She was my mom! I think mothers are the hardest people to let go of, but likewise, mothers have the hardest time letting go.

We looked thoroughly into all aspects of such a move, and after careful thought, prayer, and discussion, plans were made for me to move to Winter Park. A nice Christain couple agreed to rent me their basement which had a bedroom, bathroom, and a small den. I planned to take correspondence courses to finish my studies.

I couldn't believe I was actually going to leave. I couldn't believe I was going to live in Colorado and train! I couldn't believe I was leaving behind all the security I'd ever known—all security, that is, except God, and only because of His faithfulness and commitment to me did His security remain. Before me stretched many roads, some expected and some unexpected, but all to be traveled with haste in my quickly departing childhood.

10

Vanishing Dreams

THE FIRST BREEZES OF WINTER blew away the intense heat of the California summer of '81. My sixteenth year of life drew to an end with my fulfillment and independence in life multiplied. During the summer I had decided to have another surgery. It was a choice I alone made. The mobility in my knee had remained minimal, and the frustration of that limitation resulted in my decision. I had heard of a new amputation that was rare but sounded perfect for me. It was called a "knee disarticulation," a separation of the knee joint. I would be better off than an "above-the-knee" amputee because my weight would be focused on a joint that was naturally meant to bear weight.

As badly as I wanted to save my knee, realistically it didn't seem wise. Three years had passed since I'd started therapy, and the prosthesis I'd finally been fitted with was still not satisfactory. If I wore it in a car, I still had to stretch out in a back seat. If I went to the movies or rode an airplane I had to sit by the aisle with my leg stretched out, and my walk looked funny because my leg was so stiff.

We did, however, risk stirring again the dormant infection, but it was a risk I decided to take and was glad I did. Now it had been eight months since the surgery, and I was already walking on a different-fitting leg. Once in a while it would get sore and I would use crutches, but I could now sit in cars, movies, airplanes, nearly anywhere, with little trouble.

Along with my new leg, I also had the fulfillment of a dream all sixteen-year-olds have—a driver's license. Because my right leg was my good leg, I had no trouble driving an automatic and no trouble obtaining my treasured license.

December drifted by, leaving beautiful memories of my birthday, Christmas, and the emotional departure for Winter Park, Colorado. The good-byes at the airport were hard. I held on long and tight to my parents, trying to absorb a surplus of physical affection to carry me through the months ahead.

And then, I was in Winter Park—home of my dreams. The skiing ambitions I'd built over the past two years had simmered through the long summer months, growing stronger and stronger as winter approached. However, once I arrived, I discovered that living there wasn't all the continuous fun and excitement I'd expected. Disappointments right and left soon dimmed the flame of my cherished dream to a mere spark fighting for life.

The lodging situation I had taken at Winter Park

just wasn't working out. I talked my parents into letting me live on my own if I could find a nice, safe place to stay, and I did.

The few times my friend, Chris, could come to visit from Denver brought delight. But those times were few. Hal was no longer coach of the ski team; instead, he was putting full time into teaching new students. I saw little of the busy man who gave his life so freely to the children who crowded his office. The team members I'd known previously either trained elsewhere or gave up the sport. Both Chris and Ri lived in Denver, so their visits were infrequent. I saw Bill here and there, but he skied mostly on his own, away from others. As far as the current team members and coaches were concerned, I wasn't good enough yet to earn their attention and respect.

Most of the time I skied alone, trying to teach myself to ski like the picture in my mind of Chris and Ri the winter before. I remembered how the short outriggers seldom touched the ground; the quick movements of the one leg and ski—back and forth, back and forth; the way they kept their bodies facing downhill, relying on muscles in the lower body. The pictures of them ran again and again through my mind.

However, no matter how hard I tried, I knew I wasn't learning nearly enough. Meanwhile a hidden, silent loneliness was slowly filling my world, an isolation that began to diminish my joy in skiing.

Meeting a lovely, young Christian family kept me from total isolation. Craig and Nancy Bruns already had two children, ages ten and eight, but they gave themselves continuously to my physical, emotional, and spiritual well-being. They were truly a gift from

God during those weeks; yet I still was becoming a loner of sorts even though I dreaded that possibility.

Every day I became more lonely and depressed. The mood filled nearly all my waking hours. I sat alone during most of my free time in my private place in the midst of the beautiful Rockies. Their beauty and much of the beauty of skiing was being stolen from me day by day, and where it was being taken I did not know.

God, who had been my life and my love, was becoming a distant feeling away in the past. My cries to Him were loud, desperate, and frequent, but whenever I began to feel Him near me, I drew away. It was too painful to risk being close to God and then losing Him again and again. I didn't know why I felt the way I did, but feel it I did.

I called home two or three times a day, crying. The hug my parents had given me on that stormy day of departure now seemed nothing more than a faraway memory. I knew that I probably needed to go home—others could help fight the loneliness that tormented me—but I couldn't give up my dreams! At last I decided to stay and hope for some kind of mercy to release me from the depression. I was sure it would drown me, but unknown to me, the grace of Jesus, like an invisible life preserver beneath my arms, was keeping me afloat.

The end of February drew near after what seemed like years, bringing with it the Handicapped Regional Race in Vail. The Handicapped Ski Association had switched the program around, so everyone had to qualify in a Regional race before going to the Nationals. That way, only class A racers would be in the Nationals in March. Anyone could enter any

Regional to qualify. They could even go to more than one, and that's exactly what I planned to do.

I had little hope that I would qualify because of lack of gate training, but I was at least going to give it my best shot. I had stuck it out nearly the whole winter just to make the Nationals, and, after going through such pain and hard work, I didn't want to lose that dream. I knew Vail was going to be a hard race because that was where the really good racers would be trying to qualify.

Team members who participated in international competition were not required to qualify. However, in this particular season, there had been no international competition. Consequently, even the team members would be racing, and they would be the ones setting the pace. Despite the obstacles and my lack of confidence, I looked forward to the weekend. I hoped it would be fun. Chris and Ri would both be there, and I always enjoyed seeing them. Also, Chris had promised to help me all he could on the slopes.

Now I had something to look forward to, and I threw all my effort into preparing for the race. I wouldn't be needing my downhill ski, since there would be no downhill, but I did want my slalom and giant slalom skis in top condition. I hadn't learned anything about tuning skis, so I took them to a ski shop and had them readied. I had been given a pair of padded racing pants for Christmas, and I had them dry-cleaned, so I would look as sharp as possible.

Finally, the weekend arrived. The Bruns decided to go to Vail with me for one night so they could watch me race the next day. The drive up was filled with laughter and good times as we weaved through mountain passes. Craig bellowed loudly as his wife,

Nancy, told joke after joke. It felt so good to laugh again! I was so glad they had come. We checked into a small cozy chalet at the base of the mountain. Megan, their ten-year-old daughter, was to sleep in my room.

"Carol," Megan asked excitedly as I unpacked my bags, "do you think you'll win?"

"I don't know, Meg. We'll just have to wait and see!"

"Yeah, I know." She smiled and looked at the floor.

Bedtime was early that evening, but my sleep was restless. I waited and waited for morning, as I woke often throughout the long night. Finally the dawn approached, bringing with it a beautiful, sunny day. I dressed in jeans and stuffed my ski clothes in a bag so I could change at the area. I hoped beyond hope that maybe, just maybe, I would qualify for the Nationals.

Craig, Nancy, Megan, Josh and I went for breakfast. They ate heartily, but my nerves took my appetite. I tried hard to keep from wondering what the race results would be.

At last we made our way to the ski area. I had nearly two hours before the race would begin. The Bruns left to get their lift ticket and planned to meet me at the finish area before the race began. After locking up my skis, I hurried to find the registration area where I knew I would find Chris, Ri, Bill and all the others. As I looked around in confusion, trying to decide where to look, a one-legged skier hobbled by me.

"Hey!" I caught the stranger's attention. "Do you know where the registration for the race is?"

"Yeah," he answered, pointing up some nearby stairs. "Up there."

"Okay, thanks."

Reaching the top of the stairs, I looked for a familiar face. There were so many people I didn't know! Intimidation set in, and my excitement cooled. I couldn't find Chris, so I decided to go ahead and register.

I walked quietly to the table and went through the whole process of signing papers. Finally I got my race bib and found a chair to sit in so I wouldn't stick out so much and waited nervously, hoping to see someone I knew. I tried to look busy, so I fumbled with my bib. *Well, I should probably go and change,* I thought to myself. I took my clothes and found a restroom. After I dressed, I took my leg under one arm, my crutches under the other, and hopped back into the registration room.

The area was filled with gimps, so I didn't feel so awkward hopping around with a leg under my arm. I laid it in a corner where many other legs were strewn together. Some were black, some were white, some were short, and some were long. The sight would be unusual to many, but I had grown accustomed to it in the last year and a half. I put my crutches back on and clanked my way back to where I'd left my bib, boot, and outriggers.

I sat down casually, trying to hide my jitters. All the other racers looked as though they couldn't really care less that this was the Regionals. They laughed and poked at each other as if this was all a big reunion of old friends. I looked around at all of them and wished I could enjoy this time as much as they were.

As I scanned the room again, I caught a glimpse of a familiar pair of gold-rimmed glasses. Chris! Finally! I grabbed my crutches and hurried over to him, just as he saw me.

"Hey, Carol. How long have you been here?" He asked in greeting. Not waiting for an answer, he continued, "Are you ready?"

This time he waited for my reply. "No, not really, Chris. I'm nervous. I really don't think I'm going to make it."

"Oh, Carol, you're gonna do great. Come with me. I want you to meet a good friend of mine. Do you remember that girl I told you about who used to be on the team—Debbie·Phillips? Do you remember?"

I recalled the way Chris had spoken so enthusiastically of her. She had won her first Handicapped World Cup Downhill at the age of fourteen, and the race had been her first downhill on top of that! She had stopped racing because the wear and tear she had put on her one good knee from skiing required three knee surgeries. I had always enjoyed hearing about her when Chris spoke of her, whether it was about her skiing or the funny pranks she frequently pulled. I followed him eagerly.

Sitting at a table laughing and talking with two skiers was a short, athletic-looking girl with a shag haircut. Her dark hair was frosted with highlights. Her big smile displayed an array of white teeth, and her tanned face was creased with white smile lines.

Chris interrupted her. "Debbie, let me introduce you to someone." She looked our way and then stood, slipping her arm flirtatiously around Chris's waist. The boys she'd been talking to left. I chuckled inside as I watched her coy ways.

"Debbie, this is Carol. I told you about her on the drive up, remember?"

"Of course. Hi, Carol! Chris speaks pretty highly of your skiing. He says you're a good hopeful!"

I looked sharply at Chris. What was she talking about? Why did he have to give her ideas like that? She was going to think I was terrible when she actually saw me race.

Reading my thoughts, Chris explained. "I told her that you don't have much experience, but you have a knack for it."

She interrupted, "He says you're a natural."

Chris continued. "And you are, whether you think so or not."

Debbie began laughing and talking of other subjects, and the matter was dropped. Obviously, she enjoyed life. Soon she moved on to talk with others she knew, leaving Chris and me to talk about the race that lay ahead.

"Boy, Chris, she sure has a lot of spunk! Looks like she's pretty well liked around here."

"She is. She seems to know everyone. She lives in Binghamton, New York, so she doesn't get to see everyone very often, especially now that she's not racing. When she does see her friends, you can't hold her down for a moment." He laughed and shook his head. "She'll never change. She's a pretty neat girl. We're probably the closest friends of anyone, and I know how she really is, Carol. I'm not sure what's up, but something's really bugging her. You'd never guess by watching her, but she's really going through a hard time. She's not an amputee, you know."

I looked at him, shocked, and then I looked across the room to where she stood and studied her right leg. It only hung as long as the knee of her left leg. She was walking on crutches like everyone else. She sure looked like a gimp to me.

"Her right leg was defective at birth," Chris

explained. "Her foot is where her knee is supposed to be. It's a small little foot, and apparently it really gets in the way of her getting a good prosthesis. I was born the same way, and mine was amputated. Hers should have been, too, but she disagrees with me. Now she's really getting frustrated with the whole thing, but she still won't think of having it amputated. It's too much a part of her now."

He paused and looked at her, then back to me. "You know, Carol, you might think of asking her to coach you next year for racing. It might really be good for both of you. Don't say anything to her until you think about it, though. Hang around us this weekend and see how you two get on together. It could be a good possibility."

I looked at him, then back at her. He changed the subject and started talking about the race.

"The first race will be a qualification race, like at the Nationals where they have two groups: A and B. If you make it in B you can still qualify for the Nationals with a good-enough time on one of your races, but the chances are slimmer. The courses will be the same for both classes. After you're placed in a class you'll still have to run the slalom and G.S. I'll go over each race with you beforehand and try to explain them to you, okay?"

"All right," I answered, trying to sound confident.

The day dragged on as my nerves made the hours pass slowly. I completed the qualification run, and as expected, I was in the B. I had barely missed A but that didn't matter. I still hoped that, just maybe, I could turn in a really good run on the giant slalom and make the Nationals. The slalom course looked incredibly complex, and I tried hard to listen to the many instructions Chris rattled off. He showed me how I was to take the trick gates, where I was to turn high and drop down on the gate, where to cut a little closer, and where I should go straight through.

I didn't understand all he was talking about and ended up just hanging on to the last suggestion he'd made. "Just ski it, and pretend it's not a course." That piece of advice didn't work so well: I fell. I was so frustrated! I was really beginning to hate the slalom. I got back up and finished the course, but my time was terrible. The gates had confused me, and I had practically been lost in the maze of bamboo. I was glad to be finished with it, but now all the pressure was on the G.S. If I didn't do well in it, I wouldn't be in the Nationals.

One hour before the giant slalom was to begin, Chris took me by the course one more time for inspection. He told me where I could gain speed and where to take it easy so as not to be caught by the tricks in the course.

I tried desperately to concentrate and remember everything he said, but little was taken in. Before I knew it, the race was underway. The last racer before me was in the gate. I stepped nervously into my ski and fumbled with my outriggers, trying to get them positioned right on my arms. I dropped my gloves clumsily, and my goggles fell over my eyes as I tried to adjust them. I wasn't used to standing around in one place with my ski on, and with my leg shaking from my nerves, the ski slipped around, almost making me lose my balance. I felt as if I was about to throw up. *Why do I do this?* I wondered. *All I do is feel sick and just because I want to win a stupid race. Why do I even bother! What is racing anyhow! Maybe I should* just be content to "free ski" and not bother with races.

But something inside me loved it and each time I was finished with a race, whether I fell or not, I couldn't wait for the next one to begin.

The starter called me into the gate, and within seconds I was out and onto the course. I worked hard to pick up as much speed as I possibly could. I struggled not to bear down on my outriggers so that the metal claws which worked as brakes on the back would not dig in the snow and slow me down. Chris told me to get those claws taken off before the next time I raced. But for now, I had to bear with them. Despite my insecurity, I tried desperately not to use them. *Look way ahead,* I reminded myself, *so that the trick gates Chris pointed out won't surprise you.* I rounded gate after gate. People on the sidelines yelled their support as I skied past. I was feeling good, and my hopes began to rise. The snow flew beneath me, and each time I passed a gate, the next one seemed to be on top of me. The finish line drew nearer and nearer and I couldn't wait to cross it. That finish line seemed so close, yet so far away. Then, it was over, and a big round of applause surrounded me. The Bruns ran to me and congratulated me on a good run. The announcer spoke my time, and everyone insisted it was a good one.

I turned to Nancy and asked, "What were the other times like?"

"Well," she answered, "most of them were around the same as yours. A lot of them were slower, and a few were faster."

I nodded. "How about the girls? How many were faster than me?"

"Only one."

"Really?"

"Yep!" She smiled.

However, my excitement was subdued because I knew that only the B class racers had come down. The A class racers were still to come, and it would be the end of the day before the officials could compute the qualification time. Only then would I know whether I had made it or not.

As the rest of the racers came down, I dropped farther and farther down the list. I was still one of the top B racers and managed to beat a few A racers, too. The team members, though, blew me away!

Debbie found me, and since she wasn't racing, we watched the rest of the race together. We became instant friends. She helped take away the frustration and embarrassment I felt by making the events much less serious.

At the end of the day, the results were posted. Anxiously, I ran down the list of who had made it and who had not. My name was not there. My heart sank. Taking special note of the cutoff time, I realized I had been very close, but not close enough.

I was alone, so I let one tear drop. But I wasn't going to let it get me. I didn't want to be a baby. I'd never gain the other racers' or coaches' respect if I could not prove myself to be tough. I fought back the feelings of failure and the old depression I had felt the week before. Seeing Debbie, I went up to her and focused on having fun and shaking off my disappointment.

Chris appeared and put his arm around my shoulder, interrupting a story that Debbie was telling. He pulled me away from the small circle of people around us.

"Carol, you did good, and I'm proud of you! You skied that G.S. exactly like I told you to. Mark my words, you're going to make it some day. Just keep it up. You really are good. You have some kind of drive in you that's going to make you go for it. I can feel it! You're tough!"

I looked up at him and smiled. "Thanks. I was pretty close, wasn't I?"

"Yeah, you were. Hey, you get second in the B class women, so you'll be taking home a medal or trophy or whatever it is they're giving out!"

"Yeah, that'll be nice." I tried to cheer up at his words, but it wasn't easy.

"You know," he went on, "the girl you took second to has been skiing a while. I think she'll be a good racer, too, some day. But you've only been skiing a year, and you beat a lot of the guys!"

"Yeah," I responded.

"Why don't you go back to your room, change, and then you and Debbie and I will drive to the awards ceremonies together. I know you haven't had a chance to see any of Vail, except for the mountain. It's a beautiful place. We'll all get some dinner and see the town. How about it?"

"Sure, that'll be fun. What time is the ceremony?"

"Seven, so I'll pick you up at six-thirty."

"Okay."

I walked back to the nearby chalet. The Bruns had left an hour before to go back to Winter Park, but Chris had promised to find a way home for me.

The night that followed was one of the best times

I'd ever had. After the awards ceremony, five of us went to dinner. We were all in crazy moods and laughed the whole time. We walked arm in arm to the restaurant, forming a big line across the street. The snow beneath us was icy, so we watched our steps. Nonetheless, Debbie slipped and brought the rest of us down on top of her. Each of us, having at least one bad leg, had a heck of a time getting back up, and we fell on the slippery surface again and again.

A special bond formed between Debbie and me during our three-hour dinner. We ignored everyone else as we became engrossed in a deep, intimate conversation. Much of the talk was about God. I tried hard to answer her many questions. To my surprise, despite my own problems with God, He seemed to give me answers that satisfied and intrigued her more. With feelings of hypocrisy, I thought of the way I had felt over the last month. God had seemed to be at such a distance. However, I couldn't tell anyone *that*, especially a non-Christian. If a non-Christian knew what had been going on with me, I was afraid she would hold it against God, and I wouldn't be able to take that.

Inside I felt a continuous battle between what I thought to be honesty with people and loyalty to God. I chose the latter. Above all, I didn't want to fail God, but trying to present a less-than-honest picture caused unnecessary guilt and condemnation, which pushed God and me apart all the more. I felt unworthy even to talk to Him. If only I'd known then that God can take care of Himself! I didn't need to worry about ruining His image, for as His child I could never fail Him. Rather, I was His pride and joy.

The rest of the winter brought another bout of immense depression and loneliness, along with bronchitis that put me in bed for weeks. I fell deathly ill and had no one to care for me. (I continued to tell the Bruns that I was fine and not to bother with me.) I lay in bed, day in and day out, trying to fight the germs that killed all my body's energy. With each wrenching cough I was sure my sides would come out as well. I called Mom constantly, wishing beyond hope that she could take care of me, but that just could not be.

The last Regionals that I would have a chance to qualify for were in Mammoth, California, or Oregon. I had decided to go to Mammoth. *I've got to make that race. It's my last chance to qualify,* I thought desperately. *I just have to make it!* But I was getting sicker and sicker.

Three days before I was to leave, I tried to ski just a little while, so I wouldn't arrive totally unprepared. I was able to put my ski on and was riding the chair when I began to cough. My chest hurt so much. I gripped the center pole and rode the chilling, long incline, crying and crying as I fought the terrible pain that burned in my chest. I skied down the beginner run as fast as I could, jumped quickly out of my ski and into the car, and headed home, oblivious to the fact that I had left my ski behind.

I had made plans to fly home for a few days before going on to Mammoth and was glad I had. Mom wanted to see how sick I really was. I was more than happy to obey her wishes, for I couldn't wait to see her and home again. Even the airplane ride was excruciating. The other passengers kept their distance once they heard my wrenching coughs.

At home, the doctor examined me and discovered I

was on the verge of pneumonia. Back to bed I went, but this time I was home. Mom cared for me every minute of the day, and to have her love and attention again almost made the sickness worthwhile. The doctor called every two hours to make sure I was getting better and not worse. After two days had passed and I was still in bed, it was clear to everyone that I would have to miss the race.

Mom held me close as I cried and cried. The more I cried the more my chest hurt, and then I'd cry from the pain. It looked as if my dream for the '82 Nationals was gone. But then I remembered the Oregon Regionals. They were a long shot. I would have to leave in a few days, and I wasn't sure I would be well enough. Even if I was, I would be racing with a weak body that hadn't been on skis for nearly a month. But at least it was another chance.

As I improved in the next days, Mom and Dad gave hesitant permission for me to go. My friend, Debbie Harmes, again accompanied me—and again watched me fail. I placed in the top three, but I wasn't fast enough to qualify for the Nationals. This time it was final. My dreams *were* gone.

I tried to look ahead to the '83 Nationals, but for the present I could only mourn my lost hopes. It was March and the season was nearly over. The Nationals would be the final event. I dreaded going back to Winter Park, but I had to bring all my belongings back home. A friend had even recognized my ski and retrieved it for me.

I returned to Winter Park somewhat subdued but stayed to watch the Nationals and had a great time with friends. Again I watched the downhill, wishing desperately to be in it instead of simply watching.

Surprisingly enough, excitement began to well again. My dream was reborn as I watched the race I'd been denied. I had to make the Nationals some day, and I would give up everything until I did—health, home, everything!

11

Heading for the Nationals

COMING HOME AGAIN three weeks after my previous short visit was more than just a return to my family. The move was a return to security, rest, and above all, I felt as if I had come home to God. God seemed to abide at home in a special way. Home was my haven, and I was glad to be back.

But I wasn't to be there long. Debbie Phillips and I called each other often, and we continued to build our friendship through "Ma Bell," racking up an incredible phone bill by the end of the month. Debbie instructed me on ways to build my strength and stamina for the coming year. Before long we had agreed to work together the next season to ready me for the Nationals. I planned to move up to Binghamton, New York, where she lived so she could coach me at a small ski area nearby. She said it was good training to ski in the East, where the snow is icy. The ice would make me learn to use the edges of my skis to turn rather than sliding around on the flat of the ski. Together we planned to go to as many Regionals as we could before the Nationals so I could get some experience under my belt. When Mom and Dad okayed the plans, I began immediately the exercise program Debbie had explained to me over the phone.

My new regimen kept me busy, but not too busy to make new friends. One night I met a group of kids who attended a church which came to be known as the Vineyard. I went with them to a small group meeting they had once a week called Kinship, where they sang worship songs for a long time and then prayed for each other. I was soon attending regularly.

I also began going to the evening services at their church, which were held in a high school gymnasium. The service opened with forty-five minutes of singing, followed by the message from the pastor, John Wimber. The singing seemed to be different from any I'd ever heard before. The songs weren't *about* God, they were *to* God. The first time I attended, the gym was filled with about three thousand people. As their voices raised in song so magnificently, I began to weep because I felt God so incredibly near. They sang what the depths of my heart longed to tell God, and they sang with everything they had within them. The people sounded like a host of angels before the throne of God, and I thought the roof would tear from the rafters as the room vibrated with the music.

From that time on, I attended my father's church in the morning and the Vineyard at night. I loved the arrangement. I could dress in my Sunday clothes and go to church with my family in the morning and then wear shorts and a T-shirt to church at night. Everyone at the Vineyard dressed casually, and being seventeen, I loved it.

My time at home through the fall months was filled with fun, yet I thought continually of New Year's when I would leave for New York. I had no fears of running into loneliness and depression as I had the year before because Debbie and I would be together all the time.

The holidays came and went quickly, as they always seemed to year after year. It was a long drive to the town of Binghamton from Orange, California, but a friend of mine and I took turns driving my little Toyota Celica. Behind this we pulled a trailer full of things I would need for the winter, including a street bicycle for clear days, and indoor exercise bike for stormy days, all my ski equipment, and clothes, clothes, clothes.

Debbie left no time for goofing off. As soon as I arrived in New York, she put me to work. A three-hour workout every morning was scheduled for one month before I could go on the mountain for any kind of skiing. Our first race was scheduled for the end of January. With Debbie's plan I would ski only a week before entering that race, but she said the timing would pay off later in the season. I listened to her.

Debbie's outline for the first day of conditioning sounded grueling, but I was excited nonetheless and ready to work hard. Outside it was snowing. I had rented a small house right next door to Debbie, and I sipped a hot cup of coffee waiting for her to arrive. She had a doctor's appointment first thing this morning. During the summer she had had more surgery done on her leg and the doctor needed to keep a close eye on it. In her latest operation, they had turned the small foot attached to her knee a hundred-eighty degrees so that her heel became her knee. She was excited about having it done because of the possibilities of being fit with a good prosthesis when she was fully recovered.

I didn't have to wait long for her arrival.

"Ready to work, Carol?" she called loudly up the stairs that led to the living quarters.

"Yes, ma'am, as soon as you tell me how your doctor's appointment went."

She managed the stairs skillfully, in spite of her awkward crutches. Stairs are routine to gimps; we've all had to learn to accept them as a normal part of life.

"Oh, it went great. They said they'll be ready to start fitting me for a leg next week. I'm so excited— Carol, I just know it's going to work great!"

"That's good to hear. No more hobbling around on crutches!" I was happy for her. She was such an active girl, and being confined to crutches had obviously been hard for her. Besides a great skier, she had been really involved with competitive horse jumping. She earned her living breeding thoroughbreds and entering them in top nonhandicap shows around the nation. She had wanted to try out for the Olympics a few years before, but her horse had thrown her onto the fence she was jumping, and her back had been broken. The injury hadn't caused permanent problems, but it had put her out of the trials. Obviously, from the way she was already pushing me, she missed competing in a sport.

Debbie finished her hike up the stairs and joined me at the kitchen table. "So, Carol, do you like living in Binghamton?"

"Well," I answered, "It's beautiful here; I love the quaint town and beautiful trees. And I'm having a blast with you. But, of course, you haven't begun to crack your whip yet, so I just might change my mind when today is over!" I threw her a sidelong glance, and we both laughed.

"Well then, lazy, let's get the day over with!" She poked my shoulder with the tip of her crutch.

I hopped up like a soldier at attention. "Yes, ma'am. What first?"

"Knock it off and get down and do some stretching—twenty minutes."

I moved to the center of the living room and began a number of stretches I had learned. When I took a breather Debbie taught me some new and better ones to add to my routine.

Then she directed in a tone that warned me not to say no: "Okay, that's enough. Now, let's start with a set of fifty sit-ups, and we'll do four sets. You need to work on that slalom race, Carol. Maybe this will help a little." I obeyed and worked as hard as I could, ignoring the nausea that arose again and again. Now I understood why she had been so serious about my getting in shape before I arrived here. I had thought I was in great shape and was looking forward to pleasing Debbie, but once she started working me, I couldn't tell I'd done a single exercise back at home.

In the downhill race, the skier has to do what is called a *tuck*. She curls up in a ball with her chest resting on her knees. In the case of a handicapped skier, like me, I needed to rest my chest on my single knee, take my outriggers, and stick them directly in front of me at eye level. In a good tuck, I would look directly over the tips of the outriggers. The tuck is used to cut down on wind resistance, so you can gain more speed on the course. A good skier tries to use it every chance she can, but holding it constantly is impossible because of the turns. I had tried the year before to learn how to tuck after seeing Chris and Ri do it, but I had had a hard time. My leg wasn't strong enough.

Debbie and I both felt that the downhill would probably be one of my better races, so she had me practice a tuck in the living room with my outriggers but without my ski. I began holding it for five minutes and then ten, to develop strength and balance.

"It won't be as hard on the snow as it is here, Carol," Debbie assured me. "If you can do this on the floor, it will be a breeze on the slope. On the snow you'll have your ski and that will give you extra leverage to help you balance more easily."

I hoped she was right. I remembered the year before when I had tried to follow two girls from the team down an easy hill in a tuck. I soon gave up and watched them disappear from view.

The rest of my workout included hopping up and down flights of stairs, sitting against a wall in a chair position for five minutes, and biking.

When the three hours of torture were over, I could barely stand up. Fifteen minutes of cool-down stretches helped ease the weariness I felt, but collapse was the only thing I wanted to do. Debbie brought me a glass of orange juice and commanded me to drink it slowly. I obeyed without hesitation.

As the weeks went by, Debbie and I became nearly inseparable, except for the time she spent with her horses, which wasn't much because of her recent surgery. A beautiful prosthesis was fit to Debbie's leg. She quickly began learning to maneuver it, as she had dreamed of doing for so long.

After keeping to my workout strictly, the day came for mountain training. I was up in a flash as soon as my alarm went off. The sun was shining; frosted trees glittered brightly. Puddles formed on the sidewalks from the melting snow. The birds sang sweetly, suggesting that a joyous day lay in store, but I barely noticed. I had been getting terribly antsy to get on my ski. For nine months my heart had been crying out: ski.

Because of the warm air outside, I pulled on a T-shirt and threw a sweater over my shoulders, just in case. The padded racing pants pulled tight around my leg showing the form of my now-protruding thigh muscle. I devoured rather than enjoyed a quick, healthy breakfast, then gathered up the items on my extensive check list: three pairs of skis, one boot, outriggers, ski gloves, goggles, suntan lotion, hat, ski wax.

Somehow I managed to squeeze the load into my small car. The sun was already beating down unmercifully, and I did not hesitate to put on sunscreen. The air felt like spring despite the fact that it was only January, really the dead of winter.

As I was carefully arranging my 215-cm. skis, Debbie walked out her front door loaded down with equipment.

"Well, Carol, are you ready?"

"Are you crazy? You bet! I've looked forward to this day more than anything. Are you?"

"Yep," she answered with a broad smile on her face, "but I don't know how much I'm going to ski.

I'll have to wait and see how my leg feels. If worse comes to worst, I'll just sit in a chair at the bottom of the run and watch you come down. I can correct you and tell you what do do from the bottom. It may not be the ideal method of coaching, but it's better than nothing."

I agreed. "It'll work out. Let's go!"

"Wait a second." She grabbed my arm, interrupting my eager approach to the car door. "Did you do your stretches this morning?"

I looked at her blankly. *My stretches?* Dang, I'd forgotten. *Heck, she'll never know. It would be a hassle to do them now.* I pulled my arm away and headed for the driver's seat. "Yeah, yeah, yeah. Now let's go!"

She saw right through me. "Carol, you're a terrible liar! You didn't do them, and you know it! Now, get in the house and stretch!" She stood, arms crossed, waiting for an honest confession.

"Okay," I finally replied. "You're right. I didn't do them, and I'm a terrible liar. That's probably the only reason I don't lie more often than I do!" We laughed and went back in the house. The whole time I worked out I listened to Debbie repeat her sermon on the importance of stretching. The necessary inconvenience over, we were on our way.

The drive took only forty-five minutes, but I looked and looked, and no matter how I tried I could see no mountains. Debbie, nonetheless, assured me that a ski hill existed. When the drive was nearly over, I asked impatiently, "What are we going to—a mountain, a hill, or a valley?" There was no humor in my tone as I awaited an answer.

"Well, Carol, no matter what it is, you have to

learn how to ski all three. No matter what the conditions or the terrain, you'll never be a great skier until you can ski it all."

She was trying to avoid the question. I kept still and waited to see just what I had gotten myself into.

I soon found I had not been far from wrong. The area was not a valley, but it for sure was not a mountain. By the looks of the size of the longest run, Debbie would have no problem coaching me from the bottom. At this juncture the only thought that gave me hope for this year's training was the fact that Debbie had trained here most of her skiing days, and she had become one of the best.

We'll just have to wait and see, I thought to myself. *I hope this works.* I followed Debbie to the ticket office so we could both get season passes. The dust on the ground rose in small puffs under my crutches. I looked down in disgust. "Dirt!" I fumed under my breath. "Where's the snow? Of all things!" I looked down at the ground and shook my head at the sight.

Despite my disapproval of the area and its conditions, training that day went well. Debbie had me exercise as I skied. Instead of turning my ski back and forth as usual, I was supposed to jump from one direction to the next, lifting my ski totally off the ground. Of the many different exercises, that was the hardest, but in a way, I enjoyed it! I could tell I had been working out and working out hard. The effort was already paying off. I skied a nonstop run from top to bottom on the first day without dropping dead from exhaustion.

The skiing was hard for me, though. The varied conditions of the slope manipulated my ski until I seemed to be totally at their mercy. The top wasn't too bad, but the next section was suddenly sheer ice. Then, without warning, I hit slush.

As days of skiing this unforgivable slope stretched out before me, I began to pray for a snowstorm and some powder. Instead, the conditions became more and more difficult each day, until the slope looked like the blue glaciers I'd seen one summer in Alaska's Glacier Bay. The conditions had an advantage, however. I had to learn my ski so well that I knew how to react, how to work with it and coax top performance in any condition. My ski and I were becoming one, working sensitively together, trying our hardest to give to each other our best. I was far from good, but I could feel it coming, and I worked hard on and off the snow to help that feeling become a reality.

The week of training was over before I knew it, and I was suddenly staring a race in the face.

I did well in Powderhorn, Colorado, considering the competition I had and the little training, but my time was far from qualifying me for the Nationals. The race had not been separated into classes, so I competed against both team members and many team hopefuls. I was not much of a threat to any of them. My disappointment was not too overwhelming because I knew I had many other Regionals I could attend. I had accomplished what I had set out to do that race, which was to gain more experience. Debbie and I quickly brushed off the results of the race and focused on having a good time for the remainder of our stay.

All race participants were invited to a party at the ski lodge after the last race, and after changing clothes, Debbie and I decided to go. We were quickly welcomed into the group of racers, and Debbie, knowing a few from the team, introduced me as her new protégée. The gathering was small, designed to catch people at the end of the day before they ran off to dinner, so it was still light as people drifted in. The remaining skiers who were still enjoying their day on the mountain diminished until few were left on the mountain except some workers outside and the racers at the party. Everyone was laughing and joking and meeting new friends, and I was no exception.

As I was talking with a newfound friend, Debbie interrupted us.

"Carol." She whispered loudly to override the clamor of voices but kept her tone soft enough so as not to be overheard. "Come here." She took my arm and pulled me to the side of the room. I wondered what in the world she was up to now. The look on her face spelled trouble. Chris had warned me about her pranks, but so far I had been spared any real exposure to them.

I looked at her quizzically. "Debbie, what's up?"

Deviously she reached into her jeans pocket. Finally she pulled her hand out and held in front of me a small, silver key. I looked at her blankly.

"Debbie, what is it? What's the big deal about a little key?"

She lifted her eyebrows and smiled. "It's the key to Eric's snowmobile."

"Who's Eric?"

"He's that ski patrol guy who was helping out with our race. I talked with him a while, and I stole the key from his jacket when he laid it down on the chair over there. I had seen him playing with it earlier, and I knew it was to the snowmobile."

"So? What are you going to do with it? You know it

belongs to the area. You'd better give it back, Debbie.''

"Carol, he's cool. He wouldn't care if we took a little spin. I'm great at driving snowmobiles. Come on—let's go take it for a little while. He won't get in trouble. We'll just make sure we have it back soon. Everyone's at the party and won't even miss us. Besides, I talked for a while to the head of patrol, and he wouldn't get mad—I know it. He'd just get a kick out of it. Come on.''

As I listened, the troublemaker side of me began to rise. I was in the mood for something different and exciting. *This could really be fun,* I thought to myself. I had always been one for pranks and had been the instigator of many myself, but I wasn't really confident following someone else. I hesitated. "I don't know, Debbie.''

She looked at me anxiously, waiting for a definite answer. I looked at the ski mountain outside with its empty runs. I'd always wanted to go to the top of the mountain when no one was around. No workers, no one. I looked back at Debbie.

"Okay, let's go.''

Her eyes lit with the anticipation of causing trouble. She acted like a thirteen-year-old more often than she did a twenty-three-year-old.

"Debbie.'' I stopped her before she went out the door. "We'd better get a jacket and some gloves. It's going to be cold out there. Ours are all in the car, and I don't feel like going all the way out there to get them.''

She had a quick answer. "We'll borrow some.''

"No way! I ain't ripping off someone's stuff, too.''

"No, we'll ask them if we can use them for a little while. We'll tell them we're going for a short walk.''

"All right, but who are you going to ask?"

"I don't know! You go find someone and I'll go find someone, then we'll meet back here."

She ran off, and I began my search. I saw one guy I had gotten to know pretty well over the weekend, and he let me use his jacket without any questions. I also decided, however, that I could trust him and told him what we were up to. *Just in case something happens, somebody'll know where we are. . . .* I met Debbie again, who was now snuggled deep in a down coat and warm gloves.

We ducked quickly outside and found the lonely snowmobile. Debbie hopped in front and I climbed nervously in back of her.

"Debbie, are you sure you know how to drive one of these things?" I asked.

"Of course! I've ridden them ever since I was a little girl."

She started the engine, and off we went, fast as the wind up the mountain. As we climbed steeper and steeper, I held tightly to her waist. We hit bumps right and left and shot off the ground before dropping back into the snow.

"Debbie, don't go so fast. You're crazy!"

She kept on. We went up one ski path and across another hill, then up another path. Closer and closer we came to the top of the cold, deserted mountain. The sun was setting to our right as we continued our ascent. We sped over mogul runs, flying into the air again and again. All I could do was hold on for dear life, trying to keep from sliding off the slippery, vinyl seat.

Ahead of us lay another path for snow cats—the snow tractors that groomed the hills. Debbie headed for it without hesitation. She was making a sharp turn up the path when she missed the trail and the snowmobile fell sideways down a drop to the side of the path. Debbie and I both jumped off before the vehicle rolled onto its side, and we landed next to it in deep powder. The drop wasn't far, and after a small struggle to maneuver through the chest-deep snow, we were standing back on the path. We looked at each other and then at the snowmobile. It lay only four feet from the path but in an awkward position.

"Well, Debbie, we'd better try to get it out!" I scolded, shaking my head in frustration.

We dove again into the deep snow and, with effort, turned it right side up. Then Debbie tried the motor, but it wouldn't start. We tried again and again, until after about ten minutes it finally turned over. I looked at her in relief.

"Debbie, you drive it out, and I'll hike up. We'll have a better chance of getting it out if there's only one person on board."

"Yeah, you're right," she responded, climbing back on the seat.

She accelerated and headed for the path, but it was too steep. The snowmobile couldn't make it. She tried again and again, but to no avail. The only other way to go was down. Below us stood a mass of trees.

"Carol, look. There's a cat trail down there about fifty feet. If I can just weave through the trees, we can hit that trail and we're home free."

"Debbie, there's no way you'll make it through the trees. They're too close together."

"*Well,*" she returned acidly, "there isn't any other way. We have to try it!"

"Eric's going to kill us, Debbie. I can't believe this!"

"Don't worry, Carol. I'll get us out." She was acting like this was no big deal! I couldn't believe it! I wasn't worried so much about us (we could always hike to the bottom), but what were Eric and the patrol leader going to say? *At least the race is over, and they can't kick me out for punishment.*

Debbie turned the snowmobile toward the trees and slowly headed toward them. I crawled on all fours through the deep snow back to the path to watch.

"Oh, oh!" I heard Debbie exclaim from the trees. I whirled around.

"What's the matter, Debbie?"

"I think I'm stuck." She sat on the snowmobile, not moving. In front of the vehicle was a tree.

"Did you hit the tree?" I yelled.

"Well, not really. I think one of the blades just caught it."

"Can you get it out?" I asked nervously. From what I could see, it wouldn't be too hard to get loose, but I was kind of far away.

"I can't get it, Carol," she called in desperation.

"I'll help." I made my way down to where she stood, sunk deep in the snow. She was only five-foot-one, and the powdery snow nearly buried her.

We tried and tried. Soon we gave up. "Debbie, it's almost dark. We'd better start heading down to get help."

She looked at me with a guilty expression on her face. "I don't believe this happened," she said, obviously fearing the consequences.

"I do." I grinned back at her.

We climbed back to the path. At the top of the

mountain we surveyed the valley below. We couldn't even see the lodge. How were we going to get down? We started hiking down the steep mogul run, but our fake legs became a tremendous hindrance. We fell again and again, sliding for ten or twenty feet, then getting back on our feet. We had only walked down half the path when I heard a sound in the distance. "Did you hear that?"

"Hear what?"

"Listen."

The sound came again. I looked at her quickly. "It's a snow cat! He's out grooming the mountain. Let's go find him!"

"Where do you think he is?" The sound was getting louder, but we couldn't seem to figure out the direction the noise was coming from.

"We'll just have to guess," I offered logically. "Let's go that way." I pointed to the right. "We'd better hurry, though, because he won't be there for long before he moves to another hill." I began running as fast as I could, but I slipped over and over. I looked back to see that Debbie was having a hard time getting her fake leg to cooperate.

I yelled back, "Debbie, why don't you stay with the snowmobile? I'll go get him and bring him back. If I take too long, then just start hiking toward the bottom."

She nodded and sat for a rest in the snow. I went on. The sound got nearer and nearer. I rounded one corner of the hill and ended on another path and then another. As I approached the next hill, I saw the snow cat. I ran toward it and waved my arms, trying to get his attention.

Soon I was climbing aboard, sharing the whole

story with the shocked driver. He took me back to where Debbie sat, head in hands. At the sound of the engine she jumped up, enormously relieved to see me return with help.

The sun had now set, and the whole ski area was nearly covered in darkness. The man worked and worked, but after half an hour he gave up. He'd have to come back in the morning with some help and better tools.

"We'll be able to get it out. Don't worry, girls," he said kindly, seeing our sorrowful looks. We shivered from the cold. Our clothes were drenched from crawling in the snow, and the chill air bit at us harshly. "Come on," he continued, "let's get you two back."

We all piled in the warm tractor and headed for the bottom. As we descended, a voice came over the CB. "Hey, Hank, this is Eric. Have you seen two girls up there with my snowmobile by any chance?"

Hank looked at us and responded, "Sure have. I'm bringing them down now."

As we neared the lodge, we could see that all the lights were out. No one remained except for four figures standing outside, waiting and worrying.

Eric was so sweet; he couldn't get mad at a worm! He was worried about his snowmobile, because it did belong to the area, but his leader said it would be all right. We were simply warned never to pull a stunt like that again.

We actually laughed about it for days later, and the escapade became a favorite story to tell after a hard day of skiing, but thank goodness, the rest of our season was not quite as adventurous as our first race. Debbie did come up with a few more wild ideas, but I was quick to dampen them.

The following weeks and months became a jumble of race after race, workout after workout, airplane ride after airplane ride. We traveled from Colorado to Iowa, to Minnesota to Michigan, to Oregan to New Hampshire and North Carolina. Through it all, Debbie and I strove for improvement.

There were good times and bad times. We experienced tears and frustration, and we often fought as our strong wills struggled with each other. Our friendship, however, thrived, and the good times overrode the memories of the bad. When I became discouraged and began to lose sight of my dream, Debbie pushed me on. She kept me from dwelling on the failures, as she rekindled the hopes of making the Nationals and, some day, the team.

With the rigorous schedule of races I gained more and more confidence in the courses. I had not yet raced the downhill because few of the Regionals had them, but that event was what I longed for. In Duluth, Minnesota, we froze in fifty-below-zero weather, and I never made it out of the B class. I did take first in the giant slalom over both men and women, but I had no desire to return. When Debbie said I had to learn to ski everything, she meant everything, from ant hills to the Alps. Although I placed second and third in all the B classes I entered, I was always a hair away from qualifying for the Nationals.

Finally, in North Carolina, I did it! I won every race there was to race, and I qualified.

After the North Carolina races, things began to break loose. I began to win everything I entered, so long as there weren't team members racing. We would have to wait until the Nationals for the harder courses to tell how much I'd improved, but I seemed to have finally pulled away from most of the other women racers—except for the team members. They were my next goal. That pinnacle would be a hard one to reach, but I wanted it. The competitive spirit in me grew with every race I won.

Each day my excitement mounted for the Nationals. Every chance I had I practiced my downhill tuck in the snow, holding it for long stretches, picking up as much speed as I could before I had to slow down for other skier's safety. I was disappointed that I couldn't have any real downhill training; instead I tried to focus my attention on the slalom and giant slalom training I was getting. In between races, Debbie and I continued our skiing in New York. Debbie had no way of setting gates for me to train in, so the only gate training I really had was in the races.

The weeks went by, and I qualified again and again at the Regionals I attended. I was coming to feel that I deserved to be in the Nationals, rather than only having made it at a little race in North Carolina. As things went better for me, for some unknown reason Debbie began drawing more and more into herself. We still went out for a good time; in fact, we had great times! But she began to tire easily, and her spirits always seemed to be low.

When we were with a group of people the old Debbie would come back, but in private I could seldom get her to smile. I asked her over and over what was wrong, but she said she didn't know, so I let her be. Her new leg wasn't working right and I could tell she was discouraged, but I figured when she went back to New York the doctors would work on a new one. She tried not to let it get her down, and I could see her try with all her might to be happy for me and encourage me. I would even forget about her depression sometimes, but then it would appear again.

By the time we went to Squaw Valley for the Handicapped Nationals, both Debbie and I were ready for the season to end. She had given her all to me, but we were both tired of traveling and working so hard, and we were more than anxious for the big finale.

The Canadian Nationals were scheduled after the U.S. Nationals, but Debbie would not be going with me. She would go home from Squaw Valley. But now that we were in California, we were ready for a good time with friends and anxious to see the outcome of our year of hard training. We didn't have much expectation for my placing even close to the team girls, but we hoped I could do well in the Junior Division (eighteen and younger). There was one team member who was also still in the Juniors, but I thought I had a chance at some seconds and thirds. Most of all, I simply hoped to make it through the courses. I knew they would be different from any I'd ever skied before and far more difficult. I never had had the chance to ski hard courses but I hoped to make a good run for the money.

The day of the giant slalom was beautiful. The course was long and full of turns and on a pretty steep hill, but I fought to keep my head clear and my nerves to a minimum. After looking carefully over the first course with Debbie, I ran it through my mind over and over again so I would know it by heart and hoped I would conquer the second course as well. As in all slalom and giant slalom races, I would have to run two courses and combine my times for the final results.

When my turn came, I skied the race all the way

through, and I skied it well both times. My form was great, my confidence was firm, and I was happy with the second place that I took, right behind the team member. Next year I would try for a time closer to hers, but for this year I was more than satisfied.

"You had a great run," the team coaches said. "You have great potential." They smiled with a new kind of respect. *Maybe I'm finally on my way.*

The slalom, as usual, was not good to me. I disqualified. However, I put it aside and waited for the downhill.

Before racing the downhill, it was mandatory to take one inspection run, skiing very slowly to feel out the course. Then followed two timed, nonstop runs, so the officials could watch and eliminate anyone who skied too slowly to deserve to race or who couldn't handle the course safely. The runs were spread over two days, with the race on the third day. My training runs felt good, even as I concentrated on checking the areas that would cause me trouble and searching out the stretches where I could go for it. Each run the racers took a little faster and then the last, but they saved their all for the actual race.

Finally, the day of the downhill arrived. It was the day I had waited for since the first downhill handicapped race I'd ever seen in Winter Park. I yearned to realize my dreams of what it would be like to ski fast. *Will it be everything I think it is?* Whatever the outcome—fulfillment or disillusionment—more than anything I simply wanted to ski fast.

The time had come. All the racers before me had left the starting gate, and now it was my turn. I stood in the gate, waiting for my countdown. My head spun. I thought of my family, who had flown from

Orange to watch me race. What were they thinking
right now? Dad had seen the course with the starting
gate far away, hidden from his view. He couldn't
believe that I was actually going to ski it. He was
scared. I wondered what my mother was thinking, and
I knew she was worrying. This was their first time to
see me ski, and they were nervous and excited. I
thought of Debbie and wished so badly to make her
proud of me. My sister Jeanne and her new husband
Paul along with my little sister Gretchen also watched
in anticipation. I wanted so badly for everyone to be
proud of me.

As the countdown began, all other thoughts cleared
away. I focused on the first turn of the course and
reminded myself exactly where I planned to turn. My
leg shook from nervousness, and the helmet I wore
slipped slightly, pushing farther down on my sweating
nose. I owned no downhill suit, so I wore my racing
pants. All sounds around me seemed to shut off, and
before I knew it I was on the course and pushing for
speed. The first turn was taken beautifully, and I
quickly set myself up for the next one. I turned too
late, but instead of discouraging me the error made me
push all the harder to make up for the time I knew I'd
lost. My speed built and my stomach was nearly in my
throat, but I loved the feeling. My ski slid on the snow
with incredible ease and speed. I tried hard to set up
for each turn exactly as Debbie had directed me.

Up ahead lay the trickiest turn in the course. It
could waste a lot of time if not taken right. I
concentrated with all my might to ski it as Debbie had
said to do. I took the traverse and held it long and
steady, avoiding the natural place to turn; instead I
kept my eyes peeled for the invisible mark she'd

pointed out. I kept high, then dropped down and around the turn right where she'd said to. I could feel it was near perfection. I did it! I nailed the bottom of the course just as I'd hoped to and crossed the finish line.

The race had been everything I had hoped. I had been nervous and a little unsure, holding on to almost nothing but a prayer, but I'd loved it and I knew that love would grow.

As I came to a stop, I became aware of loud cheers. Debbie ran to me and accompanied me out of the finish area to clear the way for the next racer. My family hugged and congratulated me on a good run, and I blushed. My time was announced over the loudspeaker. I was a whole two seconds behind one of the team girls and three seconds behind the other. I was well ahead of the rest.

The third team member was not on her way down. She was only seventeen, still in Juniors, but good enough to take first ahead of me. A hush fell over the crowd as she neared the bottom of the course. I watched her. She was skiing great! She was skiing fast! She was so good. However, as she rounded the third gate from the bottom, she suddenly lost it. She was down! The crowd moaned. A mixture of feelings swept me.

This could mean I have first place! I thought, but I felt so bad for her. She had deserved to win. She was fast, and everyone knew she had trained hard the past year with racing academies for nonhandicapped skiers to reach the status she had. She tried to get up, but it was too late. Debbie jumped and hugged me. My family kissed me on every available place on my face they could find. I couldn't help being happy, but I still wished I hadn't won that way.

As expected, no other woman in the Juniors beat me, although two others in the Women's class did. They held nearly three seconds over me, but I could work on those extra seconds next year. I'd placed third overall in this event in which I longed to prevail. For now, I had more than achieved my year's goal. The finale we'd waited for couldn't have been more spectacular for either Debbie or me. What better way to seal a friendship that was sure to last a lifetime!

12

55 and Faster

DAWN BROKE OVER SOUTHERN CALIFORNIA as I strove to overcome the last length of a big hill on my bicycle. My right thigh muscle burned as it did the work of two legs by itself. My heavy breathing could be heard easily through the stillness that lay over the awakening city. Sweat trickled down my temple and spilled onto the turquoise sweatpants I wore. I'd been riding for an hour and a half, and my day's ride would be complete at the top. My artificial limb had become part of me over the past years, and now I had it strapped securely to the left pedal. However, it gave little assistance to the strong leg opposite.

I pushed and pushed until my last ounce of strength pulled me to the summit of the challenging hill. At the top I rode around in circles, trying to relax my tense vibrating leg. The first streaks of sunlight broke over the horizon, sending harsh flashes of orange and red into my eyes.

The off-season training schedule I'd put myself on (with some help from a nearby health club) took all my energy, thoughts, and time. I was awake almost every morning at four. I biked anywhere from twenty to forty miles. I incorporated both endurance riding and strength building sprints into my workout.

After the biking came an hour of swimming, which was now a daily session, and a two-hour workout with weights, which I did four days a week.

I thought of the intense, tiring work that was still ahead, and dread began to loom over me. But as soon as the negative thoughts started to prey upon me, the memory of the downhill that I'd raced months before shot back into my mind and a new surge of energy flooded me. I remembered the feel of my burning thigh as I'd held turn after turn through the long, fast course. I knew I was going to be even better this year because I was going to be in the best shape I could be before going back to Winter Park to train with the team. The coaches had liked the way I'd skied at the Nationals and had sent me an invitation to train with the team that was going to Austria in February. I accepted gladly, knowing that Debbie couldn't go through another year like the last one.

Debbie and I had talked on the phone frequently since our departure last April. Both her good knee and her short leg that had just had surgery were giving her problems with pain and immobility. Her depression intensified with each week. Once in a while she would call me in a great mood, telling me how good she was doing; then before I knew it, she was down again.

As I finished my day's worth of training, Debbie flooded my thoughts.

"God," I prayed, "what's the matter with her! When is she going to snap out of this?" I wept as I talked with Jesus. My Friend spoke nothing in return. I only felt a security that seemed to surround me like a strong fortress. Somehow, I felt as if Debbie stood outside the wall, unable to enter. The fortress didn't seem to appeal to her. She preferred the danger and adventure she had always had.

Traffic surged around my car as I fought to get home, away from the horns and the sound of motors. Everyone was on the way to work. I couldn't wait to get away from the mass of people and back home where I could have a cup of coffee, orange juice, and bran cereal. Besides a rigorous exercise routine, I held to a good diet. I had committed myself to refraining from red meats, oils, caffeine, sugar, and salt. I even made my own salad dressings with honey and mustard to stay away from excessive oil. I did cheat on certain foods, such as coffee and an occasional hamburger or steak. I was pretty good, though, because I wanted to be in the best shape I could be for the upcoming season. I was really going for it.

As I parked my car in front of the house, I noticed the empty horse corral that stood on the west side of the house. All my horses were gone now. I'd sold my first two, and Hosstar was still up north near San Jose. I missed him, but now skiing was so much of my life I knew it was best he be up there with people who enjoyed and loved him. I'd probably never see him again and I was thinking strongly of selling him, but that was too much to face right now. I just wanted to have a glass of orange juice and relax.

As I walked in the front door, the telephone was ringing. I ran and picked it up before the person calling hung up.

"Hello," I said.

"Hello, Carol?"

"Yes, this is Carol. Who is this?"

"This is Mrs. Phillips, Debbie's mom."

"Hi, Mrs. Phillips, how are you? I haven't talked to you in a long time. How's the Mister? How's the weather in Binghamton?" I had always liked Debbie's family. They had been so generous to me the few times I saw them when I was living up there.

There was silence on the other end of the phone. "Carol, things aren't going well. I have some bad news about Debbie." Her tone was solemn and serious. My heart beat furiously inside. What was it— her leg? No, it was something worse than that. I could tell by Mrs. Phillip's tone, but I was afraid to ask.

"Carol, Debbie is in the hospital. It's a psychiatric hospital . . . she tried to commit suicide last night."

I couldn't believe it! Not Debbie! I had known something was wrong, but I didn't think . . .

Mrs. Phillips interrupted my thoughts. "Carol, she's okay, but she's really scared. I thought I should call you because she can't call out. You can call in and talk with her. Let me give you the number."

I took down the number and thanked her for thinking of me, then hung up.

After talking with Debbie I felt better. She sounded like everything was going to be all right. She wanted to get better, so I knew she would. As much as I hated myself for thinking it, I couldn't help believing she had done it just for attention—which she did desper-

ately need. She had always been that way. She always
stuck out in a crowd, and she loved it. But that was
Debbie, and that's what we loved about her. When
Debbie wanted something, she could usually get it. I
hoped it was so in this case as well.

I continued to put my whole heart into training for
racing, while Debbie went on an emotional roller
coaster ride. She felt great, then lousy; great, then
lousy. Again and again she admitted herself to
hospitals out of fear. She was given drugs to take the
depression away, but they only made her worse. I
talked to her about God, but I always got the same
response:

"Carol, I wish I could believe like you. I really
want to! But for some reason, I just can't."

Finally, right before I was ready to move back to
Colorado, Debbie called with good news. She had
been in Boston at a topnotch hospital.

"Carol, we found it! We know why I've been so
depressed!" she said eagerly.

I was relieved to hear her encouraging words.

"The doctors did a bunch of tests on me. They said
that I had had so many surgeries so close together that
the anesthesia was too much for me. This whole time,
there's been like a residue of drugs in my body,
making me real tired and depressed. They said it will
go away really soon. As a matter of fact, I'm feeling
much better already.

"You know, I've also been thinking about what you
said to me a while back about trying for the Olympic
equestrian jumping team again. I have a great horse
that I know would do great! I feel like my energy's
coming back a lot, and I've even got some new legs
the doctors want to try on me." She was so excited. I

was so glad to hear her like that again. In my mind's eye I could see her short, slim figure, her face bubbling with personality, her frosted hair always in motion as she chattered away. It had been a long time coming, but finally my friend Debbie was back.

I was getting more and more excited with every day that passed before going to Winter Park. Between working out with the team and finally getting some gate training, I just knew I was in as good shape as anyone.

On top of training with the handicapped team, I also decided to work with the local Winter Park ski team. The schedules for the two teams coincided perfectly. I was ready to push. This year was going to be *great,* especially now that I didn't have to worry about Debbie so much. On top of everything, Atomic skis had decided to sponsor me with three new pairs of race skis, some clothing, and matching ski tips for my outriggers. Technica Boots supplied my boots. Things were starting to break loose. I was on my way.

During the time I was home from New York, things had gone great with God. I became involved with a new kinship and started learning how to minister to people in a small group. We prayed for each other when we were sick, and God healed us. The group was mostly young married couples with a few singles like myself. I loved them. Through the years, I had always put up defenses so I was close to only a few people. I was afraid of people liking me because of who my father was—or people not liking me—period! Through the summer, God stripped those fears away and began to build a new trust in me with the kinship. He visited me over and over again, continually reassuring me of His love and rest and giving me spiritually everything I'd missed so desperately in the winters.

When the time came to leave California, I felt torn in two. I was so excited about doing well with my skiing, for I'd worked so hard all summer to get in shape; yet at the same time I was scared I would lose everything God had done for me. Still troubled, I packed my things and left, but this time I didn't go alone. One of my friends who had been going to the Vineyard with me for the last few years, Roberta (Berta for short), graduated from high school that year. Before she knew what had happened, I talked her into moving to Winter Park with me.

Soon we were settled in our cozy little place and had assumed our separate schedules. Berta found a job, and I started dry-land training with the normie team. We had approximately one month before training on the hill again. Each person was given a U.S. ski team "stomach routine," which we had to do every day on our own before coming together as a team. The exercises took about an hour and half to do, and they were designed to build strength in the abdomen. Surprisingly enough, the abdomen is a very important part of skiing, especially racing. Those muscles pull you back up over your ski if you start to fall, and if they're strong enough, you can often recover and stay in the race. The abdomen also plays a major part in controlling how well you can lift your legs up and down for good knee movement. Since one of the major parts of racing—especially in the slalom—is quick up-and-down knee movement, having a strong abdomen is crucial.

The team workout began with a cross-country jog under the supervision of our coach. (He had previous-

ly coached at Burke Mountain Academy, a well-
known race academy for high-schoolers.) The course
included many rocks and small streams and mud.
Ironically, our dry-land training seemed to occur
everywhere but on dry land. Many times snow flurries
and small storms accompanied us, but no matter the
conditions, Coach made sure that we worked up a
good sweat.

I had never really run before I started working out
with this team. I had hobbled for very short distances
such as from one side of the house to the other, but
never for exercise. My run was more of a hop/skip,
and I had a hard time keeping up; but when I lagged
behind, the others simply ran in circles until I caught
up. They gave me no privileges or excuses because I
was a gimp, except for the times when my stump
broke out in sores and blisters from the pressure of
running. Then, and only then, was I able to cut out
running. Those times I hated to tell our coach,
because I wanted to be tough—not a baby—but
sometimes the sores were too bad to ignore.

After the cross-country jog, we ran up hills backwards. I seemed to be always slipping and falling in
the slush, but I was determined to get back up and
keep going. Next came tuck practice: leaping uphill in
a tuck position, holding tuck position for five minutes.
We were also to stand in one place and jump until our
knees touched our chests, which I never could do, no
matter how hard I tried.

Two full hours of exercise were followed by a tough
workout with weights. We practically ran from one
machine to the next. The overall pace was excruciating—no other word describes it better. Many times I
thought I would drop dead from exhaustion, but

Coach would still be asking for more. Yet in a way, I felt great—like the hero in the movie *Rocky*. I felt cool, training in the snow with about ten other kids when people drove past and looked at us as if we were nuts. I thrived on my new way of life.

The '83–'84 ski season in Winter Park brought success in many areas of my life. Not only was I skiing well and winning almost everything I entered (including a few races against other team members), I was also making friends. The only Christian friends I had were Berta and the Bruns, the Christian family from two years before, and a girl named Beth from Kansas, who lived with the Bruns now. Berta moved home after Christmas for health reasons, and Beth and I had different groups of friends who didn't know each other, so we spent little time together. I developed a deep love for my non-Christian friends, but all too often they couldn't understand why I felt, spoke, and acted as I did.

For the first couple of months, living in the beautiful Rockies made me feel very close to God. Then, as time wore on, I wearied of standing up for His kingdom alone. Separation from God began to set in. I couldn't stop talking about Him or the things I'd seen Him do, but the more I talked about Him the guiltier and lonelier I felt. I missed the closeness I had once had with Him. However, I didn't want to pay the cost to get back to Him, which to me meant giving up my dreams. Skiing was becoming my life and, in the process, pushing everything else aside.

Once in a while I would drop everything, crying out to God with all my heart. In those times He sovereignly drew me to Him and I wept as my Father held me close. Then the time would pass, and the loneliness and depression set in again.

I was growing stronger physically as I grew weaker spiritually. I skied gates every day in addition to working out with both teams. I swam every morning and worked out with weights three times a week. I entered every race I could, handicapped and nonhandicapped. I skied on my new 215-cm. Atomic downhill skis every free chance I had. Whenever a long, steep run was groomed, I was the first on the mountain that morning, making big, fast, long, arching turns, and holding my tuck for what seemed miles. People were beginning to know me as a downhiller: my coaches, my race buddies, and especially me. I learned to let my ski run free beneath me and concentrated on keeping my body up with it. As the season wore on, I became frustrated that there were so few downhill races left to enter. I knew I needed to race more of them under pressure, and because the handicapped coaches didn't set many downhill training courses, I wasn't getting what I really wanted.

February came, and with it time for the team that had been picked at the past Nationals to leave for Austria. Three girls had been picked. Most of the friends I had come to know so well during the season were on the team, and I wished desperately that I could go with them. I knew that the girls who had made it deserved to be on the team, but being left behind was hard, especially knowing how close my times had been to theirs in the past months. The team went to Austria, and I stayed in Winter Park dreaming of Austrian downhills and someday winning the international downhill. With an effort, I shifted my focus back on the Nationals.

A few days after everyone had left I went to the

area to ski. These two weeks would be slow for me with the team and the coaches away, but I decided to take advantage of the holiday and have a good time. No coaches, no training, just fun skiing.

The day was bright and lovely and the sun-rays powerful as they beat down on the crowd of locals and vacation skiers. *There'll be a lot of sunburnt faces by the end of the day if the tourists aren't careful,* I thought to myself. I was glad I didn't have to worry about burning. My face was already weatherworn and tanned from being out all season. Goggle marks lined my cheeks and my nose.

I headed toward the second floor of the lodge to a small coffee and croissant shop for breakfast. As I walked to the entrance of the lodge I noticed a big blue and gold banner hanging from the upstairs balcony. I hadn't seen it before. It read: Camel Sprint Series, Winter Park, Co., February 10–12. *I wonder what that means—some kind of race, I guess.*

A friend of mine from the Winter Park team walked by, and I flagged him down.

"Hey, T.C." He saw me and came over.

"Yeah, Carol, what's up?"

"Do you know anything about that?" I pointed to the banner.

"It's something like speed skiing," he explained. "You know, with Franz Weber and Steve McKinney and all those guys. But it's like a simplified version. Steve McKinney supposedly put it all together and he's taking it to a bunch of different areas."

Speed skiing meant racing straight down a hill, without turns. The special course was designed with a speed trap at the bottom to clock the racer at miles per hour instead of seconds and minutes. Austrian Franz

Weber currently held the world record at 129.303 miles per hour, having beaten Steve McKinney's old record.

I questioned T.C. further. "Is it today?"

"Yeah."

"Where are they running it?"

"On Hughes." He pointed as he answered, and I looked out the window to the familiar run. The course looked so short!

"That's it?"

"Yeah."

"It's so short!"

"Well, they're only letting people go fifty-five, and it doesn't take that much to get going fast when you're going straight. Besides, it's on the steep part of Hughes."

"Yeah," I agreed, "I guess you're right. You can get cooking on that part if you tuck it."

"They also say they'll move it up if the people look safe on it, but the president of the area won't let them take it much higher than fifty-five."

"Is there anyone you know doing it?" I asked.

"No, but a bunch of guys from other areas came out to ski it. Most of them are downhillers out for a kick. Apparently the series is traveling to many other areas as well. I don't know why they came here; I guess they just want to do more than one of the series. Some top speeds at other areas are supposed to hit around sixty-five or seventy. It would be fun, Carol, if you want to know what it's like to ski that fast, but personally I don't think it could ever replace the downhill."

"Yeah, I'm sure you're right, but there have been so few downhills I've been able to do, maybe this would be fun. I have nothing else to do—why shouldn't I?''

"Shoot, Carol, go for it! Worse comes to worst you'll either kill yourself trying to stop in that small finish area, or you'll bore yourself to tears.'' He smiled.

"Well, we'll see. Right now I'm gonna grab a croissant. See ya later.''

"See ya.'' He waved and we went our separate ways.

After breakfast, I headed for the registration booth, and after a few more questions I signed up. The officials decided that because of my handicap, it would be safest to time me from the lowest starting point on the course. If I did all right, I could move up. *This will be good for me,* I thought to myself. *Maybe it will take my mind off the team in Austria.*

The actual race wasn't until the following day. With each run the judges eliminated the competitors they thought weren't safe on their skis. I decided that if I was going to race, I would do my best, so I wore my downhill suit to cut down on wind resistance. Helmets were required. I was the only handicap around doing the sprints, and all the other racers stared at me, wondering what the heck I was doing. However, when they saw me go into a tuck on the first run, lifting my outriggers in front of me in beautiful form they couldn't believe their eyes. These racers had never seen a gimp tuck before, and I got question after question. I was stable with every run and moved higher and higher.

This is terrific! I shouted to myself. I loved skiing in a tuck, but when I was free-skiing on the mountain, the ski patrol would get mad when I went too fast.

Here I could go as fast as I wanted. As we went higher, though, I began to get a little nervous. Speed wasn't the problem: the movement felt a lot faster than I thought it would, but that was the fun part. What frightened me was the size of the finish area. With all that speed I didn't know if I could stop on time in such a small area before hitting the netting.

The race had reached the highest point when word came that they were going to let us go even faster than fifty-five miles per hour. The racers here were good enough.

Nearly two hundred men and women were still racing. I was one of four girls and the only gimp. The first competitor went, then another and another. I was near the back of the pack. I'd met several of the out-of-town racers during the day, and we were having a great time goofing around at the top. They were impressed with my skiing, and I was proud of it. In the background we kept hearing the times: forty-eight, fifty miles per hour at best, none higher.

Then my turn came. There were only ten others left behind me, waiting to go. I got in position. The starter released me. I pushed off hard to gain speed, then dropped quickly to a tuck. The speed built and built. The run was over in seconds, but my fears came true. I couldn't stop; I was going too fast. The fence was too close. I hit the netting, popped out of my ski, and hit the protective bales of hay on the opposite side. I never heard my time—I was wiped. My goggles had ripped off my face, and my eyes felt swollen already. A few officials ran to help. In disgust I got up and brushed myself off. I was bummed. I knew they were going to eliminate me now, and I guess I'd deserved it. My head pounded from the impact.

"Did you hear what you had?" The official was speaking to me, and gradually I became aware that the crowd was clapping and yelling.

"No."

"Well, you're not going to believe this."

"What was it?"

"You hit fifty-five. No one else is even close to you. You did great!"

He was right, I couldn't believe it! My face mirrored the shock in the officials' eyes.

Despite my triumph, the judges refused to let me move up any farther, which was probably best. Everyone knew that the speed wasn't a problem: I could handle that. I simply didn't have enough room to stop. Also there were ripples in the snow, caused by so many skiers stopping in the same place. I soon learned that at high speeds, a course for me had to be close to flawless or I would be thrown off.

I was hooked! I loved speed, and if I couldn't get a downhill, I would settle for speed skiing—at least for now.

Franz Weber wasn't at that first series, but when the pro racers came to Winter Park for the Denver Cup Race, Weber was with them. Speed skiing had made him famous, but he also competed in other races. I had no idea what he looked like, since the few pictures I'd seen of him had shown him in a big helmet with a face protector, but I heard he was in Winter Park.

Pro racers swarmed the mountain the week before their big race, and to be perfectly honest, they were starting to bug me. I assumed they were stuck-up, so every time one came near me, I ignored him rather than feed his ego. To say the least, I wasn't very "holy" in most of my encounters.

One day that week, in the late afternoon, I was headed for a gate practice that the Winter Park team had set up. At the chair lift, two pros cut in line next to me. I could see out of the corner of my eye that they were looking at me, but I ignored them. They went on before me, and I followed soon behind.

Once at the top, they skied off the same way as I, obviously headed for the same area of the mountain. When I arrived near to where our course was laid out, I saw the two pros standing in the start ready to run. Now, an unspoken rule in racing is that you never ski another team's course without first asking permission of the person who set it. I didn't know if this course was theirs or ours and the only way to find out was to ask them, since no one else was around and I wanted to run it. I skied over to them. They were conversing in French.

"Excuse me . . ." I interrupted, trying to act cool.

They both looked at me. One was totally silent; the other answered coldly, "Yes?"

I pressed on. "Do you know who set this course, by chance, because our team is supposed to have one up here, too? Could it be for both of us?"

The same skier answered shortly. "We don't know who set it, but it is our course." He turned away from me and began speaking in French again.

By this time I was convinced of my assumptions about pro racers' attitudes. He sounded like a child protecting his toy. Still, I knew I'd done the same thing before, so I shouldn't judge.

"Would you guys mind if I skied it?"

The quiet one looked casually at the spokesman, waiting for him to answer.

"No, I don't think you could handle it. It's a hard course, and I think you could hurt yourself." His French accent only accentuated the finality of his words.

That did it! *Fine, I'll show them who can't handle their stupid course!* I had on my slalom ski that day, in preparation for training. Because their course was really tight, I decided to ski the smallest and quickest and most aggressive turns I'd ever skied—even if they weren't my forte. I'd show those pros a thing or two about gimp skiers.

"Good-bye," I said haughtily. I turned quickly, lifted my ski off the snow with my weight on my outriggers, then slapped it down loudly, pushing myself off as if I'd started a race. My starts were better now, too, so I showed that off as well. Then I skied, and, man, did I ski! I didn't know I could turn like I turned. I caught a mogul and on purpose flew in the air, landed effortlessly, and continued my quick, small turns. Back and forth, back and forth. I was mad!

At the bottom, I put my leg on at the chair lift. I now had my ski pants altered (in a way I'd designed) so that I could take my leg off and on without having to take off my pants, too. I could drop my leg off at the bottom of the chair lift until I needed to walk around. As I finished putting my leg on, the skiers from the top of the slope came by. They looked at me again and again as they stood in line for the chair. I could tell by their expressions that they were surprised, even impressed with my skiing, and I was glad.

A few days before the Denver Cup, I went over to a

nearby ski area to run another speed course. This time, I wasn't eliminated at all. On one run I beat all the men and women, except for the top three, hitting sixty-five miles per hour. After the race was over, I stopped in the cafeteria to grab a bite to eat.

"Carol." I heard my name called from behind and knew immediately that the voice belonged to Steve McKinney. I didn't even turn around but kept filling my cup with hot cider.

"Hi, Steve," I returned blithely.

"I want you to meet a friend of mine, Franz Weber."

I couldn't wait to see what this guy looked like. I'd heard so much about him. I turned around while taking a sip. When I saw him I nearly spilled my cider down the front of me.

Oh, shoot! I whispered to myself. I felt like crawling under a rock. Weber was the quiet pro racer I'd been so cocky with. I tried to act like I didn't remember him and hoped he didn't remember me.

He greeted me politely, stretching out his hand. "Hello, Carol. It is nice to meet you. That was a good run you had today. What kind of ski do you ski on?"

"Atomic," I replied.

"They are good, no? I use them, too." His English carried a strong accent. "Would you like to eat with us?"

I looked at their loaded trays and then back at them. He seemed not to have recognized me, so I was safe.

"Okay."

I followed them to a table where all their friends were waiting. I ate quickly as everyone around me talked. I felt very out of place and wanted to leave. Then Franz looked at me in the middle of one of his conversations. "This girl right here," he said, putting his hand on my shoulder, "she is a great skier. Did you see her on the course?" I couldn't believe what he was saying. I felt so stupid! Now I really wanted to leave.

None of the group had seen me. They had had to work with registration, but they'd heard about me.

He continued. "I also saw her skiing at Winter Park. She is very good." He turned to the fellow beside me and repeated, "That girl can ski!"

Oh, he'd remembered. But I had been right; he and his friend had been impressed, and I could tell by the way he was talking that he meant it. I felt better. Earlier that year he had crashed into a tree during a race, ruining one of his favorite pairs of skis. The one ski was snapped nearly in two, but the other stayed perfect. One day after we ate together, he signed the good one and gave it to me. The base was made of a special graphite that was especially fast. Few skis in the world have that base. I thanked him sincerely but kept my cool until he left. Then I squealed to myself and turned the ski around in awe. One of Franz Weber's skis—what a perfect gift! It said so much: that he thought of me when he realized it was severed from its pair; that he thought I was worthy to make the most of it.

When the Winter Park team returned from Austria, they quickly heard what I had done. My friend, Reed, who had an arm missing, had done a bit of speed skiing in the past on the pro courses. He held a time of one hundred twenty-two miles per hour. He'd been trying to get me to speed ski for a while, as he had many gimps, but no one had ever taken him up. My run wasn't nearly as fast as his, but it was a start. I decided to go on the pro course and try to break one hundred miles per hour next year, if there was a course that had a smooth, long run out. With bumps or dips at that speed, I would lose it.

When I shared my plans with Reed, he laughed at me and shook his head in disbelief. Now that I had actually done it, he said speed skiing on one leg was nuts. Only two other one-legged skiers from Europe—both males—had speed skied on the big course. Their best time was one hundred five miles per hour. Deep inside me, I really wanted to beat them, but I wouldn't tell anyone. That dream was too unbelievable!

I entered two more sprints, but my fastest time only reached sixty-nine miles per hour. I decided to put my time back into training with the team, preparing for the Nationals in Jackson Hole, Wyoming, which were fast approaching. Before I knew it, it was March and I was in Jackson Hole for my first year of competition in the Women's Division.

Debbie had flown out from New York to meet me, and we roomed together for old time's sake. She was doing great. She had moved to North Carolina around Christmas time to start training her horses for the trials. While there, she also fell in love. I had gone for a brief visit and met her boyfriend before coming to Wyoming. He was a nice guy.

Mom, Dad, and Gretchen came to Jackson Hole as well to watch me race in the Nationals, and when I saw them, I hugged them again and again. I'd missed my family this year a lot but not desperately like the year before. I was older and felt more independent and stable.

The night before the downhill race, I worked hard

to prepare my race ski. The tool room was empty as I ran the file along the edges of the ski to take out any burs and to bevel them in perfect form. The sound of the file on the metal edges scraped and squeaked loudly. My breathing was heavy from the exertion and from nervousness.

The training runs had gone beautifully! I had surprised many who hadn't seen me ski since the year before. On the first timed run, the top two racers and I were hundredths of a second apart. On the second run, I'd jumped ahead two seconds! I was finally going to give the team members a run for the money. It felt great to have some of the other skiers stare at me as if I'd come out of nowhere to be a threat, and they knew they had to keep an eye on me. I didn't care too much about winning the slalom and G.S., but the downhill was mine and I wanted it! I loved that event and I'd worked hard at conquering it. I had never wanted to win a race so badly and had never felt like I'd deserved to win one so much.

The concentration I'd been holding for the past hour of tuning my ski had given me a headache. I rubbed my head trying to remove the pain. Time for bed. I put my skis in the locker until morning. As I undressed in the empty hotel room I looked out the window at the mountain, which was planted directly in front of me. The moon shone on the snow, giving it a fluorescent glow. I couldn't see the course from my window, but I could see it in my mind: the red flags directing one turn to the next, every dip in the snow, every flaw. I had that course stamped and sealed in my mind.

I was a high hopeful for winning. My coaches and buddies had said it over and over again. I had said it to

myself over and over again. I was scared, though.
One girl in particular would be my biggest threat. She
had the kind of determination that could bounce back
with ease after being beaten today.

I wondered where Debbie was. *Oh, well, I guess
she's out with friends.* I closed the curtains, crawled
into bed, and tried to find sleep.

The day dawned with brightness. Debbie lay asleep
in the bed next to mine. She looked like she'd had a
late night out, so I decided not to wake her. I got down
on the floor and began stretching. My stomach was in
knots, and I dreaded the thought of eating breakfast.
Nevertheless, I slipped into my downhill suit, put my
warmups on top, and headed for the hotel restaurant. I
saw many people—friends and family—but I kept
mostly to myself. I didn't feel like talking because I
knew what the main topic would be and I was nervous
enough as it was. I ate just a little, then headed for the
locker to get my equipment. The room was empty and
I was glad. I sat on the bench in front of my locker and
put my head in my hands.

"God," I muttered quietly, "I'm scared. I want to
win so badly but if I don't, please let me take it well. I
don't want to live for skiing so much that it crowds
You and the feelings of others out, but God, I really
want to win. It's the only thing I've ever really been
good at."

Unexpectedly, He answered back, "You're good at
being My kid." I opened my eyes quickly in surprise.
Then they filled with tears. His tone was so loving and
tender.

The words stilled me. I didn't know how to respond
until we were interrupted by a group of racers coming
into the room. I reached for my locker and took out all

my equipment. I put on my gloves, my hat, and left my goggles on my forehead. I pulled my boot on but left it unbuckled. I took my helmet by its strap, my outriggers, and my skis, and headed for the door.

I squinted as the brightness outside pierced my eyes. The chair lift was only yards away, and soon I was near the line and putting on one of my skis. Even though I only used one ski at a time, like all serious handicapped racers I needed pairs of skis. One was used for training and inspecting the course before the race. The other was kept all waxed at the top of the course until the race was ready to begin.

I put on the downhill ski I used for working out, then took my race ski in hand and laid it across my shoulder. I was used to maneuvering on one ski while carrying its twin. I'd done it often. I slipped into the chair and carried everything to the top. I skied off to the right where the course was located, to the starting area. The starters and the officials were busy checking everything out. One of my coaches was talking with the starters when I arrived but interrupted himself and walked over to see me.

"Carol, how are you feeling? Are you ready?"

My nervousness worsened at his query.

"I guess so. I like this course. It could be a little straighter and faster, but I like it."

"You sure looked good yesterday. Just do it again. This one's yours, Carol."

There was silence between us. He took my race ski and helmet from me and put them on the side of the course. "Why don't you go take a few runs to warm up? Get by yourself and just ski. Be back in forty-five minutes."

"Okay."

I headed off and skied smoothly down an evenly groomed hill. The wind blew gently and quietly about me, but my head was still spinning. The plains of Wyoming spread before me as I skied Jackson Hole Mountain, and billowy, white clouds floated lazily through the blue sky, but I became absorbed in my ski. Quickly and responsively it turned to my commands. My heart cried out for joy at the feeling of being one with the ski, one with the mountain. All my nervousness left me as I engrossed myself in the powder that lifted slightly on the sides of my ski. After a couple of runs it was time to head back to the top. I quickly joined the other waiting racers.

Finally, the race began. I tied my race bib over the top of my red downhill suit. My warmups and jacket lay on the ground beside me. At first I joked with my friends at the top, trying to forget my fears, but as my time neared I became silent. I had trained and dreamed for this day. Would my dream come true or would I be a flop and come in way at the bottom? Maybe I'd even fall or disqualify for some reason.

Peace—oh, I longed for it now—the kind of peace I'd always found when we sang the worship songs at the Vineyard. My favorite tune rang clearly in my mind as I closed my eyes and lay back in the snow.

> *I love You, Lord,*
> *And I lift my voice*
> *To worship You.*
> *O my soul, rejoice.*

To worship Him at that moment like the song said was hard, but for a few seconds everything disappeared from my mind and the Lord was all I could see. I missed Him. Hearing Him speak so clearly to me that morning had rekindled the fire in my heart for Him.

"Number 105 . . ." *That's me!* I took my place in line, and my coach rubbed my leg and shoulders to loosen me from all tension. "You're going to do great, Carol," he said in encouragement. "You've got this one!"

The starter's voice sounded. "Number 105—in the start gate, please." I took my place, and for a few seconds the mountain was hushed.

"Racer, ready?"

I looked straight forward and nodded slightly.

"Ten seconds . . . five, four, three . . . !"

I lifted the back of my ski off the snow and pushed myself from the start as hard as I could. My boot triggered the time wand forcefully. I began to fight for more and more speed. I skied that course as if my whole life depended on it. I rounded one corner, then another. I came to a flat stretch and tried to drop my tuck. I wobbled slightly and lost the extra time I was hoping to gain at that point, but I pressed on. Up ahead lay a drop, then a turn directly after. I stayed high, using the mountain's pitch to shoot me into my turn.

My red Atomic ski ran fast and smooth upon the firmly packed snow. The whiteness almost hypnotized me. My mind ran fast. I was so caught in the oneness of body and ski that the course seemed to disappear from sight. I had all the freedom in the world, nothing to hold me back—no course, no care, no fear.

I was now near the end of the course. The finish line lay ahead, only three gates away. It was a pretty straight shot with just a couple of little turns. I went into my tuck and tried to make the turns without coming out, but it was more a half tuck than a full one. I tried to press further into the tuck; the wind that built and swirled around me from the speed made it a challenge. Soon—soon it was done. I was finished.

My time came over the loudspeaker and everyone cheered. I had taken nearly a whole second off my training run! The girl I was worried about would have to take three seconds off her best training run in order to beat me.

I must have won, I thought to myself, but she had come down before me and the announcer had not said where I stood. I left the finish area as quickly as I could to find out how she'd done.

As I moved off, everyone was hugging and kissing me and congratulating me, but I only kept asking how the other girl had done. Finally I caught the results through a congratulatory remark.

"Good going, Carol! You almost had her. What a close race! I can't believe she took three and a half seconds off!"

My heart sank. She'd beaten me. I couldn't believe it. I almost started to cry, but I couldn't. *Who cries over a silly race?* Everyone would think I was a poor sport, and I didn't want to be, but I was hurt and tired after working so hard. I should have been ecstatic for taking second in my first year in the Women's Division and only my second year in the Nationals. Still, I couldn't help being disappointed.

I put a smile on my face and walked over to the winner, my friend, and congratulated her sincerely. She had deserved it, and I knew it. She was good—but now I was good, too, and everyone knew it.

In the slalom I skied extremely well for me and took a third; in the giant slalom I also took a third and took second place in all races combined. I had started off my first year in Women's Division well, but the winner and national champion was a better all-around skier than I was. She'd truly deserved all she won, as I'd deserved all I'd won. *Next year,* I promised myself, *I'm going to be on the National team to go to the World Cup—if I have to kill myself to make it!* I knew I was good enough to make the team, and that was exactly what I planned to do. The Nationals were over, but I looked at them as a door to what lay ahead.

Girls, keep a close watch behind you, because here comes Carol!

13

Tragedy and Triumph

THE SUN WAS SETTING as I drove the busy California freeway to Los Alamitos. Since I'd been away, the kinship I was involved with had formed another group. A couple I had been very close to before leaving had taken the new group. This would be the first time I'd seen them since I left. I'd only been home for a week. I was scared. I wasn't crazy about going back to the kinship because I was afraid everything would be different. I also feared no one would understand my excitement and feelings for skiing.

Most of all, I dreaded what God would say to me or to them about me, and what He would do to me for not staying close to Him all season. I knew I wasn't supposed to be scared of God. I knew that He loved me, but for some reason I was afraid of facing Him. It was spring—Eastertime—the celebration of the giving of Christ's blood and grace, but His grace seemed a million miles away.

I fought the homeward-bound traffic, and the longer I sat in the tangled mess of cars, the more I wasn't sure if I wanted to get right with God—not that I would have admitted that to anyone. If I did "get right," would I lose it again next season? The future seemed like such a vicious circle.

I approached my exit and turned off, for a moment contemplating turning around and going back home. I knew I'd have to face my friends sooner or later, so I continued on, all the more apprehensive. I parked outside their home and walked in. I was glad I was early. Danny and Joyce, the couple I knew so well, ran to me and threw their arms around me. "Carol, it's so good to see you!" they greeted me.

I was able to get rid of some of the jitters by making small talk with them. I was fidgety still, but at least I hadn't had to walk into a room full of new people! As the others began to arrive, I sat in the corner of the room trying not to be noticed by the small crowd. I hardly knew anyone. I was beginning to like this less and less. I felt as if people could see right through me. *I shouldn't have come. I just want to leave. Why did I come?*

Gradually, Danny and Joyce pulled the group together as Danny produced his guitar and led us in the worship with songs I loved so well. The words pierced my heart, and I fought to keep the tears from coming. I wasn't going to let myself break down in front of all these people. No way! I just couldn't do that. I crossed my arms in front of me and tried to think of other things. I had quite a struggle the whole thirty minutes of worship, but finally that part was over.

Danny began to speak, explaining that he thought God wanted to deal with some people and to touch some people. He gave a few words of knowledge, and everyone responded. Words of knowledge are things which God tells someone about another person that otherwise he would have no way of knowing. Many times they're for people who need prayer for their condition. God really does want to take care of them, so He tells someone about it. Danny asked if anyone else had any words. I prayed no one would get any words of knowledge about me.

Danny and others began praying for the people who'd responded to the words. Danny was praying for someone right by me, so to keep suspicion off me, I helped to pray as I'd learned the year before.

As I prayed, a lump began rising in my throat. I felt like I was going to cry. *Not again!* I thought nervously. God was trying hard to break my heart so He could restore everything the enemy had taken from me, but I fought with all my might to keep control. Just as the lump began to evaporate, Danny turned to me and placed the palm of his hand over my heart. The gesture broke my resistance: I couldn't fight anymore. I cried and cried, and my weeping turned to sobs as God stripped away the residue of hurts from the many painful years. All the defensive barriers I had built up over time began to crumble as He drew closer and closer to me. I felt naked and vulnerable in the hands of the Almighty. He came to me powerfully and tenderly and washed me clean.

After about fifteen minutes of crying while the others prayed, God finally showered on me an incredible peace. How wonderful it felt! His peace surpassed anything I could imagine. I had experienced the same feeling only one time before, when I'd first attended a meeting at the Vineyard a few years back. I had thought it was a once-in-a-lifetime healing that God had done for me, yet here I was experiencing His power again tonight in a living room chair. Little did I know I was to feel it many, many times more.

After that evening, I became more and more involved in the Vineyard. Over the weeks, God visited me constantly with his power and His love. I cried and I laughed with joy. What a precious, precious time! I wanted everything I could get from God; therefore, when I heard about a week-long conference the Vineyard was holding, I decided to attend. The topic was "Signs and Wonders and Church Growth," based on a class that John, our pastor, taught at Fuller Seminary. Nearly five thousand people from outside our church were signed up to hear John's lectures and to participate in the small workshops given by other pastors at the Vineyard.

Danny and Joyce went, too, and I was glad to have someone to be with. God continued to touch me over and over again. People were praying for me, and God came in power. I followed Danny and Joyce around and helped them pray for people when I wasn't being prayed for myself. I saw beautiful things happen all week long. It was great!

I finally began to realize the incredible faithfulness God had shown in drawing me back again. I realized He'd *never* left me, and in turn I began serving Him as I never had before. I began loving Him as I never had before. A fire burned constantly within me. Joy surrounded me, and all I could do was talk about

Jesus. I had had some times of excitement similar to this, but nothing as magnified as what I had now. I prayed for people, Christian and non-Christian, any chance I could seize. I prayed for their sick bodies, their hurting hearts, and their wounded memories. Sometimes I would just be their friend—someone to talk to. God did powerful things time and time again. I was far from a perfect servant, but God was patient—and thank goodness, He still is!

As God healed broken bodies and restored wounded spirits, He wrapped His love around their broken hearts, like a warm woolen blanket killing the bitter cold. His mercy flowed everywhere—on airplanes, hotels, on the streets—anywhere he had something He needed to accomplish.

I continued my off-season training at home with the same schedule as the summer before, but the work quickly became a chore rather than a joy. Everything for the upcoming year was ready and set. My sponsors were already lined up, and a home awaited me. I was receiving a lot of publicity from my speed skiing, and my summer was filled with exciting times. *US* magazine heard about me and wrote a feature article about the "one-legged girl who hit nearly seventy miles per hour on one ski." That article broke loose a lot of other things. Before I knew it, I was offered publicity engagements right and left.

"Good Morning, America" flew me to New York to talk with David Hartman about my year's accomplishments. Mom had bought me a lovely new outfit for the occasion, and I looked as pretty as I could while my father and I talked with the warm-hearted host. I talked freely of my active life of skiing and training and of the hopes and dreams I had of making the team and trying to break one hundred miles per hour in the upcoming year.

Following the "Good Morning, America" segment, I was asked by some financial sponsors to run with the Olympic torch in Colorado in June. I accepted proudly, for I hoped someday myself to compete in the Handicapped Olympics in Calgary, Alberta. I was flown back to the beautiful mountains I loved so for a one-week visit to carry the flaming torch for one kilometer. As I ran through a sprinkling rain, people cheered from all sides. A special fire flickered in me, too, a dream of the faraway Calgary games that I wanted to be in so desperately. A beautiful bouquet of red roses was presented to me at the end of the run and I brought them carefully home, along with my priceless engraved torch.

Olympic fever infiltrated all of the Los Angeles Basin as the time drew nearer and nearer for the 1984 games. Everywhere I went I saw posters of athletes, and the fire flared in me violently, as if to consume me. I was overwhelmed by an invitation to join Jack Gifford for the television Olympic coverage. I couldn't believe they actually wanted to talk to me when the Olympians were the stars. *Olympian*—it had such a beautiful ring to it. Would it ever be a name tagged to me? As I talked with Mr. Gifford, I thought of the millions watching and listening to the dreams of success I had for my beloved sport. Would they cheer me on with the respect and support they held for the winning athlethes during that inspiring week? I thought not, but I dreamed nonetheless.

Winter drew near. Debbie and I talked a few times on the phone, and each time we talked she sounded

more happy than the last. She told me she had given
her life to Jesus and was going to a local church. I was
so happy for her!

I was scheduled to leave for Colorado in October,
but the closer the date came, I was hesitant to leave.
Why, I didn't know. All my dreams had been funneled
into skiing, and I anticipated seeing them come true.
Yet, however deep and passionate the drive to race
was within me, something else within me dreaded the
thought of leaving. I cried to God constantly, begging
for an answer, but I heard nothing.

My kinship friends, Danny and Joyce, moved back
to their home in North Carolina, but I found a new
kinship group where I fit in instantly. When God took
away Danny and Joyce, He immediately gave me
others who would love me, guide me, and uphold me
with prayer and fellowship.

Two of my friends, Blaine and Becky, were praying
with me about what I was to do with skiing. Blaine
worked with the Vineyard. He had been very supportive about my move to Winter Park and even suggested that the Denver Vineyard send someone up to
start a new kinship. The idea appealed to me, but for
some reason I still wasn't totally certain I should go.

When September came and I still hadn't heard
anything about the subject from God, I decided to go
ahead with my training. I went to tell Blaine one
Sunday evening after church, and I will never forget
the words he said to me. They were totally
unexpected.

"Carol," Blaine said soberly, "I can feel when
God's moving in someone's life. I've seen it often. I
think God has something for you to do here."

The words were out: what I'd been feeling for so

long but did not want to admit. My heart dropped to my stomach. I knew he was right. I also knew he wasn't one to give advice. It was God. I knew I would miss everything God had for me if I went to Colorado. There was no question in my mind: I was to stay home. I cried as I told my kinship leader the story. I knew in my heart what God wanted me to do, and I knew what my decision would have to be, but it wouldn't be easy. What would everyone say when I told them the change of plans? What would my coaches say, my friends, my race buddies? What would the millions of people who'd read about me and who'd heard me on talk shows think? What would my parents and family say?

Many asked me over and over again, "Carol, why would God make you give up something that you love so much if He really loves you? I don't understand!"

I couldn't give them a pat answer. All I knew was that I loved God with all my heart, and He was all I wanted. I had to believe that my Father wouldn't take something like that from me without giving me something better in return. I trusted Him; He was all I had.

The decision was not between skiing or not skiing, racing or not racing, Winter Park or Orange County; the decision was between the presence of God or the absence of God. There was no contest any longer. I knew what I wanted.

Yet now that I wasn't skiing, I had no idea what I *was* going to do. I had nothing to live for, really, but God. I didn't want to go back to school, and I didn't know what kind of work I could do. I felt lost and insecure. I'd always had some interest in art and paste-up work, so I casually approached my brother-in-law, who had been a graphic artist for years. I began asking a question here and a question there, to see if the field was something I would be interested in.

My thoughts of racing dwindled as I prepared with excitement for a trip with my church to England. John Wimber was giving his "Signs and Wonders and Church Growth" seminar in London, and churches from all over Great Britain were signed up. Three or four thousand people were expected to attend, and I was part of a two-hundred-party ministry team that John was taking with him from many states. We paid our own way, but the expense was more than worth it.

We saw literally hundreds healed physically, in addition to the many hearts God touched in powerful ways. The sovereign work of God, touching His people in ways they didn't know He could or would, was a beautiful scene to witness. What a joy, to see the looks on the faces of people who'd never prayed for the sick before, when they put their hands on someone else in prayer and watched God heal that person. They couldn't believe God wanted to use them to extend such blessings to others, and they wept for joy at the goodness of God. My heart went out to many during the time in London and during the week we spent outside of London, when our team divided up. One woman in particular I will never forget.

One night, our meeting in London was overpacked, and we had many people on the street still wanting to get in. We had rented a huge meeting hall, but there was not enough room. Word had spread about what was happening in the meetings, and people flocked to see what this conference was all about. Many pastors who had been attending all week opened their churches for us to use, and we began instructing the crowds where to go. While the main meeting was going on, some team members and I went outside to an alleyway to talk and minister to a few who still remained. After all the people seemed to be cared for, we headed back inside. Everyone else went on ahead, and I brought up the tail end.

As I was about to walk through the door, I happened to look down the dark alley one more time. Seated on the curb not twenty feet from me sat a person with a shaved head, wearing a ragged, old overcoat. I could not tell if this was a man or woman, but I guessed male. Before I could think twice I was headed for the figure, who turned out to be a woman. She was small, but her size seemed even less as she huddled on the curb smoking a joint. Her face was weatherworn, and its toughness was intensified by the look of meanness she wore.

When I came within five feet of her, she suddenly looked up and caught my eye. "Don't you come near me!" she spit out violently. "Don't you say a word, and don't touch me!" Fire flashed from her dark eyes, but I couldn't stop. I felt as if someone else was controlling me, and I had no choice in what to do or say. Within seconds I was sitting close to her, holding her in my arms and whispering calmly, "Don't worry. I'm just going to hold you a little while."

I could see the bald places on her head that looked like they'd been eaten away by lice. The stench that rose from her clothes only deepened the overwhelming compassion I felt. I had always had a heart for street people, but I'd never felt a compassion like this. This love was different, almost like a special anointing.

Bitterness surrounded her like a cloak that she hid

beneath for safety. She spoke angrily of people who had hurt her and of people she hated. I heard little of it for something seemed to shield my ears.

I interrupted her. "Can I pray for you?" I asked quitely.

She barked back sharply, "You can pray your God will kill the people who've hurt me, that's what you can do!" Her Cockney brogue accented the wrathful words.

Without thinking, I answered, "Okay, but first, can I pray for a few other things?"

She was silent, then nodded and said, "Yes, you can."

"Okay," I answered, as I took my arm from around her and knelt in front of her. She closed her eyes as I put my hands on either side of her face. My body trembled as the power of God came on me. I sobbed as the words poured out: angry words, as I spoke to the bitterness and hatred that had bound her for so long. I was angry at what Satan had done to her, the way he'd robbed her life, and as God's grace and mercy poured through my hands, the bonds were broken. The tension in her body left her, and she slumped in peace and freedom.

She lifted her eyes to mine. All hatred and bitterness was gone now, replaced by a soft, quiet spirit. She asked in a totally different voice, "What do I do now?" The sincerity of her childlike words broke my heart, as I watched her meet Jesus. I couldn't believe what I'd seen! *To see someone change so quickly,* I thought to myself, *just can't be real! She must have been faking!* But I knew better. I'd seen the power of God.

I have never heard what happened to her. She came

with me to the meeting and met some pastors from the area. When I left her that night, knowing that I'd probably never see her again, I felt as if I'd given birth but had left the baby in the street to die. Yet I knew that I had to trust God. He loved her more than I possibly could imagine. I'd felt that love when His compassion came on me while speaking to her. That compassion had felt so different—so much more pure and powerful than any I'd felt for anyone before or since. It was the compassion of God!

I could go on and on with similar stories, witnessing to the powerful, merciful, and miraculous things that God did there. The trip changed my life and my life's desires.

After the trip, adjusting to being home again was difficult. Jet lag cut my days in two, and coming down from such a tremendously emotional high was exhausting. We'd ministered day and night, often going without meals. Coming home, I'd felt like I'd been gone for years.

The first night home, I found a message on my desk from Mom, telling me to call Debbie. I picked up the phone immediately and dialed her North Carolina number so as not to forget. No one answered.

Oh, well, I thought as I began unpacking, *I'll try again in the morning.*

I tried for three days, several times a day, but I was never able to reach her. I knew she was busy training her horses, so I simply kept trying.

A few nights later I was watching TV in my room when the phone rang. "I bet that's Debbie," I said to myself. I jumped to grab the receiver.

"Hello?" I was in a good mood and ready to talk with her, but the caller wasn't Debbie. He was a man.

"Hello, Carol?"

"Yes."

"Carol, this is Mr. Phillips, Debbie's father."

"Mr. Phillips?" I was perplexed. Why would he be calling me? Mrs. Phillips was always the one who called to chat, but the words he spoke next I would never forget.

"Carol, I'm afraid I have some bad news. Debbie has killed herself." The suddenness of his words whizzed right past me.

"Excuse me, Mr. Phillips, I didn't hear you. What did you say?"

He repeated himself. "I said, Debbie's killed herself. It happened a few nights ago. She shot herself in her boyfriend's house."

All my breath was snatched from me, as if someone had hit me in the stomach with a two-by-four. I refused to believe what he was saying.

"You're kidding. I know you are."

"No, Carol, I'm afraid I'm not."

I couldn't take it. I couldn't listen to any more. He started to explain the details about the memorial service, but I interrupted him.

"I'm sorry, Mr. Phillips, I've gotta go." Sobs slurred my words together. Not waiting for an answer, I hung up.

I screamed in horror at the news. "Oh God oh God oh God! Help!" I fell to the floor, clutching my stomach. *I have to find help.* My sister Jeanne stood in the hall.

"Jeanne," I cried.

"Carol, what's wrong?" She rushed to me.

"Debbie," I gasped for a breath, "she's killed herself."

Sobs gripped me again, as Jeanne held me close. "Where's Mom and Dad?" I asked in panic.

"They're not at home."

I ran my fingers nervously through my hair. I felt like I was going crazy. *I can't handle this. I just can't handle it!*

I left Jeanne and went back to my room. I cried and cried, and I cried. I screamed in pain until I had no tears left, and then I sat in a daze on my bed, holding the stuffed dog from my father that had been with me through all my hospital days. I clenched his soft body tightly under my chin and stared out my window at the black night. How long I sat there, I don't know. One minute I seemed to be in a dream—a nightmare. Then I'd be back in reality. My parents finally came home and interrupted the shock that gripped me.

Mom sat on the bed with me, and I laid my head on her lap. My tears stained the elegant dress she wore. We said nothing. I undressed and went to bed, leaving my mom with a limp kiss. I lay in bed on the damp pillow until exhaustion overrode emotion and I slept.

Over the next week I lived in a kind of daze, just making myself go through the daily routines and responsibilities. Memories of Debbie ran freely through my mind: I thought of her frosted hair and her round, cheery face. I remembered the time we got stuck on the snowmobile. I remembered the long, hard, strenuous workouts and the way she loved to drink her coffee, doing nothing as I strained for more strength. Had it not been for my family and the priceless friends God had given me both from the kinship and England, I don't know what would have happened. They fought for me in prayer constantly as the battle waged about me.

A few nights after the phone call, I had a class at the Vineyard. As I drove on the freeway, the rain outside pattered on the windows, but the car was filled with beautiful piano music. While the fingers of George Winston controlled the keys with style and ease, I thought back to the first time I'd heard the pianist I now listened to so often. I had been in North Carolina for a visit with Debbie. Just like tonight, the sky was throwing rain down on the earth in buckets. The beautiful, white, birch trees spread like fur across the land. Debbie was driving the van she'd just bought to pull her new horse trailer. We were going for a ride on her horses, but because of the stormy weather we sat in the car instead and talked for hours as we listened to George Winston. A clap of thunder brought me back to the present as I pulled into the church parking lot.

My mind kept wandering as my friends greeted me. Noticing my distraction, they questioned me worried-ly. I cried for a few minutes and then told them everything that had happened. For many, this was the first they had heard of the news. To talk about it had hurt too much before now. Even with my parents, when questions were raised about Debbie, I pretended not to hear. But now, I was ready to deal with the pain and the grief.

A couple of my friends took me outside and prayed for me. As one laid a hand on my heart and the other on my forehead, they spoke peace to my body. I felt like a bucket had been dumped over my head, and refreshment trickled down my arms, my head, and my legs. Rest came to my heart, and God held me close to His bosom. Incredibly, all the pain and anguish seemed to be a million miles away—just a speck in the distance.

After that night, strangely enough, the mourning seemed to end. A few times, I cried for just a little while, and disbelief would fill me afresh. However, most of the time, I was able to put it away. God acted as a buffer and a shield about my heart when the enemy tried to strike his most furious blows. God was so good to me.

The memorial service was in Binghamton, so I didn't go, but my prayers were with the family more than they'll ever know.

To many people Debbie seemed to have everything: friends, success in nearly everything she did, and a great personality. Apparently, that wasn't enough. She had many hidden wounds—insecurity, fears, confusion—as most everyone does, but the depths of the wounds were unseen and went untreated. So many times, I felt like a doctor left holding the remedy while the sickness destroyed the patient. I just didn't know how to give the medicine to her—I just didn't know. Like cancer, the illness grew and eventually killed her.

Well, this Christian soldier has wounds, too. Only I've survived, so far, the grueling war. Why? I don't know. I have nothing but the grace of God, and through His grace my wounds are disappearing from view, and some even from memory. Now, all I can say is that I know my God is on the move today, to heal the many wounded Debbies and the many wounded Carols, and I must be a part of His work. I no longer have a choice. I can live for nothing else, because there is nothing else. Until I meet my God face to face I will, for the rest of my life, sing a triumphant song:

O Death, where is your victory?
O Death, where is your sting?
Victory came through my Lord Jesus
Who walked on the front line of battle,
Keeping the arrows away,
With no knowledge from this wounded soldier
Who in the foxhole lay.
Jesus is my Victor, and to Him shall I
Be faithful unto death.

Praise for
The Adamantine Palace

"*The Adamantine Palace* tosses the reader between fascination, revulsion, compulsion, and trepidation with barely a breath in between . . . . This is a terrifying appetizer from what will surely be seen as a landmark in dragon-orientated fantasy."
—Total Sci-Fi

"A rompingly good, character-focused tale . . . an entertaining mix of Pern and Westeros, with the knowing characterization of Abercrombie and the endearment of Novik. To be recognized alongside such authors is a real achievement . . . . This is traditional-style fantasy, but written in a contemporary manner that should attract many new readers."
—SFFWorld

"A fast, furious, and entertaining book that grabs hold of the reader and whisks them off like a roller coaster. The dragons, as promised, indeed kick ass."
—The Wertzone

"In short: dragons, intrigue, poison, mercenaries and a Big Dark History. If you like that sort of thing, then this is definitely worth a look."
—Sandstorm Reviews

"Remarkable . . . Anne McCaffrey as filtered through the mind of Oscar Wilde . . . imaginative."
—*Locus*

"Roll over, McCaffrey. There's a new Dragon Lord in town."
—Gareth Wilson, Falcatta Times

"Will appeal to fans of both classic and contemporary fantasy."
—Fantasy Book Critic

"Full of everything that I like about fantasy right now: strong characters, a complex plot, and loads of dragons."
—Graeme's Fantasy Book Review

continued . . .

THE
ADAMANTINE
PALACE

THE
MEMORY OF FLAMES,
BOOK I

STEPHEN DEAS

A ROC BOOK

ROC
Published by New American Library, a division of
Penguin Group (USA) Inc., 375 Hudson Street,
New York, New York 10014, USA
Penguin Group (Canada), 90 Eglinton Avenue East, Suite 700, Toronto,
Ontario M4P 2Y3, Canada (a division of Pearson Penguin Canada Inc.)
Penguin Books Ltd., 80 Strand, London WC2R 0RL, England
Penguin Ireland, 25 St. Stephen's Green, Dublin 2,
Ireland (a division of Penguin Books Ltd.)
Penguin Group (Australia), 250 Camberwell Road, Camberwell, Victoria 3124,
Australia (a division of Pearson Australia Group Pty. Ltd.)
Penguin Books India Pvt. Ltd., 11 Community Centre, Panchsheel Park,
New Delhi - 110 017, India
Penguin Group (NZ), 67 Apollo Drive, Rosedale, North Shore 0632,
New Zealand (a division of Pearson New Zealand Ltd.)
Penguin Books (South Africa) (Pty.) Ltd., 24 Sturdee Avenue,
Rosebank, Johannesburg 2196, South Africa

Penguin Books Ltd., Registered Offices:
80 Strand, London WC2R 0RL, England

Published by Roc, an imprint of New American Library, a division of Penguin
Group (USA) Inc. Previously published in Gollancz and Roc hardcover editions.
For information contact Gollancz, an imprint of Orion Publishing Group, Orion
House, 5 Upper St. Martin's Lane, London WC2H 9EA.

First Roc Mass Market Printing, February 2011
10   9   8   7   6   5   4   3   2   1

Copyright © Stephen Deas, 2009
All rights reserved

ROC REGISTERED TRADEMARK—MARCA REGISTRADA

Printed in the United States of America

With thanks to K. J. Parker for pointing me at John Jarrold, John for putting up with me until Simon Spanton came along, and to Simon for everything since. To Peter and Jean for their support, and lots of others (you know who you are) who helped along the way. To "Ou sont les dragons?", Kyle and were-ducks. To everyone who picks this up and starts to read.

And especially to my wife, Michaela, for her patience, understanding and much, much more.

Now, on with burning stuff.

THE KINGS AND QUEENS OF SAND AND STONE AND SALT

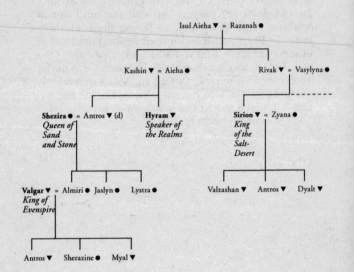

Isul Aieha ▼ = Razanah ●

Kashin ▼ = Aieha ●

Rivak ▼ = Vasylyna ●

Shezira ● = Antros ▼ (d)
Queen of Sand and Stone

Hyram ▼
Speaker of the Realms

Sirion ▼ = Zyana ●
King of the Salt-Desert

Valgar ▼ = Almiri ● Jaslyn ● Lystra ●
King of Evenspire

Valzashan ▼ Antros ▼ Dyalt ▼

Antros ▼ Sherazine ● Myal ▼

▼ Male

● Female

THE KINGS OF THE ENDLESS SEA

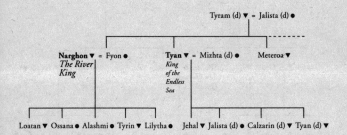

Tyram (d) ▼ = Jalista (d) ●

Narghon ▼ = Fyon ●
The River King

Tyan ▼ = Mizhta (d) ●
King of the Endless Sea

Meteroa ▼

Loatan ▼ Ossana ● Alashmi ● Tyrin ▼ Lilytha ●   Jehal ▼ Jalista (d) ● Calzarin (d) ▼ Tyan (d) ▼

Kings and Queens of the Plains

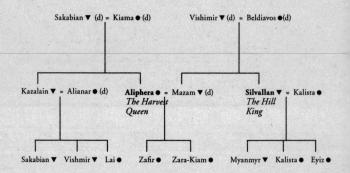

Sakabian ▼ (d) = Kiama ● (d)   Vishimir ▼ (d) = Beldiavos ●(d)

Kazalain ▼ = Alianar ● (d)   **Aliphera** ● = Mazam ▼ (d)   **Silvallan** ▼ = Kalista ●
                              The Harvest   *The Hill*
                              Queen   *King*

Sakabian ▼   Vishmir ▼   Lai ●   Zafir ●   Zara-Kiam ●   Myanmyr ▼   Kalista ●   Eyiz ●

THE KING OF THE WORLDSPINE

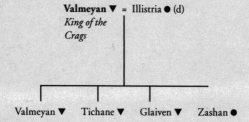

Valmeyan ▼ = Illistria ● (d)
*King of the
Crags*

Valmeyan ▼   Tichane ▼   Glaiven ▼   Zashan ●

PROLOGUE—JEHAL

Prince Jehal felt the dragon take to the air. Curled up inside a saddlebag, he couldn't see a thing. But that didn't matter. He could see it in his mind, exactly and precisely. He felt every stride as the dragon accelerated. He knew exactly when the dragon would make one last bound and unfurl its wings. He felt himself grow heavier as the dragon rose up into the air.

The bag smelled slightly of rotten meat. Jehal wriggled and stretched as best he could, trying to make himself more comfortable in the tiny space. He forced himself to breathe slowly, suppressing the edge of panic that threatened to blossom inside him. Small spaces had never agreed with him, and the smell made him uneasy. It made him wonder what the bag had been used for before. Carrying dragon snacks was the obvious answer.

Is that me? Am I the snack of the day today?

The absurdity of the thought calmed him. Queen Aliphera was as shrewd as anyone, but she was also besotted. Jehal had come to know what that looked like, even in a dragon-queen.

The dragon stopped climbing and began to glide. Officially, Jehal was indisposed. A great deal of effort had gone into his illness, every bit of it spent so that he and Queen Aliphera could be alone and unobserved. All he had to do now was stay hidden until the queen found an excuse to fly away from her riders, her dragon-knights. Months of work and then days of waiting for exactly the right weather, all for half an hour of absolute privacy.

He clenched his fists. One of his feet had cramped. He wriggled his toes. When that didn't work, he tried to rear-range himself so his feet were underneath the rest of him. That didn't work either, but by the time he gave up trying, the cramp had gone away anyway. Eventually, he fell asleep.

HE WOKE UP TO SEE gray sky pouring in above him. Every muscle in his legs was shouting at him, demanding to be stretched. He yawned, stood up and grinned at what he saw. They were high in the sky, skimming the base of the clouds. Aliphera liked to do that.

Jehal looked around, scanning the horizon, but there were no other dragons in sight. Finally, he looked at Aliphera. She was still half strapped into her saddle, but she was looking back at him, grinning. Her eyes were very wide. They'd flirted with each other for months, in little ways, little stinging touches where no one else would see.

Jehal grinned back. Anticipation, that was the key. And now she had him alone at last.

"You look a little disheveled, Prince Jehal."

Carefully, Jehal hauled himself out of his saddlebag. He crawled the few feet toward her, mindful of the thousand or so feet of empty space between him and the ground. It would be stupid to get this far only to plunge to his death.

"I want you, here and now."

She laughed, but he saw a flash of excitement in her face. "You're being silly. We'd fall."

"I don't care." He didn't let her answer, but covered her mouth with his own. One hand went to the soft skin of her neck. He let it slide down, only an inch or two, and then stopped.

"Loosen that harness," he said. "I want to ride with you. Let me hold you while you find a place to land."

"Yes." They fumbled together at the clasps and straps that held her fast. Now and then they let their fingers stray.

Finally, the last restraint fell away. Jehal lifted her up, just enough so he could slide into the saddle behind her. He let his hands run slowly down her body and felt her shudder.

"I can't tell you just how long I've been waiting for this," she breathed.

With a sudden jerk, he rammed his head into the small of her back. She staggered and gasped as he rose and drove forward, punching her as she tried to turn. Once, twice, knocking her forward. Her arms flailed and then she was gone, off into the sky. Jehal sat back down and pressed himself into the saddle, gripping the dragon with his legs while he strapped himself in. A part of him couldn't believe it had been so easy.

The dragon tucked in its wings and dived after her, but that was simply what any hunting-dragon was trained to do. It couldn't catch her. All it could do was land somewhere close by and then stay there, howling, pleading for help. Not that anyone could survive a fall like that.

He clung on and peered over the dragon's shoulder, listening to Queen Aliphera's screams, watching until the ground reached out and swallowed her whole.

"That's exactly what your daughter said," he hissed.

HATCHLING GOLD

When a dragon-rider wishes a new dragon for his eyrie, he will write to one of the dragon-kings or -queens, petitioning them for their favors. If the rider is wise, the letter will come with a gift. It is understood that the more generous the gift, the more likely the rider will receive a favorable response. This gift is the first of many payments and is made long before a suitable dragon is even born. This gift is called the Hatchling Gold.

Naturally, as dragons are few and lords are fickle, nothing is ever certain.

I

SOLLOS

There were three riders. Sollos had watched them land away in the fields beyond the edge of the forest. They'd all come down on the back of a single war-dragon, and one of them had stayed behind, keeping the dragon calm. The other two had walked straight toward the trees. Their pace was brisk and full of purpose. Sollos watched as they passed his position and then padded silently after them. They were dressed from head to toe in their dragonscale armor, and Sollos began to think they might as well have let the dragon come with them. It might have made less noise.

He took careful breaths, following behind. As long as the other men who'd been waiting for the riders to arrive didn't get a sudden case of cold feet.

A few hundred yards into the trees, the ground rose into a small mound topped with a standing stone. It had been a place of worship once, back in the days of the old gods, but now the forest had all but swallowed it. The riders went straight up the mound and stopped at the top.

"This is it, isn't it?" said one, in the kind of whisper of someone to whom the whole concept of being secretive was something of a mystery.

The other one was even worse. He leaned against the stone and started fiddling with a tinderbox. Sollos couldn't quite believe what he was seeing, or rather what he was smelling. The idiot was smoking pipeweed.

"It's almost insulting, isn't it?" breathed a voice in his ear. Sollos froze for an instant, and then relaxed. Kemir. "They're as subtle as a mace in the face."

"I wish you wouldn't do that, cousin." Sollos hissed the words between his teeth, hardly daring to make a sound. He could actually feel Kemir's lips brushing his ear, that's how near he was. He found it uncomfortably distracting. How did Kemir get that close without him ever noticing?

"Don't worry. We're downwind, and the men waiting for them are on the other side of the mound. They've been there for a while now. They're getting impatient."

"They're probably wondering why this lot didn't just crash in through the branches on the back of their dragon."

"I was beginning to wonder the same."

"The men on the other side of the mound. Are there still just three or are there more now?"

"Still three."

Sollos took a deep breath and let it out slowly. He still wasn't sure what to make of all this. He'd had his orders, whispered in his ear, and they'd been quite clear. A pair of Queen Shezira's dragon-knights were going to come to the forest around these parts. They were coming to buy something, something meant to harm the queen. He and Kemir, a pair of sell-swords, were going to stop them. The gold in their pockets came from the queen's knight-marshal, but if anything went wrong they were nothings and nobodies with no ties to anyone who mattered. That was as much as Sollos knew.

"Did you see what they brought with them?"

Kemir didn't answer.

"They must have brought *something*."

"Maybe they didn't. Maybe they're going to do our work for us and gut this pair of traitors for their gold. If they did, it's small. I didn't see anything."

The whispering voice hadn't given any clues as to what the something was, either, only that trying to buy it should cost these dragon-knights their lives. Sollos was to wait until the riders met whoever was doing the selling, then discreetly kill the lot of them. The riders would be carrying gold. He could help himself to that, the whisper had said. As for the rest, he would leave the bodies alone and untouched. They'd be found in the morning, by which time Sollos would be back in his barracks. He'd wake up as shocked as anyone else to find that two of the queen's riders had been found murdered.

Which was all very well, but there were three dragon-knights, not two.

"There's another one," he whispered. "A third rider came with them. He stayed with the dragon."

There was a long pause. He could almost hear Kemir thinking. "We have to let that one go, don't we?"

Sollos nodded. There were supposed to be two riders. From short range with the advantage of surprise, he and Kemir could be reasonably sure of taking down one apiece. A third, though, forewarned, with a dragon at his back, that was a different matter.

"What do you make of them? Not the riders, the others. The sellers."

"Nervous. They're not swordsmen. They'll run, not fight. We'll have to take them down quickly."

Sollos shuddered; Kemir's lips were still brushing his ear. He edged away. "When the purse changes hands, that's when we act. I'll deal with the rider who gives over the money, you shoot the other. Whoever is holding the purse is mine too. Then we go after the rest. Closest first." From the corner of his eye Sollos saw movement at the top of the hill. He shooed Kemir away and began to creep closer. As he did, he took a careful grip of his dragonbone longbow. It was an old weapon, taller than he was, honed from the wing of some monster of a war-dragon by the looks of it. Too long and clumsy for his liking at such close quarters, but guaranteed to punch through as much steel and dragon-scale as a man could wear and still stand upright.

"Have you got what we want?"

"Have you got our money?"

"Show me you've got what we want."

At the top of the hill three men had joined the dragon-knights. As if all the noise they'd already made hadn't been enough, now they were arguing. Sollos had a fleeting vision of simply walking into the middle of them and seeing how many he could stab before they even noticed he was there.

"Show us the gold, friend. *Then* you see what you get for it."

"No. You first."

"Oh, just show them the money. Here . . ."

One of them lit a torch. Slowly, Sollos rested an arrow against the string of his bow. One of the riders was holding what looked like a purse. Any moment now . . . And they were making it all so easy.

The purse changed hands. As Sollos let fly, he saw the other rider stagger. He didn't even look to see what his own arrow had done, but reached at once for a second.

Both riders were down. The man holding the purse was still exactly where he'd been a moment ago. Sollos could see his eyes, slowly tearing themselves away from the riches in his hands as the dragon-knights toppled over.

The dragon-knights' torch lay on the ground, still burning, lighting the faces of the three strangers still standing on the top of the hillock. Sollos fired again. This time his aim was a little low. The arrow hit the man with the purse in the jaw and ripped off half his face. Good enough. He could see the last two clearly. Still they didn't think to run. Sollos dropped his bow and charged at them, first one hand and then the other drawing a pair of long knives out of his belt.

The farthest pitched suddenly backward with another of Kemir's arrows in his chest. Finally the last one turned to flee, but by then Sollos was barely yards away and coming at a sprint. A leap and a lunge and Sollos buried both knives into the man's back, one high and one low. That turned out not to be enough, so he slit the man's throat for good measure. Then got up and looked at himself. His shirt was damp and glistening.

"Shit. I'm covered in blood."

"Better stay away from that dragon, then." Kemir was standing by the torch, his longbow held loosely at the ready.

"Are you sure there aren't anymore of them?" Sollos scurried back to where he'd dropped his own bow. Without it, he felt naked.

Kemir shrugged. "As sure as I can be. You never know."

"We should leave. There's still a rider and a dragon waiting for those two to come back. The purse is there. Get it."

He watched Kemir stoop and pick something up off the ground. Something that jingled with a very pleasant sound. Sollos smiled.

Kemir frowned. "This is a lot, Sollos. Are you sure we're supposed to take it all?"

"That's the deal."

That would normally have been enough for Kemir, but he was still standing there, frowning. As Sollos walked toward him, Kemir reached down and picked up something else. "Have a look at this."

"Put it back! Whatever it is, it's not ours."

"Yes, yes, I will, but I want you to look at it first."

Sollos shook his head. "Leave it alone." Do exactly what was asked, no more and no less. Wasn't that a simple enough rule to live by? For Kemir, apparently not, and it was this sort of thing that always got him into trouble. "Just put it back," he snapped as he reached him, so of course Kemir thrust it into his hands instead.

"What is it?"

"I don't know and I don't care." What Sollos was holding was a spherical bottle made of glass, stoppered and sealed with wax at the top. It fitted nicely into the palm of his hand, and from the way its weight shifted was filled with some sort of liquid. In the darkness he couldn't quite see.

Sollos frowned. If it was a liquid, it was a very heavy one. Then he reminded himself that he really didn't want to know. Quickly, he put the bottle back down where Kemir had found it and took Kemir's arm, dragging him away.

MUCH LATER, WHEN SOLLOS AND Kemir were both long gone, the shadow of a woman slipped out from among the trees and stepped carefully around the corpses. The woman bent down where Kemir and Sollos had stood. She picked up the bottle and crept silently away.

2

KAILIN

The dragon made one circle over the eyrie and then came in to land. Kailin stopped what he was doing to watch. He squinted, trying to make out the dragon's color, or anything else that might distinguish it. Around the featureless top of the eyrie the other Scales would be doing the same. They'd all be thinking the same question too: *Is it one of mine? Is that one I raised?*

Its shape made it a war-dragon, he decided. Hunting-dragons had long tails and long necks and enormous wings and were, to Kailin's eyes, much more graceful. War-dragons were stockier. End to end and wing-tip to wing-tip they were the smaller breed, but they weighed twice as much and ate enough for four. Their colors tended to be drab too. Hunting-dragons were brighter. Their bloodlines were more carefully recorded, their breeding more strictly managed, their diet meticulously controlled by the alchemists.

When a mount was old enough, the trainers taught them to take the saddle and the rein, and to understand their riders' commands. The rest of the work of growing a dragon was down to people like Kailin. They were the ones, if they survived, who fed the dragons, watered them, nurtured them, cared for them—the Scales, whose ruined skin, hard and flaking, marked them for life. In the end Hatchling Disease got them all, petrifying them while they were still alive. A Scales did not get to grow old.

If it was a war-dragon, it wasn't one of his. He watched it come down anyway, a steep, hard dive that made the ground quake as it landed. It folded its wings and snorted, blowing a thin stream of fire up into the air. Kailin recognized it now. Mistral. Queen Shezira's second-favorite mount.

Mistral shook himself. He took a few steps forward and then lowered his head almost to the ground. He looked hungry, Kailin thought. Already, several of the nearest Scales were running over, ready to call Mistral away to one of the feeding paddocks. Their other job was to make sure that Mistral was kept well away from the breeding females. One mistake could ruin centuries of careful breeding, and no one in the world was insane enough to get in the way of a pair of mating dragons.

A single rider slid down from Mistral's shoulders, exchanged a few words with the Scales, and then walked straight toward Kailin. As she came closer, Kailin sank to his knees and bowed his head. Queen Shezira was a regular visitor to the eyrie. Lately, circumstances had hurled Kailin into her path.

She stopped in front of him. "Rise, Scales."

Shakily, Kailin got to his feet. He didn't dare raise his head.

"How is my Saber?" Saber was the queen's hunting-dragon. A few weeks ago she'd brought him to the eyrie with a cracked rib. According to the whispers, the queen had taken Saber hunting somewhere far away, and he'd been charged while on the ground by some beast that sounded like an armored elephant, except with horns. Saber, said the whispers, had bitten the creature's head off with a single snap of his jaws.

"Doing well, I understand," said Kailin, trying to keep the tremor out of his voice. "Your Holiness knows that I am not the Scales caring for him."

"Yes, yes. When do *you* think he will be ready to hunt again?"

"If he were in my care, Your Holiness, I would beg for him to be rested another three weeks."

He could tell from the way the queen tapped her foot that this wasn't the answer she'd wanted. He heard her sigh. "Then I shall have to ride Mistral. And how is my perfect white?"

Snow, thought Kailin. *She's called Snow.*

"What did you say, Scales?"

"I-I . . ." Kailin stammered. "I'm sorry, Your Holiness. I spoke out of turn." Had he spoken at all? He wasn't sure.

"What did you *say,* Scales?"

He was shaking. The queen had a temper. Everyone knew what happened to those who made her angry. "We call her Snow, Your Holiness." Kailin screwed up his eyes and waited for the blow to come.

"Well then, Scales. Snow. How is she?"

"Still . . . still perfect, Your Holiness." He could feel her eyes on him, but he couldn't bring himself to look at her.

"You see she stays that way. And learn to mind your tongue, Scales. You and your dragon will be the property of Prince Jehal before the next full moon. He will give her whatever name takes his fancy, and he is *not* known for his forgiving nature." She laughed. "If you're unlucky, he'll decide you're a spy."

She left him there, quivering.

3

THE EYRIE-MASTER

The Scales was forgotten almost before Shezira had turned her back on him. Two more days and they were due to fly, almost from one end of the realms to the other. Another two weeks and they'd be in King Tyan's palace. Prince Jehal would be there. She would give Jehal her perfect white and her youngest daughter, and in return he would give her lordship of all the realms. Or rather, he wouldn't object to her taking it.

She smiled. Lordship? Or should it be ladyship? It wouldn't be the first time that the speaker was a queen instead of a king, but it had been long enough. Too long.

The eyrie was built on an escarpment. Most of it was tunneled underground and so, from the outside, there wasn't much to look at. Scorched rock and blasted earth and the occasional smoldering mound of dragon dung. Farther away, fields full of cattle stretched out as far as the eye could see, interspersed with tiny clusters of farmhouses. And there were the dragons, of course, always a few of them out on the rocks, being groomed or trained or saddled or fed, or simply sunning themselves.

The only structure built on top of the eyrie was a mas-

sive tower, the Outwatch. As she walked toward its gates,
they swung open. Soldiers poured out and formed up in
ranks to salute her. In their midst was Isentine, the
eyrie-master, dressed to the nines in dragonscale and gold.
Shezira stopped in front of him and he fell to his knees to
kiss her feet. He was getting old. She saw him wince as he
struggled to rise again, which annoyed her. She'd have to
replace him soon, which was a nuisance. He was competent
and devoted, and it would be hard to find his equal. But if
he couldn't bow properly . . .

"Come on, come on, get up!" she hissed under her
breath. All the soldiers were watching.

"Your Holiness." Shezira bit her lip when she saw his
face. He looked so worn out, almost defeated.

"Eyrie-Master Isentine." She forced a smile and put a
hand on each of his shoulders. "Your eyes grow ever sharper
with the years. You must have seen me coming from quite
some way away."

The eyrie-master bowed again, a little dip from the waist,
which didn't seem to trouble him. "I live to serve Your
Holiness."

"And you do it very well." She walked on past him. "We
have another hatchling, I hear. One I should see?"

"I'm afraid not, Your Holiness." Isentine took up his
proper position, walking in step with her just behind her
right shoulder. "This is another that refuses its food and
wastes away."

"Again?" A flash of irritation sounded in Shezira's voice,
and that made her even more annoyed. A queen should
never sound petulant.

"I am sorry, Your Holiness."

"That's three out of the last four. It's not usually that
many." The eyrie-master could still match her pace easily
enough, she noted, so maybe there was some life left in him.
For now.

"It is unusual, Holiness, but the alchemists assure me it
is to be expected that these things should happen from time
to time. I am promised it will not last."

"And do you believe them?" Shezira shook her head.
"Don't answer. One a month, Isentine. That's what I need
from you. One good hatchling every month. But that's not
really why I came here." They were past all the soldiers now.

They walked through the gates and into the maw of Out-watch in silence.

"Does Your Holiness desire something?" Isentine asked her. "We have made all the usual preparations. Baths scented with oils, a feast of delicacies from around the realms, men and women who desire nothing more than to serve your pleasure." He should have known her better by now, but he was old, and some habits simply wouldn't break.

"If that's what they desire, they can spend their time teaching my daughters some manners and some respect, and making them understand that above all they are required to be obedient."

It took a long time for him to digest that, which made Shezira smile. She wasn't supposed to say such things in public, and there was no proper formal response. They walked across the grand hall, a gloomy cavern of ochre stone that accounted for most of the lower levels of Out-watch.

"You should do something about this hall. Put some windows in." The echoes of their footsteps made it seem even emptier, dreary and lonely. "Maybe I should send my daughters to *you* for a while, eh?"

They reached the far side of the hall, where a maze of intertwined staircases snaked toward the upper levels.

"The study, Your Holiness?" asked Isentine.

"Yes." The hall wasn't as empty as Shezira had first thought. Here and there she saw soldiers standing guard, still as statues and tucked into little niches where they wouldn't easily be seen.

By the time they reached the top of the stairs to Isentine's study, he was wheezing. What was it? A hundred and twenty steps to this balcony? She shook her head and watched him as he opened the door and then stood patiently waiting for her to enter. This wouldn't do.

She sighed, went in and sat down. "You're getting positively ancient, Master Isentine." She watched him as she said it, and saw how much it hurt him. Which was good. He knew what was coming, and that would make it easier for both of them.

"Three score years and then some." He looked sad.

"And then some more. You've been the master here for as long as I can remember. Twenty-five years almost to the day I came here." She smiled, thinking back to the first time she'd landed at Outwatch. "Fifteen years old, betrothed to King Antros, and you were the first person I saw. I thought you looked so handsome."

The eyrie-master's throat began to bob up and down as though he was trying to say something, but the words were stuck in his throat.

"I haven't forgotten," Shezira added. "I haven't forgotten that it was you, more than anyone, who stood at my side when Antros died so suddenly. If you'd turned against me, I would not be queen now. You always had my gratitude in the years after that. You have it still."

"Then . . ." They both knew what he wanted to say. They both knew she couldn't consent.

"You may choose who will be the new master of Outwatch and my other eyries, Isentine. I will respect your judgment. But you cannot remain master of my dragons. Speaker Hyram's reign is almost done. I will succeed him. I can hide you away here, but when I rule the Adamantine Palace I cannot have a weak old man who can barely walk at my side. I am sorry." She almost reached out and took his hand, because in more ways than one he was the oldest friend she had. But she was a queen, and so her hand stayed still and only the whiteness of her knuckles betrayed her.

Isentine swallowed. He took a deep breath and slowly bowed. "I understand, Your Holiness. I will find you a man worthy to serve you as I no longer can, and I will take the Dragon's Fall."

They sat together in silence for as long as Shezira could bear. Then she went and stood by the window. The study looked out directly over the cliffs, and the drop felt almost infinite.

"Or . . ."

Isentine didn't move. She could see he was holding his breath.

"My daughters are very fond of their dragons, and very fond of you. Almiri is my heir and has children of her own. Lystra is promised to Prince Jehal and still young enough to be pliable, but Jaslyn . . . She spends a great deal of time here, or so I understand."

Isentine looked at her. He smiled and shook his head. "You may choose whoever you wish, my queen, but Jaslyn is too young to be mistress of any eyrie. She knows her dragons well enough, better than most I might say, but she has no experience . . ."

Now at last he began to see.

"She would need a mentor." Shezira kept her voice stern. "You would have to live out your years here, surrounded by these beasts. I could not permit you to take the Dragon's Fall until you were quite sure she was worthy to succeed you."

"Yes, Your Holiness. Thank you."

Shezira looked away. Isentine was almost weeping with gratitude, and that was something she couldn't bear to see. "You will not come with us to King Tyan's realm. You are too old. Instead you can stay here and think about everything you must do. It will not be an easy task for you with Jaslyn. She's willful and proud. If I said she was plain, it would be flattery, yet she turns up her nose at every suitor I put before her. Before long you might wish you'd taken the Dragon's Fall after all."

"I will make her a daughter to be proud of," whispered the eyrie-master.

I already am, thought Shezira, but that too was something she could never admit. Instead, she began to pace the floor, steadfastly ignoring Isentine's gaze. "Yes. Now, Prince Jehal. Two more days, Eyrie-Master."

"All is prepared, Your Holiness."

"Oh, I have no doubt of that, but still . . . Summon the alchemist. Haros? Huros? Whatever his name is. Let him bore me with the details of *his* preparations. And in case I fall asleep, please make sure he knows that my knight-marshal has something she wishes to discuss with him. It seems she has acquired a bottle of something that she requires him to understand for her."

"At once, Your Holiness."

Shezira watched Isentine leave. He had a spring in his step, one she hadn't seen for a long time. She could almost make herself believe that she'd done something good. A little ray of sunshine amid a much darker storm.

Two more days before I leave to buy Prince Jehal with my own daughter's flesh. Although I, above all, understand that is what we daughters are for.

4

THE SPEAKER OF THE REALMS

"How," murmured Jehal, "could anyone *not* covet it? I simply don't understand."

Beside him he felt Zafir's skin, slick with sweat, move against his own. She turned toward him. "Covet what, my lover?"

Jehal threw out his arms. They lay together in a carved wooden bed a thousand years old, swathed in silken sheets. In all four walls windows opened out to the sky and the vista of the Adamantine Palace and the City of Dragons below.

"This! All of this!"

Zafir pressed herself against him and began to stroke his chest.

"All of this," she murmured. She sounded happy, Jehal thought, and well she might. She'd spent most of the night gasping, after all.

Jehal sighed and sat up. "Yes, all of this. Wouldn't it be perfect? Ah . . . I'll never forget the first time my father brought me here. I sat in his saddle with his arms around me as we soared high in the air. The sky was a brilliant blue, the sun burning and bright, the ground far, far beneath us. Dark and green and lush. I could see distant mountains, and then beside them I saw something glitter. I pointed and asked what it was. My father said it was a jewel, the greatest jewel I would ever see, and he was right. The Adamantine Palace, glittering in the sun, the lakes sparkling around it, the mountains of the Purple Spur at its back. That sight is burned into my mind, like dragon's breath." He smiled and shook his head. "Awestriker. That's what my father's dragon was called. He was an old one even then, and long gone now. Sometimes I wish my father had gone with him. After my deranged little brother murdered our mother and the rest of our siblings, he was never the same. Lingering like this, drooling and deranged, it's not fitting. A king should live forever or else die in a blaze of glory."

Zafir draped her arms around his shoulders. "You have me."

"Yes. I have you. More than enough for any man. The most beautiful princess in all the realms."

"Queen," she whispered, nibbling at his ear. "My mother is dead. Some wicked man threw her off a dragon, remember?"

Jehal pulled her lips to his. "That is a dangerous thing to say, my sweet. Your mother had an accident. I'm quite certain of it. And you're still a princess, not a queen. Not until Speaker Hyram says otherwise."

"Will it be long?"

"I would think an hour, maybe two, before he calls you." Zafir snorted. "Why does it take him so long?"

"Have you seen how he shakes? He's an old man, and twilight is coming fast upon him."

"He's so dreary. He makes time drag."

Jehal laid her gently on her back. He gazed into her eyes, so dark and wide, and rested his hand on the curve of her belly. A faint breeze from the windows brushed his skin. "A clever trick." He grinned. "But I can make it fly."

Zafir giggled. "When I'm a queen, and you're still only a prince, does that mean you have to do as I say?"

"I will be yours to command."

"Then I know exactly what my first demand as queen will be."

"And what is that, my love?"

"As soon as I'm queen, I shall summon you back here at once." She cupped his face in her hands and pushed him slowly down on her. "More!" she sighed. "That'll be what I want from you. More ..."

Later, Jehal watched Zafir dress herself and leave. After she was gone, he stood naked at the window, waiting, wondering if anyone was watching him. The Tower of Air was the tallest and grandest of the palace towers, and Speaker Hyram had set it aside for Zafir as soon as he'd known her purpose in coming to the palace. The floors below were full of servants, a few of them Zafir's but most of them the speaker's. It wouldn't do for Hyram to know whom Zafir had taken to her bed, and yet he stood at the window anyway, daring fate to expose him.

Once he thought Zafir had been gone for long enough, he slipped on a plain tunic and a pair of slightly soiled trousers, and walked out carrying the chamber pot. In the confusion of unfamiliar faces, no one spared him a second glance.

In contrast to the Tower of Air, Jehal's own lodgings were somewhat more modest, almost the meanest that the palace had to offer. Hyram had probably wanted him banished to a leaky hut of mud and straw somewhere outside the city walls, Jehal thought. That would be too overt an insult, but the slight was not lost on him, and he made up for it by being late to Zafir's coronation, loudly bursting into the Glass Cathedral when Hyram was halfway through his tedious speech about dignity and service and the duties of kingship. Kingship, not queenship. Jehal made a mental note to mention that to Zafir once he had her naked again.

Hyram droned on and Jehal picked his nails. The cathedral felt immense and empty. A gaggle of dragon-priests hovered and twittered in the shadows at the back. A few lords and ladies of Hyram's household sat politely, but the only other person who mattered was the potion-maker, dutifully recording the event: Bellepheros, grand master alchemist and First Lord of the Order of the Scales. Jehal watched him and yawned. They could have done all this in ten minutes in Hyram's study with a bottle of fine wine. Oh, but then it wouldn't have been the *same*. Perhaps flirting with death from both boredom and hypothermia at once somehow gave the event gravitas. He should have brought a cloak, he decided. A thick, warm cloak. And a pillow. As it was, the amusement of watching Hyram shake and stutter his way through his speech would just have to do to keep him awake.

Eventually Hyram was done. Jehal slipped out and watched, waiting for Zafir, already thinking about how he would fulfill her first queenly command. But it was Speaker Hyram who came out first, and walked purposefully toward Jehal.

"G-G-Good of you t-to eventually attend," he stuttered. Every part of him was trembling. Jehal gave him the slightest of bows.

"I'm quite aware that Queen Zafir could not be crowned without at least someone else of royal blood to bear witness, otherwise I would not be here at all. Are you cold, Your Highness? There's certainly a chill to the air today. I could get a cloak for you, if you like."

Hyram spat. "D-D-Don't play the fool with me, Prince J-Jehal."

Jehal smiled and touched his forehead. "Of course, Your Highness. I forgot. Your sickness. It seems to be getting worse. It will be a terrible loss to the realms. All that wisdom. Who among the dragon-kings could possibly take your place?"

"And h-how *is* your father, Jehal?" Hyram looked like a broken old man with his constant quivering, but there was still fire in his eyes. Jehal bit his lip. *Careful, careful. He's not a fool. Not yet.*

He tried to look sad. "His mind, I think, is still as sharp as ever. It *is* hard to know. Most of the time he's rigid with the paralysis. When the shaking comes and he can actually open his mouth, none of us can understand what he's trying to say. It's a wonder we're still able to feed him. The sickness—"

"Sickness?" Hyram snorted. "I think you will f-find it is almost taken for granted that you're p-poisoning him."

Jehal clenched his teeth. "Then I must be poisoning you as well, Your Highness, for your symptoms are the same as his were in the early days. Yes, it's hard to remember a time when he could still talk and feed himself and fuck women and do everything a dragon-prince's father should be able

to do, but I would say your symptoms are *exactly* the same."
He spat and turned to walk away. "It's as well your time will
soon be done. How pitiful it would be to have a speaker
who can't actually speak. And how's your memory, by the
way? Are you starting to forget things yet?"

"Jehal."

Jehal stopped but didn't turn back. "Your Highness?"

"Queen Aliphera. They say she f-fell from her dragon."

"So I heard." He turned now, so he could watch Hyram's
face.

"I knew Aliphera. She l-loved the hunt. She rode her d-
dragons as well as any man. This notion—it's p-preposterous."

Jehal shrugged. "Yes it is, isn't it. But she'd chosen to fly
away from her escorts. No one saw what happened, or no
one will admit to it." He laughed. "You could always ask the
dragon."

"I'm asking you."

"*What* are you asking me, Your Highness?"

"D-Did Zafir do it?"

"If that's your question then you should ask her, not
me."

"I d-did. They were my f-first words after I put the crown
on her head. D-Did you kill your mother to get this?"

Jehal smirked. "I imagine that went down very well. If
you've suddenly taken to valuing my opinion, the thought
did cross my mind. I doubt Zafir murdered Queen Aliphera, though. She may have the ambition to think it, but
she lacks the nerve."

"Y-You, however, do not."

"Me?" Jehal growled. "Since it appears I have failed to
finish poisoning my own father despite a decade of effort,
perhaps I am not as able an assassin as you think, Your
Highness."

"I will send t-truth-seekers to your eyrie. T-To Zafir's as
well. B-Bellepheros already has my orders. If you make
a-any attempt to interfere with them, I will kn-know you are
guilty."

"Your faith in my character is touching, Your Highness.
By all means, send whoever you like, and of course
Bellepheros shall have everything he needs put at his disposal. I shall demand that he is as meticulous and thorough
as he can be, and when he finds nothing I shall expect you

to doubt me no less than you do now. Are you done with me, old man?"

"I-I very much hope so."

Jehal leaned toward Speaker Hyram and held his gaze. "What if you're wrong? What if I haven't spent the last few years slowly murdering my own father? What if I've been looking for a cure instead? What if I were to tell you I'd found it?"

For an instant Hyram's eyes faltered. Only for an instant, but Jehal could almost taste the victory. "Then I look f-forward to seeing him in the s-saddle once more."

"So do I, Your Highness. So do I." Jehal walked away, biting his lip, his face stony. When he was sure no one could see, he looked up to the Tower of Air.

"There," he whispered, as if the wind might somehow carry his words to Zafir. "Do you think that went well?" He began to giggle and then to laugh until he wept, and after that he didn't know whether it was the laughter or the tears that wouldn't stop.

5

SHEZIRA

The snapper pack was already scattering. Shezira picked one of them and yelled at Mistral. Obediently, the dragon wheeled and dived, tucking in his wings and plummeting toward the ground like a falcon. The snapper was going to be too quick, though. It was going to reach the trees before Mistral was in range. Shezira growled softly to herself. This was what she got for riding a war-dragon on a hunt. They were so vast, their shoulders were so broad, their wings so large, that she couldn't even see what she was doing half the time. Unless she dived like this, in which case the wind almost blinded her instead. She squinted at the scattered trees below.

"Fire!" she shouted.

Mistral spread his wings. Shezira found herself hugging scales as the dragon almost stopped in midair. She quickly shut the visor on her helm. She heard the roar and felt Mistral quiver, and a wall of heat washed over her. Then Mistral shuddered and lurched as he landed heavily and stumbled. Shezira felt branches and leaves tear at her armor and heard the crack of a tree trunk. The air was hot and filled with the smell of charred wood. When she opened her visor it was to see a swathe of forest floor a hundred yards long burning. The trees around her were blackened; some were broken where Mistral had smashed into them. Shezira couldn't see whether the blast had reached the snapper. Slowly she backed Mistral out of the wreckage.

"You missed him, Mother," shouted Princess Almiri. Her dragon was already on the ground, some fifty yards away, clutching a headless snapper in its front claws.

Shezira instinctively ducked as something huge flew right over her head, so close that she felt the wind of its passing almost lift her out of the saddle. A sooty gray hunting-dragon arched up and flew over the forest, so close that its tail slashed the treetops. Again and again, its head darted down and spat out a narrow lance of fire. Then the dragon climbed, turned and came back to land next to Shezira, squeezing into the space between her and Princess Almiri. Its rider took off her helm and waved an angry fist.

"That was my kill, Mother!" Princess Jaslyn bellowed and threw her helm away in disgust. "What do you think you were doing? You flew right into my path! Silence almost plowed into you and your clumsy behemoth. You should have borrowed one of Almiri's hunters."

"Height has precedence!" snapped Shezira. She had to shout to make herself heard. Mistral was scratching at a fallen tree, rolling it over. He could smell something.

"The *chaser* has precedence!" Jaslyn yelled back. Silence folded his wings and took careful steps sideways, until he and Mistral were almost touching. Mistral dropped the tree, shifted and hissed, and Silence hissed back. War-dragons didn't like being crowded. Shezira felt suddenly small. Dragons didn't actually attack riders unless they were commanded. Being accidentally crushed to death, however, was a very different matter.

"I *was* the chaser!" Shezira tried to calm Mistral down. Jaslyn was right. Mistral wasn't made for this sort of flying, and she should have borrowed a proper hunter.

"Only after you practically barged me out of the air!" Silence was baring his teeth at Mistral now. The difference in size didn't seem to bother him at all. *At least being on a war-dragon means I can look down on my daughter while we bicker.*

"Did you get the snapper?" shouted Almiri. She'd shuffled her own dragon sideways too, coming close enough to distract Silence. As the eldest of Shezira's daughters and the only one married with a family of her own, Almiri had taken to the role of family peacemaker. This always made Shezira smile, because she remembered a time when Almiri was every bit as bad as Jaslyn.

"Of *course* I got it!"

All around them, the other dragons were landing on the open ground and the earth trembled as each one came down. At a quick count, Shezira guessed they'd got about a third of the snapper pack, which certainly wouldn't be enough to keep King Valgar happy. Snappers were a menace. Standing up on its back legs, a snapper was half again as tall as a man, twice as fast, and if it got the chance would happily bite your head off. They were cunning, ate anything and everything they could catch, hunted in groups, and weren't averse to slaughtering entire villages. Dragons were by far the best way of keeping them under control, and King Valgar had been holding back from this herd just so they could have this hunt.

Mistral took a few steps toward Silence, barging into him, and growled. Silence hissed again. The dragons were sensing the moods of their riders. Mistral was probably hungry too, and most of the other dragons were eating their first kills now. The scent of blood was in the air, mixed with the sounds of cracking bones and tearing flesh and heavy dragon breathing.

"Would you like to swap, Mother?" asked Almiri, still shouting to make herself heard. "Have a proper mount for the hunt?"

The offer was tempting, but Shezira shook her head. "It'll be dusk before you're finished here and I need to get back to Valgar's eyrie. I should be keeping an eye on Lystra, in case she does something stupid."

"You should have let her come."

"A week before she's supposed to kneel before Jehal? You know what she's like, especially when she's got Jaslyn to goad her on. I want to present her the way she *can* be, perfect and beautiful, not the way she usually *is*, saddle sore and covered in bruises. No. It was nice to fly with you for a while, but I should go."

Almiri smiled. "It's a pity, though. I would have liked the four of us to fly together one last time."

The words cut, although Almiri surely hadn't meant them to be cruel. It seemed only yesterday that she'd given Almiri away to King Valgar. Which had been hard, but at least their clans had been intertwined by blood for centuries and their realms were close. Besides, Almiri was the oldest. She was the heir to the Throne of Sand and Stone, and letting her go had been right and proper. And she'd still had Jaslyn and little Lystra.

Somehow, over the years, she'd lost Jaslyn to her dragons; now she was about to lose the last of her daughters to a prince she barely knew, to live in a palace more than a thousand miles away. A necessary arrangement and certainly not without its benefits, but once the marriage was made, Lystra would be a stranger to her. She was going to have to get used to the idea.

Almiri must have seen something of Shezira's thoughts in her face, for she added, "Once you sit in the Adamantine Palace, you'll be able to summon all of us as often as you like. You can have as many hunts and tournaments as you want. Prince Jehal will *have* to bring Lystra with him if you tell him to."

Which was all true, but she couldn't shake the feeling that it would never quite be the same. She sighed. "There will be a day, Princess. One day. Would you spare Mistral half your carcass? He's restless."

Half a snapper was little more than a snack for a monster like Mistral, but it seemed to settle his mood. With a pang of regret, Shezira left the hunters to their fun. She turned him on the ground, cumbersome and slow as he was, and then he started to run. *That* made the other dragons sit up and take notice, for the footfalls of a running war-dragon could shake the earth enough to shatter houses, and it took a lot for a beast like Mistral to take to the air. When he did finally spread his wings and soar into the sky, though, all his ungainliness was gone. Shezira had him circle once above them and tipped a wing to wish them luck. Then she put the mountains and forests to her back and headed out over the plains. She allowed Mistral to set his own pace, and let herself enjoy the feeling of the wind in her hair and the utter sense of being alone. It wasn't often that she had the skies to herself, and yet she had long ago come to realize that that was what she enjoyed most. That was when she was truly free, free to pretend she had no titles, no burdens, no family, no daughters to marry off, no plotting nephews to watch, no subjects to rule, no obligations, no responsibilities ...

Catching herself thinking these thoughts made her laugh. *And here I am, set to become the next Speaker of the Realms. Would I really turn my back on that if someone told me I could? Would I really take Mistral and fly away across the Stone Desert to the secret valleys beyond, where no one would know me and no one would find me?*

The answer, she knew, was that she wouldn't contemplate it even for a second. Which probably made her a fool, and that in turn made her laugh even more, and by the time she reached Valgar's eyrie, she felt ten years younger.

She'd hoped the feeling would last after she landed, but it didn't. It died at the exact moment that she saw her knight-marshal, Lady Nastria, walking briskly across the scorched earth toward her. Nastria was already half in her armor, as if in a rush to leave, and was waving something in her hand. She was shouting.

"Your Holiness! Queen Aliphera is dead!"

6

HUROS

Huros knew exactly what was going on, because nothing could happen without him. He'd sat with Eyrie-Master Isentine and explained to Queen Shezira everything about the route they would take to escort Princess Lystra to her wedding. Exactly how many dragons would be flying, exactly where they would be stopping and exactly for how long.

They left King Valgar's eyrie at the crack of dawn. Huros was expecting that, because that had been in his plan. Today was the longest stage of their journey, all the way to the Adamantine Palace. They would stay there for one day, no more and no less, to let the dragons rest. He was quietly looking forward to it. He would spend the time with the highest alchemists in the realms, perhaps even with Master Bellepheros himself. It was an opportunity to advance himself, and this had filled his thoughts until late into the night. Thus he wasn't entirely awake when someone knocked on his door. He stumbled outside while the sun was still creeping over the horizon and checked his potions were all carefully packed. Then he wrapped himself in his thick and deliciously warm flying coat, secured himself to the back of a dragon and started to count the others getting ready around him. By the time he reached twenty, his eyes had grown so heavy that he thought he might rest them for a bit. The counting was rather pointless, after all. He knew exactly which dragons were with them and exactly where they were going.

Others climbed up beside him. He felt the dragon start to run and then launch itself into the air. He had a sleepy look around, and then his eyes closed.

When he woke up two hours later, as his belly reminded him that he hadn't had any breakfast, he was in the wrong place. The mountains of the Worldspine were too close. More to the point, there should have been some thirty dragons in the skies around him. Instead, he could see the white, two other war-dragons, and that was it.

"Er . . . Excuse me?"

There were two men on the war-dragon with him. One was a rider, sitting up above its shoulders. The other one looked like a Scales. Huros furrowed his brow, trying to remember the man's name. Kailin. The one who looked after the white.

"Hey! Scales!"

The Scales turned around and gave Huros a blank look. The rider was too far away to hear them over the wind.

"Scales! Can you hear me?"

The Scales nodded.

"Where are we?"

The Scales shrugged.

"Um, don't you know? Where are the others then?"

The Scales shook his head and shrugged again.

"Well. Oh. Then who *does* know?"

The Scales tipped his head toward the dragon-knight. Huros rolled his eyes and gave up. Strictly speaking, Scales were subordinate to Huros and the other alchemists, and all belonged to the order. In reality, most Scales lived in a tiny world of their own that seemed to consist of themselves, their dragons and very little else.

His stomach began to rumble. He decided to have one more try. "Scales! Um. Have you anything to eat?"

The Scales nodded and passed back a hunk of bread. Huros gnawed on it and quietly fumed. Under *no* circumstances was a squadron of dragons to split without consulting the senior alchemist present. Since Huros was the only alchemist Queen Shezira had deemed fit to bring, that was him. He would have *words,* he thought grimly. Words, yes. Strong and forthright ones.

They flew for hours, and with each hour, Huros clenched his fists ever tighter. Eventually it occurred to him that Queen Shezira might have changed her plans because of the news of Queen Aliphera's tragedy. Huros wasn't sure why that should be, but then he hadn't really been paying much attention. He'd had his own plans to worry about. Besides, that didn't change anything. He should have been *consulted.* Ancestors! He didn't even know where he was anymore, except that the peaks of the Worldspine were to the right and there were more mountains to the front. Which meant they were still flying south, away from Outwatch. He furrowed his brow. Or was that the other way round, and the mountains should be on the left?

The pressure on his bladder grew. He pressed his legs together and bit his lip, but eventually he had to give in. Dragon-knights did this all the time, he told himself, and he started to undo the straps that held him onto the dragon. Even the Scales had calmly stood up, relieved himself into a bottle and strapped himself back in again. Except when Huros stood up, the wind buffeted him and almost knocked him over, and he was so terrified that he couldn't go. The pressure turned gradually into pain, and by the time they landed, it was so excruciating that Huros was in no fit state to have words with anyone. He didn't waste any time to see where he was, but stumbled and staggered away toward the nearest tree.

Before he was done, his dragon and its rider were already taking off again, the beast lumbering away and flapping its wings, accelerating up to a speed where it could lift itself off the ground. For one terrifying heartbeat Huros thought he'd been abandoned; then he saw the Scales and a pair of strange-looking soldiers, and when he looked up, the other dragons were there, still in the air overhead. The Scales was sitting by the edge of a wide-open stretch of jumbled rocks, next to a pile of boxes and sacks that must have come from the dragon-riders. Here and there sparkling ribbons of bubbling water crisscrossed and threaded their way between the stones and among streaks and strands of silvery sand. Strips of ragged grass, perhaps a stone's throw across, lined the river's course before the forest trees took hold.

The two soldiers walked slowly toward him. They were carrying some strange contraption between them. From the way they were walking, it was awfully heavy. Huros had a moment to wonder where the queen's precious white dragon had gone, when it shot through the air straight over his head, so close that the tree beside him shook and the alchemist was almost lifted off his feet into the dragon's wake. He clung on to a branch. By the time he'd recovered, the dragon was rolling on its back in the riverbed next to the Scales, flapping and splashing its wings. Its rider was standing nearby, soaking wet, waving his arms and shouting furiously at the Scales.

The two soldiers shouted something as well and shook their fists, then carried on with what they were doing. Huros waited until they were close, and then stepped out of the trees. "You're not dragon-knights." Both soldiers had long-bows slung over their backs. The bows were white and made of dragonbone. Precious things. The alchemist wondered where they'd got them.

The soldiers looked at him. They exchanged a glance and seemed to smirk. "Clever of you to notice," said the taller of the two. "Was it the fact that we're not wearing several tons of dragonscale that gave it away, or that we're not sitting around and picking our noses?"

"We're sell-swords," said the other one.

The tall one nodded. "That's right. Currently we've sold them to your knight-marshal."

"They don't come cheap, either." The shorter one gave Huros a nasty grin. "Our swords are long and sharp and very hard." He definitely smirked.

"Lady Nastria?" Huros frowned. The thought of her sent a jolt through him. She'd given him a bottle of something strange, and he hadn't even looked at it. He was supposed to tell her what it was.

"If that's what her name is."

The tall one belched loudly. "That's the one. I'm Sollos. This is my cousin, Kemir. Since you're not the Scales, you must be the alchemist."

"Huros," said Huros.

"Well then, Huros the alchemist, make yourself useful. There's half a ton of luggage down there by the river. We'd quite like to move it up into the trees before the heavy brigade come back." The sell-sword made a rude gesture toward the rider who was still standing over the Scales, waving his arms and shouting. "I don't imagine he'll be much help."

"That was pretty good, though." The short one grinned again. Kemir. "The white one forgot she had a rider for a moment there. If he'd been any slower jumping clear when she rolled ..." He drew his finger across his throat. "Pity, really. I would have pissed myself. Still, we don't want all our luggage crushed, do we."

Huros shook himself. *Words,* he reminded himself. He was going to have words with someone. And these two were very rude. And he was *Master* Huros, thank you very much. They looked a bit big, though. And armed. He bit his tongue. "Um. Of course. Although ... Excuse me, but where have the rest of the dragons gone, exactly?"

"Their riders have taken them hunting," said the tall one. Sollos. He gave Huros a pitying look and shook his head.

"For food," added Kemir. Yes. When the knights came back, Huros would have words about these two as well. *What are they even doing here?*

"Can't have them getting hungry. Never know, they might set their minds to snacking on alchemists." The two sell-swords were leering and shaking their heads. Every day Huros spent at least some of his time with ravenous monsters who could swallow him in a blink, kept only in check by their training and by the subtle potions that he dripped into their drinking troughs. These two, though, made him far more nervous than any dragon ever had.

"Um. Clearly. I meant the *other* ones. The rest of them. Where's the queen?"

The sell-swords looked at each other and shrugged. "Keep an eye on the Scales," said Sollos. "That's what we were told. We keep an eye on the riders too. In case any of them get any bad ideas about stealing the queen's dragons." He grinned and stuck out his bottom lip. "Where the rest of them went ..." He shrugged. "Don't know, don't care. A clever man might hazard a guess that they flew off to the Adamantine Palace, just like they were supposed to. But you're an alchemist, so I suppose that must mean you're a clever man, and you'd already thought of that."

"Well ... But why ... why didn't we?"

The tall one sniggered. "I don't know. Maybe some unsettling news came of late. Maybe your queen doesn't trust your speaker farther than she could throw him. I hear he's grown quite large of late. Or maybe we don't know shit." The sell-swords looked at each other again.

"Did anyone say anything about keeping an eye on alchemists?" asked the short one. The tall one shook his head. Sollos, Huros reminded himself again. His name was Sollos. He seemed to be the one in charge.

"I don't think so."

"No, I didn't think so either."

Sollos smiled what was possibly the most menacing smile Huros had ever seen. "We're just sell-swords. We do as we're told and go where we're sent. No one gives us reasons, and we don't ask for them. Why don't you bother that rider over there, once he's finished laying into your Scales. I'm sure he'll know more than us. As long as you don't expect him to help with the luggage. In the meantime do you think *you* might help us? I believe some of it could be yours."

The short one nodded sagely. "It's the stuff at the bottom, I think. It might have been a bit squashed. Crushed even." He looked at the other sell-sword. "Come to think of it, did you see something leaking out of one of those boxes?"

His potions!

Huros ran toward the river as fast as his legs would carry him. He didn't need to look back to know that the sell-swords were laughing at him.

A shadow crossed the sun. Huros stopped and looked up. There were dragons in the sky, diving toward the river. Four of them, which was at least one dragon more than there should have been. And they were hunting-dragons, not war-dragons, which meant ...

The lead dragon opened its mouth, and the river exploded in fire.

7

THE GLASS CATHEDRAL

Being alone on Mistral's back was one of the nice things about being queen. All the dragon-knights had to share their mounts with the gaggle of courtiers from her palace, the mob of extra hedge-knights that Lady Nastria insisted on bringing and of course the alchemists and the Scales from the eyrie. Not to mention all the luggage.

Shezira sighed. Everything seemed so small from up in the sky. Over her shoulder, to the west of the realms, the volcanic Worldspine mountains ran from the sea to the desert and, as far as Shezira knew, on to the ends of the world. North of Shezira's eyrie, the dragon lands faded into the trackless Deserts of Sand, Stone and Salt. At the opposite end of the realms, King Tyan's capital was built on the shore of the endless Sea of Storms. When she stood among the mountains or in the emptiness of the desert, everything seemed so unimaginably vast. Yet from up here it was all nothing.

"I hear whispers of lands across the seas," she whispered to Mistral. "So do you suppose those are King Tyan's secrets, just like the mystery of what lies beyond the Desert of Stone is ours, eh?"

She sighed again and tried to peer around Mistral's enormous head. Somewhere down there ...

South of King Valgar's eyrie the peaks of the Purple Spur reached out into the heart of the dragon realms. Nestled in their far foothills, surrounded by the waters of the Mirror Lakes, lay the Adamantine Palace. Shezira had landed among its ramparts often enough; still, even now, the first sight of it, gleaming and sparkling like distant treasure in the summer sun, was enough to make her heart skip a beat whenever she saw it.

There! A twinkle, right at the foot of the last mountain. And sure enough a thrill ran through her, as though she was twenty years younger.

Sparkle it might, she thought to herself. For it *was* a treasure. It was a prize, a symbol of power. It was a place where marriages were brokered and alliances sealed, where kings and queens plotted their paths to greatness. It was the center, the beating heart of the realms.

Above all, it would be *hers.* Soon.

She led her flight to circle around the palace eyrie, waiting for the signal to land. She'd forgotten how immense it all was.

"Do you like it?" She patted Mistral on the neck.

A gout of fire from below told her they were ready. She let Mistral plunge through the air. Like most dragons, he seemed to like that, dropping like a stone from among the clouds. Every time, she was sure he'd misjudge and they'd smash into the stone, but always, just as she screwed up her face and closed her eyes, there would be a clap of thunder as he spread his wings. The force crushed the air out of her lungs and made the ground quiver. She loved it.

As she slid from Mistral's shoulder, Hyram was there to greet her. His shaking, she noticed, had become much worse over the months since she'd last seen him.

"Y-You're going to h-have an accident one d-day."

It was hard not to grin, but the business of being queen was a serious one, and moments of levity were strictly out of the question. In public at least. She bowed. Hyram held out a trembling hand and Shezira kissed the ring on his middle finger. *Her* ring, soon.

"Speaker Hyram. It is a delight to be in your presence again."

He nodded brusquely and waved over some of his attendants. He and Shezira walked in silence away from the eyrie, the attendants following. Mouthwatering words gushed from their lips, describing the pleasures of the mind and of the flesh that awaited her, but Shezira barely heard them. *It should be Hyram telling me these things, not his courtiers. Has the sickness become so bad that it's robbing him of his speech? How long before he can't even walk anymore?*

Carriages were waiting to take them to the palace. Then they had to wait for Jaslyn and Lystra and Lady Nastria and the other riders Shezira had brought with her, and after that there were endless rituals and formalities to observe, and then the obligatory feast to honor guests, none of which interested Shezira at all. At least Hyram had put some effort into it. Tiny alchemical lamps festooned the vast spaces of the Chamber of Audience. There were hundreds of them, thousands, strung out on lines like little glowworms, hundreds more studding the vaults of the ceiling like stars so that it seemed they were feasting outside under the sky. Statues surrounded them, larger than life, silent guardians carved in granite. All the speakers who had ever ruled the realms, watching over them. Above them, marble dragon heads reached out from the walls, peering down from the shadows, sullen and brooding. Little lamps were hidden in their mouths to make them glow. As they entered, voices hushed to whispers or stopped altogether, awed by the Speaker's hall. Then the feast began, the noise resumed and the hall filled with servants running to and fro with cups of wine, platters of roasted meat, huge pies and colorful glazed pastries twisted into the shapes of dragons and men.

An adequate effort.

She sat or stood next to Hyram for the entire time, yet she couldn't talk to him. At least not about what she wanted. At the end of the feast, when Hyram stood up and wobbled and declared that he was retiring to his bed, Shezira watched him go, then slipped away to follow him. The Hyram she remembered would almost always slip away to bed early after a feast, it was simply a question of *whose* bed. This time, though, as she watched, he staggered and meandered his way toward the Glass Cathedral. She followed him inside, half expecting to find him locked in an embrace with some dragon-priestess. Instead, she found him prostrate at prayer.

She kneeled beside him at the altar and looked up at the face of the dragon glaring down at them. Hyram stank of wine.

"I should thank you for your hospitality," she said. Hyram didn't seem to hear her. She shivered. Somehow, the Glass Cathedral was always cold.

"This p-place is a lie," said Hyram suddenly.

"What?"

"The G-Glass Cathedral. It's a lie." He turned to look at her. His face was flushed and he was either about to burst out laughing or fall about weeping.

"Are you drunk?"

"It makes the t-tremors better. Three bottles of wine and I c-can almost believe I am well again."

Shezira raised an eyebrow. It was true that Hyram didn't seem to be shaking as badly now, but he couldn't keep his eyes focused on her while he was talking, either. "Are you sure that's not the wine, lying to you?"

"Does it matter?"

"I suppose not."

Hyram nodded, as though that was the end of their conversation. He lifted his face toward the stone dragon above them, closed his eyes and sighed. "Please . . ."

Shezira shifted uncomfortably. This wasn't the Hyram she remembered at all, and she wasn't quite sure what to do with him, except maybe help him up and show him to his bed.

He started to climb unsteadily to his feet. Instinct made her offer a hand to help him, but he shied away from her as though she'd offered him a snake by mistake.

"I wouldn't even be here i-if my brother . . . if Antros hadn't died. It should have been Antros who got this place. You and him. H-He was supposed to be the new speaker, not me. That was the arrangement. I-I would have inherited my father's throne, not my cousin Sirion. I would have been a king. I was going to m-marry Aliphera. Did you know that?"

Aliphera? Shezira shook herself. She hadn't the first idea what Hyram was talking about. Did he even know what he was saying? She got up. "You *are* drunk. Let us talk in the morning instead."

"It had to be one of us, but everyone liked A-Antros better, didn't they. Except you. And Aliphera." He looked at her suddenly. "I never quite worked out whether y-you had Antros killed or whether it really was an accident."

She slapped him. He staggered back and fell over. "You are *too* drunk, Hyram. You forget yourself."

Hyram wiped his face and picked himself slowly to his feet. "You liked Aliphera too."

"I respected her."

"Well I *l-liked* her. I was going to marry her once. But then . . ." His face grew distant. For a moment Shezira thought Hyram was simply going to fall asleep in front of her. "Things happened. It would have b-been a good match, though. She was always the sensible one from that lot in the south. If I *had* married her, I'd have to have made her s-speaker after me, though, wouldn't I? And that wasn't the arrangement. S-So I did what I was supposed to do. I will honor the p-pact. That's what you c-came here to ask, isn't it?"

Shezira sighed. "I came here to pay my respects to the Speaker of the Realms. I did not expect to find myself in a midnight tryst with a drunkard."

Hyram peered at her. "Promise m-me something."

"Promise you what?"

"Promise m-me the truth. Tell me one thing, and I will p-promise that you will have this palace after me."

"I am not, by habit, a liar, Hyram."

"When Antros died, w-was it you who cut his harness?"

Shezira clenched her fists. "Everyone who was there saw what happened. We were hunting snappers, as we often do. When we saw the pack, several of the dragons dived. His went with them. He always wore his harness too loose, and on that day, he wore it much too loose. He fell. He shouldn't have, but he did, and it wasn't the first time either. For some reason, his legbreaker rope was too long. It caught him all right, but he ended up hanging underneath his dragon. He was dragged along the ground and through the trees for about a mile before we could make his mount come to ground. I've never seen a dragon so agitated. Antros was dead when we reached him. It all happened in front of a dozen witnesses. No one pushed him and no one cut his harness."

Hyram gave her a reproachful look. "You n-never liked him, though."

"Oh, I was young and he was well into his middle years!" Shezira stamped her foot. "He was going to be the next speaker one day. He'd already had one wife and she hadn't given him any children. That's what he wanted me for. Heirs. I was a dutiful wife, Hyram, and he was a dutiful husband. I was in awe of him. I didn't have time to *like* him." She sighed. "It might have been a little different if I'd given him a son, but all I gave him were daughters, one after another. He never even saw Lystra."

"Hmmm." Hyram suddenly sat down. He sounded sad. "No sons for Antros, no s-sons for me. The end of our line."

"You can still sire sons."

The speaker looked up at her, shaking. Shezira couldn't tell whether he was laughing or sobbing. "L-Look at me, woman. Who would have me? Would *you* have me? You should have done. By rights, you sh-should have. After Antros was gone, you should have married me in his p-place."

Shezira sighed. "Yes. But my childbearing ended with Lystra, as you were so keen to point out." She looked down at Hyram and shook her head. Not the man she remembered. Not the man she wanted to remember. The old Hyram had reminded her of her dead husband. This one . . . She didn't know whether to despise him or pity him. She turned away. "Besides, you blamed me for Antros. You still do. Somewhere in your heart, you think I had a hand in it."

When Hyram spoke again, his words were so quiet that Shezira almost didn't hear them. "Aliphera f-fell off her dragon too."

She laughed. "That's ridiculous."

"If Antros could f-fall off, why not her?"

"Antros was arrogant. Aliphera was always meticulously careful."

"I've sent B-Bellepheros to King T-Tyan's eyrie to find out." He grimaced. "Yes, th-that's where it happened, and that's where you're g-going. So I think I should w-warn you to have a care. P-People die around the Viper."

"The Viper?"

"Prince Jehal. H-He's a snake, you see. A p-poisonous snake. A Viper."

"Then I will be very careful. *Some* people seem to think he's poisoning his own father. Could that be true, do you think?"

"W-Why don't you find out? Because I'd very much l-like to know. A g-gift for me." He stood up and spread out his arms. "In exchange for all this."

"It's cold in here," said Shezira. She was tired, and seeing Hyram like this had killed all the joy that the palace had given her. "I shall retire. I will think on what you've said."

"I-I remember the first time I came here. I thought the Glass Cathedral would be a palace of light and color. But it isn't. It's old, cold dead stone, its skin burned glassy by dragon fire so long ago that no one can even remember how it happened."

Shezira turned slowly away. "Go to bed, Hyram. Get some sleep." She walked away.

Hyram stayed where he was, staring up at the stone face of the dragon altar.

"Th-This place is a lie," he said again.

8

THE ATTACK

A torrent of flames poured from the sky, swallowing the white dragon and her Scales in its fury. The river waters steamed. Stones cracked in the heat. Huros stood stock still. He was fifty, sixty, maybe seventy yards away. A little part of him that wasn't paralyzed with fear noted that this was too close. At the last instant he turned his face away, as a wall of hot air and steam seared his skin and slapped him back toward the woods. He caught a glimpse, as he did, of the stranded rider, the one who'd been shouting at the Scales, catapulted into the air, snatched from the ground by the dragon's tail. Of the Scales himself, there was no sign.

"Run! Get under the trees."

The first of the attacking dragons was wheeling away. As Huros watched, it flipped the rider held in its tail high into the sky. Huros didn't stop to see where the man came down; a second dragon was already diving in. He caught a glimpse of the white, curled up amid the steaming stones, its wings spread over its head like a tent, shielding itself from the fire. When he looked at his hands, the skin on the back of them was bright red. It was already starting to sting. He could smell singed hair. *His* hair.

The second dragon opened its mouth. Huros didn't stay to watch, but turned and ran, hunching his shoulders, trying to shrink into his coat. Another blast of heat punched him in the back. Where his skin was already burned, his nerves shrieked with agony. Up in the sky, when he spared a glance that way, several more dragons were fighting.

"Come on! Come on!" The two sell-swords were waiting for him at the edge of the trees.

"What? What?" gasped Huros. The pain was coming now. He'd had burns before. Every alchemist had had burns. The backs of his hands, the side of his face and neck. He tried to tell himself they weren't deep, and that was what mattered. The skin would blister and peel, but it would heal . . .

It didn't work. The pain was excruciating. His hands were the worst. They felt as though they were still on fire.

The sell-swords took hold of him by his arms and ran, almost carrying him away into the trees. A minute ago they'd been so cocksure. Now they were white with fear. Seeing that made Huros's own terror recede, just enough that he could start to think for himself again.

We're being attacked by dragon-riders. Why on earth . . . ? Who? Who would do this?

This was war. When the queen found out, there would be war. Irredeemable, irrevocable. Unless . . . Unless there were no witnesses to testify to the attack.

He shook the sell-swords off and started to really run, deeper and deeper into the forest. Another blast of hot air caught him from behind, weaker this time. He caught a whiff of smoke. *We're going to die! They're going to burn us!*

"Stop! Stop!"

One of the sell-swords grabbed him by the arm.

Huros shook him off. "Why? We have to run. They're going to kill us!" *Oh gods, oh gods, it hurts . . .*

"Look behind you."

Huros looked. Back toward the river the forest was full of smoke. He could see flames flickering.

"See. We're far enough into the trees. The dragon fire can't reach us now."

Huros shook his head. Every instinct he had said run, run and keep running until he dropped.

The sell-swords looked at each other. "We should scatter," said Kemir. "Harder for them to hunt down three of us if we scatter." Somewhere far overhead, lost behind the canopy of leaves, dragons shrieked and screamed.

Sollos nodded. "Fire from above. That's how they flush their prey out into the open. Did you see how many of them there were?"

Kemir shrugged. "Do you think they'll send men into the trees to track us?"

"Doubt it. But they might."

Huros felt himself start to panic again. Both of the sell-swords were looking at him. What did he know about hunting on dragon-back? Not much. Did snappers always run in a straight line when they reached the trees? Was that how the hunters caught them? "But, but . . . It'll be dark soon."

"Yes. Be thankful. It makes us harder to find."

"Dragons see heat," blurted Huros. He screwed up his face. His hands, they were the worst. He'd have given anything to run back to the river and drench them in blissful cold running water.

The sell-swords looked at each other again. "Mud," said Kemir. "Good for burns." He pointed higher up the valley. "I'll go that way. See if I can't lay a false trail or two."

Sollos nodded. He looked at Huros. "You make your way deeper into the trees. I'll go downriver. Keep yourself hidden, that's the important thing. Anyone comes after us on foot, we can deal with them. Once it's dark, they won't be able to find you if you keep still and you keep quiet. We'll find you tomorrow, after they're gone. A mile up the river. The way Kemir's going."

Huros opened his mouth to say something, but the words stuck in his throat. *No, no! Don't! Let me come with you!* But the sell-swords were already turning away. He watched, struck dumb, as they left him standing there. He wanted to cry. His hands, his beautiful hands . . .

It's only pain, he told himself. *There's no lasting damage.* Still . . .

He began to run. He had no idea whether he was going in the right direction, only that it wasn't the same way as either of the sell-swords. Kemir was right. Mud. Thick, cool, slimy mud. That's what he should think about. Mud was good for burns. How did the sell-sword know that? Stupid question—there were dragons in his life, so of course he knew.

He tried not to think about the dragons who might be circling overhead, or the riders who might be racing through the trees in pursuit. When he was out of breath, he stopped running and rested against a tree, careful not to scrape his burns on its bark. The forest was silent. He thought about that for a while, and decided it was a good thing. He had no idea where he was, but with a bit of luck neither did anyone else. It was getting dark too. He tried not to think about wolves and snappers and other monsters that might sniff him out. Shelter, that was what he needed. Shelter and water. Food as well, but that was probably too much to ask for.

Huros made himself think about all these things until his head spun, and then he made himself think about them some more. They were a fragile and uncertain armor, but they just about kept the horror at bay. When they failed, he dug his fingernails into the burned skin of his hands until the pain became so excruciating that it overwhelmed everything.

Stay alive . . .

BY THE TIME THE LIGHT failed and it became too dark for him to see, he'd found himself a place to shelter, nestled into the hollow of a giant tree. He tried to sleep. When that didn't work, he tried telling himself that it was summer, that the nights were short and warm, even here in the foothills of the Worldspine, that the sun would rise before long. He'd make his way back to the river, the sell-swords would be there, the queen and her riders would return, and everything would be fine.

Halfway through the night, it started to rain.

9

THE KNIGHT-MARSHAL

Lady Nastria, knight-marshal and mistress of Queen Shezira's dragon-riders, glanced up and caught a glimpse of herself in the mirror. She saw what she always saw. A short, mouse-haired, nondescript rider who shouldn't have amounted to anything much but who found herself knight-marshal to the most powerful queen in the realms. An enigma. Sometimes even *she* didn't know who she truly was.

Today, though, if she was an enigma, she was an irritated one. She was having trouble with her boots. However much she stamped her feet, they were never quite comfortable. It was as if, overnight, they didn't fit anymore.

"So? Did he or didn't he?" Queen Shezira sat lounging in a corner of the knight-marshal's robing room. She looked distant, Nastria thought. Distracted.

"Short answer: I don't know." There. Finally one heel slipped into place. One down, one to go. "If he did, he was keeping it well hidden."

"We might have been wrong about Speaker Hyram. He's not himself anymore. Perhaps we *should* have brought the white with us for him to see before Jehal gets her."

Lady Nastria snorted. "Holiness, Hyram hates Prince Jehal. He's also petty-minded and vindictive. You sent the white across the Purple Spur because if you'd brought her to the Adamantine Eyrie, he'd have found a way to ruin her, just out of spite."

"I don't think Lystra or Jaslyn thought much of our speaker either." *No. They were both too busy making eyes at Valmeyan's ambassador, Prince Tichane. When they weren't giggling at that vacuous Prince Tyrin and his brothers. Who, ancestors help us, will doubtless be waiting for us in Fury-mouth in a few days.*

"There's not much to think, Your Holiness, not anymore. He was a strong man once. Not exactly a good one, not even a fair one or a just one, but strong enough to exert his will. He's not even that anymore. The realms will breathe a sigh of relief when you take his place."

Shezira got up and started to pace. "The Hyram I remember, back when we were all a lot younger, he would have mated one of his males to my white while we were sleeping. Oh, he'd have apologized and made some gesture of penitence, but he'd claim the eggs, if there were any, you can be sure of that. But he's not that man anymore. If you had seen him last night, you would know that."

"From the sound of things it's as well I didn't. I might have been compelled to put him out of his misery there and then. Got it!" Nastria took a deep breath and sighed, as the second riding boot finally slipped around her foot. "No, I think you were wise, my queen, not to bring Jehal's gift here. I didn't uncover anything in Hyram's eyrie to damn him, but still . . . I daresay Prince Jehal would have been extremely put out if his wedding present had been spoiled." She wrinkled her nose and smirked. "All I found were whispers that Hyram's acquired a fondness for little boys of late. They say that no one's seen him with a woman for months and that his potboys keep going missing."

The queen sighed, and Nastria frowned. Shezira wasn't herself this morning. She was pensive and troubled, and all because Speaker Hyram might actually be dying at last.

"Do you think I should have married again, after Antros?"

"No!" Nastria turned away quickly before the queen could look at her and fumbled with a buckle.

"No. I suppose not. Pointless really." Then Shezira laughed and pointed to the door, and the two of them walked, and then rode in silence to Speaker Hyram's eyrie.

"It's a good eyrie, this one," muttered the queen as they dismounted. "I'll enjoy having it for my time."

"I prefer Outwatch, Your Holiness," said Nastria, but Shezira was already walking away, seeking out Mistral and her daughters, leaving Nastria on her own.

Which hardly bothered her at all. Being alone was what she did best.

Later, when they were all high in the sky, riding their dragons with the Adamantine Palace behind them, soaring with the thermals rising over the Purple Spur peaks on their way to rendezvous with Jehal's white and her little escort, Nastria wondered about a certain pair of sell-swords, and how well *they* took to being alone. Probably not so well at all, she thought.

A few hours' flight was enough to take them around the south side of the Purple Spur peaks to Drotan's Top, a dome-shaped hill with a flat crest big enough to land a whole eyrie full of dragons. Drotan's Top marked the end of the Adamantine Palace's domain. To the west the land grew ever more rugged, rising up into the Worldspine and the rule of Valmeyan, the King of the Crags. To the south stretched the realm of the Harvest Throne, of Queen Aliphera.

No, Nastria reminded herself. *Queen Zafir now.*

Drotan's Top wasn't exactly an eyrie, but Speaker Hyram had built a small stronghold there with some animal pens. The hunting was supposed to be superb in these parts. As soon as Nastria had seen her mount was well cared for, she went looking for the queen. She knew exactly where to go. Hyram had built a lookout tower on the north side of the Top, where the landscape swept sharply down into the cavernous basin of the Fury River valley, and then up again to the Purple Spur peaks, a dozen or more miles away.

Shezira was there, looking out over the valley, eyes fixed firmly to the north.

"I knew I'd find you here." Nastria stood beside her queen. "Looking for your white, Your Holiness?"

"Of course."

"They have to fly up over the mountains. They have a much harder day of it than us today."

"I know. And yes, I know they probably won't be here for hours. But still I want to look. I'm afraid I shall be poor company until I see my precious white, safe and sound."

Nastria allowed herself a secret smile while the queen couldn't see her face. "I'm a little surprised you're not on Mistral's back and flying out to meet them."

Shezira snorted. "We both know where that leads. The sky is immense; we fly along different valleys, around different mountains, never seeing one another. Everyone gets lost. No. I'll bear the waiting. Badly, mind you, but I'll bear it."

"Your Holiness, may I speak with you about Queen Aliphera?"

"If you must. I had invited her to come here and hunt with us before we flew on to be guests at The Pinnacles." She frowned. "It's a shame she's gone. I wondered if her daughter might come instead. The new queen. Which one is the older?"

"Zafir, Your Holiness."

"Yes." Shezira smiled. "Another queen who could only make daughters. All those kings out there must have thought we had a secret conspiracy between us. This Zafir. I've met her, but that was years ago. She and her sister seemed rather bland. What do you know about her?"

"No more than you do, Your Holiness."

"Really, Knight-Marshal?" Shezira raised an eyebrow. "That's very unusual for you."

Nastria felt herself redden. "We should send a rider, Your Holiness, to the new queen's eyrie. We should ask them for her blessing for our journey. If we send a dragon right away, it will delay us here another day. If we wait until the morning, it will be two days before we hear a reply."

The queen nodded. "Make it so. Send Hyrkallan. He's suitable, and he's been chafing at the bit to let his hunting-dragon off its reins. Mistral doesn't fly fast enough for his liking."

The tone of the queen's words told Nastria that she was dismissed. She bit her lip. At the door she hesitated. "I could stay, if you wish, Your Holiness. We have a few hours yet."

Shezira shook her head. "No, Knight-Marshal. Let me alone a while. I like it here. It reminds me of flying, with all this space around me; and I want to be the first to see my white coming in. Besides, don't you have a hundred and one things to do?"

"Only one, Your Holiness." Nastria smiled sadly as she left. "Only to serve my queen."

10

THE ASH DRAGON

Sollos spent the night snuggled up inside a huge hollow log. He'd covered himself in leaf mold to keep warm, and in the end he'd slept surprisingly well, even after it started to rain. No one had come after him, and when he woke up, it didn't take him long to convince himself that all the dragons were gone. He made his way cautiously back to the river in case any of Queen Shezira's riders had survived, but all he found were the charred remains of the luggage. The white was gone, no one else was there, even the body of the Scales was missing. *Washed away in the river?* he wondered. But while the river was wide, the water was only a few inches deep, and peppered with sandbars and stones.

Maybe the Scales didn't die after all.

He shrugged, washed and drank, and then, more in hope than expectation, rummaged through what was left of their supplies in case something edible had survived.

"Gotcha!"

Sollos almost jumped out of his skin. Kemir was standing right behind him.

"Anything that looks like breakfast left in there?"

"No." Sollos gave Kemir a glare. "Burned to the core."

"They really went for that white dragon, didn't they?"

"Whoever *they* were."

Kemir shrugged. "Some other bunch of lords on dragons. Can't tell them apart myself."

"It matters." Sollos sighed. "We're supposed to notice that sort of thing."

"Well I didn't see any colors, if that helps."

Sollos gave him a sour look. "Not really. Did you see what happened to the white dragon?"

"I saw it take to the air after the first couple of flamestrikes. I didn't hang around to see where it went."

"South. It went south."

"Took what was left of its Scales with it too."

"Did it?" Sollos blinked in surprise.

"Hanging from one of its claws. Maybe it was hungry. It hadn't fed, after all. He must have been dead. He was right in the middle of that first blast."

Sollos sighed. That explained why he hadn't found the remains of the Scales here. "We shouldn't stay out here. If they come back, this is the first place they'll look."

"It's the first place Queen Shezira will look too."

Sollos thought about this, trying to work out how soon the queen would realize that her precious white dragon was missing. "It'll be tomorrow before anyone comes looking for us. Anyone friendly, that is. Anyway, we ought to try and find that alchemist."

Kemir looked truly surprised. "Really? Do you actually think he's still alive?"

Sollos shrugged. "He might be. You have something better to do?"

They walked in silence up the valley, staying close to the tree line and scanning the skies, until Sollos decided they'd covered a mile. For most of the morning he wandered up and down, calling out as loudly as he dared. The alchemist never appeared. In the end he gave up. For a brief moment he wondered whether it had been right to let the alchemist go off on his own. No one had come in pursuit, despite his fears. They could have stayed together. The man had been wounded too.

No, he decided. Kemir would tell him that when dragons came, it was every man for himself, and the best thing they could have done was to scatter. Kemir would tell him exactly that, and Kemir would be right. He put the alchemist out of his mind.

When he came back, he found Kemir sitting against a tree. Next to him was something large and furry, something shaped vaguely like a rat, except it was the size of a small deer.

Kemir grinned. "Lunch," he said. "Do you think we could start a fire?"

"Absolutely not." On a clear day like this a plume of smoke would be visible for miles.

"Well you're no fun at all today. They're not coming back. You never know, your alchemist might see it. He's probably only lost."

Sollos shook his head. "Tomorrow. By then the queen might be looking for us. Then we'll have a fire."

Kemir shrugged and started to hack at the carcass. Raw meat was better than no meat at all. They had the river for drinking water. All in all Sollos thought he could come to like being out here, if he didn't have to constantly scan the skies.

Yes. And there's the rub, remember?

He got up and found things to do to fill the time, and eventually he splashed back down the river to the remains of their supplies, in case he'd missed something.

He had. The boxes and bags piled up by the river were all still ruined, and there wasn't a thing he could see to salvage, but when he turned away and let his eyes scan high up the sloping sides of the valley he saw what he'd missed. A great black scar, scratched through the trees. Before, in the light of the early morning, that side of the valley had been in shadow. Now the sun was high overhead, the wound in the forest was obvious.

He blinked and stared, and then looked again, and when he was quite sure, he raced back to Kemir and dragged him to come and look as well.

"There!"

Kemir sucked in air between his teeth. "Is that what I think it is?"

"That's not a flamestrike."

Kemir shook his head. "No. Too big."

"Much too big."

"You think there's a dead dragon up there, don't you?"

Very slowly, Sollos nodded. "Only one way to find out."

"We've got about four hours of daylight left. Do you think we can get up there in time?"

"No. But we can get a lot closer than we are now."

They looked at each other and shared a grin. A dead dragon meant dragonscale. Dragonscale meant gold, buckets of it, far more than Queen Shezira's knight-marshal had ever put in their pockets. Suddenly they were simple soldiers again. Simple soldiers out to make their fortune.

GETTING THERE TOOK THEM THE rest of that day and most of the following morning. The smell led them to it in the end, the stink of burned wood laced with something else, something sweet and fleshy. The dragon was there, tangled among the trees it had shattered in its fall. Its wings were twisted and broken, but most of it was intact and still so warm that Sollos could feel the heat of it pushing at him through the air. Here and there its scales were black with soot. Its eyes had already turned to charcoal. Tiny swirls of steam or smoke still curled out of its mouth and nose.

Kemir pulled out a knife, ran up to its flanks, touched the scales and then jumped away yelping.

"Bugger me! Ow! It's hot! *Really* hot."

There was the slightest sound from underneath one of the dragon's broken wings. Instantly, Sollos had his bow and an arrow at the ready.

"Who's there?"

Slowly, a streaky black figure emerged. For several seconds Sollos stared. Then the man wiped some of the soot off his face, and Sollos breathed out. The alchemist.

"Lady Nastria's sell-swords." The alchemist slumped to his knees. "Thank the flames. I got . . . Um. I got lost, you see. And then it started to rain, and I was cold and I couldn't sleep, so I started to climb up, looking for somewhere dry. I saw the flicker of the flames up the mountain through the trees. Well, I knew it must have been a dragon come down during the battle to still be burning. Which meant it would be warm and there would be shelter, you see, so when the sun came up I came here instead of going to the river. Um. Sorry if I caused you any trouble. How did you find me?"

"We didn't," said Kemir, and he pointed to the dead dragon. "We found this. You just happened to be here, but since you are, maybe you'd like to be helpful. You see, I'd quite like to take some of the scales off this dragon. Think of it as a bonus for rescuing the queen's alchemist."

Huros shook his head. "You can't. Not yet. It's not hot enough yet."

Sollos watched Kemir frown. "It's blistering. You could cook food on it."

"Um. Yes. Actually, do you have any? I'm a bit . . . Well, I haven't eaten anything since . . . Since you know."

Kemir moved sharply toward the alchemist. He still held his knife. "Listen, you! I want some of these scales. You can have some too. Plenty for everyone. You know about dragons, so you tell me how to get them. I know about knives, and I'm going to use this one. It can be on you or it can be on the dragon."

Which was as bald a threat as they came, Sollos thought, but the alchemist didn't seem to get it. "You can't," he said. "You simply can't."

"Why the fuck not?"

"It's not hot enough. It's only been dead for a day and a half. It's started to burn up from the inside now, but it takes days for the skin to char. Come back in a couple of weeks with a heavy hammer. You'll be able to smash the poor thing up into pieces then. Underneath the scales it'll be nothing but ash. If you've got a cleaver that's sharp enough and heavy enough, you could have a go at getting the bones out of the wings, I suppose. I don't think you'll get very far with a knife, though."

"A couple of *weeks*?"

"I'm afraid so."

"But the knight-marshal and all her riders will be back by then."

The alchemist nodded, and suddenly Sollos found himself wondering whether the man was quite so stupid after all. "Yes. I sincerely hope so."

I I

AN ACT OF WAR

When it became clear that the white and her escort weren't coming to Drotan's Top, Shezira tried to sleep. When dawn broke, she finally gave up trying. The search parties left before the sun had finished clearing the mountains. In the middle of the afternoon the first hunter spotted a column of smoke rising from a river valley close by. Dragon cries echoed through the mountain valleys, and by the early hours of the evening Queen Shezira was sitting by the side of the river yards away from where her riders had been attacked. A dozen hunters circled overhead, keeping watch. She'd already seen one of her war-dragons, Orcus, dead amid the craggy forest. Lady Nastria reported that the hunters had found another. Which left one more still missing, and of course it was the white.

Snow.

Her hands were trembling, she realized. That was how angry she was. Nastria was questioning the survivors. Dragons were shambling about the place, clumsily cracking boulders and trees alike, unattended, swishing their tails and stretching their wings, either one of which could kill a man in a blink if they happened to be in the way. It wasn't good enough. No one was talking to *her*. No one was telling her who had done this to her dragons, who was responsible, who had *dared* . . .

She stood up. "Marshal!"

Her call cracked through the air like a whip, and Lady Nastria jerked as though she'd been stung.

That's right. Come running when your queen calls you . . .

Nastria bowed, deep and low, careful to observe every protocol and display of respect, and then dropped to one knee. Shezira wanted to hit her for being so cautious. Or maybe she simply wanted to hit *someone,* anyone, whoever happened to be in her way.

"Who survived, Knight-Marshal?"

Nastria kept her eyes to the ground. "Your alchemist and a pair of sell-swords, Your Holiness. They were on the ground with the Scales and your white dragon when the attack came."

"Did they see who did it?"

Nastria shook her head. "No, Your Holiness."

A savage impulse gripped Shezira. She drew a knife and put its edge against the bare skin at the back of Lady Nastria's neck.

"Have you asked them how they dare still to be alive when my dragons are dead?"

"Your Holiness, there is little—"

"*Have you asked?*" she roared.

"No, Your Holiness." Nastria shook her head very slightly. Shezira felt the hand that gripped the knife urging her to bite into flesh.

"Who chose the dragon-riders to escort my white, Knight-Marshal?"

"I did, Your Holiness."

"Who brought in those sell-swords?"

"I did, Your Holiness."

"Who chose the route? Who chose the numbers of dragons that would fly? Who said that I should not fly my white to the palace for fear of what Hyram might do to her?"

There was a pause. "I chose the route, Your Holiness."

"Who said I should not take my white to Speaker Hyram's eyrie?"

Nastria didn't reply.

"Answer me, Knight-Marshal, or I will have your head here and now."

"Then have it, Your Holiness, for that idea was yours, not mine."

Shezira froze. For a second she seemed to go numb. Then she withdrew the knife. "Yes. It was, wasn't it? And you chose the riders, but I would have chosen the same. I wouldn't have sent sell-swords, but I don't suppose they stole my dragon. Very well. Someone has betrayed me, Knight-Marshal, and they will die for this. Get up."

Nastria rose. She was shaking, Shezira saw. *Good. You should be.*

"I will find them, Your Holiness."

"Yes. You will. Now where is my daughter?"

"Lystra is at Drotan's Top under guard." Nastria frowned, confused for a moment. "As you ordered. With the supplies and as many riders as we could spare."

"Not her. Jaslyn."

"Flying guard, Your Holiness." They both looked up at the dragons circling overhead.

"Get her down. I wish to speak with her."

Shezira looked blankly around her as her knight-marshal stumbled off. They were in the middle of nowhere, in some piece of wilderness that could have been claimed by any one of three kings, but in reality wasn't claimed by any. The steep sides of the valley were covered in trees with nowhere for dragons to land except the river. No one lived out here.

Two kings and a speaker. Valgar, Valmeyan and Hyram. Any one of them could have flown dragons here and no one would have known. I should add Aliphera's heir as well. All she'd have to do is skirt Drotan's Top, which is hardly a difficult thing to do. But which one of them did this?

She dismissed Valgar at once, since there was no way he'd be able to hide a white dragon without either her or Almiri finding out about it. Hyram then? She'd mistrusted him enough that she hadn't brought the white to the Adamantine Palace. The old Hyram, he might have done something like this . . .

But . . .

She shook her head, trying not to think of the broken

and pathetic thing that had masqueraded as Speaker of the Realms. Maybe not Hyram. This new Queen Zafir? Audacious, perhaps, to start a war within days of gaining your crown, but she wouldn't be the first. Or Valmeyan, the King of the Crags?

She paced back and forth. Valmeyan. Yes. Easy to hurl the blame at a reclusive king who hadn't left his mountain strongholds for more than twenty years and showed no interest in the affairs of the other realms. *Not so easy to prove, though, and not so easy to exact retribution against a king who has more dragons than any other two of us put together.* Shezira snorted. She didn't even know where Valmeyan's eyrie was. One rumor said far to the south, close to the sea and King Tyan's realm. Another rumor said it was much closer, near the source of the Fury River, only a day from Drotan's Top. Other rumors said other things. She would have to find out.

"Mother!"

Shezira shook herself back to the present. Jaslyn was standing rigid in front of her, looking as angry as ever.

"Jaslyn."

"You called Silence down. What do you want, Mother?"

Shezira glared. "Go back to the eyrie," she snapped. "Go now, and do not stop until you get there. Tell them that Orcus is dead, and most likely Titan and Thorn as well. Do not tell them *anything* else. Then bring every hunting-dragon I have back with you. Jehal can take his pick as a wedding gift, and I do not care which one it is or who it belongs to. The rest I will send back here and they will scour these mountains. We will need another alchemist as well, and supplies to keep a dozen dragons and their riders out here in the wilds for as long as it takes."

Jaslyn shook her head. "Send your knight-marshal. I shall stay here until all our dragons are found."

"You will not! I am your queen, daughter, and you will not forget it! You will do as I say now, and when you return from Outwatch, you will fly with me to watch your sister wed! You will have no part of this search."

They stared at each other, mother and daughter, anger burning the air between them. Finally Jaslyn cast her eyes to the ground. "If you find who did this to Orcus, I want them to burn," she hissed. "I want to *see* them burn."

Shezira nodded. "At last something on which we agree. Obey my command and I'll grant you that wish."

Jaslyn marched back to her mount, and Shezira watched her go. *You got all that was worthwhile out of Antros but without his stupidity. Such a pity you insist on spending all your time with dragons. You could have made someone a good queen. You could have had my throne when I take Hyram's ring. You'd do better than Almiri will.*

She sighed and clenched her fists. All around, her riders were about the business of setting up a camp. At other times she liked these nights with the stars over her head, with no maids waiting on her hand and foot. Not tonight, though. Tonight her dragon-knights would circle grimly overhead while she slept—if she slept—on watch for a mysterious enemy who would, likely as not, never appear.

The sun set and Shezira retired to her tent. She tossed and turned and snatched a few meager hours of fitful rest. When she rose, she almost sent them all back to Drotan's Top. Staying out here, so exposed, was dangerous. *It's what Antros would have done, though.* Perhaps that was why she stayed. She didn't know.

They found Thorn two days later, riderless but unharmed. The day after that they found Titan. The white, though, had vanished, and by the time Jaslyn returned with a dozen more dragons Shezira was resigned. The white was gone. By now she could be anywhere. One day she would find who had done this and there would be blood and fire and pain, but for now her perfect white was lost.

One little thing troubled her, as they turned their faces back toward the south, toward King Tyan and Prince Jehal, toward Furymouth and the sea. They never found the body of the Scales.

12

LYSTRA

"**A**t *last!*"

Jehal yawned and stretched. He'd taken to sleeping through part of the afternoons, simply as a way to make the time pass. Queen Shezira and her flight had been expected five days ago. Dutifully, albeit at the last possible minute, he'd left behind the pleasures of his father's palace in Furymouth and ridden to the eyrie at Clifftop to greet her. Except she hadn't come, and the eyrie was a full day on horseback from the city, and there was absolutely nothing to do except look at his dragons and listen to the noise of the waves crashing against the cliffs.

He'd been on the point of going back, but now the Queen of the North had finally arrived. Either that, or someone else was flying thirty-odd dragons toward his eyrie.

Maybe it was more alchemists. As he dressed himself, he smiled. Hyram had sent twelve of them, including the old sorcerer himself, Bellepheros. They were crawling all over his eyrie, dragging in his men, his riders, his soldiers, his servants, his Scales, even their own kind, the alchemists who served King Tyan's dragons. Every day Jehal made a point of going to watch them at their work. Every day they took a few dozen of his people and filled their lungs with truth-smoke. They asked their questions: *What do you know about Queen Aliphera's death? Do you know how she died? Did you have any part in it?* Every day they got the same answers. They were so sure of themselves, and yet, in the days since they'd arrived, they'd found out nothing. When he was watching them, Jehal would smile a lot and ask how else he might be of help, and try not to laugh at the frustration on their faces. In a few more days they'd be done with the eyrie and would move on to the palace at Furymouth. It was an intolerable imposition, of course, but one that was almost worth bearing simply to watch them fail.

The speaker's alchemists had almost unlimited power, but there were a few things they weren't permitted to do. Inflict their potions on someone of royal blood, for example. Which was a pity for them, since unless they were going to conjure up Aliphera's ghost and question her, that was the only way they were going to find out what had happened. Jehal had put a great deal of thought and effort into Aliphera's death, and so there was a certain pleasure to be had in watching the alchemists flounder.

But only to a point. Having them here was also a humiliation, an insult that couldn't be ignored and for which Hyram would have to pay.

Jehal pulled on his boots and looked at himself in a mirror, carefully adjusting his clothes to make sure everything was exactly as it should be. He couldn't really complain, he thought. This business with the alchemists would just make him feel that bit more justified in doing what he'd been going to do anyway.

There. He was shrewd enough to see through his own vanity, and he could cut a dashing figure when he wanted to. He nodded to himself in the mirror and walked briskly away, to the stairs that would take him down to the landing fields. It wasn't going to be enough to simply murder Hyram, he decided. Something more was called for. Some sort of vivisection, that would be more like it.

He marched out through the gaping doors of Clifftop and into the open air. Hundreds of soldiers were running to their positions, forming up into wedge-shaped phalanxes. Jehal wasn't sure whether this was supposed to be a show of strength or a display of respect. He ignored them, as he was sure Queen Shezira would do, and looked up. Dozens of dragons were circling overhead. Four were already coming in to land, plummeting toward the landing fields in near-vertical dives. Jehal put Hyram out of his mind; for now he had an entirely more delicious problem to deal with.

The four dragons unfurled their wings, three slender and elegant hunting-dragons and one brutish war-beast. They hit the edge of the landing field hard and at exactly the same time; even at that distance the air shook and the earth trembled under Jehal's feet. All four stood exactly where they had landed without taking a single pace forward. Which, he supposed, was meant to show him how skilled the riders were. *Well it doesn't. That's the dragon doing the work, not you. All you're showing me is that your trainers and your Scales are as competent as they ought to be.*

He almost expected to see the four riders slide out of their saddles and march toward him in perfect synchronization; instead, if anything, they seemed to be arguing.

Then one of them—it had to be Queen Shezira—took the lead and the others fell in behind. Jehal and his eyrie-master, Lord Meteroa, walked out to meet them. In the periphery of Jehal's mind he noted all the other things that were happening: the guards of honor carefully formed up, marching to exactly where they were meant to be, the Scales taking the visiting dragons to the feeding paddocks while the best of his own were lined up for inspection, harnesses and saddles polished and gleaming. None of this mattered at all unless someone made a mistake, and since Meteroa never made mistakes, Jehal largely ignored it. He needed his attention for the queen whose daughter he was about to marry.

Shezira stopped an instant before Jehal. She met his gaze with a stare of her own. Her eyes weren't exactly cold, he thought, but certainly not warm. And relentless. Above all, that was his impression of her.

Good. I could do with a decent challenge. He smiled and took one further step. Queen Shezira held out her hand, and Jehal bowed to kiss the ring on her middle finger. As he did, he was already looking past her, at the three women behind her, who were presumably her daughters. One with a plain flat face, beady little eyes and an angry look; one rather more delicious, clearly the youngest, shy and nervous but not *too* shy and nervous, peeking back at him through her eyelashes. And the one at the back, who looked the oldest, plain and unassuming, with her eyes cast to the ground and much darker skin than the others. There was something kinetic about that one, as though at any moment she would burst into violent motion. She set Jehal on edge.

O gods and dragons, I hope it's the young one she's here to give me.

"Queen Shezira." Jehal bowed again, deeper this time. "Welcome to Clifftop."

He watched her look around. She didn't say anything, but her face told him all he needed to know. *Adequate,* she was thinking. *Adequate.* He felt Lord Meteroa bristle behind him. Apparently her face was telling him the same thing.

He waited. This was where Queen Shezira was supposed to introduce her daughters and he got to find out which one would be sharing his bed before the month was out. And then she was supposed to explain what had taken her so long, and why he'd had to spend days out here when he could have been back in Furymouth, slipping into Queen Zafir's bedchamber every other night and helping himself to an occasional cousin in between.

Finally, Queen Shezira nodded.

"We met," she said, "a long time ago. When Hyram was made speaker. Do you remember? Your father was showing you off."

Jehal smiled and bowed and gritted his teeth. *As if I could possibly forget.* "Yes, Your Holiness, I remember very well."

Shezira stepped to one side. "This is my middle daughter, Jaslyn." She was pointing at the plain one. Jehal breathed a small sigh of relief. "You won't remember her, because she only wanted to stay with the dragons and spent all her time hiding in the palace eyrie."

Jaslyn's face tightened a notch. Jehal bowed to her. "Grown into a most beautiful princess. Dragons are our life, Princess Jaslyn. They are what sets us apart, and without them we are nothing. You are welcome to spend as much

time at Clifftop as you wish. We will set aside rooms for
your exclusive use while you are here."

Jaslyn seemed to soften, although only a fraction.
Shezira's face didn't change at all. "The lady at the rear is
my knight-marshal, Lady Nastria."

*Ah, the dangerous one. Good. I don't have to be nice to
her.*

"And this is my youngest daughter, Princess Lystra."

Princess Lystra bowed to him, but her eyes still never
quite left his own. Jehal tried to hide a smirk. *Sweet, with a
hint of spice. Now, is that the way you really are, or have you
simply taken the trouble to find out what I like?*

"Princess Lystra." Jehal made a point of not bowing in
return for a second or two. "I . . . I . . . am overwhelmed. I
have heard of the beauty and elegance of the ladies of the
north, but you must surely be the most delightful, the most
sublime, the most radiant . . . Why, I'm not sure I can marry
you, for if I do, you will be the fairest of my father's subjects,
and every lady in Furymouth will seethe with jealousy."

Princess Lystra blushed prettily. *So . . . she might be
clever enough to recognize flattery when she hears it, but she
still likes it. Good.*

"Would that not be the case whoever Your Highness
marries?"

Jehal blinked. Queen Shezira clearly didn't approve of
her daughter being so forward, but Jehal found that he
rather did. *Apparently I like a little flattery too. Well who
would have guessed?*

"You are too kind, Your Highness." He smiled and gave
a little sigh, and then gestured to the walls of Clifftop. "Shall
we clear the landing field, Your Holiness?" He spoke to
Queen Shezira now, who gave a little nod of her head. The
best bit, Jehal thought, of being a prince, was that you only
had to do the interesting things. The tiresome logistics of
dealing with all these dragons, all the riders that Queen
Shezira had brought with her, servants, alchemists and so
on and so forth, all that was entirely Lord Meteroa's
problem.

As they walked, Jehal stole a glance at the skies, looking
for Shezira's fabled perfect white. He was wasting his time,
though. The other dragons were all still too high to make

out any coloring, all circling silhouettes and shadows. He was itching to ask, but that would have been crass.

They paused for a moment at the doors to Clifftop. Queen Shezira was obliged to survey his men, all dressed up in their gleaming dragonscale. For a moment, all was still and silent except for the distant waves crashing against the base of the cliffs.

"Your riders are a credit to your father, Prince Jehal," said Queen Shezira, and Jehal couldn't decide whether she meant it, or whether she was simply saying what she was supposed to say.

Either way, there was only one correct response. He bowed. "You're too kind, Your Holiness. My father will be delighted to hear your compliments. Your own are known throughout the realms for their strength and their splendor." Which was rubbish, of course. If anything, the riders of the northern realms were known for quite the opposite.

Queen Shezira's face didn't flinch, but Jehal caught a flicker of disdain from Princess Jaslyn. *Full of fire and fury, this one. All austerity and determination and not even a flicker of fun. I can thank my ancestors that she's not the one I'm marrying. A real joy she's going to be at the wedding feast.* The thought made him shudder. There were certain duties that fell to elder sisters at these times. *Poor Princess Lystra . . .*

"Excuse me, Your Highness, but may I ask what's making that sound?"

Jehal's thoughts fell into disarray. "Pardon me?"

Lystra was looking straight at him again. "What is making that sound, Your Highness?"

Jehal cocked his head. "I'm sorry, Princess Lystra, but I don't hear anything."

"She means the sea," muttered Shezira.

For a moment Jehal almost forgot himself. "Have you not . . . ?" *Never seen the sea?*

Lystra bowed her head, looking abashed. "I have seen the Sea of Sand and the Sea of Salt, Your Highness."

Jehal smiled. "And I have seen neither, and they are doubtless mighty and magnificent. We have a different sea here, and I will show it to you at once." He glanced at Queen Shezira. "If Your Holiness will permit."

Shezira gave a curt nod. Lord Meteroa and the stewards

of Clifftop would doubtless start pulling their hair out at this diversion from the precise script of the day, but Jehal couldn't help himself. *Never seen the sea?*

He led the way around Clifftop toward the edge, where the land fell away, sheered and shattered by some unimaginable violence.

"Have a care, Your Highnesses. The edge is treacherous. It's a long way down, and many people have fallen over the years. The sea pulls them down, somehow." He stopped a couple of feet from the edge and offered Princess Lystra his hand. "The sea, Your Highness. The endless Sea of Storms."

Lystra took his hand, and so he gave it a gentle squeeze and hoped that Queen Shezira wouldn't notice.

"It's ... breathtaking." The cliffs dropped a hundred feet to the roaring, crashing waves. The sea went on forever, a churning maze of white-capped waves stretched as far as the eye could see, fading into the gray haze of the far horizon, a mighty monster that could sometimes make even a dragon seem small and tame. Jehal smiled at Lystra. Up here on the edge you could feel the spray and even taste the salt in the air. Lystra was staring, mouth agape. "It goes on and on and doesn't stop! Like the Sea of Sand, except made of water!"

Jehal gave her an indulgent smile. "The Taiytakei say that if you sail far enough, and can navigate the storms, there are other lands across the waters, so distant that you would have to cross from one end of the realms to the other to even begin to understand how far away they are." Mentally he congratulated himself. *There. That didn't sound patronizing at all.*

"All that water ..." Lystra took a step closer to the edge. Jehal tightened his grip on her hand and she stopped. The cliffs plunged vertically down into the sea.

"There is a path, from the back of Clifftop, that runs down to the sea," he said. "The steps are worn and slippery and the way is treacherous, but there is a cave there that can only be reached by those steps. To truly see the waves crash on the rocks and send their plumes of spray up into the air, there is no better place than that cave. I will take you there one day."

Jaslyn suddenly walked right up to the edge and looked

down. For a moment it seemed to Jehal that she swayed in the wind that whipped and swirled up the face of the cliff. If she did, though, she quickly caught herself, and the next thing he knew Lystra had slipped her hand out of his and was standing next to her elder sister, laughing.

13

FURYMOUTH

Shezira had little choice but to bite her tongue and hold her anger. As soon as they entered Clifftop, the rituals began in earnest. First the breaking of bread with Prince Jehal and his lords to assuage the hunger that came after a day on dragonback. Then there were scented baths and massages to ease sore muscles. After that she had to dress, and then came the formal feast, which ran from dusk until the middle of the night and beyond. Parts of it might still have been running when Shezira rose again at dawn.

Then she had to dress for the journey to Furymouth. That was the trouble with being a queen. She always had to be somewhere or do something, which meant there was no time left to keep an eye on her daughters, and it was up to Lady Nastria to make sure they looked the way they were supposed to look, and that they appeared in the right places at the right times. Without Nastria, Shezira was quite sure that Jaslyn, at least, would have sought out Prince Jehal's secret steps and spent the whole time in his cave. Likely as not, Lystra would have followed her.

Finally, the carriages to Furymouth were ready to go. All

her riders were mounted up as escort, there was nothing left for her to do and she had her daughters to herself again.

"What do you think you're doing?" she snapped as soon as the carriage wheels were rolling. "Both of you! Talking back at him? Holding his *hand*?"

Lystra bowed her head and peered back through her eyelashes, but it was Jaslyn who answered.

"He offered it. It is him you should take issue with."

"And I will." Shezira glared back. "But that does not excuse the taking of it. And besides, Lystra should be speaking in her defense, not leaving it to you, as always. *You* will not be here a month from now."

Jaslyn's eyes flashed. "No, and I shouldn't be here now. I should be in the mountains, hunting down whoever killed Orcus and stole our Snow."

Snow. That was the name the Scales had given it, wasn't it? Shezira growled. "You are a royal princess, whether you like it or not. You go where your duty takes you. And you do *not* dance about like some farmyard peasant."

"They are more . . . forward in these parts of the realms," said Lystra softly.

Jaslyn and Shezira both looked at her. "What did you say?"

"Since I was forbidden to go to Outwatch for months and months before we left, I spent some of my time in the library. I thought I'd try to find out a bit more about where I was going." She leaned toward Shezira and her voice dropped. The carriage picked up speed. "I think they are more, uh . . . Mother, do you know what a southern wedding is like? Have you been to one?"

Shezira shook her head. "Knight-Marshal Nastria assures me that their customs are no different to our own."

"Did Lady Nastria mention what you have to do on the night of the wedding?"

"Me?" Shezira blinked.

"Yes, Mother. You. And Jaslyn."

A smirk died on Jaslyn's lips. "What are you talking about, little sister?"

Lystra leaned forward even more, until all three of them were huddled into the center of the carriage. She whispered: "It's about the consummation."

"Lystra!" Shezira's feet began to fidget. She reminded

herself that she was supposed to be angry with her daughters.

"Mother, I *do* know what happens on a wedding night. I've been watching dragons mate since I was five."

Inside, Shezira squirmed. This was not the conversation she'd been meaning to have. "Little Princess, it's not quite the same . . ."

"Oh don't be silly, of course I know *that*. There are lots of books in our library."

Antros. Antros and his library . . .

"*Picture* books, Mother."

"Lystra!"

"Well that's what you get for not letting me fly dragons with Jaslyn." She smiled like the sun for a moment and then glanced at her sister. "And you can stop laughing, big sister, because you and Mother are going to have to strip Prince Jehal naked and take him to my bridal chamber, and before you let him in you are obliged to make certain that he's quite definitely ready to fulfill his nuptial duty." She giggled.

"Lystra! How dare you! That's preposterous." Shezira clenched her fists and sat back, half filled with fury. The other half of her had gone numb with horror.

"That's what the books in the library say. *With* pictures."

"Ridiculous." The queen glared at her daughters, one after the other. *Bloody Antros. It can't be true though. Can it? Are they* that *different from us here?* "You should not believe everything you read in books. Whatever they may do in this part of the world, you are my daughters, and you will behave as *I* have taught you. If Jehal wants to parade you like a whore after he marries you, that's his business. But until then, by all the ancestors, you will deport yourselves as princesses should or you will never fly from my eyries again. Do you understand me?"

After that there wasn't much to say, and a sullen silence filled the carriage. At midday they stopped for a while beside a tranquil rocky bay. A small army of servants was already there, clearly having camped the night to be ready for them. Course after course of cold meats and breads and a hundred varieties of strange vegetables marinated in oils were passed in front of them, until Shezira thought she would burst. At least this time her daughters behaved themselves impeccably. Prince Jehal remained flawless, flirting effortlessly on the edges of decorum without ever quite crossing the line. If she was honest with herself for a moment, Shezira could see exactly why Lystra was so taken with him. He was both handsome and charming, after all.

Just a pity he's poisoning his father, eh? Oh, my precious girl, what have I brought you to?

"I spoke to our knight-marshal," said Shezira when they set off again in the afternoon. "It seems little Lystra is partially right. Fortunately we are merely invited to take part in this ritual, not obliged. So we can all thank our ancestors for that."

Lystra giggled, and Shezira couldn't help but smile, and even Jaslyn was grinning and laughing, and the air in the carriage was much better after that.

"What else did your books tell you?" asked Jaslyn.

"Preferably the ones without pictures," added Shezira.

"I know that King Tyan's realm is the richest."

"You don't need a library to tell you that."

"Their eyrie is so far away from Furymouth."

"Another thing I can see for myself. Did they tell you why?"

She frowned. "Ships. Dragons don't like them. A pair of ships belonging to the Taiytakei traders was burned by dragons in the time of King Tyan's great-great-great-grandfather. The survivors said that the Taiytakei would never come back unless the dragons were moved away from the city, and so that's what the king did."

"He moved his eyrie?" Jaslyn looked shocked.

Even Shezira raised an eyebrow.

"Hard to believe," she said, "and a story I've never heard before. What of the Taiytakei, then? What did your books say of them?"

Lystra shrugged. "I think they might be some sort of wizards."

There wasn't anything Shezira could think of to say to that. Antros had filled his library with all kinds of rubbish. Shezira had never quite understood why, since as far as she knew, he'd never read a book in his life. She'd been the same, far too busy raising daughters and flying dragons and then ruling her realm when Antros was gone.

Maybe I should have gone in there sometimes. Then I'd know about southern wedding-night rituals. The thought made her smile. *Maybe when I'm too old to ride anymore . . .*

Outside, the countryside rolled past—sandy beaches, little farming villages, fields filled with cattle and corn; wagons and oxcarts, men leaning on staves, gawping as the carriages passed by. *Hot,* Shezira mused, as her eyelids grew heavy. *I'd forgotten how hot it is in the south.*

She dozed. When she woke up again, the sun was darker and the sound of the carriage wheels on the road had changed. *Cobbles.*

She snapped awake, sat up and looked out of the window. They were driving between houses packed together so tightly that they were piled on top of each other. They leaned into the street, reaching out toward each other ever closer, until rooftops almost touched and the sky was pushed out of sight. Now and then crossroads punctured the gloom, bright flashes of sunlight as the carriages trotted past. These other streets fell away, sloping down toward the sea, and with each one Shezira caught glimpses of the harbor, of masts and rippling waves, and the sun glinting on the water. Shielded from the winds by the curves of the bay, the sea here was still and calm. Lystra still couldn't tear her eyes away.

"Now it's just like the Mirror Lakes!"

Shezira nodded. The view from King Tyan's palace, built at the summit of the hill that overlooked the city, was better. She dimly remembered peering over his walls, sitting on someone's shoulders, gawping at the strangeness of it all. The ships with their flags and their masts and their sails had seemed like weird water monsters, and all the cranes around the harbor walls were like a forest of strange trees with no leaves. And the smell, the smell of the sea, reaching out over the ubiquitous stink of the city . . . She'd been five, maybe six years old.

"You'll see many strange and different sights here, Lystra. Keep your sense of wonder, but keep it to yourself or people will take you for a fool."

Jaslyn tutted and rolled her eyes, but Shezira could see that Lystra understood.

"Let your eyes sparkle at everything you see, but say nothing. Do that and Prince Jehal will be yours to command." She laughed, thinking of Antros. "And he won't even know it."

"As long as you spread your legs whenever he asks and give him plenty of sons," muttered Jaslyn, which made Shezira want to slap her. She didn't, though, because the carriage was slowing to a halt. A moment later the door opened, and Prince Jehal was standing there.

"Your Holiness." He bowed and offered his hand. "Welcome to Furymouth."

They were at the foot of King Tyan's palace now, and the view out over the sea was unbroken. Close into the harbor, dozens of small fishing boats bobbed in the water. Farther out, three much larger ships sat in a line.

"There should be dragons, Your Holiness," said Jehal. "I told the Taiytakei that the next Speaker of the Realms was coming to give her daughter away to be married, and there should be dragons filling the air with their fire. In recompense the Taiytakei offer you this, Queen Shezira, in your honor. A sight never seen before in any realm."

As Shezira stared out over the sea, tiny streaks of fire shot up into the air from the three ships. High in the sky, they burst into dazzling showers and swirls of color. Shezira couldn't help but stop and stare. She'd never seen anything like it. She'd never even *heard* of anything like it.

It lasted for a minute, perhaps. When it was done, Jehal bowed to Lystra. "A pale, ephemeral reflection of your beauty, my princess. You will light up my father's palace as the Taiytakei light up the sky."

"I trust we will have the opportunity to thank your guests for their most novel and inspiring welcome?" Shezira slipped carefully between Lystra and Prince Jehal.

Jehal smiled. "Of course. An ambassador of the Taiytakei will be at the wedding. I'm quite sure he'll wish to speak with you, if you will grant him an audience." He sidled closer, and his voice dropped until he was almost whispering. "You should know, Your Holiness, that they have only one desire. They have been coming to our shores for more than a hundred years. We sell them slaves and dragonscale, but that is not why they come. They will flatter you and shower you with gifts, just as they did with Speaker Hyram and my father, but they only want one thing."

"A dragon's egg, perhaps?"

"Most eggs fail, and they know this. A living dragon, Your Holiness. A hatchling. That's what they want, what they've always wanted, and they will do anything to get it. Anything at all. Why is Clifftop so far from the harbor? To keep our dragons away from the Taiytakei ships?" He laughed. "No, Your Holiness, it is to keep the *Taiytakei* away from our *dragons.*"

14

THE SEARCH PARTY

Sollos poked at the fire with a stick and glanced up the side of the valley toward the black scar among the trees where the dead dragon lay. Sometimes it would smoke. Sometimes, at night, he saw the flicker of flames. Then it would rain and the smoke and the fire would go away, and when the rain stopped the wound in the forest would steam instead. Today, though, it was quiet. Still and dull.

"You're looking again," grunted Kemir.

"I know, I know." The queen had been gone for six days now. Which made it twelve days since the attack. Two weeks, the alchemist had said. Two weeks and a big hammer. Well, he had the big hammer now.

"Hoy! You two! Get that fire going and boil up some water!"

"Aye, milord." What he also had was the company of a dozen dragon-knights, seven hunting-dragons and the alchemist. Sollos poked the fire again and threw on another couple of logs. As the dragon-knight turned away, he muttered an obscenity at the man's back. The dragons probably didn't mind what happened to their dead brother, but the riders and the alchemist certainly would. And while half of them were away searching each day, the other half had nothing better to do than sit around, stuck with guarding the camp.

"Are you sure we couldn't murder them all in their sleep?" muttered Kemir. "Maybe we could poison them."

Before Sollos could think of a reply, a piercing rumbling cry echoed along the valley. The first of the dragons was coming back. Every day six went out searching for the queen's white while the seventh circled high overhead, keeping lookout. Since the attack they'd not seen any dragons other than their own, and Sollos was quite sure that they were wasting their time. By now the queen's white was far away.

Still, if it meant waiting here until the dead dragon up the slope cooled down and there was a chance of looting some dragonscale . . .

"He's a bit early." Kemir was watching the arrival glide down toward the river. Sollos tore his eyes away from the forest and watched the dragon descend. Before it had even come to a stop, the rider on its back was standing up, unstrapping himself from his harness and sliding out of his saddle.

Kemir belched and threw a stone toward the river. "You don't suppose they actually found something, do you?" he said. "They're not usually back for hours yet."

Sollos shook his head. "And there I was looking forward to another peaceful afternoon sucking on grass stalks and scratching my arse."

"Yeah, and staring up at that dead mound of dragonscale and charcoal up there."

"We're not going to get our hands on it. You know that, don't you?"

"A *part* of me knows that. We could buy land, you know. Our own little village with our own little subjects. Our own little manor house. With a brewery."

"And a brothel."

"Aye, and that." Kemir sighed. "Like I said, are you sure we couldn't poison them?"

"Even if we did buy ourselves a title, we'd still answer to the queen."

"Oh bollocks to her! We could set up somewhere out here, in the mountain valleys."

"And serve King Valmeyan instead?" Sollos snorted. "I don't think so. Not him."

Kemir's voice dropped to a growl. "No. Not him. Not him at all. Do you think . . ."

The rider from the dragon was running toward them. A couple of the sentries were close on his heels.

"Uh-oh." Sollos let his hands drop to his sides and unconsciously fingered the knives at his belt. Kemir stooped down and picked up his bow.

"You two!" The rider from the dragon stopped a little short of them. "Sell-swords!"

"Sell-swords with names," muttered Kemir. Sollos took a deep breath, gritted his teeth and bowed.

"Rider Semian. How may we serve?" Semian was the third or fourth son of Duke Semian. Sollos could never remember which, nor did he particularly care. There were some sisters too. They all lived in the vast tract of arid wasteland known as the Stone Desert and the duke served Queen Shezira as Guardian of the North. Sollos wasn't quite sure exactly what the duke was supposed to be keeping at bay up there, other than perhaps the use of first names. This particular Semian was about twenty, skinny and buck-toothed. If he'd been born with a different name, Sollos thought it most likely that he'd have grown up as the village idiot somewhere. As it was he was a Semian, so he'd grown up as an idiot who rode a dragon.

"We have found a town, of sorts. Hidden in the mountain valleys."

Sollos exchanged a glance with Kemir. "Then it most likely falls under the dominion of King Valmeyan, Rider Semian." *It's obvious why Queen Shezira didn't take you south with her.* Rider Semian's helmet was slightly too big for his head, Sollos noticed. It kept slipping forward. *Less obvious why she thought you fit to be part of the search for her precious white. Unless she already knows this is a waste of time.*

Now *there* was a thought. What if the queen herself had been the architect of the attack?

"It is built on the edge of a lake. There is nowhere for a dragon to land. When I passed low over the place, they *shot* at me."

"And what did *you* do, Rider Semian?" asked Kemir. "Did you burn them, Rider Semian?"

The dragon-knight took a step back, clearly unsettled by the edge in Kemir's voice. "Certainly not, sell-sword."

"Rider, there are, here and there, settlements among the Worldspine that claim freedom from the dragon-kings and -queens." Sollos spoke carefully. "They are home to hunters, trappers and others who live off what the mountain forests provide. They are, to a large degree, harmless."

"I would have to disagree with you, sell-sword. I am quite aware that such places exist, and that they are dens of vice and corruption. They do not survive off the forest at all. They survive by polluting the realms with Soul Dust, sucking the life out of their hapless victims."

"Rider, it is true that Soul Dust comes from these mountains, but it is not made in places like the one you have seen. It is made in secret camps that you would not see, flying overhead."

"Perchance you are right, sell-sword, but how does it permeate out into the realms at large? Through places such as the one I have seen today, that is how."

Sollos decided he would have to revise his opinion of Rider Semian. Maybe he only *looked* like an idiot. He bowed his head. "That may be true of a few, Rider, but not of most. And if something *is* to be done about them, it is King Valmeyan's place to do so."

"The queen tasked us to find her white, and that is what *we* will do. These outlaws may have seen something. They may have heard something. News travels, does it not, among these places?"

Sollos nodded, slowly. "I see where this is going, Rider. King Valmeyan burns such places now and then, and whether they're filled with honest men or villains seems not to bother him. They see a dragon and they run deep into the trees. They see a knight and they hide. But perhaps a sell-sword . . ."

Rider Semian nodded. Sollos heard Kemir give an exasperated sigh.

"Sollos, you know they won't—"

Sollos held up a hand to silence him. "Rider Semian, we are servants of the queen. We understand our duty."

"Knight-Marshal Nastria was quite explicit. You know these mountains and these settlements."

Again, Sollos nodded. "Yes." *Now how did she know that?*

"There will be a reward, if you find the white."

This time Sollos grinned. "Yes," he said. "I'm sure there will." And it took every ounce of willpower that he had not to glance up the valley to where the dead dragon lay waiting for him.

15

GIFTS

Zafir ran her fingers down Jehal's chest. "So what's she like, this girl you have to marry?"

Jehal smiled. They lay naked together, side by side under the sun, in one of the solars. Over the years Jehal had made a few nests like this around the palace. Private places where he and others who knew of them could come and go unobserved through hidden passages. Small places, but with tall windows to let in the light and the air. Most of this solar was filled by a large sumptuous bed. Others served more delicate purposes.

"A girl, as you say." He began idly stroking Zafir's thigh. The solar was thick with the smell of incense. "Naive. Full of wonder at the world, and almost completely lacking in any experience of it, I would say."

"Stupid, then."

Not at all. "Yes. I think she very probably is. Of course, she was barely allowed to open her mouth."

"Queen Shezira would not want you to know you were marrying an idiot. You might change your mind."

Jehal laughed. "Were it possible to avoid this marriage, it wouldn't matter if she was the most clever princess in all the realms. She would still not be the most desirable." He turned to face Zafir and cupped her cheeks. "She did speak, though clumsy and out of turn. I daresay she earned herself quite a rebuke as soon as Queen Shezira was able to give her one in private."

"Is she pretty?"

Yes. "Not particularly. She was dressed up nicely enough, but she didn't wear it particularly well." Which was true, he thought. Although unfortunately rather intriguing.

"Tell me she's ugly and deformed."

"I'm afraid I could only say that about her sister."

"Then I wish it was the sister that you were marrying. Why can't you marry her instead?"

"It was all arranged, my love, long ago, when my father was still well. My family has given a pledge, and I must honor it."

"You could still marry her sister."

"I will ask, if that pleases you, if I might have the choice. I doubt that Queen Shezira would agree."

"You like her, don't you?"

Jehal's face didn't flicker for a second. "I hardly know her, my love. She is a doll. All dressed up to look as pleasing as she can, but still a doll." *Still, I would have to admit to being interested.*

"And you can't wait to unwrap her, can you?" For a moment Jehal was quite sure that Zafir was about to sit up and pout and become unbearably tedious. Instead she pulled him closer. "I'm afraid I'm going to have to spoil your wedding night. If you have to fuck your doll then so be it, but you'll be thinking of me while you do it."

Jehal growled contentedly. For a moment, though, he hesitated. "I should go. Lord Meteroa will already be waiting for me with whatever news there is from the eyrie."

"Which do you want more? Me or Queen Shezira's white dragon?"

"You, my love. Always you."

"Then let him wait."

"He's not stupid. He'll find out about us if we're not very careful."

"But he's *your* man, is he not?"

"Yes." Said with only the slightest hesitation.

"Then let him wait."

Jehal let him wait, and then wait some more. The secret passage out of this particular solar led him right through the palace and back to his own bedchamber. Still he ran, and by the time he reached his own room he was out of breath.

He burst through the doors into his private anteroom. "Lord Meteroa! I was resting. I do apologize for keeping you waiting. You should have knocked." He couldn't help glancing at the floor to see whether Lord Meteroa had worn a groove in it with his pacing back and forth.

Meteroa wrinkled his nose. He didn't bother to bow. "Resting? You stink of a woman, Your Highness. Should I wonder who you've got in there?"

"See for yourself if you wish."

Meteroa met his gaze. There was something unnerving about the eyrie-master's eyes. They were somewhere between blue and gray, watery and incredibly pale, and the man never seemed to blink. It was like locking stares with a snake. "Ah. In one of the solars, were you? Which have you got up there? A princess or a queen?"

Jehal pursed his lips. "Perhaps I had both at once." He picked up a plum and tossed it through the air. "Try something sweet to take that sharpness off your tongue."

Meteroa caught it and tossed it back. "Thank you, Your Highness, but I had my fill some time ago."

"Tell me, Uncle, since you're so insightful this morning, how is it that, when their lover's thoughts begin to stray, even a blind woman can see through the most finely crafted lies as though they were glass?"

The eyrie-master gave a harsh bark of bitter laughter. "*You* are asking *me*?"

"I learned from a master."

Meteroa's face became unreadable, the way it always did when he was remembering things from a long time ago. "That's women," he said. "Shower them with pretty words and they'll be insensible to almost anything. Why's that? Because all their capacity to think is occupied with watching every movement of your eyes and listening to every nuance of your voice, searching for the infidelity that they secretly know must be there. Treat them like dogs and they'll fawn at your feet. Throw them a bone now and then and they'll show you far more gratitude."

Jehal grinned. "Your advice is as uncompromising as ever. Now tell me about the alchemists. Are they done yet? No!" Jehal clasped his hands together. "But first tell me about my white dragon. Is she as beautiful as she should be? Is she perfect?"

"So far, Your Highness, she is invisible."

"She's what?"

"There is no white dragon, Your Highness."

"*What?*"

Meteroa raised an eyebrow and a faint smile played around his lips. "Queen Shezira hasn't told you?"

"Told me what?"

"Apparently the wedding gift you were hoping for has not arrived. Queen Shezira has quite a few hunting-dragons resting at Clifftop, but none of them is remotely white." Meteroa cocked his head and raised his other eyebrow. For a moment Jehal felt an almost overwhelming urge to punch him. He carefully unclenched his fists.

"The best dragon in her eyrie. That is what I was promised."

The eyrie-master bowed. "I have made some inquiries. As always, it is the alchemists who have been most pliable. It would seem that some sort of incident occurred on the way. As best I can make out, Queen Shezira came here by way of the Adamantine Palace, but the white did not, and someone took advantage of the opportunity to seize it while it was poorly guarded. However, although there were survivors, including the original alchemist who set out with Her Holiness, none of them has come here. A firsthand account is sorely lacking. You are agape, Your Highness."

Jehal closed his mouth. "And so I should be, Lord Eyrie-Master, for what you're telling me is preposterous."

Meteroa snorted. "If I didn't *know* that none of your dragons has been away, Your Highness, my first thought would have been that this was *our* handiwork."

"Yes, but since you know that it wasn't, that leaves a rather intriguing mystery, doesn't it? I hope you can solve it swiftly, Eyrie-Master. That white is mine." He frowned. "Besides, why would I steal my own present?"

"Why indeed? Shall we move on to the alchemists, Your Highness? I understand they've nearly finished."

Jehal spat. "Forget the alchemists! I want to know what

happened to my dragon. Unless . . ." He grinned. "Unless Queen Shezira stole it from herself, just so that she didn't have to part with it."

Meteroa shook his head. "She isn't you, Your Highness. I think it unlikely."

"Then who?"

Jehal scratched his head. To look after a dragon you needed an eyrie, and no one could be stupid enough to imagine that a pure white dragon would remain a secret for long, wherever it was hidden. So most likely the dragon would return before long. Meteroa was probably right about Shezira, so what was the point? Attacking Queen Shezira? Wasn't that incredibly dangerous? A huge risk to take, and for what? What could be worth such a gamble? What could anyone possibly gain?

A sudden chill seemed to fill the room. What might he do, confronted with this news? Why, someone who didn't know him too well might wonder if he'd call the wedding off . . .

No. No, she couldn't . . .

He turned his back on Lord Meteroa, waving him away.

"The alchemists, Your Highness? Grand Master Bellepheros wishes a discreet audience."

"Yes, yes, yes. Let him come. Now go. I need to think."

"Yes, Your Highness." Jehal felt Meteroa bow and begin to back away. "Once you have finished thinking, Your Highness, I trust you will share whatever wisdom you have found?"

16

THE OUTSIDERS

Sollos squelched through the mud with Kemir behind
him. To his right, it grew deeper and stickier until it
slipped beneath the waters of a mountain lake. To his left,
the mud didn't seem to get any better at all, but the forest
was thicker and there were even more roots and dead
branches in the way. The sun had already dropped behind
one of the peaks surrounding the lake, and in another half
an hour it was going to be dark. *At which point,* Sollos
thought grimly, *we're buggered.*

A couple of hours ago it had seemed a reasonable idea.
Rider Semian had flown them deeper into the mountains.
Sollos guessed they were about fifty miles southwest of
their own camp when Semian had started to descend, and
then banked in a half-circle around the shore of a lake. The
settlement had been obvious enough, and Semian had
found a place to land only a mile or so farther around the
shore. The day was nearly done, but the distance was short,
and Sollos had been confident that they'd easily reach the
settlement before nightfall.

Then they'd hit the mud.

"What we need are some boards," grumbled Kemir. "A

pair of long wide boards. Our own mobile path. With a couple of eyes bolted into them to thread a bit of rope through so you can pull them back up out of the mud again. Do you remember that?"

"Aye. Going back a bit, though."

"Yes. Being out here does that. I can't wait to get out of these shitty mountains. I really don't know why you were so keen to come back here."

Sollos shrugged. In a way, it went against his own better judgment as well.

"Not that it matters now, I suppose."

They trudged on. The sun sank lower, the sky darkened, and the mud didn't get any better. The settlement couldn't have been more than a quarter of a mile away. Sollos's legs were starting to burn with the exertion.

"My boot's stuck. Can I hate you yet?"

Sollos only half heard Kemir's complaint. He stopped. He had the distinct feeling he was being watched.

"Oh . . ." Among the trees, he saw a slight movement. Something *was* watching him. A snapper. Very slowly Sollos slipped the dragonbone bow off his shoulder. He began to string it.

The snapper advanced slowly. One of its feet sank into the mud. It took a step back and returned to watching.

"Do you—"

"I see it," muttered Kemir. "I was just thinking that the one good thing about this mud was that nothing big enough to eat us would be as daft as we are and try to walk through it."

"It's on firm ground over there."

"Oh good. Let's walk *toward* the half-ton man-eating ravening beast then."

The snapper stepped into the mud again. This time it didn't withdraw. Instead it took another step, and then another. Sollos looked about, but trying to run away wasn't going to work. Most people faced with a snapper simply ended up eaten. The ones who survived usually did so by climbing a tree and managing not to starve to death before the snappers got bored.

Still, Sollos had a bow powerful enough to take down a dragon-knight. So if he hit the snapper in the right place . . . Except it was going to charge, any second, and his bow still wasn't strung. His hands slipped toward his waist, and to the two long knives he carried there. Waste of time really, facing a snapper with anything short of a lance. He could forget about his armor too. A snapper could bite through anything short of a steel plate, and its back claws were worse. Even so, he couldn't bring himself to simply roll over and die. There was always a chance. He could always get lucky . . .

They hunt in packs, remember.

The mud would slow it down, though. From moving like lightning to merely very, very fast . . .

Shit. I'm going to die.

The snapper opened its jaws and charged, and time seemed to slow. Even through the mud, Sollos felt the ground shake with its each step. He dropped the bow and pulled out his knives. It was coming for him. For a split second he seemed completely unable to move.

At the last possible moment, his arms and legs finally remembered what they were for. He didn't bother trying to step out of the way, but let himself fall sideways, out of the monster's path. As he moved, he twisted. One knife jabbed straight at the snapper's face, trying to distract it. The other arced in a vicious backhand toward where he hoped the creature's throat would be.

All completely wasted. Maybe if it hadn't been for the mud . . .

The first knife missed. The second hit something and was wrenched out of Sollos's hand, and then the snapper smashed into him, the sheer force ripping him out of the mud and tossing him into the air. Teeth tore at his shoulder. There was a sharp pain from one of his ankles, and then he landed on his back, hard enough to knock the breath out of his lungs. The snapper was flying toward him, all teeth and claws. And yet there was something not quite right about it . . .

He thrust the knife up toward the monster with both hands and closed his eyes. The snapper fell onto him, jaws gaping. He felt a searing flash of pain, and then everything went mercifully black.

He was in a pool, deep in a cave, far beneath the World-spine. In one of the secret places that only the Outsiders knew. The water was icy cold. The darkness was absolute and

*the silence immense. He was alone. He was alone because
this was what his clan did when a boy became a man. Except
his clan was gone, and he was more alone than anyone had
ever been. Only him and Kemir . . .*

*Something snatched his leg. He didn't feel it coming, and
it dragged him down so fast that he didn't even have time to
breathe. He vanished with barely a ripple and sank like a
stone. The water became colder and colder until it began to
burn, and then the darkness blossomed into light, and the
water wasn't water, but white-hot fire, stripping his flesh and
searing his bones to ash, and there was a face, the face of a
dragon.*

Something slammed into him. He opened his eyes and
the world and the pain came flooding in. He was lying on a
damp dirt floor. Everything hurt. His cheek was pressed
into the toe of someone's boot.

"Morning," said a voice that was both too loud and too
far away. His head hurt. He started to retch, but that sent
such spasms of pain through his ribs that he stopped. He'd
seen someone once, in Queen Shezira's eyrie, caught by the
idle swish of a dragon's tail. They'd flown about a hundred
feet through the air and they hadn't got up again. If they
had, Sollos thought, this is how they'd have felt.

Unless . . .

What happened when you died? He remembered the
snapper well enough, so that had to be what had happened.
The dragon-priests said that everyone went to the great
dragon in the sky to be forged into new souls in the great
cosmic fire. But the dragon-priests were mad.

"Are you going to lie there all day?"

"Kemir?" He tried to move. Bad idea. "The snapper . . ."

"Got an arrow through its head. And so did its friend."

"This really hurts." For a moment Sollos had the almost
overwhelming urge to get up and look himself over, just to
make sure there were no bits missing. One bite was all it
took to lose an arm or a leg, after all.

Even the thought of moving triggered fresh spasms of
pain. "My ribs . . ."

"Best I could tell there's nothing broken. Nasty wound
on your shoulder. That'll need seeing to. The rest of you

looks all right. You took a mighty thump when that thing crashed into you, though. You're probably bruised all over. Lucky it didn't land on top of you."

"It did. Didn't it?"

"Half and half. It sort of bounced off you and ended up lying to one side. Otherwise only the ancestors know how I'd have pulled you out of that mud. Bloody stuff."

Very slowly, Sollos rolled onto his back. He started to take a deep breath and then quickly thought better of it. "My head hurts. Got any water?" He frowned. Instinctively, his hands reached for his knives, if only to make sure they were still there. They weren't. "Where are we?"

"We're in the Outsider settlement, my friend. Home sweet home."

"Where are my knives?"

"All right. We're *prisoners* in the Outsider settlement. That would be more accurate."

Sollos blinked. Carefully, he looked around. Walls made of ill-fitted planks of wood surrounded him. Soft sunlight filtered in through the cracks. "Prisoners? Why?"

Kemir shuffled his feet. "There were . . . words."

"What did you say?"

"Oh, nothing to get so upset about. I blundered into the place in the small hours of the morning, which probably didn't help, and since I had you slung over my back, I wasn't in much of a position to argue. And they asked if we had anything to do with the dragon they'd seen earlier, and I said yes, and they asked if the dragon-men were going to come back and burn the place, and so I said yes, probably, since that's what they usually do, either that or the rider was just scouting for a good place to buy dried fish, which, let's face it, was about the only thing this lot have to trade. They didn't take that too well."

Sollos rolled his eyes. He could do that, he discovered, without anything hurting.

"Don't get all crotchety! Like I said, it was the middle of the night and I woke them all up, so they were pretty grumpy. All right, I might have shouted at them a bit as well, but I'd been carrying you through that fucking mud for hours. I'd lost count of how many times I fell over and I'd had enough. Bloody stuff was bad enough when it was just me."

"All right, all right." Sollos forced himself to ignore the pain. He took a deep breath, sat up and then stood. And nearly fell down again.

Kemir caught him.

"Shit! You didn't tell me I'd broken my ankle."

"Really?" Kemir bent down. "I didn't spot that. Let me have a look."

"No! Don't . . ." He hopped back and forth, trying to keep his balance. "Ow!"

"That's not broken. That's just a sprain."

"How do you know? *Ow!* Stop that!"

"See. No grating bones. Strap that up and you'll be fine. Well, maybe in a couple of days."

Standing on one leg wasn't working out. Sollos tried sitting down, but then his ribs shrieked at him. He ended up flat out across the floor, back where he'd started. "So we found the settlement, and now we're stuck here."

"That's it." Kemir shrugged. He gave the walls a good shake. The hut seemed ready to fall apart. "Not exactly stuck. We can leave whenever we want, and I doubt they'd stop us either. Of course, with no bows, no knives, no armor and you being in the state you're in, we wouldn't get very far. Not that we'd know which way to go in the first place."

"That's fantastic, Kemir. Thank you."

Kemir snorted. "Better than being eaten by snappers, I thought."

"One way to look at it, I suppose."

"Not as dull as picking our arses back in the valley with those stuck-up knights, either."

"Since you put it like that."

Kemir lay on the floor next to Sollos. Together, they stared up at the ceiling. "I did pick up one thing while we were all busy shouting at each other."

"What's that?"

"Rider Semian wasn't the first dragon they've seen in these parts lately."

"Really?"

"Could be they've seen another. Could be it was white."

"Could be they want to give us our stuff back and then show us where it is?"

"Could be they don't."

For a long time they lay in silence, looking up at the thatch of reeds.

"Lot of spiders up there," said Kemir after a while. "You know, we could . . ."

"No."

"But there's always—"

"Certainly not!"

"Right."

Sollos could hear men talking outside. Mostly they were the loud confident voices of people going about their normal business, but he could hear whispers too, much closer. Eavesdroppers. He knew exactly what Kemir was thinking, but that was a last resort, something to be kept to themselves until they truly needed it. When they were tying him to a stake and lighting the pyre around his ankles, *then* he might tell them about the dead dragon.

17

❦

BELLEPHEROS

Bellepheros, grand master alchemist, bowed low. Prince Jehal sat on King Tyan's throne. Queen Zafir was to one side of him and Queen Shezira to the other, and then King Narghon and King Silvallan. Both of Queen Shezira's daughters were there, and Bellepheros counted at least a dozen other princes and princesses, not to mention almost every lord or lady of any significance within King Tyan's realm. All here for the wedding.

And this is what passes for a discreet audience?

Strictly, Bellepheros answered only to the Speaker of the Realms. Strictly, no one in this room had any power over him. Strictly . . .

"Your Holinesses." He bowed to each king and queen in turn. "Your Highnesses." Now to the princes and princesses. "I have been charged by the Speaker of the Realms to conduct my sacred duty. I have completed this charge, and now it is my duty to report to you, Your Highness," another bow, this time for Jehal, "on what I have found."

Prince Jehal smiled and looked bored. "We're all gagging to hear it, Master Bellepheros. Tell me first, though, so that we all might hear it—have you had every cooperation from my eyrie-master?"

Bellepheros bowed again. "Yes, Your Highness. Every cooperation."

"Have you been able to question every one of the men who serve him?"

"Yes, Your Highness."

"Has anyone been missed? Has there been anyone you've sought and not found?"

"No, Your Highness."

"And what of Queen Zafir's men? Her Holiness has remained here as our guest since her mother's death. She has not permitted a single one of her riders, her keepers or any of her men or dragons to return to her own eyrie. Has their cooperation also been complete? Have you been able to question every one of the men who serve her too?"

"Yes, Your Highness."

Prince Jehal clasped his hands in front of him and leaned forward. "So in short, Master Bellepheros, you have left no stone unturned, and no obstacle has been placed in your way?"

"The only people I have not questioned under the smoke are yourself and your eyrie-master."

Jehal nodded. "Those of royal blood. But you have questioned us yourself, without the smoke, and you have found nothing to contradict what we have told you."

"That is the case, Your Highness." Inside, Bellepheros felt the first pangs of unease. Jehal was backing him into a corner.

"So then. To your findings. The speaker sent you here because he believed that Queen Aliphera's death could not have been an accident. Was it?"

Bellepheros smiled. "Now that I cannot say, Your Highness, for that is *not* what the speaker charged me to learn. My sacred charge here was to determine whether any other man or woman had a hand in her death."

"There's a difference?"

"A subtle one, Your Highness. And I shall report to the speaker that Queen Aliphera harnessed and loaded her dragon herself on the day that she died. All her fixings and fastenings were checked by one of her own Scales. I have questioned that man myself under the truth-smoke, and he is innocent of any wrongdoing. I am convinced that no one tampered with Queen Aliphera's mount before she left. Indeed, it seems that the late queen was unusually involved in seeing to her dragon herself on that particular day."

"Did someone kill her or not?" growled Prince Jehal.

"It is a conundrum, Your Highness. I have every reason to think that Queen Aliphera left Clifftop with her harness fully secured. If there was an accident or, for that matter, any malice, it did not originate within your eyrie, Your Highness. I assure you, I will make this very plain to the speaker. Also, there is no possibility that Queen Aliphera was attacked while in the air. The evidence is absolute on this. Her harness was not cut or torn or burned. It was simply undone."

Jehal cocked his head. "You haven't actually answered my question, Master Bellepheros. Did someone kill her?"

Bellepheros shrugged. "I cannot say, one way or the other. No one saw her fall. She had sent her riders away. It is not my place to speculate as to why she would do such a thing, or what she was doing when she fell." He'd given the truth-smoke to almost every man and woman in Clifftop and found out nothing, except that the queen had insisted on preparing her mount herself. He looked around the room, looking for clues in the faces of the assembled dragon-kings and -queens. Still nothing. Nothing at all. He sighed, and bowed again, this time to Queen Zafir. "I am sorry, Your Holiness."

Queen Zafir gave him a curt nod.

Prince Jehal was looking annoyed.

"So you will not say whether this was murder, or that it was an accident. So in fact you say nothing at all, and you have not discharged the duty placed upon you by our speaker despite every possible assistance."

Bellepheros bowed deeply. "My apologies, Your Highness." Understandable, he supposed, that Prince Jehal wanted this to be over, for him to stand up and say it had been an accident. It would be the easy thing too, and yet he couldn't quite bring himself to do it. *Call me a perfectionist, but something is not quite as it should be.* "If the speaker is not satisfied and demands an opinion that I cannot substantiate, Your Highness, I will say that Queen Aliphera took her own life."

Queen Zafir almost spat at him. "And why would she do that?"

Bellepheros bowed again. "I cannot say. What I can say is that the actions that Queen Aliphera took when leaving Clifftop lead me to suspect she took something with her and that she intended no one to know of it." He glanced at Prince Jehal. "Many riders took to the sky that day. Even your eyrie-master, Your Highness, and eyrie-masters, in my experience, do not leave their eyries when they have visitors. Not without a pressing reason. Eyrie-Master Lord Meteroa flew that day, and when he returned, he also took great pains to conceal something. One might speculate that Queen Aliphera meant to meet with someone in absolute secrecy, and that she took with her something of great value."

Jehal sneered at him. "And what might that have been, Grand Master Alchemist?"

"I cannot even speculate, Your Highness."

"Then have a care with what you imply, alchemist. Trysts? Secret meetings? Suicide? You will find yourself suggesting that my uncle and Queen Aliphera were lovers next." Which drew a laugh from some of the less civilized, since it was well understood that eyrie-master Lord Meteroa's preferences lay firmly elsewhere. Jehal waved him away, and Bellepheros was glad to go.

ALTHOUGH FOR NOW HE COULDN'T go very far. Jehal's wedding was only days away, and the ritual litany of feasts and games and extravagance was already well under way. Bellepheros would have much preferred to disappear to Clifftop among the dragons, or else hire himself a carriage and get back to his laboratories in the Adamantine Palace. But he was grand master, and that meant that Prince Jehal had to invite him or risk being rude. Which meant he had to accept, lest he cause any offense. He had exactly long enough to change from one set of clothes into another, and then he was back among the same kings and queens and princes and princesses as before, only now they were in a completely different part of the palace and dancing. No one paid him any attention now, which suited him well enough. He would wait, he decided, until he could disengage and retire. Tomorrow, he would hire that carriage to take him back to the Adamantine Palace. He wasn't entirely sure whether he was invited to stay for the wedding or not, but he could always cite his overriding duty to the speaker.

"Grand Master. A pleasure to see you." Bellepheros jumped. He looked around. Queen Shezira was standing next to him, along with a lady knight he vaguely knew. Her knight-marshal, perhaps?

He bowed, deeply. "Your Holiness."

"How are you finding the entertainment?"

"Most impressive, Your Holiness." Of all the people here, Shezira was the one he least wanted to talk to. She would be the next speaker, and thus the one to whom the Order answered. Generally, history had taught that grand masters should keep a very low profile when a new speaker was imminent.

"You seemed very sure of yourself when you reported to Prince Jehal. Up to a point. And then very *un*sure of yourself."

He bowed again. "I am confident, Your Holiness, that no sabotage occurred in Prince Jehal's eyrie. What happened after Queen Aliphera left Clifftop, I cannot say."

"Well, I'm quite sure that wasn't the answer Prince Jehal wanted to hear. Especially that nonsense at the end. Nor will it be what Speaker Hyram wants to hear, for that matter."

Bellepheros blinked. "I do not understand, Your Holiness."

"Oh come, Grand Master. Prince Jehal wishes you to report that Queen Aliphera's death was an accident. Speaker Hyram wishes to hear that it was murder, preferably with Jehal found crouched over her bloody corpse with the knife still in his hand. You give us neither."

A chill ran down Bellepheros's spine. Even in his most informal reports he would never have been so direct. For the second time in as many hours he felt himself thoroughly cornered. He bowed once more. "I give you the truth as well as I can uncover it, Your Holiness."

Shezira nodded, already losing interest. "And let us make up our own minds, which we would have done anyway. I'm sure you tried your best, Grand Master."

Her tone was patronizing, and Bellepheros had already taken a few cups of wine. "I have a concern, Your Holiness, that I must share with you," he said. There. The words were out. No going back now.

"And what is that, Grand Master?"

"I understand that one of your dragons is missing."

It took a moment for Queen Shezira to realize that they weren't talking about Queen Aliphera anymore. Bellepheros savored it. She gave a very slight nod. "Yes. That is true."

"Your Holiness, you are a queen of a dragon realm, and so you know the true purpose of our order. We are in every eyrie. We keep meticulous records of the dragon bloodlines and mix the potions needed to make them grow into their different breeds. However, our most vital and most secret task concerning the dragons is somewhat different. Your Holiness, I do not concern myself with the politics of the realms, but from what I hear it is by no means clear that your dragon has found its way into another eyrie. I hear her keeper has not been found."

"Yes," said Shezira sourly. "One of yours."

"Your Holiness, the dragon-lords may play their games, but we alchemists are charged with the ancient duty of keeping the dragons in check. Even one dragon allowed to reach its full potential is a threat to every king and queen in the realm. I will be obliged to inform the speaker."

"Grand Master, what is your point? If the dragon has gone rogue, I have eyries filled with many scores more with which to hunt it down. Across the realms there are more than seventeen hundred, as you very well know. How is one wild dragon a threat to the realms?"

Bellepheros bowed yet again. "My point, Your Holiness, is that my order is at your disposal to help in any way that it can, and that I shall return shortly to the Adamantine Palace, but as I am bound to travel by land, there will be some delay before I arrive."

Queen Shezira nodded. "Your offer is noted, Grand Master. I assure you, I am already conducting a quite thorough search. I *will* find my white, and when I do—and I find who took her—there will be blood. Good day."

The queen moved away. Bellepheros wiped his brow. After that, he decided, he might as well start thinking about who his successor should be. It took him a few seconds to realize that the queen's knight-marshal hadn't followed her mistress away. She leaned into him and spoke quietly in his ear.

"Grand Master. A private word, if you please?"

HE LEFT FURYMOUTH THE FOLLOWING morning, in a carriage supplied by Prince Jehal and escorted by a company of soldiers. The other alchemists at Clifftop would just have to find their own way back to the Adamantine Palace. Tucked under his seat, carefully packed in straw, was a spherical bottle made of glass, stoppered and sealed with wax. It fitted nicely into the palm of his hand, and from the way its weight shifted, was filled with some sort of liquid. A very heavy liquid. Unlike the knight-marshal, Bellepheros knew exactly what it was. What he didn't know was where it had come from, or how several such bottles would have found their way into the possession of one such as Shezira's knight-marshal. It would be a long journey home, though, with plenty of time to ponder and plenty of inns with wine to help him think.

He didn't get the chance. Two days out of Furymouth his carriage was stopped. Masked men with knives tore open the door. Blood glistened on their blades. He could see bodies on the ground outside. He had time to open his mouth, but before he could shout, a hand clamped over his face.

18

THE PRICE

Twice a day the door to their hut opened and half a dozen Outsiders armed with spears and knives would be clustered outside. One of them would very gingerly place a bucket of water on the floor, together with some dried fish and half-rotten fruit. On the first day, Sollos told them that they had six days before the dragon-riders came. Every morning he reminded them that they had one fewer day to let him go. It took until he was down to two before the Outsiders made up their minds. In the middle of the day the door opened again, and this time there were nearly a score of them. One stepped forward, a heavyset man in his middle years with a thick curly black beard.

"What do you want?"

"Some food that doesn't give me the runs would be nice," muttered Kemir. Sollos shushed him.

"First of all to thank you for your hospitality." Sollos smiled. "Second, I'd like my bow and my knives and my armor back. Then I'd like to know about the white dragon."

"And what then?"

"We find the dragon, we go away and leave you in peace."

"We've seen dragons every day since you came." Curly Beard looked tired. He was frightened.

"We're all looking for the white dragon. You weren't very friendly when they came by, so they sent us instead. When they find what they want, they'll go away. They don't fly for the King of the Crags and neither do we."

Kemir spat. "Doesn't mean they won't burn you out if they don't find what they want."

"What if we help you find the white dragon. What's in it for us?"

"Not being burned?"

Sollos glared at his partner. "What do you want?"

"Money." Curly Beard set his face hard. "A hundred gold dragons."

"So you've seen one then."

Curly Beard nodded. "Could be. Could be we know of someone who's seen one."

"All right. A hundred gold dragons. That had better buy me a lot of help." Sollos could feel Kemir behind him, almost unable to contain himself.

"Up front."

Sollos snorted. "You must think I'm an idiot."

"There's been a white dragon seen a few times in these valleys. Not here but somewhere else. I can take you to where they've seen it. And that's all you're getting until I see gold."

"If you're lying, you know you're going to get burned."

"Could be that might be coming anyway. So I'll take the gold first, if you please."

Sollos shrugged. "All right. Not my gold anyway."

Ten minutes later they were free. Another half an hour and they were in a boat, rowing across the lake with Curly Beard and two of his friends. They were a bedraggled lot, these Outsiders, thought Sollos. Their clothes were ragged and crude, a mixture of animal pelts and cheap cloth that had gone rotten in the permanent damp. Everything they had looked worn and well used, the handles of their knives shiny and smooth and molded to the shapes of their hands. A few had belts, the leather hard and cracked, the buckles tarnished and bent. Others made do with string. Most of them, Sollos realized, were scarred or damaged; some were missing fingers, others had whole limbs or even faces that had broken and then healed out of shape. Apparently, life was hard as an Outsider. Harder than he remembered.

Sollos had been born and raised somewhere out here. He ought to sympathize, and yet he didn't, because he didn't want to. What was the point, when it was all long gone and burned away?

Curly Beard rowed them to the gravel flats a little way from the settlement, the place where Sollos and Kemir had first landed. They waited for half the morning, patiently standing in the steady rain, until around noon Curly Beard pointed. There was a dragon skimming across the lake toward them. A moment later the three Outsiders were off, fleeing into the safety of the trees. Sollos stood and watched the dragon. He waved.

"I hope that's one of ours," muttered Kemir with a glance toward where the Outsiders had gone. "Now would be a fine time to run into whoever started all this."

The dragon circled over them once, close enough that Sollos could recognize it, and then landed, the wind from its wings spraying a cloud of gravel into the air. Rider Semian beckoned them over. He didn't bother to dismount.

"I almost gave up on you," he shouted through the rain. The dragon, Sollos saw, was steaming very slightly.

"Well, we're very glad you didn't," shouted Sollos back. Belatedly, he remembered to bow.

"And? What news?"

"They claim to have seen her. They claim they know where she is."

"Where?"

"Not here, but they claim they can take us to her." Sollos hesitated. "They want gold."

"How much?"

"Two hundred dragons."

Rider Semian didn't flinch, but his dragon suddenly snorted and snapped at Sollos, who fell over in his haste to get out of the way. The dragon glared at him.

"You ask a lot, sell-sword."

"I don't ask for anything, Rider," yelled Sollos, picking himself up and warily watching the dragon. "That's the price the people who live here are asking."

"Tell them no."

"Then you'll never find the queen's dragon, Rider Semian."

The dragon bared its teeth. Its tail was up in the air, flexing and flicking back and forth like a whip. Among their own kind, dragons usually lashed out with their tails when they were annoyed. It was meant as a warning. But when they did it to humans . . . Sollos closed his eyes and tried not to think about it.

"Tomorrow," shouted Semian. "Meet me back here tomorrow." Abruptly, the dragon turned and began to run, launching itself across the flats. The stones hissed and danced with each colossal stride, and Sollos fancied he could see the whole lake ripple. Then the monster unfurled its wings and with a clap of thunder hurled itself into the air and was away. He watched it go. He could actually see it rise through the air with each beat of its wings, he realized, and then dip again between them.

"You should have asked for a thousand," said Kemir, suddenly standing beside him.

"Apparently so." Sollos shrugged. "I suppose it's not his money either."

19

THE TAIYTAKEI

Any other dragon-lord, mused Jehal, wouldn't have these sorts of problems. Any other dragon-lord would simply have gone to their eyrie, looked at the dragons and then gone back to their palace again. Any other dragon-lord would have built their eyrie conveniently *close* to their palace. *He*, though, had to ride out to a field a little ways outside the city to look at Queen Shezira's dragons. Not that he minded all that much, but the fact that he had to go meant that everyone else had to go too, and that meant shuffling everyone into carriages. What should have been a twenty-minute jaunt on the back of a horse had taken them an hour and a half, and now the whole wedding was running late. Knowing that the dragon he wanted wasn't going to be here didn't help either.

He tried to keep himself amused by mentally undressing his guests. Zafir's little sister Princess Zara-Kiam was going to be worth undressing for real quite soon, he decided. There were a few cousins and other minor relatives out there who might be worth some attention too: Queen Fyon's youngest, Princess Lilytha, for example, if her brother Prince Tyrin hadn't got to her first. He narrowed his eyes, looking at them standing next to each other, trying to decide.

He sighed. Everyone had been telling him how weddings were supposed to be wonderful days filled with joy and happiness, but looking around him he couldn't see much sign of either. His guests were grumbling and shifting on their feet, already overstuffed with a hundred pointless delicacies. Queen Shezira looked tense. She hadn't actually told him that the white wasn't here, so there was always the chance that no one else had told him either. Jehal had already decided to have some fun with that. Queen Zafir had a permanent angry scowl etched into her face. For himself, he couldn't shake the feeling that the whole exercise was a waste of time. The only person who seemed to be enjoying herself was Princess Lystra.

They sat next to each other on their wedding thrones, shaded by a makeshift awning while everyone else burned up in the summer sun. If he wanted to, he could have reached out and taken his bride's hand, but apparently he wasn't supposed to do that yet. As best he could tell, they were in some sort of interim state between being not married and being married. They'd had a dawn ritual and then a morning feast. After that came the giving of gifts, and then everyone kicked their heels until the evening. There was another feast, a dusk ritual, then the whole humiliating bit about being drugged and stripped naked in front of all the wedding guests. What was that? Revenge for having to stand around and be bored all day?

Finally, after the consummation, once the whole thing was over, they never had to look at each other again, if that was what they wanted. Maybe it was *supposed* to be an ordeal. A warning of things to come? A test of strength?

Someone was parading a pair of horses in front of him. Strictly speaking, they were parading them in front of King Tyan, who sat in his own throne next to Jehal's, drooling and snoring. He was still king after all. Jehal smiled. They were wonderful beasts, pure white, with gold and silver livery. A stallion and a mare. Jehal stifled a yawn.

"Very nice," he said. "They will be the most beautiful creatures in my stables. Tell . . ." Oh, now this was going to be a problem. He'd let his mind wander so far that he hadn't heard who they were from, and now he was going to look stupid and insult someone all at once. "I am in awe. Bring them closer." He glanced around in search of helpful clues. *Horses. Who likes horses? People always give the sort of gift they'd like to receive.*

"King Valgar is too kind," said Princess Lystra quietly. For the first time since the wedding had begun she wasn't smiling. "He meant them to go with the dragon. To take us to and from your eyrie."

So she assumes I know. She doesn't know that her mother hasn't told me. He could have some fun with that too.

"King Valgar is too kind indeed." He smiled, waving the horses away. Valgar wasn't here so there was no need to waste any time on flattering his presents. "Let King Valgar know that they are the most beautiful horses in my realm, and that Princess Lystra and I shall ride them to and from Clifftop for a year, as a mark of our respect for his generosity." He leaned toward Princess Lystra. "Is the dragon as pure?"

She turned to him, startled, with a wonderful look of horror. "You don't know?"

"What don't I know?" He smiled again, all innocence, as various shades of panic flew across her face.

Lystra turned toward her mother, sat on the other side of her, and started whispering.

Jehal tapped Lystra on the back of the hand. "Sorry, did you mean the theft of your white dragon? I know about *that.* Terrible business. I'm sure it doesn't matter." She was shaking, completely flustered, like a rabbit caught by a farmer's lantern. He kept his smile in place, warm and reassuring, glancing at her from time to time, making sure she caught his eye. *Terrible business?* That was putting it mildly. *I'm sure it doesn't matter?* Of course it bloody mattered. At the very least everyone who had anything to do with the theft was going to die. With a bit of luck, open warfare might break out. There would be trials and tribunals in the Adamantine Palace. It was quite easy to imagine an entire realm falling. Now *that* would be fun.

Somehow, though, tormenting Princess Lystra wasn't as satisfying as it ought to have been. She still looked pale and worried when her mother's dragons were finally brought down to the field and Jehal stood up to inspect them. He picked one quickly, said something nice about it and waved the rest away. He'd had his bride squirming in her seat, and instead of reveling in her discomfort, he found he felt . . . well, vaguely guilty. And that wasn't right. That wasn't how it was supposed to be at all.

Maybe it was the heat. He sighed, stood up and made a pretty speech about how this was the start of a new era, and how proud he was to be joined to such a great clan and yet humbled too. When he was done, he hoped that at least a few of his guests had paid more attention to it than he had.

Riding back toward the palace didn't help either. Having a wife had sounded like a simple enough business, and it had all been arranged so long ago that he'd never thought to question it. However, meeting her in the flesh was some-how . . . disconcerting. She would be his queen one day, per-haps sooner rather than later. Which was fine, as long as she was the *right* queen. A simple queen with a demented ob-session for needlework or embroidery or something like that, who stayed in her tower all day, had no interest in the world around her and paused only from her handicrafts to pop out a steady stream of heirs, preferably male ones. That was the sort of queen he needed.

"Terrible business," muttered a voice beside him. Jehal snapped out of his reverie. Lord Meteroa was riding next to him. "I'm sure it doesn't matter, Your Highness."

"What do *you* want?"

"I'm afraid you have to attend a little diversion, Your Highness. After all, no one can leave the ceremony of gifts until you and King Tyan lead the way, and yet somehow everyone is required to be in place for the wedding feast before you arrive. In the normal course of things, this would simply oblige you to take a particularly tortuous path from one part of the palace to another, with perhaps a dalliance in the gardens to kill the time. As things are . . . ."

Jehal raised an eyebrow. "What, with several hundred relatives all rushing back to the palace as fast as they can, all getting in each other's way? And that's just Aunt Fyon's family."

Meteroa smiled and nodded. "Your Highness must be delayed."

"And do you have something in mind, Eyrie-Master?"

"I do indeed, Your Highness." Meteroa flashed Jehal a knowing look and kicked his horse into a trot. After a mo-

ment Jehal followed him. They turned off the road and galloped down a narrow track lined with trees, then off into
the fields. Behind them, a dozen of Jehal's dragon-knights
followed, keeping at a discreet distance yet never too far
away.

"You weren't thinking about the dragons at all when you
picked one, were you?" shouted Meteroa.

"On the contrary," called Jehal. "My thoughts were entirely devoted to how none of them was white."

"Really? I could have sworn your mind was somewhere
else. I certainly wouldn't have made the same choice as you
did."

Jehal felt a flash of irritation. Lord Meteroa was clever
and loyal and ran Clifftop like a precise machine, and his
frankness was usually a refreshing change from the sycophancy that infested the rest of King Tyan's court. Sometimes, though, the eyrie-master seemed to forget that Jehal
wasn't King Tyan's little boy anymore.

"Well, it was mine to choose. Queen Shezira can thank me
for not taking the best she had to offer." Mentally, Jehal
kicked himself. He'd *meant* to choose the ash-gray, the dragon
that Princess Lystra's elder sister rode. He'd completely forgotten about that, and now he had no idea which one of
Shezira's knights would be flying home without a mount of his
own. He sighed. He ought to find out. Doubtless he'd made
himself another enemy there.

The ground was starting to get rocky. Lord Meteroa
dived down another track, where the trees and undergrowth pressed in so close that Jehal kept having to duck
while thorns tore at his cloak. *Better change into a new
one as soon as we get to the palace. That'll keep everyone
waiting another few minutes.* After a little while the wood
gave way to great slabs of rock, and the mud below became sand. They were in the Stone Forest, a maze of
spikes and spires and walls of rock woven with tracks and
trails and clearings, caves and tunnels. Jehal knew it like
the back of his hand. It was the perfect place for a secret
meeting.

A perfect place for an ambush too.

He slowed and stopped, then glanced over his shoulder.
"What *is* this diversion of yours, eyrie-master? I'm not so
sure I shall like it."

"Wait here if you will, Your Highness. I will fetch them to you."

"And *who* will you fetch?" Something about Meteroa's manner made Jehal uneasy.

"No one who means you any harm, Your Highness."

Jehal looked behind him again. His knights were emerging from the woods, funneling into the cleft between the rocks.

"This is not a good place to stop, eyrie-mas—" He broke off. Emerging from the shadows between the stones, three riders approached, their horses stepping slowly in the sand. They were strange folk, dark-skinned with overly ornate clothes studded with gold and jewels and dazzling rainbows of feathers. They stopped a dozen paces short of where Lord Meteroa waited, dismounted and bowed.

Taiytakei.

The middle one, who wore the brightest clothes, came a few paces closer and then carefully kneeled in the sand.

"Your Holiness," he said. "We pay homage on this auspicious day."

With slow deliberate movements, like a cat stalking its prey, Jehal dismounted. He drew nearer, never taking his eyes off the man.

"Sea traders," he whispered. He glanced at Meteroa. "What is this?"

"We bring you a gift," said the dark man. "A gift for you, O mightiest of princes, to honor your wedding day."

Jehal forced a smile. "Forgive me, but it is said that the Taiytakei do not deal in gifts, only trade, and that what may appear at first as a gift will always turn out to have a price."

The kneeling man beckoned one of his fellows, who brought over something under a cloth and then quickly withdrew. "We wish nothing more than to bring to you what you desire, and take from you that for which you have no need." Slowly, the man placed the object on the ground and then backed away, still on his knees. When he reached the others, he rose and turned. All three of them mounted and rode slowly away.

Jehal watched them go, and only when they were long gone did his eyes move slowly to what they had left behind. He took a step toward it.

Meteroa jumped off his horse.

"Let me, Your Highness."

"Why did you bring me here?"

"Forgive me, my Prince, but I will show you. The Taiy-takei wished to give this to you in person and in private. You will see why." Meteroa tore away the cloth. Under-neath was an exquisite box carved from black wood, inlaid with vermilion and gold.

"Open it."

Meteroa lifted the lid. Inside lay three strips of plain silk, two black and one white, and two tiny golden dragons with ruby eyes.

"Pretty." Jehal shrugged. He would have said more, but one of the golden dragons turned its head and looked at him.

Meteroa pulled out one of the silks and snapped the box shut. "Best that others do not see," he murmured. "Here." He handed Jehal a strip of black silk. "Wear it around your eyes. You will not be disappointed."

Jehal smiled. Meteroa seemed to be in deadly earnest, and so he wrapped the black silk across his eyes. Immedi-ately the world seemed to shift and shimmer. Voices spoke inside his head: *You are the speaker in waiting, and we are the gift of the Taiytakei.*

For a moment he thought he saw himself, as if looking through another's eyes. He ripped away the silk. Meteroa was still holding the box, but now he had it slightly open again. Four glittering ruby eyes peered up at him.

"In the sunlight they can fly. Or when you will them to," murmured Meteroa. "Wear the silk and they will obey your thoughts. They will see and they will listen and you will have their eyes and ears. There will be no secrets you cannot un-lock." He closed the box again and smiled. "Was I wrong, Your Highness, to bring you to the Taiytakei, so that you might receive their gift?"

"No." Jehal shook his head in wonder. "No, Eyrie-Master, you were not wrong."

He looked at the box and grinned to himself. *You are the speaker in waiting . . .*

20

KNIGHTS

Rider Semian, when he came back the next day, didn't bring only gold. Three more dragons arrived with him, and on the back of each dragon were three knights. Semian himself brought the alchemist. They landed on the same gravel flats in a flurry of wings and spray. Sollos watched while the alchemist and the riders dismounted and rearranged themselves. Most of the knights stayed on the ground, crouching cautiously behind a protective wall of shields with the alchemist in the middle, while the dragons took to the sky again.

Archers. They're afraid of archers. Which made Sollos think of the last time he'd watched a dragon-knight hand over a purse full of gold to a mysterious stranger.

He stood his ground, out in the open, waiting. Kemir was beside him. Curly Beard and his friends had scuttled off to hide among the trees and watch. Semian emerged from the midst of his men and advanced slowly, looking around, scanning the shore of the lake. Up above, the dragons circled.

Sollos bowed. "Riders," he acknowledged. He knew some of the other dragon-knights only by their faces. Despite two weeks of sharing a camp together, they'd never asked his name, never called him anything except sell-sword. Not one had spoken to him other than to order him around.

Semian gave him a disdainful look. "Where are your outlaw friends, sell-sword?"

"Hiding and waiting to see what you do. Did you bring the gold, Rider?"

"One hundred coins. They may have the other half when we have found the dragon."

Sollos silently clenched his fists. "That's not going to work, Rider. They know perfectly well that you'll simply burn their village if they try to steal from you. They expect you to burn it anyway, before you leave."

"I will honor our bargain if they do the same."

"I don't doubt it, Rider, but these people are used to King Valmeyan's men, and the King of the Crags is hated here. They expect nothing but treachery and betrayal, and they're not wise enough in the ways of the world to know the difference between one knight and another. They probably haven't even heard of Queen Shezira." Sollos sighed. "I suppose we'll have to wait until tomorrow for the dragons to come back, and then another day for the rest of the gold."

"Sell-sword, they will either take us to the dragon today or they *will* burn. That's the only offer I will make. A hundred gold is a fortune for most men."

Sollos gritted his teeth. *Yes, it would have been.* He shook his head and held out his hand. "Then give me the gold and I'll see what I can do."

"No, sell-sword, I will give it to them myself, when they have taken us back to their settlement."

"With all respect, Rider, that isn't the arrangement."

"Then change it."

Sollos shrugged. "If that's what you wish, but I certainly won't be coming with you. I say again, Rider: these people fully expect your dragons to burn their village whether they honor our bargain or not. Once they've got your gold, I can't see why they shouldn't simply murder us all in our sleep. Either way, your dragons will burn their homes."

Semian seemed to consider this. "Then what arrangement do you suggest?"

"These men and women have not seen your white

dragon, Rider, but they have heard of others who have and they will take us there. We have to go to another settlement, a smaller one, about ten miles from here. We go directly there. They'll come with us to show us the way. Tomorrow morning, when we're somewhere between here and there, you give them the gold. One or two of them will stay to take us to the man who's seen the white." It had taken almost an entire day of arguing with Curly Beard to find an arrangement they could agree on.

Rider Semian narrowed his eyes. "And this other man, will he too demand a hundred gold dragons?"

He will if I have anything to do with it, thought Sollos. "I'm sure you'll find a way to convince him, Rider." *Yes. With the point of your swords, no doubt.*

With a curt nod, the dragon-knight turned away. "Tell them we agree. But *I* will give them the gold, not you, and it will be one hundred dragons, not two. And, sell-sword?"

"Rider?"

"We travel in the open, where we can be seen from the skies. Make sure they understand that. Make sure they understand that every step we take will be watched from above."

"They're not stupid, Rider."

As Sollos and Kemir walked away toward the woods where Curly Beard was hiding, the knights retreated as far from the woods as they could. Sollos looked up. The dragons were still there, distant specks high in the sky. Which was a pity, because even five minutes of Rider Semian's company was already making him wonder if there was some deal he could cut with Curly Beard that would result in six dead knights and his pockets full of gold.

Probably not, though. Curly Beard would kill him and Kemir as happily as he'd murder a dragon-knight. You were either an Outsider or you weren't, and that was that.

"Well, that went well," muttered Kemir. "I thought you said he was an idiot. Are you going to tell Curly Beard he can only have fifty?"

"He won't take it. No, he'll get his hundred."

"Nothing for us then. Hurrah. You should definitely have asked for a thousand."

Sollos shrugged. "There's still the dragonscale too. Let's not forget that."

"Give up. We're never going to get our hands on that."

"And a reward for finding the white."

"If we find it," grumbled Kemir. "If they pay it." He snorted. "Why did they bring the alchemist?"

Sollos shrugged. "Don't know, don't care. All we have to do is make sure that Curly Beard and Rider Rod-Up-My-Arse stick to the agreement and don't start trying to kill each other. Should keep us busy enough, don't you think?"

"Let them kill each other. I'll help if you like. When they're done, we can have the gold. Suits me."

Sollos twitched his lips. "Don't tempt me."

"You know, we *did* make an oath, a long time ago. We could always—"

"No!" Sollos stopped and took a deep breath. "No, Kemir. These riders serve Queen Shezira, not the King of the Crags."

Kemir shrugged. "A knight's a knight. They all think they're little gods. We could—"

"I said no!" Sollos stamped his foot.

"Look, I'm not saying we should try and overthrow Valmeyan; I'm just saying that sticking a knife into a few dragon-knights would give me a sense of fulfillment, that's all."

"Those days are gone, Kemir. That oath . . ." He shrugged. "It was a stupid oath. Besides, there are six of them and two of us, and their dragons are watching us."

He saw Kemir look up at the sky and wince. "They have to sleep, you know."

They do. Yes, they do. Sollos shook his head. However much a part of him agreed with Kemir, murdering one dragon-knight or even ten wouldn't change the world at all. As long as there were dragons, there would be men and women who rode them.

As long as there are dragons.

21

THE WEDDING

Meteroa, of course, timed it perfectly. When Jehal returned to the palace, everyone was waiting for him. He walked briskly into the feasting hall with Princess Lystra at his side and a spring in his step. *You are the speaker in waiting* . . .

"Drink!" he cried before he'd even reached the throne at his lolling father's side. "Drink! A toast! Not to us, but to everyone! To each other! To life!" Then he spun Princess Lystra to face him, kissed her, and then shot a glance along the tables and made sure he caught Zafir's eye. "Drink!" he shouted again, into the shocked quiet. "Drink to the pounding of hearts! To the thunder of wings and the wash of fire! To the clash of swords, to the moment of the kill, to the drunken passion of lovers! Drink and shout for joy or shout with rage, I care not which, but do not fill my feasting hall with silence!"

He sat down and thumped his goblet on the table. Everyone was looking at him. This wasn't how a wedding feast was supposed to start, but he simply didn't have the stomach for hours of tedious politeness. Far better that everyone got roaring drunk.

He peered past Princess Lystra at her mother. "Isn't this more what you're used to, Your Holiness?" He grinned.

Queen Shezira's face remained carefully blank. "Your exuberance would, perhaps, be more appreciated in my halls than in your own."

"I mean to make your daughter feel welcome here."

Shezira said nothing.

"Am I a monster?" he asked her, much later, when the food was almost gone and he'd drunk too much wine. "Is that what you think of me?"

She met his eyes. "In another few hours you will be my son," she said coolly. And that was all.

After everyone had gorged themselves, a troupe of musicians struck up and the dancing started. Princess Lystra came first of course, with her big wide eyes and drooping lashes and that startled look she'd worn since the day had started. Then her mother, which was like dancing with an iron statue, cumbersome and awkward and with nothing to recommend it. And then, out of nowhere, Zafir slid into his arms, sinuous and sensual, pressing herself close and filling his nose with her perfume. Jehal felt himself stir. Her hand slid up his back to the skin of his neck, and he felt a slight pricking sting. He jerked.

"What are you doing?"

Zafir looked at her hand. On one of the rings she wore was a tiny spike, and on that spike the slightest drop of blood. She touched it to her tongue and then wrapped her arm around him again. "Reminding you that you're not immortal," she whispered.

"I *feel* immortal." He pulled her even closer, but this time she resisted.

"I am a dragon-queen, Prince Jehal, not some courtesan, and eyes are watching us."

"Is that a poison ring you're wearing?"

"Of course."

"Am I about to die?"

Zafir smiled. This time, when he tried to pull her closer, she didn't resist. "Not today, my love." She leaned into him for a second and he felt her breath on his ear. "I saw the way you looked at her today, your little starling-bride," she murmured. "Enjoy the novelty, but remember that it's *me* who can give you what you want. If you plan to toss me aside for her, you may as well take your dagger and run me through and let us both die here and now."

Jealous? She was *jealous*? For a second he thought about it. "If you want to see which of you I want, then let us slip away and I will show you," he said huskily.

She pushed him sharply away with a brittle smile. "Your starling can have you today. Afterward . . . we shall see." She waved her fingers at him, letting him see the ring again, still wet with a drop of his blood.

You are the speaker in waiting . . .

He watched her go. Before he could launch himself after her, another pair of arms took hold of him.

"Princess Jaslyn!" Jehal forced a smile.

"Prince Jehal."

"I cannot say why, but I did not think you to be much for dancing." Her movements were sharp and aggressive, not like her sisters, and as far away from Zafir's as it was possible to be.

"I prefer to dance in the air."

"With a somewhat more scaly partner, no doubt." Jehal smiled. "So do I. So we have something in common."

Jaslyn looked at him with scorn. "We have my sister in common now. I am only dancing with you so I can say this quietly, where no one else will hear: whatever hurt you bring her, I will return to you tenfold."

"And if I bring her joy?"

"Then I will have misjudged you." She bowed and spun away.

"That hardly seems an equitable arrangement," he called after her, but she didn't turn back. *Poor Lystra.* He'd expected to see her weep at the prospect of leaving her family and being forced to give herself to a man who she'd doubtless been taught to believe was a monster. Yet she hadn't. If anything, she almost seemed excited.

And now I begin to see why.

Another princess appeared in front of him. Jehal screwed up his face, trying to remember who she was. One of King Silvallan's brood, he thought, as they swept through the crush of bodies. Over in one corner, over the music, he could hear some sort of commotion. Drink had got the better of a pair of his knights. Others were quickly pulling them apart. He thought he heard the scrape of a sword being drawn, but there were no screams and the music didn't stop, so presumably nothing came of it. He tried to dance his way to Zafir's sister, to start laying a few foundations there, but all he got was an endless stream of distant relatives, and they all wanted something.

Suddenly, he was immensely glad that the day was nearly over. Tomorrow the dragon-lords and their courtiers would be on their way back to Clifftop, where they could be Lord Meteroa's problem for a night before they finally left for palaces of their own. He slipped away from the dancing and made his way outside. His head was foggy, and when he tried to shake it clear, it only got worse. Too much wine? Or had Zafir poisoned him after all?

Meteroa appeared at his elbow. "It's nearly time, Your Highness."

"I'll be glad when this is done."

"I would have thought you'd be enjoying this, Your Highness. Prince Tyrin and Princess Jesska have vanished, one suspects to one of your solars; Prince Loatan and Princess Kalista got as far as drawing knives on each other before your guards intervened, and those are merely the highlights. I shall of course have a detailed report waiting for you at your convenience, once you are free of your bride."

My bride. "Tell me, Eyrie-Master, about my bride. How do I look at her?"

Meteroa frowned. "I would say, with an expression of intrigued interest. Magnificently played."

Except I wasn't playing. "Mmm. And how many queens and princesses have been unable to resist the temptation to fondle a drunken prince when he's naked?"

"Queens Shezira and Zafir have both politely declined and will be attending Princess Lystra. Queen Fyon, however, accepted with great enthusiasm. I believe she forbade her daughters from joining her."

Jehal groaned. Queen Fyon—*Aunt* Fyon—was Narghon's wife. She was gray and sagging, at least ten years older than Aliphera had been. Rumors had once abounded in both palaces that she and King Tyan had been lovers as well as brother and sister. The number of heirs she'd borne for King Narghon certainly spoke of her enthusiasm.

"Princess Jaslyn will also attend you, I believe."

Jehal almost choked. "I think you must be mistaken."

Meteroa looked hurt. "I am an imperfect servant, Your Highness. On occasion."

"She made it quite clear in there that she hates me."

"I'll see to it that she doesn't poison you, Your Highness."

Jehal snorted. "See to it that Queen Zafir doesn't poison my bride, if you please. I want Lystra wide awake when I take her. Zafir has an assassin's ring on. Keep an eye on her." He thought he saw Meteroa smirk, but before he could launch a rebuke a bell began to toll. Meteroa clapped him on the back.

"It's time."

"A long time ago kings and queens married in the same way as everyone else." Jehal took a deep breath and rubbed his eyes. His head still felt fuzzy. In the sky above, the stars shone brightly. A silver crescent moon hung on the horizon, out over the sea. A breeze blew up from the harbor, bringing a strange mixture of smells: of the sea and rotting fish and ammonia, and of rose and myrrh and sandalwood from the incense burners strewn across the palace gardens.

"That was before the Seven Princes and the War of Thorns." Meteroa started to guide Jehal back toward the feasting hall.

"I know, I know, and Speaker Vishmir finally locked Prince Halim and Queen Lira in the Tower of Air and refused to let them out until Lira was pregnant with an heir, and that was the end of the matter. Much as I admire Vishmir's no-nonsense approach, I don't think he meant it to become standard practice."

"Heirs are important." For a moment Meteroa's face went as blank as a mask. Then he smiled politely. "Ask Hyram."

Jehal laughed. "Heirs are dangerous. Ask Aliphera. Oh, wait, you can't. She's dead." He sniffed the air again. "Whoever arranged the incense burners should be whipped; they're not doing their job at all. Did you put the scent vines around the east window of the bridal bedchamber as I asked?"

Meteroa nodded. He pushed Jehal back toward the feasting hall. The dancing had stopped. Princess Lystra was standing in the middle of the floor. Everyone was looking

at him, but he didn't have time to see anymore before a
gang of knights launched themselves at him. The next thing
he knew, he was whisked off his feet and being carried high
in the air. People were shouting and cheering. When he
strained his neck to look, he could just about see Princess
Lystra being escorted away by two queens, her mother on
one side, Zafir on the other.

He closed his eyes. They weren't even out of the feasting
hall before groping hands started to tear his clothes away.
Over the ribald jokes of his riders he could hear Queen
Fyon laughing. He shuddered. The women were always the
worst.

They carried him high over their heads, parading him in
front of everyone they could find, until they reached the
Sun Tower in the center of the palace. They almost dropped
him there, trying to carry him up the narrow spiral stairs,
but apparently they were quite prepared to risk that rather
than let him walk. By the time they got him to the top he
was dizzy, but he wasn't given any time to think about that.
Someone was already pressing a goblet into his hands. One
of Silvallan's nieces. What was her name?

"Maiden's Regret!" shouted a voice to a chorus of laughter. "The Maiden!"

He drank it down as he was obliged to do, and prayed
silently that the riders around him weren't as drunk as they
seemed. Mentally, one part of him listed all the dragon-kings
and -queens who'd been poisoned on their wedding nights.
Another part slowly started counting, ticking off the seconds before the Maiden's Regret took hold of him. It would
be longer than most, he'd made sure of that.

They finished stripping him and put him into his wedding shift, a pointless wrapping of cloth designed to fall
apart at the lightest touch. By now the room was spinning,
but he still had a few minutes before the potion took him
completely.

One by one, the riders, the princes, the princesses came
to him with ritual offerings of advice for the night to come,
and then left.

"Maiden's Regret loosens the tongue!" shouted a voice.
True, he thought. *That's what the alchemists were using in
my eyrie, with their truth-smoke. On my Scales and on my*

soldiers. He grinned. *What a waste. All those men and women left half-mad with lust.*

"It loosens everything." More laughter.

Meteroa must have been beside himself. I must write to Hyram, thanking him on behalf of Clifftop's whores. He started to laugh.

"Are you murdering your father?" Jehal blinked. The question seeped into his consciousness like honey dripping off a spoon. Jaslyn. That's who the voice was. Princess Jaslyn. Because hadn't Lord Meteroa said she was coming? And he didn't remember seeing her before.

Why not? urged a voice inside him. *Why not tell her the truth and be done with it. Everyone wants to know. Make her go away.*

He opened his mouth, but a hand shut it for him. "Get out of here, you little witch. How dare you! Shoo! Shoo!" The hand let go of him. "I'm so sorry, nephew. Treat your bride kindly but not too kindly. I'll wager she likes a little roughness, that one. Most of us do."

Jehal looked up and smiled. Queen Fyon, but she was going now, turning away. Hadn't he been about to say something? Whatever it was, it was gone.

It seemed that he blinked, and his knights were gone too. *That's right. Maiden's Regret fools with your sense of time. You haven't got long before it takes you now. Not long at all.*

There was a door. That's what he was supposed to do. Go through the door. And before he'd even finished thinking it, it was done, and up another spiral of stairs, and the stupid wedding shift was already falling off, and then he was naked and standing in a room with eight sides, with windows in all the walls, every one open, with a floor strewn with pillows and blankets and mattresses stuffed with everything from down to straw, and Lystra was standing in front of him. She was far gone with the Maiden, swaying slightly from side to side, and her eyes were black and immense.

A little droplet of fire seemed to fall inside him and gently explode. Princess Lystra opened her mouth and reached for him. He swayed toward her.

Not yet not yet not yet!

He had seconds before he lost any idea of what he was doing. With all that was left of his will he started counting windows. *Second on the left from the door. Faces east. That one . . .*

He pushed Princess Lystra toward that window. "Stars," he murmured. "Look up at the stars." He stood behind her, wrapping his arms around her, and peered through the air to another tower and another window. The window was still dark. Queen Shezira wouldn't have had time to get back to her rooms yet. A pity, because he'd wanted her to see him take her daughter. A sort of prelude to everything else he was going to take, and she wasn't even there.

But then the Maiden came, and Lystra was grinding herself against him, and there could be no more waiting.

22

SCORCHED EARTH

It took the rest of that day and most of the next to reach
their destination, picking their tortuous way along the
floor of a valley, among hundreds of rivulets that bubbled
and splashed among a sea of strewn rocks and streaks of
sand and gravel. On either side of them forested slopes rose
sharply toward rocky peaks. It rained relentlessly. Every
now and then one or other of the riders missed his footing
and slipped. By the end of the first day all of them were
limping.

Which serves them right for trying to hike in heavy armor,
Sollos thought.

In the evening Curly Beard and the other Outsiders sat
sullenly silent, huddled under the thickest of the trees, seeking what shelter they could get from the rain. When they
looked at the dragon-knights, their eyes glittered with a
mixture of greed and hate. The knights glowered back. Sollos and Kemir took it in turns to snooze, but no one else got
much sleep. Strangely, the alchemist seemed the most anxious of them all.

As soon as dawn broke, Curly Beard jumped to his feet
and declared it was time to move on. With great reluctance,

Rider Semian handed over the promised gold. Curly Beard disappeared back down the river with three of his friends and the sack of coins, leaving two of the Outsiders to guide the knights onward.

"If we went after them, we could still catch them," muttered Kemir.

It took barely an hour for the other two Outsiders to abandon them. The first slipped away in the woods when one of the knights fell and broke his hand. The other one, when he saw that he was the last, simply ran, trusting the sureness of his feet on the rocks, knowing the knights could never catch him. Rider Semian declared the man a traitor and ordered him shot, but by the time Sollos had his bow strung, the Outsider was too far away. He sent a couple of arrows after the man to keep Semian happy and then pretended to listen while the knight told him how poor a shot he was.

Slowly, Sollos realized that the knights didn't know what to do. He watched them dither and wondered what profit there might be from leaving them to their fate. Six riders and one alchemist, alone in the mountains . . .

He looked up. Sure enough, high above, he saw a speck in the sky. The knights had someone to watch over them.

"You! Sell-sword!"

Sollos looked around. He assumed it must be one of the knights, but it was the alchemist, pointing a finger at him.

"Master Huros. Enjoying yourself?"

"I, um . . . Certainly not. I require your help. It is clear that the correct course of action is to proceed in the direction we were being led. Please explain this to Rider Semian."

Sollos cocked his head. "Why don't you explain it to him yourself, Master Huros?"

"Because Lady Nastria made it quite plain that you two had knowledge of these mountains." The alchemist made a noise in his throat. "Um. He will listen to you, and we must press on."

"Must we? I thought we might go back. Burn those naughty Outsiders for being so ill-mannered."

"No, Sword-Master Sollos, we *must* press on. If, uh . . . if those men were telling us the truth, we cannot be far from the dragon. Turning back will waste days. I repeat, we *must* press on, before—"

"Before what, Master Alchemist?"

"Um. None of your concern. All that matters is that we reach the dragon quickly."

Sollos thought about that. There didn't seem much to gain from leaving the riders to fend for themselves, but in the end what made up his mind was that the alchemist had actually bothered to call him by his name. With a sigh, he hauled himself to his feet. He didn't bother telling the riders where he was going and didn't bother looking back when they shouted at him, simply gestured at them to follow. Eventually they did.

KEMIR WAS THE FIRST TO notice the smell. The rain had stopped in the middle of the day, and for the last few hours they'd walked on in glorious sunshine. Apart from his feet, Sollos was feeling almost dry when Kemir abruptly stopped and sniffed the air.

Sollos stopped as well. He wrinkled his nose. There was . . . something, something slightly familiar.

"Soul Dust," muttered Kemir, keeping his voice low so the dragon-knights, a few dozen yards behind them, wouldn't hear.

Sollos shook his head. "No. There's something right enough, but it's not Dust. Dust doesn't smell like that."

"It does when you burn it."

Sollos shrugged. "It can't be. No one here burns Dust." He swept his hand across the empty landscape. "Do you see anyone burning Dust?"

Kemir glared at him. "No, obviously I don't, because if I did, I'd be pointing at them. Just because you can't see the shit on the bottom of your boot doesn't mean it doesn't stink, and I'm telling you, that's the smell of burning Dust."

Five minutes later Sollos sniffed again. This time he smelled smoke.

They looked at each other. Then Kemir started to run as best he could over the scattered rocks. The riders shouted. Sollos paused for long enough to yell at them to smell the air, and then set off after Kemir. Around the next bend of the river they skidded to a stop.

Kemir pointed to the scorched scar at the edge of the forest. "Do you think that's the settlement we were supposed to be finding?" A few charred pieces of wood were still smoldering. The rest of whatever had been here was ash, but that wasn't what caught Sollos's eye.

"Bugger the settlement." He pointed up the river.

At first glance it might have been a huge white boulder, but there was something too regular about it, too smooth. The boulder, when Sollos looked closely, had eyes that looked back. As he watched, the boulder slowly unfurled its legs, wings and tail and turned into a dragon.

Kemir gave a little whoop of joy. "Finder's fee!"

Sollos touched Kemir on the arm, a gesture of caution. "Something isn't right about this. There's no rider."

"Of course there isn't. We were there, remember. When the other dragons attacked? Fire, shouting, running for our lives? Am I ringing any bells?"

Sollos edged sideways, out of the middle of the riverbed, heading for the cover of the forest. The dragon was watching, and there was something altogether too intelligent in the way it was looking at him. "We never found the Scales."

"That's because he's dead."

"Then why this?" Sollos began to step faster. "Dragons never flamestrike unless someone tells them to."

"Maybe it was hungry."

"Maybe it still is."

The dragon moved. Sollos grabbed Kemir and ran.

TIPPING THE SCALES

For ten years, as the dragon is matured, the gifts must continue, and those whose gifts are found wanting will find their dragon, when they take it, perhaps a little dull in its scales, not as vigorous in its flight or as tight in its turns as they had hoped. When his dragon has finally matured, the rider will visit the eyrie for one last time. A final round of gifts is made, and then rider and dragon are introduced. The dragon is his.

Before the rider leaves, it is customary for one last payment to be made: a small gift to the Scales, the man or woman who has fed and watered and nurtured the dragon since it was an egg. The dragon-princes call this gift Tipping the Scales.

23

※

SNOW

A torrent of flames poured from the sky, swallowing her and the Little One beside her in its fury. The river waters steamed. Stones cracked in the heat.

She felt the presence of the other dragons in the sky long before she saw them. Different minds, different thoughts made up of different sounds and colors, but that didn't bother her at first. Other dragons came and went all the time, and the Little Ones never seemed afraid. And then she'd felt their thoughts change, the colors darken and sharpen and fill with fire. She knew what was coming.

An instant before the flames struck, she spread out her wings, tenting them over her head and over the Little One beside her. Instinctively. Protecting her eyes and the Little One. The other Little One, the one who'd been angry and shouting, the one who rode on her back and told her what to do, he was too far away for her to save. She felt his thoughts snuff out, and that made her a little sad. Little Ones burned so easily.

A second flamestrike engulfed her. The fire warmed her, but didn't frighten her. The Little One was afraid, though.

Sharply, suddenly filled with fear. She felt it from all of them, but especially from the one beside her. And pain. The Little One was in pain. And panic. And terror. The emotions rolled into her from the Little One. She didn't know what to do with them. She'd never felt these things before. Bad things that made her want to run away.

The newcomer dragons were still close. She could still feel their thoughts, hot and fierce. They were circling around. They meant to come back.

She seized the Little One gently in her left foreclaws and hurled herself down the river, picking up speed with each stride. One of the other dragons swooped over her. She felt its thoughts and held the Little One close as the dragon above raked her with fire.

It passed over her head. As it did, she launched herself into the air and snapped at its tail. She still clasped the Little One tight to her breast. It was out of its mind, screaming and thrashing. Its thoughts were a jumble, disconcerting and incoherent. They made her feel strange. When another dragon swooped past her, she snapped at that one too and lashed it with her tail. She felt its surprise as it veered away.

Up, up, up. Faster and faster. Away. Sometimes she thought the Little One was trying to tell her to let it go, but its thoughts were chaos, broken and messy, and it kept contradicting itself. Three of the new dragons were following her. They were bigger than she was. They felt older. They had Little Ones to tell them what to do too. She could feel their determination, their hostility.

Another dragon dived from the sky above. A dragon she knew, one of the strong ones. One of the dragons that had come from her nest place. It shot down like an arrow and smashed into the closest dragon behind her, sending them both tumbling toward the ground. She heard the shrieks of other dragons echoing around the valleys, and with them came a surge of excitement. The dragons behind her were all gone, spiraling down together, snapping and lashing at her nest-mate.

She felt a shriek of terror from one of the Little Ones, abruptly cut to nothing. Then they were all gone, too far behind for her to hear their thoughts anymore.

The excitement faded. The Little One held in her claws was calmer now, and her own thoughts were less confused. A part of her wanted to go back and play with these new dragons, but the Little One's thoughts were clear: it wanted to get away. Far, far away. It didn't know which way she should go and it didn't care, so she flew whichever way caught her eye, along valleys, between mountains, over lakes. She'd never seen this land before, or anything like it, with all its strange shapes and colors and so much sparkling rushing water. She dragged the tip of her tail through shimmering mirrors, soared and dived and snapped at waterfalls, and spiraled around mountains, riding the currents of rising air.

Eventually the light faded, the sun set and the Little One's thoughts went quiet. She could feel herself slowly getting too warm, but the landscape was simply too fresh and exciting to ignore, and so she flew on, playing with it until the heat inside her was positively uncomfortable. Then she landed by a lake. She carefully put the Little One down on the ground, out in the open where she could see him, and bounded into the delicious ice-cold water. She splashed and played under the stars until she was cool again, and then curled up around the Little One and went to sleep.

She dreamed. Far, far away, things were happening. Immense things. Somehow she was a part of them, but they were so far away, she couldn't see them, couldn't hear them, couldn't remember them. She tried to fly toward them, but they kept moving away, eluding her, darting out of the way when she lunged for them.

Abruptly the sun was in the sky again, creeping over the surrounding peaks. She yawned and stretched out her tail and arched her back. The Little One was awake again. She could feel its thoughts. It was hungry.

Yes. Hungry. *She* was hungry too. She looked at the Little One and bared her teeth, as she always did when it was feeding time.

"I'm sorry, Snow. You'll have to find your own breakfast."

She looked around. She didn't understand most of the

noises that the Little Ones made, but sometimes their
thoughts were enough. He didn't have any food for her. He
was in pain too. And he was afraid. She didn't like those
thoughts. They made her feel anxious, and so she stopped
listening to them. She thought about being hungry instead,
waiting for the Little One to do something about it. When
he didn't, she bared her teeth at him again.

"Hunt," he said. "You have to hunt."

Hunt. She knew that noise. It meant flying and chasing
and, yes! Catching and killing and eating.

She rose onto all fours and then lowered her neck, inviting the Little One to climb onto her back.

"I can't, Snow. I'm a Scales, not a rider. I'm not allowed."

The noises made no sense. *Hunt* meant that a Little One
sat on her back and told her where to go. She lowered her
neck even more, rubbing it against the stones on the ground.

"They'd put me to death if they knew." The Little One
started to walk in circles. Its thoughts were confused, still laced
with pain, still frightened. "Only riders ride dragons. That's the
law. We should go back. What happened? Were we attacked?"
It shook its head. "Oh, I wish you could speak. What if they're
still there? The queen won't be back yet, will she? Oh, what to
do? I can't ride with you, Snow. There's no saddle; I'd fall. But
we can't stay here, and you can't find your way home on your
own. I don't even know where we are. Do *you* know where we
are?"

She rubbed her neck against the ground again and bared
her teeth once more. *Hunt. Hungry.*

"You want to eat. Yes, you must be hungry. Oh, but there
aren't any alchemists here. You have to drink the water they
make for you. You'll get sick otherwise. We'll have to go
back."

Hunt. Hungry. She made the gestures again. She was
starting to get frustrated, and the Little One's thoughts
were confusing her. She couldn't make any sense of them.

"I can't climb on your back, Snow. There's no harness.
I can't reach." The Little One walked to her left foreclaws and tried to open them. She didn't understand
what he wanted to do, then she caught a picture from his
mind, of flying through the air at night, and she was carrying him.

Yes. The way they'd come here. Carefully she raised herself onto her back legs and held out her foreclaws. The Little One nodded and made noises, and in his thoughts she saw that she'd understood him. He climbed into her claws, and she gently closed them around him.

"Hunt!" he said.

Hunt. That was something she understood.

24

A MEMORY OF FLAMES

They hunted. She ate. The Little One ate too, and then they climbed into the sky together again. The Little One wanted to go somewhere, but it didn't know which way to go, so she flew again as the fancy took her, into a wilderness of crags and broken stone and boulders the size of castles. She tried to hunt there too, but the land was barren and empty. When night fell, she found a place to land and went to sleep. The dreams came again, as distant as ever.

The next day they flew back out among the valleys and rivers. It rained. She liked that, liked the feel of it. The Little One started telling her which way to go. She understood its thoughts: *left, straight, right, up, down.* She knew the noises too, but when they were racing through the air, the noises were all lost in the wind, and she had to pluck the thoughts out of the Little One's head. She began to wonder whether this Little One was somehow broken. The other Little Ones that sat on her back had thoughts that were much clearer.

"We're lost," said the Little One. She didn't understand, but she could see in his thoughts that he was anxious. He was always anxious. Mostly she blocked him out.

They looked for dragons but they didn't find any. The next day was the same. And the next. But at night, when she slept, something was beginning to change. The dreams were coming closer. She didn't notice it at first, but after a few days a strange understanding came to her. She wanted the dreams. More than anything else, she wanted them. They were important. More important than food or shelter or even than the Little One. She didn't know why; they simply were. With that one revelation came another. They would come to her as long as she stayed here, away from the others, alone.

The day after that she chose her own way to fly. Instinct drove her toward ever higher places. The Little One was even more upset than usual. It shouted at her. It was angry with her, and that made her feel very bad. She was supposed to do what the Little Ones wanted, and this Little One was the most special Little One of them all, the one who'd been with her since she'd first opened her eyes.

That night the dreams were even closer. She could almost smell them, almost touch them. They were filled with fire and ash and burning flesh. In the morning, when she woke up, she left the Little One behind and went to hunt alone. She felt its anguish and despair as it watched her fly away. It was still there when she came back. It felt joy to see her return and made lots of noises that she didn't understand. When she slept again, the dreams finally let her touch them.

SHE WAS A TINY PART OF *something vast. She couldn't see or hear, but she could feel the thoughts of hundreds of dragons, bright and sharp and clear. She could feel other beings too, huge and powerful. Far beneath them she felt a hum of lesser thoughts. Little Ones, she realized with surprise, but that didn't make any sense, because the Little Ones seemed so dull and dim next to the other dragons, and the truth she knew was the other way around.*

She tried to grasp the dream, to unravel it, but it fluttered away only for another to come in its place.

She was flying. The air around her was thick with dragons, and on the back of each was a single rider clad in silver. She wheeled and dived and saw that the ground far below was alive. It was crawling, heaving, moving as far as she could see with Little Ones. Thousands upon thousands. Millions upon millions.

Arrows. She closed her eyes and felt them batter against her scales.

She flew over their heads as she would skim over a forest. Little Ones wrapped up in their crude skins of metal. Spears and axes rattled off her scales. She opened her mouth and let the fire burst out of her, filling the world with screams, filling her heart with joy. Everywhere other dragons were doing the same. She could feel the power from the man of silver on her back, driving her on, urging her to kill, kill . . .

The Little Ones were so many. She burned them by the hundred and they died, and the dead were swallowed up by the horde as though they'd never existed.

And then the dead rising back to life, burned and broken, turning on the living, grasping and clawing. The silver creature on her back was making it so. He laughed, and so did she.

And then something happened, and the silver creature on her back wasn't there anymore, and her wings wouldn't fly, and she couldn't move or think, as though a giant claw had seized her mind and was slowly crushing her.

She remembered crashing into the ground, scattering Little Ones around her, as the claws in her mind sank deeper, and then she remembered nothing.

No. Not nothing. She was an egg again. She was a tiny part of something vast. She couldn't see or hear, but she could still feel the thoughts of hundreds of dragons, bright and sharp and clear.

SHE WOKE UP. MOST OF THE sky was still dark, although the first glimmers of dawn were peeking through between the mountains. The dreams were still there in her head, hundreds of them. They didn't feel like dreams now; they felt like memories. But that couldn't be right. There weren't even a hundred other dragons in her nesting place, never mind a thousand. They didn't feel the same either. The dragons in her dreams had thoughts that shone like cut diamonds. The dragons of her nesting place were simple and dull.

She'd never flown far from her nesting place. She knew that. She hadn't been to the places she was remembering.

She'd never felt the presence of one of these silver men whose minds burned like the sun. As for flying over a sea of Little Ones, burning them . . .

Above all the rest, that memory stayed in her mind. She'd enjoyed it. More than that; it was the most exhilarating thing she'd ever done.

But she hadn't done it. She couldn't have done it. They were dreams, not memories, and they couldn't be real. She struggled to make sense of it, but it was far too difficult, and she was already hungry again. She got hungry a lot out here in the mountains. There was plenty to eat, though, if you knew where to look.

She launched herself into the sky as soon as the sun was up, leaving the Little One behind again. She felt his sadness as she went. He didn't like to be left on his own. She didn't understand that. In her nesting place there were always other dragons nearby, and Little Ones too. Even at night in the dark she felt the presence of their thoughts. She'd never been as alone as she was here, and yet she'd never felt so strangely wonderful.

Without the Little One to slow her, she roamed far on her hunts. She looked for river valleys and then followed them, soaring high in the sky, watching and waiting for prey to emerge from the forests to drink. Sometimes it would be a bear, sometimes a few deer, sometimes a herd of snappers. She had to be careful because the animals were never far from the edge of the forest, and once they got among the trees they were as good as lost. So she'd watch them for a while until she was sure they were coming out to drink, and then she'd tuck in her wings and dive. If she could, she'd seize them with her claws and bite off their heads. If they saw her coming and ran, she'd lash at them with her tail, wrapping it around them or sending them flying through the air to pounce on while they were still stunned. If she had to, she'd burn them. They tasted better raw, though.

Today the sky was gray and a steady rain was falling. Rain and clouds were good. She could fly a lot lower before anyone would see her, and that meant they had less time to get out of the way when she fell out of the sky at them. She ate well, and yet something drew her on, farther and farther down the valleys, as if a part of her knew that something was waiting for her.

There was. She'd flown for half the day, perhaps a hundred miles, when she felt the tickle of stray thoughts. Little Ones. When she looked down, she couldn't see them, only the endless treetops and the little scar of the river flowing between them. She circled down toward the trees and finally landed in the river, peering into the gloom of the forest. Her eyes found nothing, but she knew nonetheless. They were close enough that she could feel their thoughts, each one of them. And they didn't even know she was there.

For a while she wondered what to do. Then she launched herself up into the sky once more.

25

CINDERS AND ASHES

The dragon trotted a few paces down the river, sending boulders splashing and tumbling, and then stopped and watched them. The air stank of damp charcoal. Here and there, as they dashed for the shelter of the forest, Sollos had to step over charred remains that had once been men and women. Outsiders burned by a dragon. The sight brought back too many memories. It set him on edge.

"Bastard," grunted Kemir.

Sollos shook his head. "There has to be a rider. I told you, dragons don't flamestrike unless someone tells them to, and they don't burn their prey. They like their meat fresh."

They peered through the trees. "Should we go back and tell Rider Rod?" asked Kemir. "Or would it be more fun to lurk here and see what happens?"

"No point." Sollos clucked his tongue. "It's leaving." He ran back through the trees to the river. By the time he got there the dragon was already airborne. He watched it go, skimming along the bottom of the valley, barely above the treetops, until it vanished around a bend. *South,* he thought. *It went south.*

He looked behind him, back down the river. He could see the riders and their alchemist now, picking their way through the stones.

"Sollos!"

He couldn't see Kemir through the trees but he heard the urgency. He darted back into the shelter of the trees. "What?"

"Survivor. Sort of."

Kemir, when Sollos found him, was kneeling beside a tree. Propped up there with him was an Outsider. Given how badly the man was burned, it was a miracle the man wasn't dead.

"Shit! Give him some water!"

Kemir grunted. "Done that. He's not going to last. His mind's already gone. He keeps wittering about the dragon talking to him."

The man groaned and nodded. "The dragon spoke. It spoke in my head."

"See." Kemir shrugged. "Gone."

"Go and get the alchemist. He might be able to do something."

"*You* go and get the alchemist."

"Get the alchemist!" Sollos pushed Kemir away and crouched beside the dying man. "We saw the dragon. A white dragon. It left when we arrived. Did it do this?"

"No, it was a careless bloke with a pipe," muttered Kemir. "Daft bugger."

Sollos stood up. This time he shoved Kemir toward the river, screaming at him. "Go and get the fucking alchemist!"

Kemir jogged off grumbling. Sollos sat down beside the man again.

"We're getting help. Did the white dragon do this?"

The man nodded. He whispered something, too quietly for Sollos to hear, until Sollos bent over and almost pressed his ear to the burned man's lips. "It spoke. I heard it speak."

"Who was riding it?"

The man shook his head.

"Was it a dragon-knight?"

The man shook his head again. "No rider," he breathed.

"A man then. Not a knight but a man." *The Scales. We never found the body.*

Another shake of the head. "No ... rider ... just ... dragon ... on ... its ... own."

Sollos had never heard of such a thing. Maybe Kemir was right. The man had to be in unbelievable pain judging from his burns. Maybe his mind *had* already gone.

"It spoke." The man sighed and closed his eyes, and for a moment Sollos thought he was gone. Then his lips moved again. "It spoke in my head. I heard it. It came for Maryk."

"Maryk? Who's Maryk?"

The man didn't answer. His chest was still rising and falling, but his breaths were fast and shallow and ragged. Sollos stood up. "Kemir!" *Where's that cursed alchemist?*

The alchemist was too late, of course. Sollos watched the man's chest heave one last time and then he was still. He'd been gone a few minutes by the time Kemir returned with the alchemist and the dragon-knights.

"He's dead," said Sollos. He looked at Kemir. "You told them what we saw?"

"I told them they owe us a bag of gold."

Semian sneered. "All we've seen is the aftermath of a fire. For all I know you're lying and the white was never here."

"If you'd been a bit quicker," snapped Sollos, "this man might have told you the same story."

Kemir pointed up through the trees. "If your dragon-riders up there didn't see it, they need new eyes."

"Um ... how long has this man been dead?" asked the alchemist.

"Our dragon-riders are elsewhere, as I'm sure you noticed. And as for this man, perhaps I should look him over for wounds, in case you slid a knife into him to make sure he couldn't contradict you." Rider Semian cocked his head.

"So there's no one watching to see what happens to you?" Kemir looked ready to hit him. The alchemist was kneeling down beside the burned man now.

"Tread very carefully, sell-sword. Before you raise your hand against me, I would remind you that there are six of us and only two of you."

Kemir gave him a nasty look. "I wouldn't dream of sullying my sword with you, *rider*. Why would I, when all I need to do is nothing at all?"

The alchemist picked up the dead man's hand by the wrist and held it to his cheek.

"You're a long way from your eyrie here, rider. All I need to do is watch and laugh from a distance while you—"

Sollos tugged sharply on Kemir's arm. "Enough. Leave them."

Kemir snorted. "I'd like nothing better."

"I require an, um, assistant," said the alchemist. He was squatting by the dead man now, and was pulling things out of his pack.

"You would, would you?" sneered Rider Semian. "Then let us part ways. You clearly have nothing to contribute after all. We will simply return to our search from the air. It'll be *us* watching *you.*"

"Your, um, *help,* sell-sword."

The alchemist was offering Sollos a short curved knife, the sort he might have used for paring fruit. Sollos took it. "What do you want?"

The alchemist tore open a square of waxed paper. Inside was some black powder, which he sprinkled into a small clay cup. He held it out to Sollos. "Knife."

Sollos took the cup and gave him the knife. With a grimace the alchemist drew the edge along the flesh of his arm.

"Hold the cup so that it catches the blood." The alchemist clenched his fist. Blood ran down his arm to his elbow. When it dripped into the cup, the powder hissed.

"What is this?" Sollos frowned.

"None of, um, your concern, sell-sword, that's what."

"Looks like witchcraft to me," muttered Kemir. He took a step away. Even the dragon-knights had fallen silent.

"He's dead," said Sollos. "Potions can't help him. If you'd come sooner . . ."

The alchemist glared at him. "Where did you get your name, sell-sword? Sollos. It's an, er, alchemist's name, not a soldier's. Clearly a, uh, mistake. Or did you choose it yourself?" Inside the cup the powder and the blood had mixed into a paste. The alchemist lifted his arm and wrapped a strip of white linen tightly around his wound. "Um. You're right that it's too late to help him live. But not too late to help him talk."

"Master Huros?" Semian sounded edgy. "I am not easy with this. Blood magic is—"

"Is what?"

"The queen does not favor such practices. They are outlawed."

"In, er, her realm perhaps. Not here." The alchemist gave a little sigh. "If I smear this on his tongue, he will speak. Um . . . if my means don't please you, rider, I am sorry." He tugged the cup from Sollos's fingers. "Take this and burn it, if you prefer."

Semian fidgeted. After a few seconds, when he didn't take the cup, the alchemist shrugged. He dipped his finger into the paste and, before anyone could stop him, smeared it in the dead man's mouth.

26

AWAKENING

Day by day, Kailin watched Snow change. Dragons, he'd been told, were like little children. If that was so then Snow was growing up fast right in front of him. She was frightening, and yet he felt a strange pride and a sense of wonder watching her. There had never been a dragon like her, not with her purity of color. She was sleek and perfect, and now she was becoming something else as well. Often she terrified him, but at the same time he was her Scales. He'd been waiting for her since she first started tapping her way out of her egg and into the world, and he'd been with her for nearly ten years now. Slowly he understood. Their roles had changed. He'd cared for her, nurtured her, fed her, and now she was doing the same for him.

They developed a routine. Each morning as the sun rose over the mountains, Snow uncurled and launched herself into the air. Kailin watched her go, peering into the sky long after she'd vanished. Then he sat by his fire, drank some warm water and ate some leftover meat. After that there really wasn't much to do but wait for Snow and wonder if today was the day when she wouldn't come back. Usually he made his way across the mountain, through the snows, to the nearest stand of trees and collected some more wood. When the wind blew, cold enough to flay the skin off his flesh, he huddled up in the lee of some nearby rocks and simply waited. When Snow came back, she always knew where to find him. She would be almost too hot to touch, and her warmth melted the snows, dried his clothes and the firewood, and stopped him from freezing in the night. Each day she brought him food to eat, the headless remains of some animal she'd caught. He'd cook it over his fire, and she'd watch him. When he was done, she'd swallow what was left in a single gulp. He knew perfectly well that without her he'd quickly starve or freeze to death.

He talked to her when she was there. Not expecting any answer, but simply because the mountain was so cold and lonely and he felt better hearing the sound of his own voice. Sometimes, from the way she looked at him, he wondered if she was listening.

He got his answer to that when he trod on a loose stone. The first thing he knew, one of his feet was sliding out from under him. The world tumbled, hit him on the head and wound up lying on its side, dim and blurry.

Hurt? asked a voice inside his head.

He tried to move, but for a moment that didn't work. *Yes,* he decided. *I am hurt.*

The next thing he knew, Snow was standing over him, the tip of her face inches from his own, blotting out the sky, the scorching-hot wind of her breath almost pinning him to the ground. He put up a hand, flinched away, and she retreated.

Is it hurt? asked the voice again.

He groaned and sat up. His head was starting to throb. When he touched it, his fingers came away with blood on them. Slowly, he looked up at Snow.

"Did you speak?" He laughed and then winced. Dragons couldn't speak except in myth.

Its head is broken. Is it going to—

Am I going to what? The thought formed inside his head, but the last part of it didn't make any sense. Something to do with getting hotter and hotter and fading away and then waking up wrapped up tight inside an egg.

Snow peered at him and cocked her head. *Die?*

To Kailin, it seemed as though a giant hand had slapped him in the face. He went numb. The pain in his head washed away. He stood up and staggered away from Snow. "You . . . you . . . I heard you thinking."

Snow snorted and shook her head, the way she did when she was excited. *It hears! Understands!*

Kailin was trembling. "You understand me! You understand Kailin!"

Kailin? He got a sense of incomprehension.

"That's my name."

Name? What is a name?

Kailin didn't know how to answer that, but Snow didn't seem to mind. She seemed to pluck the answer out of his head.

All Little Ones have names. Do I have a name?

"Snow."

Snow. Why?

Kailin picked up a handful of snow. "Because you're white." He held it up to show her and then pressed it against the wound on his head.

Hurt? He could feel the tension in her thought.

"A little bit."

THEY TRIED TO TALK, ON into the night until the sun was long gone and stars filled the sky. Most of the time Kailin couldn't make sense of the images that flashed in his head, nor did Snow seem to understand him, no matter how ferociously he thought. He would feel her frustration build up inside her, and then something would burst and their thoughts would somehow align. It would last for a few seconds, maybe a little more before they drifted apart. Eventually he fell asleep, drained. The last thing he felt from Snow was how awake she was, how filled with wonder and awe.

For days afterward the thoughts that appeared in his head were strange and alien. They rarely made sense, and he would have to ask again and again what Snow was trying to tell him. As time went by, though, they grew sharper, brighter, clearer. He talked to Snow whenever she was there, and she responded. Every day she was changed, filled with new discoveries. Clearer, more articulate, more intelligent than she'd been the day before. A voracious sense of amazement and adventure infected her every thought, and his as well. No Scales had ever experienced what he was seeing, this blossoming.

It is like a veil is lifted in my mind each night, she told him one day as she left to hunt. He spent the rest of the day wondering what use a dragon would have for a veil, until he understood: she wasn't hearing his words anymore, she was seeing into his mind. And when she answered him, she was looking inside him for things that *he* would understand.

"We have to go home," he told her when she came back from her hunt with fresh blood still on her claws. "I have to show you to the others."

I am different. Why?

"I don't know, Snow. It's a miracle."

Miracle? He felt her confusion. *No. Little One Kailin, I feel as if I have awoken from a sleep that has lasted a hundred lifetimes. I do not understand how I have awoken, nor do I understand how I fell into such a slumber. Nor even how much more is to come.*

"We'll go back home. We can ask Master Huros or one of the other alchemists, or even Eyrie-Master Isentine—"

NO! She snapped her jaws. Kailin scrabbled away from her in sudden terror, before she bowed her head to the ground, a dragon gesture of submission. *I did not mean to frighten you, Little One Kailin. I will not hurt you, but nor will I go back to that place.*

"Why?" Kailin watched warily.

My brothers and sisters there are awake yet asleep. I could not bear to be that way again.

"But all dragons are like that. Except you. You're the miracle."

No, Little One Kailin. I do not think so. I think we were all this way, a long time ago. I have dreams. Memories of other lives I've lived. Many, many lives, but all of them long ago. I remember when my kind flew in our hundreds. I remember the silver gods and the breaking of the very earth itself, then a hundred lives of bright thoughts and flying free. And then, Little One Kailin, something changed, and everything since has faded into an eternal dull blur, dim and impenetrable. Out of reach. All my kin are still sleepwalking their lives. Somehow, you have awoken me. How, Little One Kailin? How did you awaken me? I will not return to my kind until I have that answer. Until I can bring that knowledge back to them.

"I don't know."

I know. Your thoughts speak for themselves. There are Little Ones who know far more, who may have the answers. You know of them. You wish to take me before them.

"You would be the wonder of the realms."

I am not so sure, Little One Kailin. Would you like to see the memories I have of your kind from my lives long ago?

"Of course."

Visions burst into his head. He saw armies of men, hundreds of thousands, more than anything he could have imagined. He saw himself land among them, lashing with his tail, scattering them like leaves, scores of them, smashing them to pulp in their little metal shells. He felt the fire build in his throat and burst forth. The air grew heavy with the stench of scorched flesh. And he felt the appetite growing inside him. For more, more, more . . .

He screamed. The vision abruptly vanished.

Do you understand? In my dream your kind were never anything more than prey, and your thoughts were always filled with hopeless terror. Why would you wish to return to such a world?

"No, no, no!" Kailin shook his head. "Dragons and men have lived together for hundreds of years. We helped you. You were dying. We looked after you. We've always looked after you. No." He shook his head again. "Go back to the eyrie, Snow. Our queen is good and wise. She'll know what to do."

The dragon cocked her head. *You have seen what we were, and yet you are more afraid of this queen? Curious. I can see that you truly believe everything you say. Perhaps . . .* Snow lifted her head off the ground. She rose onto her back legs and flapped her wings a few times. A sign of warning.

No, she said at last. *I will not go back to the place you call the eyrie, Little One Kailin. Not yet.*

27

THE BURNED MAN

The dead man's lips began to move. He gave a soft sigh.
The dragon-knights shifted away, shuffling uncomfortably. Sollos heard them muttering under their breath.

"He's all, um, yours," said the alchemist. "I don't know, um, how long he'll last. He hasn't been dead for long, so you've probably got at least, um, half an hour."

Rider Semian was looking at the dead man with a mixture of horror and disgust. "Ask him what happened here."

"You can ask him yourself, if you wish, rider."

Semian's lips curled in distaste. "No, Master Huros. You made this abomination. It's yours now. The sell-swords will guard you. We will return to the river."

The alchemist shrugged and turned his attention to the dead man.

"He kept on about the dragon speaking to him," said Sollos, when the knights had gone. "It was the white. He said there wasn't a rider. And something about someone called Maryk. I don't know what that was."

"Leave me with him, Sword-Master Sollos. This isn't for your ears."

Sollos snorted. "You heard Rider Semian. We're to watch over you."

"Thank you, but that's not necessary."

"Master Huros, there *probably* aren't any snappers or wolves lurking around after a dragon's been here, but you never know. I don't overly mind if you get yourself eaten, but I'm quite sure that Rider Semian would delight in holding us to account for it."

The alchemist shrugged. "Stay if you must." He settled himself and turned to the dead man. "Um. What's your name, corpse?"

"Biyr," said the dead man. Sollos shivered. The dead man spoke perfectly normally. He sounded much better than when he'd actually been alive and racked with the agony of his burns.

"Well, Biyr, what happened here?"

"A dragon came out of nowhere. We had no warning. It burned us. I was walking away from our tree shelters when the fire came."

"Did you see the dragon?"

"Yes."

"And, er, what color was it?"

"White."

The alchemist nodded, pleased. "Did you see who was riding it?"

"No one was riding it."

Huros frowned and shook his head. "Ah. There must have been a, um, rider. Perhaps you missed it? Um . . . When did you see the dragon? When it was in the air? Did it land?"

"It came down in the river after it burned us. I saw it then, between the trees."

"Did you see it in the air?"

"No."

The alchemist nodded. "There, you see. Um . . . whoever was riding her had probably already dismounted. Besides, it's not a good view from here through the trees to the river. I'm sure you could see something the size of a, uh, dragon clearly enough, but it would be very easy to miss a man."

"I didn't see anyone get on its back before it went," said Sollos quietly.

"That's because it didn't have a harness on," grumbled Kemir. "I kept telling—"

"It spoke," murmured the dead man.

Huros shook his head. "Dragons don't speak."

"It spoke in my head. I heard it. It came for Maryk."

"Um, no. You must be mistaken. That cannot be. Dragons do not speak."

The alchemist's knuckles had gone very white.

Sollos asked, "Who's Maryk?"

"One of us," said the dead man. "The dragon came after him."

"How do you know?"

"That's what it said. It had come for Maryk. I heard its voice inside me, full of hate and fury."

The alchemist shifted uncomfortably and frowned.

"Was this Maryk here?" asked Kemir.

"Yes. He was in the shelters," said the dead man.

The alchemist raised a hand. "Enough. Um . . . sell-sword, go and bring Rider Semian to me."

"So he's probably dead then." Sollos made a face. "Pity."

"You should leave now," said the alchemist.

Kemir grunted. "I want to know about this Maryk. Where did he come from? Why did the dragon want him?"

"I want you to, um, leave us now, sell-sword. Bring Rider Semian. Um, right now." The alchemist was chewing his lip in agitation.

"Do dead men lie?"

The alchemist turned and looked at Kemir. For a timid man, there was something very fierce in his eyes. And frightened too. "About as much as living ones do, sell-sword. I said go!"

Kemir rolled his eyes. "I'm only asking. Maybe when Rider Rod comes back, you could ask Crispy here whether we stabbed him. Just to make sure, you know."

"There are no, er, wounds," said Huros, between gritted teeth. "It is patently obvious that you did not kill him. Now *go!*"

Sollos turned and left, pulling Kemir away with him.

Kemir chuckled to himself.

"Well, he didn't seem very happy."

"Do you *have* to annoy them so much?"

"Do I annoy them?"

"Does the sun rise in the morning? One day, one of those dragon-knights is going to lose his temper with you."

"Let him. I'll put an arrow through him before he can remember which side he buckled his sword."

"Yes. And what will you do about the other five?"

"Run like buggery, I expect." Kemir laughed again and slapped Sollos on the back.

"I'm not finding this funny." Sollos wrinkled his nose and loosened his shoulders. "Something isn't right about this."

"You keep saying that. As far as I'm concerned, what's not right is that we're helping dragon-knights."

"We've been helping dragon-knights for months, remember?"

"Then let's just say I liked this work much better when we were helping dragon-knights by killing other dragon-knights. They're so stupid. They deserve to die."

Sollos shook his head and pulled away, walking briskly toward the river.

"Well they *are,*" Kemir shouted after him. "No obvious wounds? That's easy. Force open a man's mouth, drive a skewer up into the soft bit in the roof of his mouth and wiggle it about a bit. Or in through his nose, if he's totally out of it. Or up his arse, like Rider Rod. Need a bigger skewer for that, of course."

"Will you shut up!" Sollos shook himself in exasperation. Whatever they both thought of dragon-knights, a fight wasn't going to help anyone, and Kemir was going to have to understand that sooner or later. Preferably sooner.

"Sell-sword!" Sollos emerged from the trees. Rider Semian was there, waiting for him. Sollos sighed. He couldn't bring himself to bow, so he settled for a slight nod.

"Rider. Master Huros has requested your presence. I suppose he has information he thinks you should hear."

Semian looked at him askance and Sollos braced himself for the inevitable scornful tirade, but it didn't come. "Very well, sell-sword. You can make yourself useful here instead. I require a fire."

Sollos looked around at the smoldering embers all

around him. "That shouldn't be too difficult." *Even for a dragon-knight.*

"I need smoke, sell-sword, and lots of it. No more walking through these cursed riverbeds. We're finishing this search as we should have started it. On dragonback."

28

NADIRA

The Outsiders came while Snow was hunting. She'd taken Kailin down from the snows of the mountainside into the rain and the constant damp of the mountain valleys. Water was everywhere. Tiny streams boiled down the forested slopes into wide rushing rivers and long still lakes. Whatever wasn't a river or a lake or a sheer piece of rock had a tree growing out of it. Vines grew on the trees and tufts of grass grew on the vines, and all of it was moving and alive.

Kailin was sunning himself on a boulder beside a river when he heard the first scream. He looked up and saw a woman running through the river toward him, leaping from one stone to the next. As he sat and stared at her, he saw that she wasn't alone. Half a dozen men were a little ways behind her.

"Help me!" she shouted.

Heading straight for him, she reached his boulder and fell to her knees, clutching his hand. She looked exhausted and terrified. "I don't know who you are, but help me, please. They're going to kill me." Then she looked at him, saw him properly, saw his hard flaking skin and screamed.

Kailin screwed up his face and thought of Snow, but he felt nothing. The dragon must be miles away. He stood, paralyzed. As the men came closer, they slowed down. There were six of them and they were armed with clubs and knives. Evil anticipation spread across their faces. He stared back, unable to move.

One of the men looked him up and down with obvious revulsion. "What the fuck are you?" Then he jumped forward and swung a club at Kailin's head. Kailin raised his arms to fend off the blow. The club glanced off his elbow. Everything from his fingers to his shoulder erupted in pain and then went numb. He whimpered, and then the rest were on him, beating him down to the ground until everything faded away into a sea of pain.

"Nice one, Maryk," he heard someone say.

KAILIN RETURNED TO THE WORLD gradually, reluctantly. His arms felt as though they were being wrenched out of their sockets. His ribs ached. His head was filled with thunder and lightning.

He opened his eyes. He was hanging from a branch by a rope tied around his wrists, about ten feet off the ground. A thick canopy of leaves and branches blotted out the sky above, filtering the sunlight to gloomy shadows. He was facing the river, overlooking the boulder where the men had beaten him senseless. They were still there, taking it in turns with the woman. Her face was puffy and swollen, and there were fresh scars on her back. They were cursing her, but they swore with such venomous hate that Kailin could barely understand them. *Whore. Thief.* That was all.

When they were finally finished with her, two of them held her down while a third pulled out a knotted length of rope and started to whip her. She spat and kicked at them then, but it was a short one-sided fight, and in the end all that was left were her screams. Eventually even those stopped. Her back was a bloody mess, but the man with the rope only stopped when one of the others put a hand on his arm.

"Leave her. She's almost dead already."

The one with the rope wiped it clean, then used it to hog-tie the woman. Kailin closed his eyes as they turned away from her, looking up toward him.

"Enjoy watching, did you, cripple?" shouted one of them.

"Hey! Thief! Wake up!" A stone hit him in the stomach, and then another one, this time in the shoulder. He managed not to flinch.

"Ah, leave him. He's not going anywhere."

"Look at him! He's diseased."

"Well *I'm* not touching him."

"Was it worth it, thief? Thing? Whatever you are? Look! Look what she got you! Almost nothing. Here, you can have it. Make sure you give your whore her half. She worked for it." Kailin had no idea what they were talking about.

"When the snappers come by, don't forget to pull your feet up. They can reach you if they're hungry enough to jump. Your whore's not going to be enough for them."

"They probably wouldn't touch him. Look at him. Diseased, I tell you."

They went away laughing. When the voices were long gone, Kailin opened his eyes. The woman was still there, tied up, motionless. His arms felt as though they were on fire.

"Hello? Hey?"

She didn't answer, but he saw her move, very slightly.

"Hey! Hey!"

After a while he gave up. He screwed up his face against the pain across his shoulders and tried to pretend he was somewhere else. Maybe that was what the woman was doing, why she was ignoring him. Not that either of them could help the other. All he could do was wait for Snow.

By the time she came, he was so consumed with his own misery he didn't even notice until she landed. Until he heard the woman's screams over his own whimpering.

Little One Kailin! She was crashing down the river, running on her hind legs, flapping her wings for extra speed, straight toward him. With her wings outstretched, Snow was almost as wide as the river, a hundred feet across and more.

The woman's shrieks grew louder and more hysterical, until they turned into a high-pitched keening wail.

You are hurt!

"Get me down from this tree!" shouted Kailin.

How did this happen? Snow skidded to a stop, flapping her wings and scattering boulders the size of Kailin's head.

Her head darted forward; her teeth closed around the branch above Kailin's head. She bit through it as though it was putty and lowered Kailin carefully to the ground. Kailin hugged his arms to his chest. The relief was blissful.

I cannot untie you. Snow peered at Kailin, and then sniffed at the woman. *Where did this one come from? Why is it bound? Is it food?*

The woman's wailing subsided to whimpers.

"Snow, leave her alone. Don't hurt her. She's terrified."

I know. It feels pleasant. It is the way I remember it.

"Talk to her." Kailin struggled to his feet and started to walk back into the trees. "Let her know you don't mean her any harm."

You are in great pain, Little One Kailin. I feel it. I cannot help you. Why did you do this?

He could feel the confusion in Snow's thoughts. The dragon had no idea.

"Other men did this to us. Bad men, Snow. I don't know why." He tilted his head toward the woman. "She might." He winced and walked gingerly among the stones until he found one sharp enough to cut the rope around his wrist. It was painstaking work, but at least when he was done the woman wasn't screaming anymore. She was looking at Snow with an expression of bewildered terror. Kailin went over and unpicked the knots that bound her. Once she was free he slumped down against a boulder. The woman hugged her knees. She was shivering badly. He tried to give her his flying furs, but when he came close, she shrank away. He put them close by and then stepped away. Her back was still a bloody mess.

"I'm Kailin," he said. "This is Snow. She's my dragon."

The woman looked at him as though he was mad. She seemed to be almost as afraid of him as she was of the dragon.

Her name is Nadira. She is terrified of you. She thinks you mean to hurt her. She sees you in armor, with a sword and a lance, as most men who ride dragons clothe themselves. And she thinks there is something wrong with you.

He sat down on a stone and watched her carefully. "I'm not a rider; I'm just a Scales. Do you know what that means? It means I look after a dragon. I do the feeding and the grooming. Like a stable hand. I look the way I do because of her. When they come out of their eggs, dragons carry a disease. It did this to me. Even with the potions from the alchemists, it does this. Don't be afraid, though. This happened to me a long time ago. It's dormant now. Until the next hatchling I'm given to care for. I'm not allowed to ride her, by the way. She says your name is Nadira."

She is confused. She doesn't understand how we got to be here. She still believes we will hurt her.

"We got lost," said Kailin. "We came from Queen Shezira's eyrie. I don't suppose you've heard of her . . ."

No.

"Queen Shezira's daughter is marrying King Tyan's son. Snow and I were supposed to be wedding gifts. We were attacked by other dragon-knights. I don't know who they were. We escaped and ran away. We've been lost in these mountains for weeks. I don't suppose you know where we are?" Kailin stretched his shoulders and winced.

Very slightly, the woman shook her head.

Little One Kailin, what is Soul Dust?

"I don't know." Kailin looked at the woman. "What's Soul Dust?"

She flinched and looked away, and Kailin saw her eyes pause on something lying among the rocks. A tiny leather pouch.

Men who make it bought her for pleasure. She wants it. She needs it like food or drink. She took some and ran away. She was being punished for this. Punishment. Revenge. Retribution. Yes, I understand this. It is wasteful. Foolish.

"They did this to her because she stole from them?"

That is what is in her mind. Another Little One, Maryk, he is the one who did this. I see that name in your thoughts too.

"They raped and beat her and left her to die. They left me to die too. Why?"

We are alike. We both miss our own kind in the same way. We miss what they could be, or should be, but not what they truly are. I have to go now, Little One Kailin. I have not finished hunting for the day. I will not be long.

Snow turned and Kailin watched her launch herself down the river, the same way the men had gone. That could have been coincidence, but something in the tenor of Snow's last thoughts said otherwise. She'd gone to find them. She didn't look back, and by the time he made himself stand up and call after her, she was too far away to hear his thoughts anymore.

When she came back, he meant to ask her what she'd done and to tell her that it was wrong, but he never got a chance. Even as the thoughts were forming up in his head, she came crashing into his mind.

More dragons are coming.

29

THE HUNTERS AND THE HUNTED

When the white dragon came back, she caught them all by surprise. Sollos had barely started on the fire when a great shadow flashed over his head. The knights looked up and stared as the dragon wheeled overhead. She was clutching something in one claw, Sollos saw. She flared her wings and stretched out her massive hind claws, swooping down like an eagle toward them. When she landed in the riverbed and took a few steps to steady herself, the mountains seemed to shake. Then she stood there, still, poised on her hind legs, wings not quite fully folded, head raised a little on her long neck, her massive tail stretched out straight behind her for balance.

Sollos retreated slowly from the beginnings of his fire toward the woods. He'd seen dragons stand like that before. So had the riders, who began to fan out across the riverbed.

"How long before your own dragons get here, Rider Semian?" Sollos muttered. Semian wasn't there to answer, but Sollos already knew as much as he needed to. *Not for some time.*

Slowly, the dragon reached down with one forelimb. She opened her claws. There was a man curled up in there.

Holy Ancestors, Sollos thought when the man got up. *It's the Scales.* He looked well enough. A bit stiff and battered perhaps, and he walked a little awkwardly, but for a man stuck on his own in the Worldspine for a month he was remarkably alive. *Maybe having skin as hard as stone that flakes like slate helps with that.*

Rider Semian and Master Huros came running out of the trees. They ignored him and went straight toward the dragon. Kemir came after them and stopped at his shoulder.

"Oh well! That's going to make all this a lot easier." He grinned.

"She's very tense."

"Who?"

"The dragon, you idiot. Look at her."

"Mmmm." Kemir nodded. "Ready to run. Wouldn't you be? Do you suppose she even remembers her knights after all this time. How do you know she's a she—"

Sollos shushed him. The Scales was walking toward the dragon-knights. He seemed very unsure of himself.

"That's enough!" Rider Semian held up a hand and stopped the Scales when they were still a good twenty feet apart. Semian had the alchemist beside him and one other knight. The rest of the riders were still slowly spreading out, edging toward the trees. Sollos did the same.

"Um, what is your name, Scales?" shouted the alchemist.

The Scales replied, but quietly. Sollos couldn't hear him.

"Scales Kailin. We, er, are here to take you home. You and your dragon."

"Queen Shezira will congratulate you herself," called Rider Semian. "Her dragon is still intact, and has not been lost. She will be greatly pleased. There may be a reward."

The Scales said something else. Sollos screwed up his eyes and strained forward, as if that might help him make out what the Scales was saying.

Then Kemir had a hand on his shoulder and was tugging him back toward the forest. "I don't like the way this is going."

"Did you hear him? What did he say?"

"He said no."

Kemir was right; Sollos could see that by the way the alchemist and Rider Semian were standing.

"This is not a request, Scales," shouted Rider Semian. "This is an order!"

Kemir was still edging back into the trees. He was stringing his bow.

The alchemist suddenly stepped forward and walked up to the Scales. Sollos had no idea what they were saying, only that the alchemist looked very determined, and the Scales looked, well, if anything, he looked stunned. Aghast.

Something in the air changed. Sollos felt an irrational anger build up inside him. The Scales was gesturing frantically at the alchemist, trying to make him . . . Trying to make him stop? The dragon had lowered itself to all fours. It was utterly still. Sollos could feel the tension radiating from it like waves of heat.

Kemir put a hand on his shoulder again. "You know what? I think we should back off a little way farther."

"Yes." He took a step backward. Then another. "Yes, I think we should."

When the dragon moved, it was so quick that Sollos barely saw it. Its head and body stayed exactly where they were; its tail, all hundred feet of it, flicked like a whip. In the blink of an eye it flashed over the dragon's head. The tip coiled around the alchemist, lifted him up into the air and held him inches from the dragon's bared teeth. For long seconds everyone froze except for the Scales, who sank to his knees, wrapping his arms around his head. And then everything happened at once.

30

THE WORDMASTER

The City of Dragons stood behind the Adamantine Palace, squashed against the mountains of the Purple Spur and the Diamond Cascade Waterfalls. The city was a small one by the standards of the realms, but rich, filled with jewels and knights, lords and ladies. To either side of both the city and the palace lay the shimmering waters of the Mirror Lakes. To the southwest, the only open approach to the speaker's domain, were the Plains of the Hungry Mountain, the fertile grain basket of the central realms. On a good day a man in the palace looking out of the windows at the top of the Tower of Air could see all the way over them to the Fury River gorge, a hundred miles south of the city. Today, though, someone had built a very tall temporary wooden tower not very far from the palace gates, and the air beyond was hazy and tinged with gray. A keen pair of eyes might have made out two figures standing on the top of the tower. They might too have made out that the haze over the plains was the dust kicked up by the ten thousand marching men of the Adamantine Guard, preparing themselves for the ceremonies of the weeks to come.

It would have taken exceptional vision, though, to see

that those figures on the tower top were the speaker himself, Speaker Hyram, and a master alchemist of the Order of the Scales. Or that the speaker's shaking was worse than usual, that his face was flushed with what might have been excitement but was more probably rage, and that the master alchemist was looking decidedly pale.

"N-Nothing?"

The alchemist was Grand Master Jeiros, Second Lord of the Order of the Scales. The possibility that he might now be the first lord accounted for a good part of his discomfort. He bowed as low as he could without falling over.

"Nothing, Your Holiness. Grand Master Bellepheros stated his conviction before the whole of King Tyan's court. No one tampered with Queen Aliphera's mount before she left and she was not attacked in the air. If there was murder, it did not originate within King Tyan's eyrie."

"A-And that is all?"

"Prince Jehal pressed him hard in front of many witnesses. Master Bellepheros would not say whether Queen Aliphera's death was malice or misfortune, although he did allude to some sly goings-on between Aliphera and Tyan's brother. Prince Jehal was considerably displeased."

The speaker spat. "Tyan's brother? That gelding Meteroa? Nonsense! W-What of Q-Queen Zafir?"

"We have found nothing to implicate her."

Hyram growled. "A-And then B-Bellepheros disappears."

The second lord scraped another bow. "Taken by force. Prince Jehal reports that all his guards were found dead, most with their throats slit. Of the master himself . . ." Jeiros shrugged.

"P-Prince Jehal says!" Hyram spat. "D-Don't believe a word f-from that viper."

"Your Holiness, Master Bellepheros chose his words to the court of King Tyan with great care. Implications were presented, not in what he said but in what he did *not* say. He did *not* say that Queen Aliphera's death was an accident, Your Holiness."

"Of c-course it wasn't!" Hyram stamped impatiently. "D-Do what you need to f-find out who took him, Jeiros. N-Now, concerning the other matter? H-Have you got to the bottom of h-how Prince Jehal is k-killing King Tyan yet?"

Jeiros squirmed. "Your Holiness, there is still no evidence that King Tyan is being poisoned at all." He pursed his lips. "We have learned, Your Holiness, that there may be some truth to the rumors that Prince Jehal has found something that improves his father's condition. It is a little ..." He frowned. "It is unclear, Your Holiness. There are ... there are hints of some potion he has acquired."

Hyram snorted. "I-If it's a potion, i-it's from one of you. G-Get to the point!"

"Your Holiness, that is the point. It does *not* come from the order. We ..." He hesitated, but there was no going back now. "We think it comes from outside the realms."

Hyram's face went dark; he started to cough and his tremors seemed to grow more pronounced. It took a while for Jeiros to realize that the speaker was laughing at him.

"Y-You have singularly f-failed, Master Jeiros. Y-You have no answers for me, a-and now this? S-So be it. Go, M-Master Jeiros. I will summon Queen Zafir and P-Prince Jehal and *I* will f-find out who murdered Aliphera, a-and then I will tell *y-you* which alchemist is making p-potions for Jehal."

The alchemist backed away, bowing as he went. It was a long way to the bottom of the tower, down narrow stairs and rickety ladders. Hyram found himself hoping that the second lord might trip and fall. A broken wrist or some such inconvenience—that would do, nothing more. For all his blathering, Hyram preferred not to lose his second lord as well as his first.

He sighed, alone at last, and let his eyes drift out across the plain. His legions were formed up, twenty phalanxes each of five hundred men. They would be out there every day until the dragon-kings and -queens gathered at the palace to see him pass his mantle on. Part of the legacy that each speaker handed to the next: ten thousand exquisitely trained soldiers, raised from birth to fight. It struck him as strange, watching them, that so many men should dedicate every moment of their lives to such perfection, and yet be content never to fight. Their loyalty, he was assured, was total and unswerving, hammered into them from the moment they could speak. Their strength and their fearlessness too were total, forged in their relentless and brutal years of training, and then quenched in the alchemical potions that emptied their minds of any doubts that might remain; in their legends, even the dragons couldn't stop them. But didn't they secretly hate him? Didn't they despise him? Didn't they look at their own potency and then look at him and wonder, *Who is this fading king? Who is he to leash us?*

He looked away. A year ago he'd have laughed at such thoughts; then, a year ago he'd been a different man. Still strong, still fooling himself that he was younger than his years. Still with dreams that his days as speaker might go on and on, that he might compel Shezira to wed him as the price of naming her as his successor. Or, old treaties and dusty parchments be damned, marrying Aliphera and naming her instead. Still bedding women as the fancy took him, instead of lying helpless in his sheets, stinking of his own soil after one of the fits caught him unawares, screaming for his potboys to clean him.

Now Aliphera was dead, Shezira wouldn't have him, and even the potboys kept running away. In another year or two he'd be like King Tyan, dribbling and useless. How fitting that would be, the two of them, old foes that they were, side by side, forgotten, each lying in his own pool of drool. No, he'd rather die a quick death than that. Let them chop him up and feed him to his own dragons, like the speakers of old, before Speaker Narammed clipped the dragon-priests' wings.

He heard the stairs squeak behind him and turned to see a head emerging from the belly of the tower, up into the sunlight. The head didn't have much hair left, and what there was was white. The face beneath it looked pained and out of breath.

"You called for me, Your Holiness?"

Hyram shook his head. "N-No, Wordmaster Herlian."

"Then I shall take myself back down into the shade, Your Holiness, and you may tell our dear second lord that I shall corner him when he's sitting down one day and rap his ankles with my stick. I am too old to be climbing these stairs. He seemed to think you wished to issue a summons or two."

"T-To Prince J-Jehal and to Queen Z-Zafir, but it could have waited. S-Since you're here, though, come and stand with me."

"If I must, Your Holiness." The wordmaster struggled out onto the roof. "But you'd better tell me what there is to see. My eyes are as old as the rest of me."

"I-I want to know, W-Wordmaster. What will your b-books say of me?"

"Ha!" Herlian's cackle sounded like the snapping of old dry twigs. "If I write them, they'll say you were a foul-tempered little boy who never attended to his lessons, didn't listen to a word his elders said to him and made his tutor's life an endless sea of misery." The wordmaster hobbled to the edge of the tower and looked down. "Long way. Heh. I suppose I might also mention how a headstrong dragon-knight took on the duty that should have fallen to his brother. I know you didn't want it. I don't mean being the speaker, either. I mean being the eldest."

"H-History, Wordmaster, that's all."

"History is all I am, young Master Hyram. If it's flattery you want, get yourself a flatterer to walk up all these stairs. I know what you're thinking. You're thinking that there are books and books full of the stories of Vishmir and other speakers of old. Heh. I don't forget, you see. I still remember how your eyes used to light up when I'd finally consent to read to you about them. Your story will be much shorter, Your Holiness. Ten years of peace and prosperity in which nothing of any great significance happened to the realms, and all the little people were left to live their lives and get old and fat. That is what the story of a truly good speaker should be. Let that be enough."

"I-Is it, though?"

Herlian shrugged. "It is for the rest of us. If it's not enough for you, then tell me what is. I'll write wars for you if you want. Great victories, epic quests, strings of princesses fawning at your feet. Whatever you like. As much glory as you want."

"N-No, Wordmaster, that won't b-be necessary." Hyram shook his head, trying to push away the suffocating weight of hopelessness that seemed to press down on him these days. *That's it, is it? I'll be remembered as a fine speaker, because no one has bothered to write anything else? But then why remember at all?* He sat down, knowing that doing so would allow Herlian to sit as well. "D-Do you have your q-quill? Let us start with a summons to P-Prince Jehal. M-Maybe you can add an execution as a f-footnote to my reign."

31

QUEEN ALIPHERA'S GARDEN

"I have a gift for you." Jehal put on his best smile. Zafir glanced at him through her eyelashes. They were walking together, side by side, among many-colored shrubs and rainbow flower beds. The summer sun was bright and warm and a faint breeze ticked Jehal's nose with strange scents, a heady mixture of perfumes and spices.

"Do you like my gardens?" asked Zafir. "My mother grew them." They walked just far enough apart to be sure they didn't touch, even by accident. Behind them a little knot of Zafir's ladies followed them around, not too close but never so far away that they were out of sight. In case they were needed to testify that nothing improper could possibly have happened.

"Indeed, Your Holiness." He *hated* that, having to call her Holiness just because she was a queen now, and he was a mere prince. That would have to change. "Queen Aliphera's Gardens are justly famous throughout the realms. Even as far north as ..." He let that hang.

"You mean even dear Princess Lystra has heard of them? It defies imagination." Her words had edges like razors. "Is she well, your wife?"

Jehal pretended not to notice Zafir's venom. "When I left, she was a picture of health and very bored."

"You should have brought her with you. It would have been a delight to welcome her as a guest within my walls."

Yes. Especially now that she's carrying my heir. Of course, he didn't know for sure that Zafir knew this; in fact he didn't even know for sure himself, but the signs were there, and as far as he could tell Zafir's spies were making sure that she was at least as well informed as he was. *I should probably ask her whether it's going to be a boy or a girl.*

He smiled again. "She would have been overjoyed, I'm sure. Given her condition, however, I have had to order that she be confined to the palace. It is concern for her health, you see. The risk of miscarriage." Zafir didn't blink. *So that's that, then. She knows.*

Zafir sniffed. "I'm told that my mother was still flying three days before I was born. Queen Shezira probably gave birth to one of her daughters while still in the saddle."

The risk of miscarriage that would come from letting you anywhere near her. "Dear Queen Zafir, it should be plain to you that I've been seeking an excuse to lock my darling wife away since before I married her. Would you deny me my freedom?"

For a moment Zafir didn't answer. Then she stopped and turned to face him, and her face lit up. "Is marriage so unhappy for you?"

"Deeply."

"I'll help you get rid of her then," she said quietly. "I have a debt of that sort, after all."

"In time, my love." Jehal glanced back at the ladies-in-waiting. They were twenty, maybe thirty yards away, chatting among themselves, casting the occasional glance toward their queen. Well out of earshot.

"But not before she gives you an heir?"

"It *does* keep her out of the way, my sweet."

"I suppose you, of all princes, can find a way to make sure she never gives birth. What a string of tragedies she has to look forward to."

"Actually, I was thinking of birthing them in secret and then sending them away with the Taiytakei to be raised in secret in some far-off foreign land."

She smiled. "To come back in twenty years and challenge you for your throne? How romantic. And stupid. Get rid of them, Jehal. Them and her."

"As soon as I can, my love. When I find the right potion."

She drew a little closer, almost close enough to touch. "Where do you get them from? Do you have a pet alchemist? He must be very good."

Jehal bowed. "Why, I make them myself, Your Holiness."

"No you don't!" She laughed.

"I have a new one now. Something that makes my father's illness subside, at least for a while. I have a few flasks of it with me to dangle under Speaker Hyram's nose. Doubtless, he intends to accuse me of killing your mother yet again, though without a shred of evidence. He's going to start sounding quite foolish soon. When he's done, I shall let him taste a little of my bottled salvation so that he can see how much better he might be, and then he'll never, *ever* taste anymore." He shook his head and laughed as well. "Well, unless he makes me speaker, but I can't see that, can you?"

"I think he'd rather hand himself over to the dragon-priests."

"Yes." Jehal scratched his chin. "Would he rather go slowly mad, though? I suppose he would, but it will be fun to find out."

"Make him suffer. After he crowned me, he took me aside and asked if *I'd* killed her. I couldn't believe what I was hearing. And then he asked whether it was you."

Jehal put on a face. "Well, I hope you told him no."

"Of course I did. Still, I think he had rather more of a secret desire for my mother than I realized."

"I don't think it was *that* secret." *Not that secret at all. Just not reciprocated.* "Don't worry, my sweet, it's me that he wants to hang, not you. Smile him a pretty smile and he'll melt like butter."

"Like this?"

"Exactly like that. I feel my blood quickening already." He glanced back at the watching courtiers and sighed. "Is there some way we could . . ." he whispered.

Zafir's smile faded. She shook her head sadly. "No. Not until this is done. That's what you said."

"I know, but . . ." He grinned and bared his teeth. "Now I'm here, it is a physical pain that I can't touch you."

She blushed and looked at her feet. "Do you like this dress?" she asked.

"On you, it's perfection."

"It was my mother's. I think she wore it on the day she first met Speaker Hyram. I had to make some adjustments, of course. I spoke to some of my mother's old servants and learned how she carried herself, how she dressed herself, how she wore her hair. When Hyram sees me, it won't be me he sees—it will be my mother, as she was when he fell in love with her. I shall drive that dagger in deep and then twist it until the blade breaks."

"Oh, that's cruel." Jehal grinned. "Between the two of us, we should have him weeping on his knees."

Zafir shrugged. "He accused me, moments after he *crowned* me."

Jehal grinned some more. "Well, he *was* right."

She peered at him and pouted. "You said something about a gift and then wandered off into all sorts of unpleasantness. Is it a *nice* gift? Shall I want it?"

"Oh yes, I think you shall want it very much."

She wagged a finger at him. "We agreed, remember."

"My love, it's not *me* I'm offering. Well I am, but not here and now. Although . . ." He glanced back at the courtiers again. "I have a steel sword as well as the one *you're* after. I could butcher them all and then we could—"

"Jehal!"

"I'm sure they're all very tedious."

Zafir laughed, and Jehal felt a tension inside him ease and fade away. He still had her. That was what mattered. However much she hated him for marrying Princess Lystra, he still had her. He handed her a strip of black silk.

"You have to put this on," he said, "like a blindfold. No! Not here!" He lowered his voice until he was absolutely sure that no one else would hear. "But it's not a blindfold, my love. When you put it on, you will see things. You won't want anyone else to know, so do it when no one is watching you." He offered her a box. It wasn't as pretty as the one the Taiytakei had given him, but it was close. This one, though, only had room for one little golden dragon with ruby eyes.

Zafir ran her fingers over the carved wood. He could see the hunger in her eyes. "What is it?"

"Open it when you're alone. Take a good look at it, and then put on the blindfold. When you do, you'll understand. I could tell you a lot more, but where would be the fun in that?" He winked and his voice dropped even lower. "Anticipation is often the greatest pleasure."

"Oh really?" She was almost purring. "Will you be staying in the City of Dragons after you've finished taunting poor old Hyram?" He could see the desire flashing through her. *A real shame that we can't—* He bit his lip. *Not yet, not yet. Not while Hyram's watching us so closely.*

"Of course. Though no one will know of it."

"How can you be sure?"

"Leave that to me. Do you trust me, my love?"

He wasn't sure what to make of the look she gave him, but decided to take it as a cautious yes. He smiled as he felt the hairs prickle on the back of his neck. They'd dallied for too long, and the queen's chaperones were drawing closer. Slowly and cautiously and giving plenty of notice of their advance, but nevertheless with the same relentless purpose as a hostile army.

Later, when everyone was supposed to be asleep and he was alone in his carefully guarded and watched bedchamber, Jehal opened the shutters on his windows, slipped out the second strip of black silk and wrapped it across his eyes.

So, my love, let's see how far you've got.

32

THE ADAMANTINE GUARD

Watching Zafir play with her new toy was far too much fun, and of course the first thing she did, as soon as she discovered she could make the little dragon fly, was to send it to spy through his window. He took off the black silk and then let her watch him for a while, tossing and turning in his sleep, then pretended to awaken. The tiny dragon flew up to his face as if to announce its presence. He tried to look sheepish.

"You are very wicked," he whispered in the dragon's ear, "and if you were here, I would show you *how* wicked you are."

The tiny dragon danced around him, taunting him, and then darted back toward the window.

"Zafir," he hissed, and the dragon paused and hovered. "Nothing I've given Lystra comes near to this. Send it to watch us, if you want, and you will see."

The dragon paused and then left. Jehal shuttered the windows behind it and then put the black silk back across his eyes.

* * *

BOTH OF THEM ROSE LATE the next morning, and as Zafir rode with him to her eyrie, she seemed to glow.

"I'm sure you have another one," she whispered in his ear as he prepared to mount his dragon, Wraithwing. "We could watch each other when we're apart."

Or I could tell her about the second silk, he thought. *Tell her that I can share the eyes of her little spy with her, that I can watch her through its eyes whenever I want, if she keeps it near.*

Tempting, very tempting, but that wasn't why he'd given it to her. "Wait for me, my love," he said thickly. "I'll find you, after we're both done with Hyram."

"Hmmm." Her eyes flashed. "You'd better."

He climbed into the saddle and wiped his brow. *Maybe the Taiytakei can get me some more.* That made him laugh as he watched Zafir and her courtiers back away from his dragon. *For all I know, these are the only two such creatures ever made, and I ask for more simply so I can watch my lover when she's not in my bed? Not that they'd know, of course, but still.*

"Fly!" he shouted, and immediately felt the huge muscles of the dragon stir beneath him. Wraithwing lifted his head, rose onto his hind legs and began to run across the flat ground. Jehal closed his eyes. He could feel every stride as the dragon accelerated. He knew exactly when it would make one last bound and unfurl its wings. He felt himself grow heavier as it rose up into the air, and he sighed. Nothing, but nothing, compared to that moment, the second that the ground let go. Such a pity that it only lasted for an instant; then it was gone, and everything that followed was tame and flat. He thought about getting out the black silk again and letting his eyes ride with one dragon while his body rode on another, but that was just a quick way to lose the silk to the wind. He tried to think about Hyram instead, but Zafir kept getting in the way. He wondered sometimes if he should have spurned Princess Lystra and taken Zafir to be his bride instead, but that would have ruined everything. It was a shame, though, because one day, because of what he'd done, Lystra was going to be in the way. Maybe he should have turned them both away. He could have done that. Rejected Lystra because

Queen Shezira hadn't brought the perfect white dragon that she'd promised him.

He smiled. Instead, in a few days he'd be joining the search for it, even though he was absolutely sure that the dragon was safely locked away in some distant eyrie. Shezira was putting on a very good show. She'd kept it up for two months, and all sorts of little rumors leaked from her camp.

Another thought crossed his mind. Maybe it *was* all a ruse, just not the ruse he thought it was. She had some two dozen dragons and a hundred riders in the search, and all of them so very, very close to the Adamantine Palace. A lot closer than anyone else.

Yes, he thought. *Definitely worth a look,* and he let his mind wander over the possibilities as Wraithwing powered through the air. They flew over miles of rolling hills covered in trees, and then the ground fell away, faster and steeper, diving down into the Fury River gorge, which effectively cut the realms in two. To the south, Queen Zafir ruled. To the north, the speaker. Jehal thought about that too, as he guided Wraithwing down into the gorge and shot along the roaring river. He skimmed the line between the two as closely as he could, while Wraithwing dipped his tail into the waters and threw up a cloud of spray behind them.

He flew along the gorge for an hour and then climbed out again, veering north across the dullness of the Hungry Mountain Plain. He made Wraithwing fly high. *No point in scaring all the peasants.* For a while he closed his eyes and dozed, but as the Purple Spur mountains slowly grew out of the haze and he could see the first glitter of the Adamantine Palace, he saw that there were other dragons in the air. Hunting-dragons, by the look of them, half a dozen or so. At first Jehal wondered what they were doing there. Then he saw that Hyram had his legions out.

Perfecting them so he can show them off before he stands down as speaker. Jehal nudged Wraithwing into a tight spiral, diving straight through the other dragons toward the men on the ground. As he fell toward them, each legion bunched together, presenting a seamless wall of gleaming shields toward him. The shields were made of dragonscale, large enough to hide a man, and if he'd ordered Wraithwing to flamestrike, the fire would have stopped at the shield wall. As he passed over the heads of the soldiers, the shields came down and a hedgehog of scorpions popped up in their place. Each could fire a bolt the size of a javelin with enough force to punch through a dragon's scales, but it wasn't the dragon they'd be aimed at; it was the rider.

When he was past them, Jehal climbed again and had Wraithwing tip his wings to salute them. *Best to be nice. One day they're going to be mine.*

He landed at the Adamantine Eyrie, almost expecting to see Speaker Hyram waiting for him with a posse of guards, ready to drag him straight off to the dungeons. Not that the old goat would dare such a thing without any proof. Not when Jehal was married to the next speaker's daughter. *Ah, Lystra, all these little uses I have for you. A pity I'll have to be rid of you in the end.*

He frowned. Thoughts like that left him feeling strangely uncomfortable, so he set them aside and concentrated on what was around him. Instead of the almost-expected armed escort, the eyrie was almost deserted. A couple of hunting-dragons were ripping into a pile of freshly slaughtered cattle. A few Scales were going about their duties; one of them ran to help him dismount and care for Wraithwing. There were soldiers too, but not very many, and he supposed that he'd already passed most of the Adamantine Guard out on the plains. He'd brought a dozen riders and half as many dragons of his own in case he needed them; now he felt almost foolishly overdressed. All in all, he had the distinct impression that the eyrie-master, when he came running out of his little tower, hadn't even known he was coming.

"Prince Jehal!"

"Copas." Jehal smiled. The man looked horrified, taken completely by surprise. "Did the speaker not warn you of my arrival?"

"Ah, of course, Your Highness. We were expecting you tomorrow." Lies. Jehal could see straight through them. *Strange. Why would Hyram assume I would ignore his summons? Does he think I'm scared of him?*

Well, if he did, he was in for a shocker of a day tomorrow. Jehal widened his smile and let out a few more teeth. "I can't help but wonder why, since it always has been and always will be a three-day flight from Furymouth, and when the speaker summoned me, his words were quite terse and direct. 'Immediately' I believe was his demand." *I shouldn't blame him. Most of the men here belong to the order, not to Hyram. One day he's going to be mine too.*

"Your Highness, I am at a loss. Do you intend to proceed directly to the palace? I can arrange accommodation here, if you would prefer."

"In case no one at the palace is expecting me either?" Jehal cocked his head. "No, thank you, Copas. It's hardly your fault if the speaker's staff failed to warn you. I'm sure they can't have made the same mistake twice. However, my riders will stay here, if you would so oblige me." *If Hyram does plan me any ill, they'll do me no good in the palace.*

He watched as various Scales unloaded his baggage into a pair of carts. For a few minutes he wondered whether he was going to have to ride perched on the back of one of them. Eventually Copas brought up one of his own horses. He hung his head.

"I'm sorry, Your Highness. We have disgraced ourselves."

"Someone has. I'm sure it's not your fault."

Copas had at least managed to send a rider ahead so that the palace gates were open and the servants and the guards could pretend they hadn't been taken entirely by surprise. But everything took far longer than it should, and by the time he was finally alone, he had to admit that whatever mad game Hyram was playing, it was starting to work. What was it that Hyram thought would keep him away? *What is it that I don't know?*

It turned out to be two things. The first he discovered when he unpacked his precious potions and found all but one of them were missing. The second became clear when the Adamantine Guard smashed their way into his room in the middle of the night.

33

THE ALCHEMIST AND THE DRAGON

Kailin was terrified. He had no idea what he should do or say. In front of him were dragon-knights from Queen Shezira's eyrie. He didn't know them by name, but some of the faces were familiar. And the alchemist, of course. He knew Master Huros. They'd all want him to bring Snow back home, and a Scales always obeyed. That was his life. Look after the dragons and do as he was told. Except that behind him was a dragon who didn't want to go home. He walked through the shallow rushing water of the river as though lead weights were shackled to his feet.

"That's far enough!" The dragon-knight standing next to Master Huros held up a hand. Kailin stopped. They were still a good twenty feet apart. The other riders were spreading out, edging toward the trees.

Snow spoke in his head. *Make them understand that I will not come back. Not yet. They should cease their pursuit of us.*

Kailin winced. *I don't know how. They won't listen.*

"Um, what is your name, Scales?" shouted Master Huros.

Kailin looked at his feet, too used to averting his eyes from his masters. "Kailin," he said.

"Scales Kailin. We are here to take you home. You and your dragon."

"Queen Shezira will congratulate you herself," called the knight. "Her dragon is still intact and has not been lost. She will be greatly pleased. There may be a reward."

He didn't know what to say. He shook his head. He couldn't force the words out of his mouth. As soon as he did, they'd kill him. They'd take him back to Outwatch and string him up for all the other Scales to see, and then they'd very slowly execute him. *This is what happens to a Scales who does not obey.*

Tell them no!

He was shaking. He glanced up at the dragon-knight and at Master Huros, pleading with his eyes. "I can't. I don't know how to. What if . . . Snow doesn't want to—"

"This is not a request, Scales," shouted the knight. "This is an order!"

Master Huros stepped forward. He walked over to Kailin and put a hand on his shoulder. "Um, listen to me, Scales. Whatever has happened out here, it, er, it doesn't matter. If you've ridden the dragon, that doesn't matter. Whatever petty crimes you may have committed, they can be forgiven. The rules that we live by do not extend to circumstances such as these. You've done your duty and done it well. The dragon is intact but, um, she *must* come back to an eyrie at once."

Kailin still couldn't meet the alchemist's eyes. "I can't. She won't."

Tell them no! Or I will.

"Scales, you do not understand. There are, er, things you don't know. She must come back to an eyrie. If she doesn't, she will change. You might even have noticed little differences in her behavior already. We have to take her back."

Change? He could feel Snow's curiosity grow.

"I should not even have told you this much, Scales. These are the secrets of our order, but you must believe me, and so I tell you that without the elixirs I and the other alchemists at the eyrie will prepare for her, she . . . she *will* change. She will become a wild thing. She'll be dangerous, not just to you but to everyone."

What does he mean? Ask him what he means!

He felt the edge in Snow's thoughts, the suspicion, the horror, the incipient fury. He felt it in himself. "No! Stop!" He wasn't sure whether he meant it for Master Huros or for Snow.

The alchemist suddenly looked very surprised. "Yes," he said. "Yes, that's right. More intelligent. More independent. How did you know?"

Kailin went rigid. "Master, Master Huros, please—"
Leave him be!

"How did you know this, Scales?" The alchemist's voice had dropped to a whisper and he was glancing back at the knights. "Yes. They remember things. That's exactly what happens, and that cannot be, cannot be *allowed* to be! But, but you shouldn't know this. *How* do you know this?"

Something in the air began to change. The anger inside his head was growing, blooming, pouring into him. "Master Huros! She's in your head! She's reading your mind! She knows!"

He caught a glimpse of abject horror in the alchemist's eyes, and then Snow moved so fast that Kailin didn't even see it happen. One moment the alchemist was in front of him, the next he had shot up into the air, the tip of Snow's tail wrapped around him. He dangled helpless in front of Snow's face—shrieking, screaming, pleading—while everyone else froze and watched. Stray thoughts flickered through Kailin's mind, thoughts that weren't his and were filled with such a frenzied rage that he fell to his knees in the water, clutching his head. *Preparations? Memories? How? How long? How long have you done this? HOW LONG?*

He didn't see the moment when Snow squeezed the knot in her tail and crushed the life out of the alchemist, almost splitting him in two. He saw the body, though, flung through the air like a stone from a catapult, straight into one of the knights, so hard that the force of it lifted him off the ground and both sprawled like broken rag dolls. He felt the sky go dark as Snow leapt straight over his head. She landed, shaking the ground where the knight had been, and snapped up another in her claws. The man screamed as she crushed him, and Kailin heard the metal plates of his armor bend and break. The other knights were bolting for the cover of the trees. Snow's tail whipped around again, casually flinging a rock the size of half a man. It caught another rider, smashing him into a tree. He didn't get up.

Then came the fire. She swept her head from side to side, sweeping the edge of the forest with torrents of flame. The knights, if they were quick enough, would cower behind their dragonscale shields and the heat would pass them by.

But if they were crouched behind their shields, they weren't running. Snow sprang out of the river and up the bank to the forest. The fire came again, and this time her tail cracked into the trees. She plucked out one knight, cartwheeling him a hundred feet into the air, and then another, this one smashed headfirst into the stones of the riverbed. Kailin whimpered and covered his face. He couldn't bring himself to watch. He heard men scream, branches crack, tree trunks bend and break.

Sprinting footsteps splashed through the water toward him. He heard a voice: "What are you doing? Are you mad?"

Arms roughly pulled him up and gripped him tight. Raw steel touched his throat.

"You tell that dragon to fucking stop, right?"

Another voice: "Kemir! Get away from him, you idiot."

Kailin screwed up his face. "I can't." *I can't stop her. She's not listening to me.*

"Kemir! It's gone berserk! You can't stop it!"

"He's right." *Snow. Stop! Help me!*

The man with the knife at his throat tensed as if preparing to make his killing cut. "Well then, you're coming with us." He started to drag Kailin out of the river. "If it's going to burn us, it's going to burn you too, you bastard."

The man was doomed. They were all doomed. Kailin knew it as soon as they started to move. He could feel Snow had sensed his plea. She wasn't done with the other knights yet, but as soon as she was . . .

"Shit!"

They had almost made it when Snow exploded out of the inferno on the other side of the river, showering ash and embers and burning branches all around them. The fire flashed again, and the other man shrieked.

"Sollos!" Kailin's captor stumbled and the two of them went down together on the soggy grass. The man didn't let

go, but rolled so that he was lying on his back with Kailin
on top of him, both of them staring up at Snow, who glared
back down at them. Her teeth were bloody, her eyes blazed,
and she had someone in her tail again. Through the haze of
smoke and gibbering terror, Kailin thought he recognized
one of Knight-Marshal Nastria's sell-swords.

"Let him go!" roared the man with the knife. "Let him
go or I'll kill your rider."

Where are the alchemists? The thought hit Kailin like a
hammer. *Where are they? Burn them! I will burn them all!*

Don't know! Don't know! Inside, Kailin curled up into a
little ball and just waited to die.

Where are the others? Where are they?

"I know where they are!" shouted the man with the
knife. "I know how to find them."

The fire in Snow's eyes died. She snarled and dangled
the man held in her tail close. Kailin could see him clearly
now, and he *was* one of the knight-marshal's sell-swords.
Sollos. He couldn't remember the name of the other one.

Tell me!

Kailin blinked. High up in the sky he thought he could
see a dark speck or two moving against the clouds.

34

JEHAL'S CURE

There were seven or eight of them, all wearing veils to hide their faces. They dragged him out of bed and away through the palace. He shouted and screamed but they ignored him. When he struggled, one of them hit him hard enough to split his lip and knock loose a tooth. They took him out into the courtyard, across to the Glass Cathedral and to a hidden staircase behind the altar. Far underground, they hauled him through dim passageways murky with smoke and into a gloomy cavern of a room. A scattering of torches shed enough light for him to see the torture machines lining the walls. Hyram was sitting in the middle of the chamber, a small brazier glowing beside him.

"Are you mad, old man?" shouted Jehal. "Have you completely lost your mind?"

Hyram didn't say anything, only watching as the veiled guardsmen chained Jehal to a wheel.

"No one will stand for this—Narghon, Silvallan, Zafir, even Queen Shezira and King Valgar. Even the Syuss will rise out of the sand to shake their fists at you."

Hyram simply watched, trembling slightly. The veiled

guardsmen finished their work and slipped away into the shadows. Jehal and Hyram were alone.

"Y-You missed someone."

"Yes, even the King of the Crags might swoop from his lofty throne if he ever finds out that you've imprisoned a dragon-prince."

"Y-You know, I simply d-didn't think you'd come." Hyram rose painfully to his feet and snapped his fingers. "I-I am not imprisoning you, Jehal. I'm t-torturing you. When I'm done, you can g-go." Another pair of veiled men emerged from the shadows in the corners of the room. "I have h-had letters from Queen Zafir. She says that you and Queen Aliphera were lovers." Jehal's heart skipped a beat. *Letters from Zafir? Ancestors! What's she done?*

Hyram was pacing up and down. The two men with veils were standing patiently, waiting. "Z-Zafir blames you. She thinks that her m-mother killed herself because you were about to marry s-someone else. Were you lovers?"

Jehal spat at him. "Does your interest in my bed stem from the emptiness of your own, old man?"

"Were you l-lovers, Jehal?"

"None of your concern, Speaker, but yes, I fucked her every way you can think of. She couldn't get enough of it." Even in the gloom he could see Hyram's face tighten. The speaker gave a little nod, and the two torturers set to work. One pulled his head back so he couldn't see what the other was doing. He could feel it, though, the waves of agony they sent through him.

"No!" he shrieked. "No, we weren't lovers!"

Hyram gave another nod, and the torturers let go and stepped away. Jehal hung his head, slowly catching his breath as the pain faded away. Sweat dripped down his face. He didn't even know what the second torturer had done. *Have they marked me? Scarred me? If they have, I will return the favor a thousand times.*

"No. Q-Queen Aliphera was t-too wise not to see through you, Prince V-Viper. I want to k-know why you had her k-killed. And how."

"I didn't."

The torturers reached for him again. This time they didn't stop for a long time. Jehal gritted his teeth, but in the end he screamed and sobbed like everyone else. There was only one thing he could cling on to: *I didn't have her killed.*

Eventually it stopped. Jehal slumped, exhausted. Hyram looked him up and down.

"C-Can you still hear me, Viper?"

Jehal made no response. Best to pretend he'd passed out. Then Hyram slapped him.

"Don't p-play coy with me, boy. My man knows h-his work. I know you can h-hear me. Would you like a r-rest, Jehal?" Hyram dragged the brazier closer. His hands were shaking.

"You should get some help with that, old man," breathed Jehal. "Before you hurt yourself."

"M-Master Bellepheros gave everyone in y-your eyrie the truth-smoke."

"Master Bellepheros stood up in front of my father's court, in front of King Silvallan, Queen Shezira, King—"

"Yes, yes. He found n-nothing. Q-Queen Shezira found nothing. She even s-sent her daughter to ask you while y-you were reeling with M-Maiden's Regret and f-found nothing."

Ah. So that's what that was about. "Because there is nothing to find, old man."

Hyram finished moving the brazier closer to Jehal and sprinkled dust over the coals. Wisps of white smoke coiled up into the air. "I will show them h-how it is done. Master Bellepheros could not bring his s-smoke to you. N-Not allowed. But I can. Breathe deep, Prince V-Viper. The torture was only a b-bit of fun for me. Now you'll c-confess it all and be hanged. I w-win." Hyram began to totter away.

"This is a war you're starting, Speaker. Everyone will turn on you. *Everyone!*"

"N-No they won't." Hyram almost seemed to smile, but the twitching muscles in his face twisted it into a sneer. "Even if I'm wrong. N-No one cares, Jehal. Why b-bother? In a few months I'll b-be gone anyway, one way o-or another."

"If that's truth-smoke, old man, then ask me about the potion I brought with me. The one that eases my father's pain. The one that might cure your symptoms. Ask me about that, you old cripple, and then ask me what it would take from you to ever, *ever* get your hands on any of it. Ask what you'd have to give me. You're sick. You're dying, and it's the slowest, most degrading death you can imagine. I will relish every day of watching you ebb away. Ask me, Hyram!"

Hyram seemed to chuckle. "W-What makes you think I would have to g-give *you* anything at all?" He walked away and Jehal was left alone. The smoke rising from the brazier grew thicker and thicker. He could smell a sweet aroma with a strange sickly perfume. Truth-smoke.

Now what? Truth-smoke wasn't perfect. The alchemists liked to pretend that it was, but a clever and determined man could still fool an inept interrogator. *Or do the alchemists spread that rumor too, so that we always pay them to do our truth-seeking instead of doing it ourselves? Never mind. I'm clever. I'm determined. Is Hyram inept? No. He's clever too. But what if . . . I have to make him stupid. How? Can I do that? We'll have to see.*

The smoke was getting to him. His head was light and he was starting to lose track of where he was. *I didn't have Aliphera killed. She fell off her dragon. It was an accident. I wasn't there. I was sick in bed.* He stopped. He couldn't remember what he was thinking about. There was someone else in the room. He couldn't move and he wasn't sure why. And he was hurt. He couldn't remember how that had happened either.

"You were m-mumbling to yourself," said the voice. Jehal forced his eyes to focus properly. Ah yes. Hyram.

"You're old." He giggled.

"They say that the w-words a man mumbles to himself as the s-smoke takes him are the lies he wants to tell. What do you think about that?"

Jehal grinned. "I think that sounds very clever." A very distant part of him, he realized, *did* know where he was and what was happening to him. It was as though that part had been locked away in a faraway place. It was jumping up and down and shouting at him, trying to tell him things, but he couldn't hear it.

"So. L-Let's start with what you said. You didn't have Aliphera killed. I-Is that true?"

"I didn't *have* her killed." Jehal yawned. "I was there. Why can't I move my hands?" The faraway part of him was shouting and screaming something. If he tried, he could *almost* make it out.

"Because they're t-tied to a wheel. You were there? What do you mean you were th-there?"

"I was with her." He stared at Hyram. "On the back of her dragon with her when she fell off. I wasn't ill that day. Your alchemist was so close to the truth of it. She *did* hide something when she flew out of Clifftop, and Prince Meteroa too, when he came back. Me. We went to such trouble, she and I, so that no one would ever know I was with her. Weeks of careful thought. And now here you are with your silly smoke and now you know."

"You were w-with her?"

"Why, Speaker Hyram, you don't look well at all. I was in her saddle pack. I'd been seducing her for months. Little glances, little touches. She wanted me, old man. Oh, she *ached* for me. I just had to look at her and she got wet. So she smuggled me onto her dragon so that no one would know, so we could fly away and just fuck all day." He leered at Hyram.

"No!"

"Yes, old king."

"I a-asked you if you were l-lovers. You said n-no!"

"You were torturing me. I lied so you'd stop. You didn't want to hear it, but you should have believed Queen Zafir. Devious little bitch that she is."

Hyram's shaking was getting worse. He was clenching and unclenching his fists, pacing up and down in front of the brazier. The faraway voice in Jehal's head was still shouting things. Something about Hyram. Jehal frowned.

"Does it bother you, old man?" he asked. "Does it trouble you?" He twisted his head from side to side, trying to hear what the voice was saying. *Goad him? Make him angry?* He looked at Hyram again. "Does this make you angry?"

Hyram hit him. "Yes. D-Did you kill her?"

Good. There was blood in Jehal's mouth. "The ground did that. When she fell. Do you want to know why she fell? You do, don't you? Do you want to know why she wasn't strapped into her riding harness? Can't you see it for yourself? Do you want to know whether her body was naked when they finally found her?"

Hyram hit him again.

"Did she fall or did I push her? Is that what you want to know? Or do you want to know whether it was before or after I'd had her?"

This time Hyram hit him in the stomach. "Shut up!"

"Maybe you'd like to know how many times I took her?" *"Shut up!"*

Jehal coughed. "No. You wanted to know the truth, old king, and so that's what you're going to get. I was her lover. I was with her when she died. I wanted to have her on the back of her dragon. Have you ever fucked on the back of a dragon in flight, old man? It's a thrill, but it's stupid. People fall." He cocked his head. *Keep talking.* "Do you want to know what she was like, Aliphera? Do you want to know how she moaned when she came? Do you want to know what she liked best of all? Do you want to know that she liked it from behind? Do you want to know what she would whisper when I slipped my fingers inside her? Is that what all this is for? Because you can never have her for yourself and you want to know what it was like? Ask away, old man. I can tell you *everything.*"

That was as far as he got. Hyram, rigid with rage, let out a roar. He swore and screamed at Jehal, hitting him again and again. When it stopped, Jehal had a vague idea that it was because some men in veils had finally dragged the speaker away. Throughout it all Jehal grinned.

I win.

35

⁘

KEMIR

He was lying on his back. He was soaking wet and freezing. Ice-cold water rushed around him. The tumble of stones that littered the riverbed pressed into his back. He had a death grip on a man he vaguely knew, a knife held at the man's throat, and an enraged dragon glaring down at him. It already had Sollos, crushing him in its tail. Kemir's mind froze. He couldn't think. He was going to die.

Where are the alchemists? The words came from somewhere. He was staring at the dragon's mouth, waiting for the moment when the fire would come. Its mouth didn't move, but the words came anyway. *Where are they?* They filled him up on the inside, as big as the dragon itself. *Where are the others? Where?* He thought his head would explode. *Alchemists! Where?*

He could feel the Scales's skin, soft underneath, hard and brittle as glass where it was flaking away. *Will a knife even cut him?* "I know where they are!" he shouted, if only to make the noise in his head go away. "I know how to find them."

The rage in the dragon's eyes faded to a simmering anger. It peered at him and snarled, and then it threw Sollos up into the air and caught him with its tail again, holding him head down just inches above Kemir's face.

Tell me!

"Don't tell it!" croaked Sollos, and then he screamed as the tail tightened around him.

Kemir squeezed his arm into the Scales's throat. "If I tell you and let this one go, you'll burn me."

Mountains. I see mountains in your mind. They are close. Tell me or I will burn you both.

"There are mountains all around you, dragon. Burn me and you'll never know which one." Above him, Sollos screwed up his face in agony as the dragon flexed its tail again. Then the monster looked up. Abruptly, it let go of Sollos, turned and ran down the river. A few seconds later, it was rising into the air. Kemir could see two dark dots moving against the clouds high above. Reluctantly, he let go of the Scales and ran to Sollos.

"Are you all right?"

Sollos sat up. Blood covered his face from a shallow gash in his scalp and he held his left hand gingerly. "Nothing that won't get better."

"Do your legs work?" Kemir glanced over his shoulder. The Scales was standing up, looking into the sky, dazed and lost. Sollos got up.

"Well enough."

"That's good. I'll grab him. Let's get running."

"Wait! The riders."

Kemir grimaced. "What about them? They're all dead."

"No, they're not." Sollos pointed. In the middle of the river an armored figure was staggering to his feet. Kemir grinned. *Rider Semian. What luck!*

"Well, that can soon be corrected." He raised his voice. "Hey! Rider Rod! Over here."

"Wait."

"I'll make it quick. We'll get out of here before his friends come back."

"Wait!"

Kemir growled. "What?" Rider Semian was stumbling through the water and the stones toward them.

"Who was telling the white dragon what to do?"

"I don't think *anyone* was telling it what to do."

"But that's not right."

Kemir shrugged. "Maybe, maybe not. I know shit about dragons, except what they do when they have riders on their backs." He fingered a knife. Semian was getting closer. He looked bewildered, as though he hadn't the first idea what had happened. *Easy prey.*

"Let me talk to him." Sollos picked his way over the stones toward the dazed dragon-knight. From above, a series of soul-rending shrieks echoed through the valley. Kemir winced.

"Rider! Rider Semian! Are you all right?"

Semian didn't say anything. His face was strangely blank. Kemir felt the hairs on his neck prickle. *Danger!* He took a step toward them. "Sollos!"

Semian's mouth was half-open, his eyes vacant and distant, but when he moved, he moved with a sudden speed and purpose. In the blink of an eye he had drawn his sword and run Sollos through. Sollos gave a little grunt and doubled up. As Semian pulled free his sword, Sollos crumpled and fell into the water. Kemir found he couldn't move.

"Sollos!"

Semian lifted his sword and thrust down, burying the point in the exposed skin at the back of Sollos's neck.

"Sollos!"

Semian turned to look at Kemir. The vacant stare had gone.

"You *bastard*! " Kemir hesitated. Fury and revenge surged through him, demanding retribution, immediate and bloody. Yet Semian was armored. He was a knight. And he'd been so unexpectedly quick.

I'm afraid of him. The realization was horrifying, almost as bad as seeing Sollos die. *If I fight him, he might actually win. I'm afraid of him. And he's not afraid of me.*

Semian came slowly toward him. There could be no doubting his purpose now. He knew exactly where he was and exactly what he was doing.

"You and me, sell-sword. That's what you wanted."

"He never drew his sword. He was trying to help you. You're filth. You and your kind."

"It's clear." Semian's eyes were wild. "You were a part of this all along. Both of you. You made a fool of me, but I will redeem myself with this." He waved his sword in the air. "Now I have the vile stain of a traitor on my blade, I can barely bring myself to hold it in my hand. Quick now, man, before I can stand the stink no more. Let us be done. Kill me if you can, or add your blood to his."

Kemir took a step away, keeping his distance. "Killing you here and now, that would be too quick. I want to watch you die slowly."

"Are you too great a coward to fight me, sell-sword?"

The rage surged again, but the fear kept it in check. "One day there'll be a shadow in an alley, and I'll be in that shadow with my bow, waiting for you. You'll never know. You'll never see it coming." Kemir scuttled away through the rushing water and the rocks, putting more distance between them. Semian would never catch him dressed in so much dragonscale, and he didn't try. The knight simply stood and watched him retreat.

"Coward."

"You'll never know!" Kemir turned and ran. When he'd crossed the river and reached the trees, he looked back again. Semian was still standing there, stock-still, out in the open. A perfect target. Kemir took his bow from his shoulder and started to string it. *Seventy, eighty yards. A man in armor. If he's stupid enough to stay still, I'll probably hit him. I won't kill him. Then I can finish him slowly. Yes, that would be perfect.*

He'd almost forgotten the dragons when there came another shriek, so loud and close that he flinched. A moment later the entire river exploded. Water and stones flew everywhere as two dragons crashed into the riverbed, locked together, teeth and claws sunk into each other. One of them was the white. The other was dark brown with flashes of iridescent green on the insides of its legs. It had a rider on its back, but he quickly disappeared as the dragons thrashed and rolled in the water. Then the thrashing stopped and the dragons parted. The white dragon was limping. The darker beast got up, nosed at something in the water and roared. One of its wings was clearly broken, and it seemed to barely notice the white now.

It was still in the way, though. Kemir ran a few dozen

yards through the trees, following the river, but Rider Semian had gone.

The Scales was still alive. Somehow. Stumbling blindly through the stones. The white dragon picked him up in one claw, turned and ran.

Kemir watched them go. Inside him something broke.

36

THE DRAGON-QUEEN

Hyram went out to watch Zafir's dragons fly in to the Adamantine Eyrie, but his mind was still on Jehal. After the debacle of the truth-smoke, he'd been left with three choices. The most appealing was simply to have Jehal killed while he had the chance, but that would have been war, and, above all, the point of the speaker was to make sure there was never another dragon-war. Keeping him in the dungeon had some appeal as well but wouldn't achieve anything. When Shezira succeeded him as speaker, she'd let him go however much she thought he was guilty. Better to set him free sooner rather than later and see what he did.

Except that hadn't worked either. Instead of flying south, where Hyram could have kept an eye on him, Jehal had flown west, to Drotan's Top. From there he'd gone north, supposedly to join Queen Shezira's interminable and futile hunt for her missing dragon. Shezira knew all of her riders far too well for Hyram to have a spy among them, and so now the Viper was at large. He'd show up sooner or later, but Hyram would have felt a lot more comfortable knowing what Jehal was up to. *He wants to be speaker. He knows I'd die rather than betray Shezira for someone like him, so perhaps he's thinking of who comes next. Who will she name in her turn? Does he think that marrying Princess Lystra will make it him? She'll name Valgar surely? If he's still alive.*

Queen Zafir's dragons landed one after the other. A twitch started in Hyram's cheek and wouldn't go away. *Valgar's getting old. In ten years he'll be as old as I am now, and Jehal the perfect age. Maybe that's what he has in mind.*

After everything he'd learned in the last few days, he wasn't sure how he should approach Queen Zafir. She'd told him that Aliphera and Jehal had been lovers and she'd been right. She'd told him that she didn't think Jehal had murdered her mother, and she might have been right about that too. He wasn't even sure he cared anymore. Aliphera had soiled herself with the Viper, she of all people. She deserved to die. If her death was an accident, Hyram's only regret was that she hadn't pulled Jehal down with her. *I should put her out of my mind. Even if Jehal didn't kill her, he's still murdering his own father. He could hang for that. Best that I forget her forever.*

Except there she was, standing in front of him, exactly as he remembered her from twenty years ago, glorious, radiant, beautiful beyond compare. He felt a fool and ashamed of himself. Old and crippled. How could he stand before her?

"Your H-Holiness." He bowed. *It's not her. She's gone, remember. It's her daughter. But she looks so much like her. I'd never really seen it before, but she does.*

Queen Zafir bowed and kissed his ring. "Speaker. You flatter me."

He looked at her. He couldn't stop looking at her. She was Aliphera at her best, her hair piled up on the top of her head to show off the curves of her neck, the same deep red riding clothes, the same carved amber dragon hanging at her throat, the same russet folds of furs to keep her warm against the wind. Everything about her glowed.

"Y-You're wearing your m-mother's furs."

Zafir bowed her head. "Since she died I've taken to always wearing something that was hers. To honor her memory. I hope you're not offended."

"C-Come." Hyram offered her his arm, which she took with a smile. "I-I have to apologize to you, Queen Z-Zafir.

I once l-loved your mother very much. I should n-not have said what I did after you were crowned."

She met his eyes with sadness. "No, Speaker, you should not. Prince Jehal killed my mother. We both know that now."

He looked away and bit his lip. "I d-don't know. I-It may have been an a-accident."

"I think he was on her dragon with her when she died."

"I kn-know he was."

For a moment Zafir tensed. "You know?"

"Y-Yes. H-He told me. I was n-not very kingly while he w-was here, but I did learn a g-great deal."

"Then I am keen to know more." She was still tense. Idly, Hyram wondered why.

"I know that e-everything you told me was true. I kn-know I should have paid more heed to your l-letters. I know I d-did you an injustice. P-Please forgive me. Tell me, how are the rest of your family?"

She seemed to relax. "My sister still grieves. Uncle Kazalain has sworn an oath of vengeance. He stomps and shouts and drinks and bellows for war and has no idea who he should fight." She gave him a thoughtful look. "Mostly he vents his anger at Queen Shezira. He has this foolish notion that you might have defied the old pacts and chosen Aliphera to succeed you. He has his sons beside him, but that is all. As for the rest, the whole realm is shocked with sadness." Then she smiled at him, and he couldn't help himself.

"Y-You are every bit as beautiful as your m-mother, Queen Zafir. I hope you know that."

"You're too kind, Speaker. But tell me more about Jehal. I came here thinking you would ask me lots of questions, and how clever I would seem to know even some of the answers. But you already know far more than I do."

He led her to the edge of the eyrie, where a line of carriages waited to carry Zafir and her entourage to the palace. There he left her while a hundred servants buzzed about, carrying cases and sacks and boxes to the four corners of the palace. He'd given her the Tower of Air again, hoping she'd understand that he meant to honor her. When he'd summoned her, a part of him had meant to accuse her. He might even have treated her as he'd treated Jehal, with a bit of mild torture and the truth-smoke. Now the thought appalled him. What was he thinking? The Viper deserved it for a hundred and one other things, but Queen Zafir?

She was exactly as he remembered her mother. Her clothes, her hair, her jewelry, the way she spoke, the way she held herself. A part of him knew that she must have done it deliberately; another part didn't care.

In the evening they dined in the great hall of the palace, with the golden carved heads of the previous forty-four speakers looking down on them. Zafir walked in with a dozen gleaming dragon-knights behind her, all dressed in the deep reds and autumn browns that Aliphera had favored. She wore Aliphera's own favorite dress, and the sight of her brought tears to Hyram's eyes. *So much regret.*

As they ate he quietly told her everything he'd done to Jehal, and everything Jehal had said in return. She listened quietly. Her eyes seemed to tell him that he'd done the right thing.

"It doesn't matter whether he pushed her or whether she fell," she said softly, when he was done. "He is responsible, and I hate him for it. I used to like him. There was a time when . . ." She looked down. "There was a time when I hoped he would marry me and not Princess Lystra. But now . . ." She shuddered. "She's welcome to him. I should have listened to you a long time ago, and so should my mother. There will not be a war, Speaker, I promise you that. But I will have vengeance. I can promise you that too."

He got drunk. It lessened the symptoms of his illness, but that was only ever an excuse. Mostly, it lessened the bitterness and the regrets and the pain, the other illness that ate away at him from deep inside. Except tonight it didn't; it made him worse and filled him with maudlin sighs, until he found himself telling Zafir everything. It was all he could do not to break down into tears. In front of all his knights and hers that would surely have been the end of him. Through it all, she watched him. She didn't say anything, but her eyes seemed filled with sympathy. He'd expected her to tell him that he was stupid, that he was a fool, that what he'd done to Jehal threatened the peace of the realms, that he was an idiot for mourning a woman he'd barely known, and that death was death and he should be glad of the years he'd had. Instead, when he was done she leaned toward him and spoke into his ear.

"I can't bring my mother back, Hyram," she whispered. "But your sickness, if it truly is the same as King Tyan's, now there I may be able to help you."

"The V-Viper claims he has a p-potion," Hyram slurred. "The a-alchemists know nothing about it. You s-said you had some i-information. In your letter."

She leaned farther toward him. "He gets his potions from the Taiytakei, but I can do better than that." From somewhere she produced a small vial. "He was bringing a sample with him when he came to the palace to answer your summons. I daresay he meant to taunt you with it." She giggled. "I stole it when he spent the night at my eyrie on his way here." She opened the vial and poured a few drops into his wine and then a few into her own. "I thought about asking my alchemists what it was, but you know what they're like. A year from now they might come back with an answer or they might not. I've had it tested." She lifted up her goblet and swallowed. "It's not poison, I know that much. It's a bit . . ." She giggled again. "It's a bit like a mild dose of Maiden's Regret. Of course, I don't know if it will help you with your sickness, but I'm sure it can't do you any harm. If you can believe anything Jehal says, it doesn't make the sickness go away, only keeps it at bay for as long as you take the potion. If you stop taking it, the sickness comes back again."

Hyram stared at his wine. He sniffed it.

"It tastes terrible. It doesn't go well with wine either. Brandy is better."

"Y-You tried it before?"

Zafir shrugged. "I wanted to know what it would do before I offered it to you. Obviously I didn't try it until I knew it wasn't poison."

"B-But it came from the Viper." Hyram shook his head. The room was blurring before his eyes. "It c-could be anything."

She sat back in her chair, moving away from him. "You don't have to drink it, Speaker. If you do, and it works, I have more."

"How m-much more?"

Now she laughed. "Enough for a few months. Enough to see you to the end of your time here. I know where he gets it too. I can tell you, if you want me to." She leaned into him again. "Drink it, Hyram. Don't let Jehal win. Be young and strong again, the way my mother wanted to remember you."

Her closeness, the warmth of her through his clothes, made him shiver.

"What have you got to lose?"

He stared at his wine. He was still staring at it as the feast came slowly to an end. When he meandered away to his bed, he took the goblet with him, still half full. *In the morning,* he decided. *In the morning I'll ask her for another dose. Jeiros can take it. He can tell me what's in it. He can tell me if it's safe. In the morning.* He put the goblet on the table beside his bed and tried to sleep, but sleep wouldn't come, and the goblet seemed to stare at him.

If you were Antros, you'd drink me, it seemed to say. *If you were you, you'd drink me. If you don't, then who are you? Queen Zafir is right. What have you got to lose?*

"Everything," he whispered, and hoped the goblet would hear him and leave him be, but instead it seemed to laugh.

Everything? You've already lost everything. And here I am, offering it all back again, and you turn me away? Who are you? What are you? Are you already a ghost?

Trembling, he reached out and took the goblet in his hand. She'd put some into her own cup, hadn't she? And drunk it down. He'd seen her do it. She was right, wasn't she?

That's right, murmured the goblet, as he put it to his lips. *Drink me down. Be a man again. Be a man.*

Be a man.

37

❧

AN ACCOMMODATION

K emir crept out from the trees. In the middle of the
river the wounded dragon paused from its howls and
turned to look at him; quickly Kemir retreated, but the
dragon didn't seem very interested in him. He couldn't see
Rider Semian anywhere.

Maybe he got crushed in the fight.

That would be too much to hope for. Kemir ran through
the forest beside the river until he rounded a bend and the
dragon couldn't see him. Then he crossed over and crept
back again. Still no Semian. The dragon hadn't moved either. He watched it for a while, searching for the courage to
go out into the water where Sollos lay.

When he finally found him, he wondered why he'd bothered. Sollos was dead, and he'd known that from the moment he'd seen Rider Semian drive down his sword. He
helped himself to Sollos's bow, his arrows and his pack.

"Goodbye, cousin." He turned Sollos over and very gently removed an amulet from his neck, then turned his back
on the body and picked his way into the trees. He carefully
buried the amulet. Next he set about looking for any tracks
that might have been Rider Semian's; he didn't find any, but

as the sun slipped behind the mountain peaks two more
dragons swooped silently into the valley and landed in the
river. Kemir watched them come in through the trees. He
strung his bow and crept closer until he could see them
properly. The dragons were splashing in the water, cooling
themselves down, while their riders clustered by the shore.
Four dragon-knights. No, five.

He clenched his fists. He could see Semian again. Still
alive. He strained his ears to hear them. The breeze, such as
it was, carried their words toward him.

"We saw Storm's Shadow on the way in as well," said
one of the others. Kemir couldn't see his face. "Mias was
riding her, wasn't he? No sign of him though. What happened?"

"We found the white. The Scales was with her. He
wouldn't give her back. He set her on us." Semian shook his
head. "All the others are dead. The alchemist too. Everyone
except one of the sell-swords. They were in with the Scales
somehow."

Kemir nocked an arrow to his bow. The breeze carried
the scent of the dragons too, a light whiff of ash and charcoal. He savored it. If he could smell them, then they
couldn't smell him. *You lying, murdering bastard. I could
kill you where you stand. Right now.*

"Mias and Arakir got back before they were done. The
white attacked them in the air. I didn't see what happened
to Mias. The white must have got him." Semian glanced toward the dragon with the broken wing. "Arakir was on Tempest. I saw him and the white come down into the river,
fighting each other. Arakir was crushed, Tempest has a broken wing and I think a broken foot as well. The white was
hurt too. She headed upriver. She was limping and I didn't
see her fly. The Scales was still with her and the surviving
sell-sword escaped as well. I suppose he's long gone now."

No, I'm right here. Kemir squinted down the length of his
arrow. *Where should I shoot you, Rider Rod? In the face? In
the throat, as you did for Sollos? Not in your heart, because
there's nothing there.* Slowly he lowered the bow. This was
too easy. Semian could die here and now. Vengeance would
be served, but Sollos would still be dead.

There was the little matter of the four other dragon-
knights too, but they were armored and Kemir was sure he

could vanish into the forest before they could turn their dragons on him. But merely putting an arrow into Semian wasn't going to be enough. There had to be pain and suffering. He had to die slowly, piece by piece.

"We saw the white. It's a couple of miles farther up the river," said one of the other riders. "We'd seen Storm's Shadow, and then we saw Tempest. Ancestors! What do we do? Should we go on to the white? It's getting dark."

Piece by piece. Kemir raised his bow again.

"No." Semian screwed up his face. "Yes. No. Was Storm's Shadow hurt?"

"It's hard to say."

"Go and find out. If Storm's Shadow can fly, take her back to the camp. Tell them what happened and that we need another alchemist. Tell them we've found the white and bring them back here. Someone will have to stay here with Tempest. The rest of us—"

The first arrow struck Semian in the leg, just above the knee. Semian howled, staggered and fell back into the water. The second arrow struck one of the other riders in the back. The third arrow hit the wounded dragon in the neck, which only made it hiss and snap. Kemir didn't stop to fire a fourth; instead he jogged a little deeper into the forest and then turned and followed the path of the river. The knights wouldn't follow him into the trees, he was quite sure of that, and the dragons would never find him in the dark. Not killing Rider Semian, he discovered, was immensely satisfying. Killing him was something he could only do once. He smiled to himself. *I can put arrows into his arms and legs again and again and again.*

It took him well into the night to find the white dragon and the Scales. The dragon was curled up next to the water, sleeping. The Scales was huddled next to it. As he crept closer, he saw another body too, gently snoring. He slipped up to the sleeping Scales, crouched beside him, slid out a knife and slowly pulled back the man's cloak.

"Scales!" he hissed, glancing up at the dragon. He gave the man a gentle shake. "Scales!"

The man stirred. The dragon's breathing didn't change. "Scales!"

The Scales opened his eyes. Kemir touched his lips with the point of his knife. "Quiet, Scales. If I was going to hurt you, I'd have already done it. But if you wake up your dragon . . ."

"Who are you?" The Scales was looking up at him, still dazed with sleep, not quite understanding.

"My name is Kemir. I was a sell-sword working for your queen until one of her knights murdered my cousin. I want to help you."

The Scales blinked and rubbed his face. A part of him looked terrified; another part looked vaguely surprised and seemed to be looking past Kemir rather than at him. Kemir felt a coldness. He started to turn and caught a glimpse of the tip of the dragon's tail snaking through the air toward him. He swore and dived away, but the tail was too quick. The next thing he knew, he was being lifted up into the air.

"Scales! Damn you! Call it off! I'm here to help."

Help? What do you mean?

The thought seemed to come from outside him, but that was a ridiculous idea and he dismissed it. "You left one of the dragon-knights alive. Now there are more of them. They're coming. I tried to slow them down, but they're coming after you. Call it off!"

How many are coming?

"Four knights. No, five. But two of them are too hurt to worry about." This time he couldn't shake it. The question had come into his mind, but the Scales hadn't uttered a word. "How . . . ?"

The ground fell away. The dragon was rising, lifting its head, lifting him up into the air at the same time. He hung helpless as it snorted and growled. A rush of warm rancid air engulfed him.

How many dragons are coming?

Very carefully, Kemir looked down at the Scales standing on the riverbank twenty feet below him. The one who'd been sleeping, a woman he now saw, was looking up at him as well. She looked pasty and pale in the moonlight, and was shaking.

"Scales. I think your dragon is talking to me." *Have I gone mad?*

No. How many dragons?

"Snow!" The Scales was wringing his hands. "Don't hurt him. No more! Please!"

Thoughts tumbled through Kemir's mind so quickly that

they tripped over one another. *The dragon can think.* That was terrifying enough. *The dragon can hear what I think.* That was worse. *The dragon killed half a dozen knights.* That was better. *It did it because it wanted to, not because someone told it to.* That was either the best or the worst; he wasn't sure which.

He regarded the dragon. A calmness settled inside him, a mixture of hope and resignation. Shitting himself wasn't going to do much good just now. "Two new dragons. They were going to send one after you. To watch. The other was going to go for help. By the middle of tomorrow morning there might be a dozen dragons looking for you. You want to escape, don't you?"

I want to free the others of my kind.

"My name is Kemir. I want to help you."

No, Little One Kemir, you do not. All I see in you is death and vengeance. You want to kill dragon-riders. I am simply a means to that end.

"No dragons, no dragon-knights."

The tail squeezed a little tighter. *Your fear has a sharp and pleasant tang to it. How will you help me, Little One?*

Kemir tried to pull himself free. The dragon hadn't pinned his arms, but all his struggles were futile. He still had the knife that he'd used to threaten the Scales. If he stabbed the dragon's tail, would it drop him? Would it even notice?

I will crush you before you blink, Little One. Again: how will you help me?

"I'll help you kill dragon-knights. Any way I can."

I do not wish to kill dragon-knights. I wish to free my kind.

"Then I'll help you kill alchemists. You asked where they were. I can tell you."

The dragon looked at him for a long time and then slowly lowered him to the ground. *Then we have an accommodation, Little One Kemir. Alchemists. So be it.* The dragon turned to look at the Scales, but Kemir still heard its voice inside his head. *More dragons come, Little One. We must fly. Now.*

38

THE MIRROR LAKES

The Mirror Lakes, clustering around the City of Dragons, were generally thought to be perfectly round and perfectly bottomless. The ground didn't slip gently and gracefully away under the water; it simply stopped. In the myths of the dragon-priests the Divine Dragon molded the world from clay and then baked it hard in the flames of his breath. The people of the city weren't the most religious of folk, but they generally agreed that if the priests were right, the Mirror Lakes must have been where the dragon-god stuck his claws into the clay to hold it tight while he did his work. Strange and monstrous creatures were rumored to inhabit the lakes, rising to the surface sometimes in the middle of the night, swallowing boats whole and then sinking again, disappearing without trace.

From where Jehal sat, perched at the top of the Diamond Cascade falls, one could see that the lakes weren't perfectly round at all. He was fairly sure they weren't bottomless or inhabited by monsters either, but no one had ever proved that, one way or the other. Vanishing boats, he thought, were more likely to be the work of thieves, and any monsters that inhabited the lake were probably of the human variety.

He could see the city too, and the Adamantine Palace, all laid out some half a mile beneath him through the haze of spray from the falls.

Mine. It's all going to be mine.

Behind him Wraithwing splashed in the waters of the Diamond River. A shadow passed overhead and moments later another dragon came in to land. The two dragons looked at each other curiously. The newcomer dived into the water and started to drink. Its rider sauntered toward Jehal. She took off her helmet.

"I was wondering whether you'd come. You have some explaining to do," said Jehal. He had to speak loudly to be heard over the roar of the waterfall.

Zafir smiled. She didn't say anything but sat beside him and looked over the edge.

"You should be careful," said Jehal. "You could fall."

"We could both fall."

"I watched you come up from the eyrie. You didn't bring any riders with you. No one knows where you are. No one knows who you're with."

She put a hand on his arm. "Did *you* bring any riders, Prince?"

"Of course not. You never know who might have lined their pockets."

"How far did my mother fall?"

Jehal shrugged. "We're higher now. You stole my potions. And you've been writing letters to Hyram."

She didn't look at him. "You've been to see your new family. How *is* Queen Shezira?"

"Do you feel threatened, my love?"

"Not at all. Do you?"

"Not in the least."

"I didn't steal your potions. I took them because you told me to."

"I told you to take *one*."

"Hyram's got them now."

"I know."

She looked at him, and the flicker of a smile played at the corner of her lips. "And I know you know. I saw your little golden dragon sitting on the windowsill, watching us with its beady ruby eyes. How manymore of those have you got?"

"Only that one and the one I gave to you. They were a wedding present from the Taiytakei."

Zafir raised an eyebrow. "It was almost worth marrying your little starling then. And what do they want, the Taiytakei?"

Jehal shrugged. "To see me prosper, I suppose."

"That doesn't sound like the Taiytakei."

"They want what they always want and what they can never have. A hatchling." For a few seconds Jehal stared out into the void over the city below. Sitting up here with his feet dangling over the empty air, he almost felt he could fly. No dragons, just him. It would be easy, wouldn't it? To let go and soar and be free of it all. No more Hyram, no more Shezira. No more watching his father's glacial crawl toward death. No more constant battling of wits with the Taiytakei and all the others that surrounded him, fawning at his feet for favors while all the while hiding poisoned daggers behind their backs. No more—

No more Zafir. He turned and looked her squarely in the eye. "Well?"

"Well what?"

"Did Hyram tell you that he tortured me?"

"No. He said he hadn't been very kingly." She spat. "As if that was somehow a change."

"Well he's not a king, is he, so I suppose we shouldn't be surprised. He wasn't very good as a torturer either. Maybe I should send him one of mine for next time. In fact he was so inept I had to show him how to make a proper job of it. We're beyond words now, he and I. I think I have to muster my dragons when I go south." He shook his head. "I'm at a loss. I didn't think he'd dare anything so bold." Now he laughed. "I almost had some respect for him, for a moment, until he let me go. Now if he'd killed me outright and taken the consequences, why I think I might even have given him a round of applause. And then I think of him rutting with you after I left, and I just want to paint the palace with his blood."

"Don't!" Zafir shuddered. "He doesn't deserve even to exist in your thoughts."

"Ahh." He took her hand and kissed it. "You're very sweet, my lover."

Zafir pulled her hand away. "Don't touch me. I don't want anyone to touch me. I tried to think of you when I let him have me, and now when I think of you, I think of him." She shivered. "It's horrible."

"Antros was always supposed to have been quite the lover. Hyram didn't share his talents?"

"He was drunk, selfish, boorish and pathetic. I had to do everything for him. Didn't you see with your little Taiytakei toy?"

"I saw you writhe and wriggle under him. I heard your squealing too. Quite a show, I thought."

"Mercifully quick." She made a face. "If you saw it all anyway, don't ask me any more. What's Shezira up to in the Purple Spur? She's making Hyram nervous, and you going there didn't help that at all."

Jehal laughed. "Really? Why now, I would *never* have thought of that. Yes, a little more distrust between them can never hurt, but I'm afraid Queen Shezira has returned to her eyrie. I had her delight of a daughter to waste my charms on instead."

"Almiri?"

"No, not the nice one; the one that's made of the same flinty stuff as her mother. The one that thinks she's a dragon born human by mistake. Jaslyn. The one who asked me whether I was poisoning my father while the Maiden's Regret had me." He laughed. "I shall have to thank Queen Fyon for that. She's a bit sharper than I've given her credit for. No, I had a frosty welcome to say the least. I might have said one or two things out of place. Perhaps she was kind enough to put that down to my exertions of the previous days." He laughed again. "They were still trying to find their missing dragon, and now they've lost another one."

Zafir raised an eyebrow.

"Seems they tracked their white down, and it turned on them. Princess Stone did her best to make sure I didn't find anything out, but there's a dragon out there with a broken wing. They've lost an alchemist and I saw a rider in a pretty poor state. Apparently someone put an arrow in his leg, so the white's not flying around aimlessly on its own, that's for sure." Not *the* white. *His* white. "When I left, they were try-

ing to work out how to put their injured dragon down."
Jehal scratched his chin. "They had quite a lot of alchemists
there, now I think about it. More than I would have expected. And of course I now know exactly how many dragons she's got out there and have a shrewd idea how many
riders too. She didn't like me paying attention to that sort
of thing." He shrugged. "Still, I'm quite impressed. They're
up to something, and I still haven't got the first idea what it
is."

Queen Zafir shook her head and looked away. "Prince
Jehal, that won't do at all. They may make Hyram nervous,
but they bother me too—so many dragons so close by." She
stopped and peered down at the city. From the Adamantine
Eyrie the tiny distant shape of a dragon was rising into the
air. "You're going to have to go." She stood up.

"Pity. I'd been hoping to have you for rather longer."

"I'm sure you had." Zafir whistled. Her dragon looked
up from where it was splashing in the river with Wraithwing. "But we can't risk anyone seeing us together now. You
need to be gone before that dragon gets high enough to see
Wraithwing and Emerald Mirror together."

Reluctantly, Jehal got to his feet. He was going to have
to explain to Wraithwing that he couldn't simply throw
himself over the precipice and spread his wings, that he'd
have to take to the air the hard way. He sighed, and then to
his surprise Queen Zafir launched herself into his arms,
pressing herself against him.

"I wish we had longer too," she murmured.

Jehal stroked her hair away from her face and purred, "I
thought looking at me made you think of Hyram."

Zafir made a face. "It did until I got up here. Now it just
makes me think of you without your clothes on."

He kissed her and let his hands begin to wander. "It
won't be for much longer, my lover."

"Give me the strength not to murder him in his bed,
Jehal."

"Give me the patience to wait for you."

"*I* have to lie with that crippled oaf. All I think of is you
with your starling-bride, and then all I want to do is slit his
throat and then hers and be done with all this."

With a great effort Jehal let her go. "You keep that

thought close to your heart, my Queen, and keep your mind on Hyram."

She snorted. "No fear there. For as long as I can bear it, he'll think of nothing but your potions, my mother's face and the hole between my legs."

Jehal reached out to stroke her face one last time, then turned toward Wraithwing. He waved over his shoulder. "Once he marries you and makes you speaker, you can cut as many throats as you like."

"I'll hold you to that, Jehal," she called after him. "He'll be first. You can choose who comes second, you or your starling."

39

THE RAVINE

The dragon was hurt. Kemir hadn't noticed that when they'd taken to the air in the middle of the night. In fact, he hadn't noticed much, clutched in the dragon's claws and hurtling through the night air at speed. The ground flashed past in the moonlight, not far beneath him but quite far enough to smash him to pieces if the dragon let go. The monster's wingbeats rippled through the air like thunder. For the second time in his life, he prayed.

In the dragon's other foreclaws the Scales held on tight to the woman, whoever she was, while she in turn screamed and shrieked herself hoarse.

The air got colder. Finally the dragon landed in a field of snow, tumbling in a spray of powder, while Kemir thought for the umpteenth time that night that he was going to die. The beast took them to the edge of a narrow ravine and jumped in, gliding down into total darkness. When it landed at the bottom it let them go and fell asleep almost at once. Kemir huddled up against the dragon's warmth and fell asleep as well, drained beyond exhaustion.

When he woke up, he knew something was wrong. The dragon's breathing was labored, and the Scales was sitting by its muzzle, stroking its nose. This close, in the daylight, the dragon seemed even larger than it had the night before. Its head dwarfed the Scales; its amber eyes were larger than an open hand; its teeth . . .

Kemir didn't want to think about its teeth. Instead he looked up. The ravine was steep and narrow, so narrow he was surprised that a dragon could fly into it at all. He wasn't sure how any of them were going to get out again, and he was hungry. And if it wasn't for the dragon, they were all going to get very cold very quickly. The Scales didn't have any flying furs, while the woman, it seemed, didn't have anything else.

"I've seen you before," he said to the Scales. "What's your name?"

"Kailin." The Scales didn't look up.

"What about her?"

"Her name's Nadira."

"What's the matter with her?" When she wasn't screaming, she looked dull and vacant. She was sweating and shivering.

The Scales didn't answer.

"Who is she?" The Scales didn't answer that either. Kemir shrugged. "What's up with your dragon then?"

"Her name is Snow. She's hurt."

"Is it bad?"

"I don't know. She must have damaged herself when she fell into the river with Tempest. It looked like she broke Tempest's wing." Kailin shook his head sadly and looked nervously at Snow. "If she did, they'll have to put Tempest down, poor thing."

"Poor thing?" Kemir scratched his head. "How *do* you put a dragon down?"

The Scales flashed him a warning glance. "Be careful. She's sleeping, but you saw what happened in the river. I don't know for sure, but I've heard stories that the alchemists give them something in their food. They go to sleep and then they burn from the inside."

"I've seen that." Kemir nodded. "That's what happens when they die."

"I wouldn't know. I've never seen a dragon die."

"Well, if it happens with this one, we won't have to worry about staying warm for a while." He looked up at the walls of the ravine. *No. Just staying fed.* "I don't suppose you have any idea where we are?"

The Scales shook his head. It didn't take long to discover that the Scales didn't have any food, water, shelter, spare clothing or any of the basic necessities for surviving out in the wilderness. He'd had a dragon, though. Apparently that was enough.

He left them to it and set off down the ravine, following the trickle of water that bubbled along the bottom. As he pressed on, the ravine grew gradually steeper and narrower. He passed countless caves. *That's the Worldspine for you. Riddled with holes like a honeycomb. Yawning caverns big enough for an army and tiny holes barely enough for a man to crawl into.* He began to see overhanging trees above, casting everything into shadow. The sides pressed in closer and closer; the trickle of water grew into a rushing stream that ran faster and deeper around every bend. Abruptly the cliffs on either side fell away and he emerged into the middle of a steeply sloping forest. He circled around to the top of the ravine and sat on the edge, looking out through the gap in the trees. He was high up in the side of a mountain valley. One that looked exactly the same as every other mountain valley.

Great. Nice one. That really helped. Shall we walk all the way back now?

He sat there for a long time, staring, until finally he muttered something and Sollos didn't reply, and it hit him, hard, that his cousin was gone forever. They'd spent a good part of their lives with only each other for company, although it hadn't always been that way. They'd roamed the realms, selling their sword arms, but this was where they'd been born, here in the Worldspine. They'd killed perhaps a dozen dragon-knights between them, but only because other dragon-knights had paid them to do it.

And now Sollos was gone. Their contract with Knight-Marshal Lady Nastria was finished and he was back where it had all started. He had his bow, his knives and his wits, which ought to be enough to survive out in these valleys. He didn't owe anything to the poor fools he'd left in the ravine. He was entirely free to do whatever he wanted.

And entirely trapped. He couldn't walk away from what he and Sollos had been. Not on his own. Not while Rider

Rod was still alive. And then there was the dragon, and the glimmer of a possibility that he couldn't ignore no matter how unlikely it was to bear fruit. Trapped. Utterly trapped. Revenge was what he wanted. Revenge, not just for Sollos but for all the others, for every Outsider who'd ever burned. Which meant staying with the dragon and the Scales and the woman, whoever she was.

Which meant keeping them alive.

"Bollocks!"

The shout echoed around the valley and faded, lonely and unanswered. He sighed, clambered down from his rocky perch and strung his bow. It took him a couple of hours to track down a decent meal and another hour to skin and fillet it. Hiking back up the ravine took twice as long as walking down it. By the time he got back, he was exhausted and hungry. As far as he could tell, he'd been gone for about ten hours and none of the others had even moved. Maybe the woman had rearranged her legs. He threw himself down and closed his eyes.

"Is your dragon up to starting a fire for us?" he asked.

The Scales shook his head. "She's in torpor. They do this when they're hurt. She'll sleep until she's better."

"Well how long is that going to be?"

"If she's broken a rib, two or three weeks."

Kemir opened his eyes again and looked up at the sky framed by the sides of the ravine. He laughed. "Two or three weeks?"

"Yes."

"So all we have to do for all that time is hide her from Queen Shezira's riders and not starve to death. Oh, and we can't actually move from this spot, because if we do, the two of you will die of exposure." He closed his eyes again and shook his head. "Curse you, dragon. Curse you for everything." And he set about keeping them alive.

THE SCALES WAS USELESS; ALL he did was sit beside his dragon and stroke her scales. The woman spent her time staring into space with her mouth hanging open. Or else she shivered and shook and screamed about things that made no sense. Some sort of fever, Kemir thought, and it went on for so long that he was sure she'd die. She didn't though, and eventually the fever broke. At least when she was well again she had some idea of how to survive. After the first few days she took to coming with him. She didn't even have any boots, but it didn't seem to bother her to clamber over the stones and the moss in bare feet. Each day she came with him to the end of the ravine and then waited while he hunted. When he was done he'd start a fire, and they would sit and watch the flames. They didn't speak, but there was a sense of something shared between them. Of surviving whatever the cost. Every day he'd give her the choicest piece of whatever he'd killed, and then they'd lie down next to each other and doze. She didn't say much, and she often seemed to drift away. Lost somewhere far away. Or else she had fits and screamed. She seemed to understand when he wanted to be alone. Sometimes, when he touched her, she flinched and froze. And sometimes, when he remembered again that Sollos was gone, he saw in her eyes the same fierce hunger for revenge as he felt inside.

She suited him, he decided. He didn't mind keeping her alive.

As each day began to fade they slowly made their way back, chewing on raw pieces of meat. The Scales was always there when they returned, waiting for them. Every day they came back later than the last, but he never said anything. He didn't eat much either. He was slowly wasting away, waiting for his dragon to come back from wherever she'd gone.

Twice Kemir saw other dragons in the distance. He watched them, little specks in the sky, until they were gone. They never found Snow's ravine.

Snow slept for four weeks, not two. By then the Scales was little more than skin and bone. Kemir and Nadira had left him there with his dragon as they did every morning. When they came back, after dark, he was gone. The dragon was awake. The air smelled of gore.

Meat!

Kemir froze for a moment, then pushed Nadira back the way they'd come. "Run! Now!" He lowered the remnants of the wild pig he'd killed to the ground. He could feel the dragon inside his head, almost insane with hunger, eyeing him up.

"Alchemists," he said loudly. "I'm going to take you to the alchemists, remember. Eat me and you'll never find them." He stepped back away from the pig. The dragon lunged forward and snapped it all up in a single gulp.

Hunger! Feed! There was a tinge of anger in there as well.

"Where's Kailin?"

The dragon withdrew slightly. He could feel something in its thoughts that might have been shame.

Little One Kemir, it spoke in his head more quietly this time, *I have been gone for a long time. I am very, very hungry. I need to feed, and I cannot hunt until I have sunlight. It is best that you leave.*

Kemir retreated back down the ravine and spent the night huddled with Nadira, shivering, trying to keep warm. Without the heat of the dragon, a night on the mountain, even out of the wind, was unpleasantly cold.

By morning the dragon was gone. They made a quick search for Kailin, but there was no sign of him, and Kemir's heart wasn't really in it. When the dragon came back, late in the afternoon, its snout and claws were stained with blood, and its breath was foul. It looked fat, Kemir thought.

They flew north because that's where the alchemists laired. The dragon never said what had happened to the Scales, and Kemir never asked.

THE DRAGON-KING'S TITHE

The rider, if his Hatchling Gold has bought him favor, may visit many times before a suitable dragon is hatched. On each visit he will bring a gift to the eyrie-master, and these gifts are of the utmost importance, for their quality and generosity will determine the care with which the chosen dragon is raised. When a suitable dragon is finally hatched, a price will be set by the dragon-king himself. This price is the Dragon-King's Tithe.

Usually the tithe is agreed far in advance, yet until the price is paid the rider can never quite be sure that it will not change. Sometimes the tithe is everything that the rider possesses; sometimes it is nothing at all.

40

❧

PARTING

Jehal awoke from a restless sleep. His dreams had been troubled—always running, always being watched, always chased, always having to look over his shoulder—and everywhere he ran the walls, the trees, even the rivers would burn and melt and the heat would force him to run again.

He slipped out of bed and padded to the window. Kazah, his potboy, was slumped on his stool, snoring loudly. Jehal opened the shutters to let in the light. Kazah didn't stir. That was what Jehal liked best about the boy. Aside from being a deaf-mute and blessed with a loyalty that put Jehal's hunting dogs to shame, Kazah slept like the dead. Jehal could have an all-night orgy, and the boy would be none the wiser.

Outside, the sun was creeping over the horizon. Ships bobbed on the water out in the estuary of the Fury River. In places the water seemed to be on fire, burning in the dawn sun. Jehal shuddered and turned away. The sight of it reminded him too much of his dreams. There wasn't a little golden dragon with ruby eyes perched on the sill outside. That was the important thing.

He padded back to his bed, sat down, pulled a strip of

white silk out from under his pillow and wrapped it around his eyes. His sight blurred, shimmered and shifted, and then he was somewhere else. He was in the Tower of Air in the Adamantine Palace. In Zafir's bedchamber, out of sight under the bed.

He listened. He could hear breathing. *Her* breathing. Relaxed and restful, as though she was asleep. He didn't hear any snoring. If Hyram had been there with her, there would have been snoring. Then again Hyram rarely came to her, and when he did, he rarely stayed. Usually Zafir went to him and then slipped back to her own bed once he was asleep. Sometimes when she came back in the middle of the night, barefoot, hugging her clothes to her, she looked desperately sad. Other times she looked angry. Yet other times she would look around the room, searching for his little golden dragon, and then she would stand in front of it naked, and blow him a kiss, or mime being violently sick or slitting someone's throat. Whether she meant him or Hyram, he was never quite sure.

Sometimes, in the morning, she would look for him too, and if they were both alone, they'd whisper to each other through little golden ears and watch through little ruby eyes.

That would be later, though. This was much too early for Zafir. Under her bed the little golden dragon twitched its head and skittered across the floor. It flapped its wings, so fast that they vanished into a blur, and lifted off the ground; then settled itself at the head of the bed, a couple of feet away from Zafir's head, and stopped, staring at her. Jehal took a deep breath. She was fast asleep. Sometimes when she was sleeping, she was breathtaking. He could have stared at her for hours.

He shook himself, took the white silk off his eyes and slipped it back under his pillow. Then he put on the other silk, the black one.

Well, my lover, let us see who you've been spying on today.

The answer wasn't much of a surprise. Zafir's Taiytakei dragon had secreted itself in Lystra's room, where it usually was. Zafir clearly had nothing better to think about than how often he was sharing Lystra's bed. Which was pleasantly predictable of her. Jehal grinned to himself and kicked

Kazah's stool. The trouble with Zafir's jealousy was that it was a challenge. It made him want to see how many times he could bed his wife without his lover and her spy-dragon catching them at it.

It was depressingly easy too. But then if it had been harder, he'd probably have done it even more.

He kicked Kazah's stool again. The potboy jerked upright and then fell over sideways. He jumped to his feet, ramrod straight, and saluted.

Message for my wife. Jehal and Kazah had their own sign language, a bastard hybrid of the signals that the dragon-knights used when they were flying together, the signs that some thieves used, and other bits that they'd simply made up themselves. Jehal was having the boy taught to read and write too, but he was so slow that one of them would probably be dead before he got anywhere.

Kazah nodded. Having a private language meant no one else understood what Jehal was telling Kazah to do. Several times he'd sent Kazah to Lystra to arrange a rendezvous knowing full well that Zafir was watching him.

Wake her up. She is to come to my bed. Tell her I want her. Kazah smirked and Jehal grinned back. *That* gesture wasn't particularly hard to translate. *Tell her to shut all windows and doors first. Tell her that eyes are watching her.* He gave Kazah a kick and watched the boy scurry away. Then he closed the shutters, blocking out the dawn light, lay back in his bed and sighed.

He didn't have to wait long. He heard footsteps outside and then giggling, and then Kazah slipped back in with Lystra behind him, still in her nightclothes.

Jehal grinned. "Did anyone see you?"

Kazah shook his head. So did Lystra. "Only the guard you put on my door." She flung her arms around him and snuggled her head against his chest. He always flinched for a moment when she did that. It reminded him too much that he was going to have to let Zafir have her way one day.

But not yet. He pushed her gently away and put a hand on her belly. She had his heir inside her, and that made her the safest person in the world just now. He'd have to wait another couple of months before he could feel it move, they told him, but he put his hand on her anyway. After this morning they might not see each other for a while.

She held his hand there for a second, then moved it up to her breast. "I still don't see why I can't come with you."

Of course you don't. He smiled at her. "You need to conserve your strength."

"Oh Jehal, I hardly know it's there."

"You're sick every day. Don't pretend you're not."

She made a face. "That's nothing."

"Besides, you're safer here."

"But why? At the palace I'll have you and my mother and my sisters and all their riders as well."

He laughed. "You know the answer. There might be people who would prefer your mother not to take Hyram's place." *Me, for example.*

That was the trouble. She simply didn't understand that anything might happen, that someone might break their word, that the dragon-kings and -queens weren't all fast friends working together for the good of them all. Which made it very difficult to look her in the eye sometimes. And if she'd really thought there *was* any real danger, she'd either insist on going to be at her mother's side, or else insist that he didn't go so he'd be safe too. She didn't insist on things very often, but when she did it was a timely reminder of who her birth-mother was.

He kissed her lightly. "I don't want to trouble you."

"I think you're just bored with me."

Inside his head Jehal rolled his eyes. *That* old chestnut again. *How* many times had he heard that? And from *how* many different women? "If I was bored with you, my love, would I have risen at dawn and called you to my bed for one last time before I leave?"

She stuck out her bottom lip and then took hold of his other hand and put it on her other breast. She smiled. "I suppose not."

She stepped a little closer, until he could feel the heat of her right from her knees to her neck. Jehal swallowed. He looked at Kazah and nodded at the door. The boy was smart enough to know when to make himself scarce.

"I'm leaving in the middle of the morning for Clifftop," he said thickly. "Everything is packed. It'll take me—"

Lystra put a finger to his lips. "I know, husband, I know." She called him that a lot, and for some reason his head went fuzzy every time she said it. "Four days to reach the palace, a week as Speaker Hyram's guest, and then a week more after my mother succeeds him. And then another four days back to Clifftop and yet another day to return here. Almost a month. I know it all by heart, my Prince. Every day, where you'll be and what you'll be doing." She smiled at him. "One very long and lonely month. I might come out to Clifftop to meet you when you come back."

"You shouldn't."

"Yes, but you won't be here to tell me not to." She pressed herself against him and kissed him, and he lowered her down onto his bed.

"I shall miss you greatly," he said, and was surprised to find that he meant it.

"But not as much as I shall miss you."

He rolled her over and silenced her with his lips. Best not to let her say anything else. Sometimes when they were together like this he found himself questioning his whole purpose, and that wouldn't do. Instead, he set about making sure she really would think of him for every single day that he was away. Together, for an hour or so, they stopped time.

When they were spent she fell asleep in his arms, which was something she always did if he let her. To his surprise he fell asleep as well; the next thing he knew, Lord Meteroa was banging on the door, shouting at him that it was time to go. Lystra yawned and stretched. She got up and looked at him, a muzzy smile on her face.

"Do I have to go?"

"I'm afraid you do." Jehal shouted at Meteroa to leave them alone for a few minutes and started to look for his clothes. "Don't go back to your rooms for a while. Go out for a ride. Or go to the baths. Send someone to air them while you're away."

"Why?"

"Because I ask you to."

"But I wanted to wear—"

He looked at her sharply. "Humor me. A favor to me for giving you this time."

For a moment she looked hurt and he felt as though she'd knifed him. Then she smiled. "If that's what you want."

"It would make me happy. Listen!" He cupped her face. "While I am gone, trust Meteroa. Don't trust Princess

Jesska, Prince Iskan, Prince Mazmamir or any of their clan. We might have the same blood, but we also have the same ambition. Trust Queen Fyon but don't trust her sons, particularly Tyrin."

When she was gone, he called Meteroa in to help him dress. "Keep her safe while I'm gone. Whatever happens to her happens to you, my friend. You understand?"

Meteroa gave him a skeptical look. "Then I shall eat a lot and get fat for you, but please be back before she gives birth, Your Highness."

"There's always the chance I won't come back at all."

Meteroa cocked his head. "Then I shan't have to worry about her. Tell me, Your Highness, which one pleasures you the most? Your wife or Queen Zafir?"

Jehal felt his chest tighten. He snarled, "Get out!"

"Your Highness—"

"I said get *out*! Before I find something sharp."

Alone, he slowly finished dressing himself. Meteroa was getting above himself, he decided. The man would need taking down a peg or two after this was all done.

He's right, though. It's a question that demands an answer, and I don't have one.

The last thing he did, before he left, was take the black and white silks from under his pillow and tie them around his wrists. Southern knights often tied strips of cloth to their arms; worn on the left they were signs of conquests, on the right they signaled obligation, which made it an easy way to keep the Taiytakei silks innocently to hand. Generally, Jehal wore the black one on the left and the white one on the right. It seemed right, somehow.

Almost as an afterthought he took the black silk off again and put it across his eyes. The little golden dragon was still in Lystra's room, buzzing madly about the place, looking for a way out.

Jehal smiled. As he left, he started to whistle.

41

*

ARTS OF WAR

Jaslyn called Silence into a tight turn and dived. Five of Queen Shezira's riders, flying in a tight line alongside her, suddenly scattered, seemingly at random. The ground was straight ahead now, rushing to meet her. In the center of her vision a cluster of soldiers raised their dragonscale shields. Silence belched fire at them and then spread out his wings, pulling out of the dive. An immense hand pressed Jaslyn into the dragon's neck, knocking the breath out of her. She didn't have a chance to see whether the fire had done anything useful, but she doubted it. The soldiers were a half-legion of the Adamantine Guard and they'd had plenty of time to lock their shields together. Then again, the point of the dive hadn't been to burn them; the point had been to distract them, to give her knights a chance, to lead them into battle in such a way that she didn't get herself killed.

Behind her, the five knights strafed the soldiers from five different angles at once, wheeled and flew away. They'd spent years perfecting that maneuver, all for this one day.

When she was safely away from the soldiers on the ground and their vicious scorpions, Jaslyn let Silence pick up a little height and turned to look for her riders. Three of them were following her; the other two were already on the ground. Which meant that, after they'd sprayed their fire and turned away, the soldiers had managed to hit them. Which meant that, had this been a real fight, they'd be dead.

"Two?" Jaslyn patted Silence on the neck. "They got two. Did you see that? Do you think Mother's going to be angry?" She smiled to herself as she flew Silence over the soldiers, tipping them a salute. "So much for our clever plan, eh? Do you suppose we got any of them?" From up in the air it was hard to tell whether any of the soldiers had been burned. Even if their shield wall failed them, their dragon-scale armor would deflect the worst of the flames.

Scattered around the Hungry Mountain Plains, other legions of the Guard were under attack, as each of the dragon-kings and -queens put them to the test. Jaslyn circled for a while, watching in case any of the attackers had come up with something original, but as far as she could see, none of them had. In the distance she saw one group of knights try exactly the same ploy she'd used herself. They didn't get the timing right. When the first knight unleashed his fire and pulled up his dragon, the other five should have been right there and they weren't. They weren't out by very much, only a few seconds, but it was enough for the legion to adjust its wall of shields and scatter the flamestrikes. A hundred and sixty years ago, when Master of War Prince Lai first demonstrated the technique, he'd left a hundred men dead or injured behind him.

Jaslyn sighed. For every pattern of offense, the legions had a counter. Nothing ever changed. It was almost like a ritual dance where everyone knew all the moves by heart. Supposedly, Prince Lai had invented four of the fifteen recognized tactics. The other eleven were even older.

She turned Silence away from the battlefield and spiraled down. In the middle of the legions Speaker Hyram had his tower, where he and the dragon-kings and -queens who weren't participating in the mock fights could stand and watch. Her mother was there, and Almiri too. Lystra had stayed in the south, slowly getting fat with Prince Jehal's heir. As she flew past, she searched the tower for Prince Tichane but she couldn't see if he was there. The thought of the Crag King's ambassador left a strange sensation inside her, one that she usually reserved for her dragons.

She pushed all that away, landed Silence at the foot of the tower and handed him over to the alchemists and Scales who'd set up a makeshift eyrie around the tower. Then she bounded up the steps. Out over the plains, most of the other dragons were circling now, waiting to come back, watching the few who were still sparring with the legions.

"You lost two of my riders," said Shezira as soon as Jaslyn reached the top of the tower.

"Prince Lai's pattern of Autumn Leaves." Speaker Hyram smiled at her. "Ambitious. Difficult to execute properly."

"Which you didn't," added Shezira.

Jaslyn clenched her teeth. "What do you mean?"

"Your timing was wrong. The knights behind you were too slow. The legion had time to adjust." She shook her head. "Don't feel too bad. Someone else tried the same pattern and made the same mess of it."

"Prince Jehal." Hyram spat out the name. "Your execution of the pattern was better."

Shezira shook her head. "I disagree. They were both equally poor."

Jaslyn looked around, taking in all the faces. There were two men she'd never met who were Speaker Hyram's cousins, and a cluster of advisers around him. Next to her mother, Knight-Marshal Nastria was staring out across the plains, seemingly oblivious. Behind her, King Tyan sat in a chair with his tongue hanging out, his head lolling and his eyes staring up at the sky, constantly quivering. She recognized a few others from Lystra's wedding too. Queen Fyon, who smiled at her while her eyes filled with daggers. And Valgar and Almiri, of course.

Almiri caught her arm. "The signalers on the field flagged seven injured from your attack. Their shield wall wasn't quite perfect."

"And Prince Jehal?"

"Four."

For some reason that made everything better. "It feels strange, burning men I don't know for no better reason than entertainment. I hope they weren't killed."

"The signaler indicated injuries only."

"Who's winning?" Jaslyn tried to sound like she didn't care.

Almiri laughed. "Not you. Queen Zafir. Six dead, thirty injured."

"What?"

"She lost all her five riders doing it. She charged them. On the ground."

"She did what?"

"She put her five knights on their dragons on the ground, and they charged the legion as though they were cavalry. Ran straight into it. Scattered men everywhere. Broke their shield wall completely. Then she flew in behind and burned them. They got all the men on the ground but they didn't get her."

"But that's *cheating.*"

"Not according to Speaker Hyram. He let it stand."

Jaslyn clenched her fists and ground her teeth. "There are traditions! No contact. No one would land their dragons to attack a real enemy. They'd be killed at once! They're not supposed to do that."

"The riders who charged across the ground would all have been dead. Speaker Hyram has ruled that, since it was Queen Zafir's dragon who did all the damage, and since she escaped unscathed, the score stands." Almiri put an arm around Jaslyn's shoulder and led her toward the far corner of the tower roof, away from twitching ears. "If you want my advice, you don't say anything."

"It's *cheating,*" Jaslyn hissed again.

Almiri forced her to sit down. "It's only cheating if the speaker says so, and the speaker doesn't. When was the last time you saw Speaker Hyram? Before this, I mean."

Jaslyn spat over the edge of the tower. "On the way to Lystra's wedding. When Mother practically invited someone to steal our white dragon." She frowned. "If Prince Jehal can get King Tyan onto the back of a dragon to come here, why can't he bring Lystra with him too? That's not fair."

Almiri ignored her. "Have you noticed anything about Speaker Hyram?"

"Not really." Jaslyn shrugged.

"Have you noticed that he's not shaking or stuttering anymore?"

Jaslyn glanced back at the speaker. "Oh. Did he use to?"

"Little sister, do you notice *anything*?" Almiri laughed. "Speaker Hyram has been slowly dying for this last year. Alchemists' disease. Do you know what that is?"

Jaslyn shook her head.

"It's what King Tyan's got. Take a look at him."

"I know he's sick."

"It starts with trembling and shaking. Over the years you slowly lose all your capabilities. Eventually you probably die, but generally people either starve because they can't feed themselves anymore, or else their family sends them quietly on their way. King Tyan has had this disease for nearly a decade." Almiri shook herself. "Anyway, what I'm trying to tell you is that Speaker Hyram has been sick, but now he's better, and it's Queen Zafir who found him the cure. There are quite a lot of other whispers about Speaker Hyram and Queen Zafir too, so if I were you, I wouldn't say anything to his face."

Jaslyn sniffed. "Cheating is still cheating."

Almiri grabbed Jaslyn's arm and squeezed it hard. "Listen to me, little sister. You do nothing to annoy the speaker. You say nothing about Queen Zafir. Do you understand?"

"Why?"

"Because Mother will tear off your head if you do. She's nervous. I haven't seen her like this for a very long time. She thinks Hyram might change his mind about who's going to be the next speaker."

"But he can't."

Almiri's grip tightened until it started to hurt. "Yes he can. He's the *speaker*."

"We have a pact!"

"Which can easily be broken."

"But . . ."

Almiri let go. Her mouth twitched with amusement. "Little Jaslyn, these are kings and queens, not your dragons. They don't simply do what you tell them."

42

KINGS AND QUEENS

Hyram put down his cup and stood up. He looked around the immense ten-sided table at the kings and queens, the knights, the lords, the master alchemists, the priests. He couldn't remember the last time he'd felt so young, so strong, so powerful. His head buzzed with Zafir's potions. They left him on edge, hyperactive, almost priapic, but they made the shaking go away, and the stutter—that was what mattered. He wore the Speaker's Robe and held the Speaker's Spear, and the weapon's power coursed through him. He couldn't remember the last time he'd felt so strong.

Around the table the masters and mistresses of the nine realms interrupted their feast and gave him their attention, one dragon-king or -queen on each side of the table. Beside him on his side of the table sat Sirion, the loyal cousin who had inherited his crown and throne when he, Hyram, had become the speaker. On the tenth side, opposite him, sat the grand master alchemists and the dragon-priests who would anoint his successor. As expected, one side of the table was almost empty: the King of the Crags hadn't deigned to join them. *No surprises there.*

He banged his cup and cleared his throat. "These words are said once every ten years. You will hear them today. Some of you have heard them before. Some of you have heard them twice or even three times. They are old words and wise words. They are not my words, but the words of all speakers, crafted and honed over the decades. You will hear them now, and then you will not hear them again for another ten years, so I beg you to listen and remember." He looked around the table from face to face. Some were listening, some were simply pretending to listen. It didn't matter. His voice sounded strong, and he wondered if any of them could understand the simple joy of being able to speak again, to have the words come out of his mouth pure and fully formed, not wrecked and ruined by the twitching that used to plague him. In particular, he looked at King Tyan, his old friend and enemy. Now there was one king who wasn't listening. Tyan was asleep. Trembling a little, but mostly still.

Prince Jehal, sitting next to Tyan, caught Hyram's eye and cocked his head. Hyram bared his teeth and moved on.

"We keep histories of our dragons now." He nodded toward the alchemists at the end of the table. "We know when they were born, who was their sire and who was their dam. We breed them to our liking, but it was not always so. They were once wild creatures. We have no histories of them from that time. Not because there was no ink, nor because there were no books, but because they were all burned. There were no towns, no cities, not because there were no bricks and no mortar, but because they were all burned. There were kings and armies, perhaps, but they are forgotten, because they were all burned. We hid in the forests where the dragons couldn't reach us. We lived as the Outsiders live, filthy and starving."

He let his eyes wander over their faces again, and then banged his cup on the table a second time. This time the kings and queens banged the table with him. "That was before the alchemists came." He raised his cup to the far end of the table, where Jeiros gave an embarrassed nod. "Now the dragons are tamed and we are their fragile masters. You, Kings and Queens of the Nine Realms. *You* are their masters. You want for nothing and you answer to no one. Except . . ."

Now was the time. He took the Speaker's Ring, carved into the likeness of a sleeping dragon, from his finger and put it gently down. His finger felt strangely naked. Then he laid the adamantine spear beside it.

"Except to these," he said. Strange. He'd dreamed of doing this so many times, and it had always felt like the end of his life, as though it was the only thing keeping him together. He'd take off the ring and put down the spear and feel himself immediately begin to fade. Yet now, when the moment was real, he felt light-headed, as though this was the beginning of something and not the end.

He picked up the ring again and held it out for all to see. "This. This ring binds you. Binds you to ancient pacts made long ago between the ancestors of all our clans. Every ten years you shall choose from among yourselves one who will take this palace. To be the judge of your actions and the arbiter of your disputes. Ten years ago you and your forefathers chose me. My time is done. In one week you will choose another. I will guide you, but the choice, in the end, lies with you."

There. Done. The speech they'd all heard before, the speech made by every speaker since time began. His last duty. Speaker Hyram was no more. He wasn't even "Your Holiness." Just another dragon-lord sitting at the speaker's table. He put the ring down and banged the table with his cup one last time.

Someone started to clap. Very slowly. Jehal. It had to be Jehal.

"What a fine speech." The Viper was smirking at him. "Pity I've heard it all before. Yet unexpectedly clear. I confess I've been dreading it. Th-Th-The l-l-long a-a-ag-g-gonizing w-wait for each word. Truly, the potions that your darling lover stole from me have worked wonders."

Around the table everyone froze. Some paused only for a moment and then continued to eat. Others stopped, waiting. No one said anything. They were all looking to Hyram. His feast, his hall, his palace, his job to admonish such crass behavior. Even if the insult was directed at him, Jehal was making fools of them all by being so direct.

Hyram sat slowly down. He smiled and folded his arms. "What *did* make you think I would have to give you anything for your elixirs?" He felt strong. Strong enough to challenge Jehal to a duel of the sword and the axe. He could do that now. One of the perks of being a simple dragon-knight again. Yes, and another perk was that he didn't have to be the diplomat now. It wasn't up to him to keep everyone in line anymore. "Never mind, eh? Go back home. Go back to poisoning your father." *I can say that now. In public. In front of everyone.*

That got them all. Even Zafir, even Shezira, who'd tried to pretend that Jehal hadn't said anything, even they couldn't ignore that. They stared at him in mute horror. All except the Viper, of course, whose mouth would probably still spew its villainous bile long after the rest of him was dead.

"Oh no, I couldn't do that. Since it seems you're going to live a while longer, I suddenly have something to keep me from growing bored again. I'll not forget your hospitality, Hyram. Perhaps now I'll be able to repay it one day." Jehal turned and stroked his father's head. "Or perhaps not. The potions haven't done much for King Tyan. He's too far gone. How long, do you suppose, before you follow him?"

"Perhaps he'd get better if you *stopped* poisoning him?"

This time Jehal got slowly to his feet. Several others rose as well: Narghon, Shezira, a couple of Hyram's own cousins. The rest were too stunned to move. Jehal leaned across the table. "Slander me one more time, old man, and I'll take you out to the challenge fields. I won't kill you, but you'll wish I had."

"Slander?" Hyram stood up as well. "Or the truth?"

"If it's the truth, why don't you show all these worthy lords and ladies some evidence? Oh!" Jehal slapped his forehead. "What a fool I am. Of course. That's because you *haven't got any.* Not one little shred."

"Then challenge me. I accept. Axe and sword. Ahh, please, *please,* little Viper, let us play."

Someone slammed a fist into the table. It took a moment for Hyram to realize that it was Shezira. "Enough, both of you. Hyram, don't be a fool. Prince Jehal, you began this childishness. Perhaps you should leave."

Jehal shot Shezira a look of pure hate. "Of course, Your Holiness. How rude of me to be accused." He took a step back and bowed. "King Narghon, King Silvallan, King Valgar, I bid you and yours a pleasant evening. The rest of you can choke."

In silence the table watched him go, his riders and King Tyan with him. When the door slammed, Queen Shezira resumed her seat. King Narghon was still on his feet. He shook his head. It made his jowls wobble.

"Lord Hyram, Prince Jehal is right. You should show us your evidence or still your tongue. And Queen Shezira, why should Prince Jehal be forced aside when he is the one who has been wronged?"

"Because, save for those of you who choose to be blind, we all know that I'm right," Hyram spat.

Shezira drummed her fingers on the table. "King Narghon, this is Hyram's hall until another one of us takes that ring. He cannot be sent from his own hall, and one of them had to go. Hyram, you might be right that there are several around this table who have their suspicions. Nevertheless, you have no proof. I am quite certain I know who was responsible for the theft of my white dragon."

"Aye, the King of the Crags. Pity he didn't bother to come. Where's Tichane to answer for him, eh? Not here either." Hyram smirked. The potions and the wine were making him light-headed, but for once it didn't matter. He didn't have to care.

"Does he ever come?" asked King Valgar.

"I'm not sure he even exists anymore. How would we know?"

Shezira cleared her throat. "When I have *proof,* I will pursue them, *whoever* they are"—she glared at Hyram—"to the end of the world. Until then I will keep my silence, and I suggest you do the same."

"I've had enough of silence."

He stopped. Zafir was leaning forward to catch his eye, shaking her head. "The wine is making you reckless," she said, quietly enough that most of the others wouldn't hear. "And the potions."

Hyram blinked. "Queen Zafir is quite right: I have made a fool of myself. Perhaps it is the prerogative of any man relieved of such a burden, but King Narghon is also correct. If the Viper has insulted my table and all who sit at it then so have I. Queen Shezira, it is me you should have sent away, not Prince Jehal."

Shezira pursed her lips. She didn't reply.

"Oh, I think you should both have stayed," said Queen Zafir pleasantly. "I was looking forward to watching you spill that murderer's blood!"

Narghon shot to his feet again. "I will not have these accusations!"

Zafir raised an eyebrow. "Didn't you know? Prince Jehal was with my mother when she died. They'd slipped away for a little tryst, and only one came back. I have drawn my own conclusions. You may do the same." Her brow furrowed. "Maybe she fell, or maybe she was pushed. Who knows? He did it, though. Either way, Prince Jehal has her blood on his hands. If he pushed her, I have to wonder why. Why would he do such a thing? If Aliphera had been here instead of me, what might have happened? Would Lord Hyram still have honored his brother's pact? Of course he would. So I can't help but wonder what madness is going through the minds of those who suggest that Prince Jehal would have killed her to remove a possible alternative successor." She was looking straight at Queen Shezira now. "Or to guarantee his bride. Or to ensure that he would be speaker one day."

The air chilled. It took Hyram a second or two to unravel what Zafir had said. By the time he'd worked it out, Shezira was already bright red.

"*Who* suggests?" she hissed.

Zafir shook her head. "Utter madness. So perhaps Aliphera wasn't pushed; perhaps she simply fell, but I'll call him—" She coughed and gagged. "I'll call him—"

She started to rise, slipped and fell to the floor, clutching at her throat. Whatever she was going to call Jehal, the dragon-kings and -queens never found out.

43

❖

POISON AND LIES

The Adamantine Eyrie was full. It was more than full. Makeshift pens had been set up out on the Hungry Mountain Plains, more for the herds of cattle to feed the dragons than for the dragons themselves. The speaker had laid out a tented village to shelter all the extra workers that had been drafted in. Some dragon-lords had also brought a few men of their own. And with the eyrie workers and the drivers and carters came the hangers-on, the traders, the fortune-tellers, the fortune seekers, the thieves, the pickpockets and the desperate, all of them sucked out of the countryside, drawn in by the knowledge that wherever there were dragons, there was wealth. The tented village had grown into a tented town long before the last dragon arrived. It was a crowded chaos where every other face was a stranger.

For two riders set upon a very private piece of business, it was perfect. They didn't look like riders; they looked like simple soldiers, sell-swords perhaps, or a pair of off-duty swordsmen of the Adamantine Guard. They moved with purpose through the stalls and traders, right to the heart of the makeshift town, certain that no one would recognize or remember them.

They were wrong. A boy, not quite a man, in a dull brown cloak and with a dirty face had been following them for quite some time, ducking and weaving through the throng. But the riders didn't know anything about that, not yet.

Near the center of the market they stopped at a little table set up in front of a tiny tent barely large enough for a man to stand inside. There *was* a man there too, a strange fellow with uncommonly dark skin. The clothes he wore were tattered and faded, but they'd been rich and ornate once. Any gold and jewels were long gone; only a dazzling rainbow of feathers remained. The riders seemed unimpressed by his strangeness. The boy hung back and watched them all with an expression of puzzled interest.

A purse changed hands. A heavy one by the looks of it. The dark-skinned man vanished into his tent and appeared again a moment later. He held out a leather satchel. The taller of the two knights took it and they moved quickly away. Too quickly. Too quickly to be innocent at any rate. The boy followed them to the edge of the market and into a large beer tent. In the middle of the day there weren't many people inside. The boy glanced at the riders and then padded across the sticky straw floor and sat down at a table.

"Oi! You! Clear off!"

It took a while before the boy understood that the shout was meant for him. He didn't look up but fished in his pocket and put a silver quarter down on the table in front of him. Out of the corner of his eye he watched the two men he'd been following. The taller one reached into the satchel, took something out and stuffed it inside his coat.

"Where'd you get your grubby hands on a bit of silver then?"

The boy still didn't look up. Off to one side, the satchel had passed to the shorter of the two.

"Thieving, is it? Picked some rich pillock's pocket, did you?"

The tall one was getting up now. Leaving. The boy didn't move.

"Ah, what do I care." A mug of something bitter-smelling

landed in front of the boy, splashing across the table. The
boy reached out and sipped at it. Eventually, the other rider
got up and left. The boy followed. He eased closer this time,
inching into the man's shadow until they were side by side.
The boy waited for exactly the right moment.

He snatched the satchel from the rider's shoulder and
dived down a narrow gap between the tents, skipping over
the ropes that held them up. The man roared and gave
chase, hurling himself after the boy, shouting and screaming
for someone to stop him. The boy was the more agile of the
two, but the rider was fast and strong and made a good
show of keeping up. The boy led him away from the center
of the tented town and in among the cattle pens that surrounded it.

Away from the crowds, the boy turned a corner. Instead of
running, he hunched down into a corner among the shadows.
When the rider barreled round a moment later, the boy let
him pass and then stood up behind him.

It was done in an instant. The man's steps faltered as he
wondered which way to go. A blade, blackened so it
wouldn't catch the sun, flicked out of the boy's sleeve and
into the rider's side in one fluid stroke. The boy was already
running again before the man even knew he'd been stabbed.

The rider launched himself after the boy again. He
took a few steps. His hand went to his side, and then he
stopped. He looked at his hand and at the blood streaming out of him. Inside he was suddenly burning. He
couldn't speak. The pain grew and grew, filling him up
from his core to the tips of his fingers and toes, and yet he
couldn't speak, couldn't move, couldn't even scream. Mercifully, when the pain reached his head, everything went
white and then dark.

The boy dropped the knife and kicked it aside. He zigged
through the maze of wooden pens out of caution, but no cry
went up behind him. He sprinted. He'd chosen the place to
murder the knight quite carefully, but now time was against
him. He ran to the edge of the pens, to where another rider,
this one in full dragonscale, was waiting with two horses.
When Rider Semian saw the boy, he nodded and climbed
into his saddle.

"Is it done?"

The boy gave a curt nod and mounted the second horse.

"What about the other one?"

"I recognized him. He's another one of Jehal's." The boy threw off his cloak. When he took off his hat, long dark hair streamed out. He wiped the dirt off his face and suddenly wasn't a boy anymore, but Lady Nastria, Knight-Marshal to the Queen of the North. "Go! We need to be quick."

Nastria wheeled her horse and pushed along the muddy paths between the pens, retracing her steps. As they got close to the dead dragon-knight, a couple of old women got up and ran away. They hadn't had time to steal much more than the dead man's purse, and Nastria didn't begrudge them that. The two dismounted and tied the body across the back of Nastria's horse. Together, they galloped toward the Adamantine Palace and the City of Dragons. As they drew close, Nastria dismounted again, put her peasant cloak and hat back on and led both horses up to the palace gates.

"Rider Semian, pledged to Queen Shezira," declared the knight. The gate guards looked him up and down, took a good look at the body on the other horse, then nodded and let him pass. Nastria carefully stared at her boots. The guards barely noticed she was there at all.

They made their way to the Tower of Dusk in the western wall of the palace. There were many towers scattered through the palace, and each one had been given over to a different dragon-king or dragon-queen while the next speaker was being chosen. Queen Zafir resided in the Tower of Air. King Valgar had been given the Tower of Dawn on the eastern wall. King Tyan had the smallest of them, the Humble Tower. Kings Narghon and Silvallan had the Tower of Water and the City Tower over in the northern section of the palace. The Tower of Dusk had been given over to Queen Shezira. Nastria led the horses right up to the tower doors. Rider Semian opened them and they went in, dragging the body of the dead knight with them.

Inside, several other of Queen Shezira's riders were waiting. As soon as the doors closed behind him, Nastria threw off her disguise again. She pointed at the body. "Get that down to the cellars. Where's the queen?"

"The queen is with the speaker."

The riders parted as Lady Nastria pushed between them. Two reluctantly picked up the body by its arms and legs. "Your Ladyship, this man isn't dead."

Lady Nastria paused and frowned. "Just get him down there. Let Master Kithyr know that he's needed."

The knights exchanged nervous glances. Nastria shooed them down the stairs. In the wine and food cellars they cleared a heavy wooden table and laid out the body. Nastria looked him over. They were right. The man wasn't quite dead after all.

She slapped his face. "Can you hear me, traitor?"

The man didn't move, so Nastria moved around him and jabbed a finger into the wound in his side. This time he moaned and opened his eyes.

"Hurts, does it?" She pushed her finger farther in. The man wailed and screwed up his face. "Rider Tiachas. A few months ago, you flew your dragon out of Outwatch with your two other brothers in treachery to the edge of the Barnan Woods. You took them to meet some outlaws. They went to buy something. You took them to the edge of the woods and they never came back. Do you know what happened to them? They were killed. I paid a pair of sell-swords to do it. I often wondered what went through your mind when they didn't come back. Were you afraid? And then, slowly, as the weeks turned into months and no one came for you, there must have been hope. Pointless, useless hope, Tiachas, because there's always been someone watching you. Can you hear me?" She wiggled her finger and Tiachas squealed. "All I want to know, Tiachas, is who poisoned your soul. I was there, just now, when you bought the poison from that Taiytakei clown. I saw you with Prince Jehal's man. Was it Jehal, then?" She forced open his eyes and held out the satchel. "What is this, Tiachas? Some sort of poison? Did Jehal pay you to murder our queen?"

Tiachas rolled his head from side to side. His tongue lolled out of his mouth. Blood was pouring freely from the wound in his side again, pooling on the floor under the table. Noises bubbled in his throat, but if he was trying to speak, the sounds made no sense.

"No? Are you trying to tell me that I'm wrong?" Nastria pulled a knife out of her belt and started to toy with it. "I don't think I believe you, Tiachas, but I don't mind. You're trying to pretend you still have some courage and honor, and that's a good thing. So I'll humor you. All I want to know is who, Tiachas. Who bought you?"

The head-shaking intensified.

"I *will* torture you, Tiachas, and you *will* tell me. And when you have, I will parade what's left of you in front of every court in the realms before I hang you. I will destroy your family, root and branch. They will lose everything, and they will hate you because *you* were the traitor who brought this down on them. Do you understand?"

Tiachas lunged at her, but he was feeble and slow, and Lady Nastria moved easily out of the way. The pair of riders caught him and held him down before he could roll off the table.

Nastria turned away. "Let him go, and leave us. Please encourage Master Kithyr to hasten himself."

The riders released Tiachas. They seemed uneasy and left slowly. Nastria watched them go.

"You know what disturbs them so, don't you? No, perhaps you don't. Master Kithyr is not a torturer but a blood-mage. So you *will* tell me what I want to know. And if you were hoping to die before I found out what I wanted, I'm afraid you're going to be disappointed there too."

Nastria walked slowly around the cellar. Everything here had been laid in by Speaker Hyram's stewards for Queen Shezira and her knights. Hyram must have done the same for all the dragon-kings and -queens. How easy it would it be to poison an entire clan.

She put that thought aside. No speaker in two hundred years had murdered a guesting king or queen, and she doubted Hyram was about to start. She selected a bottle of wine, opened it and poured some for herself. Eventually she heard Kithyr padding across the stones toward her, but she didn't look around.

"Tiachas is a tool," she said softly. "I want to know who the craftsman was."

It took the sorcerer an hour. There weren't even any screams, but then that was always the way with Master Kithyr. Always quiet. Throughout it all Nastria didn't look around. She stood statue-still, sipping at her wine, and by the end the bottle was empty. She didn't feel even slightly drunk. Instead she felt cold. Blood-magic. Another necessary evil. Like sell-swords.

When the blood-mage was done, she heard him padding softly back toward her.

"Well? Am I right? Was it Jehal?"

"No," whispered the sorcerer. "The Taiytakei."

She thought about that for a while. The mage didn't move.

"He met one of them, who gave him something," said Lady Nastria after a while. "A flask. Filled with liquid silver. Like the last one. I still want to know what it is and what it's for."

"Ask your alchemists. There are plenty of them. You know there's only one liquid that is of interest to me, and it is not silver in color." She could hear the sorcerer's disdain.

Nastria spat. "Every time I do that I lose another alchemist. Huros, Bellepheros . . ." A second of silence passed between them.

"What should I do with the body?" asked the sorcerer. "Shall I leave it here?"

"No, Master Kithyr. Make it go away. Where no one will ever find it."

She sighed as the sorcerer went about his work. So much for parading her traitor in public. It simply wasn't the same when all you had was a collection of bits.

44

❧

A CRACK IN THE STONE

High above the city, perched on a tiny plateau of rock overlooking the top of the Diamond Cascade valley, Hyram and Queen Shezira stood side by side, watching the water rush by, hundreds of yards beneath their feet.

"Queen Zafir. How is she?" Shezira stood inches from the edge. Hyram was even closer. The tips of his boots were actually sticking out into the void. One good push and both of them would be dead.

"Recovering well."

"That's good to hear. So was she poisoned or wasn't she?"

"She's been a little unwell of late."

Shezira cocked her head. "A little? Hyram, when she collapsed everyone thought she was dead."

"She choked. That's all."

"Well then I'm sorry for you that she ruined what was left of your feast."

Hyram laughed. "We both know it was ruined already. When Queen Zafir collapsed, most of you couldn't get out of my hall fast enough. She was doing you all a favor. Giving you a polite excuse to leave."

"Very kind of her, I'm sure." Shezira swayed slightly as a gust of wind whistled along the valley. "I would prefer to return to the pavilion now."

Hyram didn't move. "This always used to be one of my favorite places when I was younger. You can see right across the realms from up here."

"I prefer to be on dragonback."

"I know. But standing here is a reminder of how far the likes of you and I can fall. One missed step and we plunge to our dooms. It's been more than two years since I came here, you know. I couldn't stand like this when I was sick; I would have fallen."

"Hyram, when we ride we wear harnesses to secure us to the backs of our dragons so we cannot fall, no matter what we do. That is what the dragons do for us. We can be as foolish as we like and our dragons will save us."

"They didn't save Aliphera. Or Antros."

"They won't save anyone who refuses to wear a harness." Shezira turned away. "If you stand there on the edge for long enough, Hyram, you *will* fall. Learn from your brother's mistake."

Set back from the edge was the small pavilion built by Speaker Mehmit some two hundred years ago. The Purple Spur mountains were littered with little follies like this. Most had fallen into ruin, but this one had been popular with the speakers who'd followed him. From the bottom of the cliff it was invisible, and even from above it was almost impossible to spot unless you already knew it was there. It had become a little secret that the speakers had shared, passed down from one to the next. It was also an excellent place to spy on the Diamond Cascade, which had always been a popular place for dragon-lords and dragon-ladies who hungered to be away from the eyes of the palace court.

She went inside. There wasn't much to the pavilion, only a single airy room with open arches instead of windows. At the back were two wide alcoves, both generously piled with luxurious furs and soft cushions. It wasn't hard to guess what the speakers had used *those* for.

Has he brought Queen Zafir up here? Shezira pursed her lips. Of course he had.

She heard Hyram come in behind her and turned. "It's good to see you in such good health, Hyram."

"I can promise you, no one is more pleased than I am."

"Are you going to marry her?"

That stopped him. For a moment Hyram froze. "I think Queen Zafir stole the secret of the potions from the Viper to spite him. She knows how I feel about him."

"*Everyone* knows how you feel about him." Shezira cocked her head. "But I'm not quite sure I understand it."

"He's poisoning his own father."

"Is he? Is he really?"

"I am certain of it." Hyram's brow furrowed. "Can't you feel it from him? The coldness? He's not human like the rest of us. He's vicious, callous, arrogant, self-obsessed—"

"You could be describing any of us." She smiled slightly.

"You don't understand, do you?" Hyram shrugged. "Ask Queen Zafir. She knows exactly what I mean. Maybe she'd be able to explain it better."

Shezira's smile faded. "Yes. So are you going to marry her?"

Hyram didn't smile. "Yes, Shezira, I am."

"And are you going to name her speaker, so you can carry on in the shadows behind her?"

This time he didn't say anything.

"Does she understand that she has to give up her throne, her crown? Does she have an heir ready to take on those burdens?"

That made him laugh. "Do you?"

"We have a pact, Hyram. If you name Zafir instead of me, I will challenge her. And you will make a bitter enemy of me. Isn't Jehal enough?"

He looked at her. After a few seconds he turned away.

"I think I shall leave now." Shezira strode past him back out into the open air. She signaled to the dragon-knights circling high overhead to take her back down to the palace. Almost at once a dragon tipped its wings and almost fell out of the air toward her, landing perfectly on the flat area of rock outside the pavilion. The rider threw down a rope ladder but didn't change position. Shezira frowned. Her riders knew better than that. Whoever it was should have moved aside so that she could take the reins.

When the queen didn't move, the rider lifted her helmet. "Are you coming up or not, Mother?"

Jaslyn. Shezira climbed up to sit behind her daughter.

"I would like to fly Silence back to the palace, please."

Jaslyn looked at her as though she was mad and didn't move. Shezira bit back her irritation and buckled herself into the second harness. Jaslyn clucked at Silence, who ambled toward the edge of the cliff and flopped lazily into the air, gliding down over the Diamond Cascade valley, out over the falls and into the immensity of space over the City of Dragons.

"You're upset, Mother," shouted Jaslyn.

Shezira kept her lips tightly pressed together. *Upset? Upset?! I'm furious, you stupid girl. More than furious, and you would be too if you knew. If you had any ambition, you'd be seething!* There wasn't any point in saying anything to Jaslyn, though. *I suppose I should be grateful that she's noticed anything at all.*

"Mother, you're making Silence anxious."

For an instant everything went red. She twitched in the saddle, half of her set on lunging forward to wring Jaslyn's neck, the other half determined to stay in control. Underneath her she felt the dragon twitch too, and lurch suddenly forward.

"Mother!"

Shezira clenched her fists. Jaslyn could tell something was wrong because her *dragon* could tell something was wrong. *That* was much more like her daughter.

"Take me straight to the palace," she snapped.

Jaslyn tipped Silence into a dive. The dragon tucked his wings into his body and simply fell, headfirst, tail stretched out behind him, toward the palace. They dropped like that, half a mile vertically through the air. The wind was immense. It was impossible to say anything; by the end, as the palace spread out before them, it was almost impossible even to *feel* anything except the rush of it, and the sharp terror, tightly held in check, that they were going too fast, that they couldn't possibly stop . . .

Silence spread out his wings. Shezira pitched forward, helpless as the dragon slowed. She couldn't breathe. She must have blacked out, because one moment there was a crushing weight on her back and everything was gray, and the next the weight was gone, and they were floating down in looping circles, already below the tops of the palace towers. When they landed, Jaslyn threw down the ladder.

Shezira climbed down very slowly and carefully. She was shaking. When she got to the bottom, Jaslyn was looking down at her with a big grin on her face.

Shezira didn't smile. "Hyram is going to name Queen Zafir the next speaker," she said. "Why don't you take her for a ride and see if you can crush *her* to death?"

She turned away and strode toward the Tower of Dusk.

45

❧

SEMIAN

Rider Semian's leg still hurt. On the outside the wound had scarred over and healed weeks ago. Inside, though, it ached. If he tried to run, the ache got worse. Climbing the stairs of the Tower of Dusk left him sweating at the pain. Even if he simply stood still, it slowly grew worse until he had to sit down. The sell-sword's arrow had hit the bone in his thigh. He must have chipped or fractured it, and it was never going to be quite right ever again. He tried not to let it show, but the other dragon-knights were slowly realizing that he was a cripple.

He stood stiffly straight as Lady Nastria climbed wearily up from the cellars. She looked very tired, more drained than Semian had ever seen her. A strange smell wafted up from behind her. Something bitter and acrid. Then the sounds started. Soft tearing sounds at first, then bones cracking. He shuddered and tried not to think about it.

At the very moment that Lady Nastria emerged from the cellars, a dragon landed in the yard outside. Semian recognized it at once. Silence. Others opened the door as the queen strode in. She looked angry and shaken.

"Your Holiness." Lady Nastria stepped out in front of her. "I have found—"

Queen Shezira waved her away. "Hyram is going to name Queen Zafir the next speaker."

Everything in the room stopped. People froze. Whispers died. Everyone stared at the queen.

Shezira cocked her head and looked at Lady Nastria. "You were saying?"

Nastria bowed deeply. "One of your knights has betrayed you. He has been bought."

"Ah." The queen pressed her lips together. "Another poison plot, Knight-Marshal?"

Lady Nastria nodded. "I believe so, Your Holiness. I have the poison. I need to take it to the alchemists' redoubt to identify it."

"Out of the question." Shezira shook her head emphatically. "Now that Hyram has betrayed our pact, I need you here. I will challenge his decision, and I need to be sure I have enough dragon-lords behind me. I would not wish this to become a war." She paused and looked suddenly thoughtful. "Send Princess Jaslyn. Let her do it." A slight smile crossed the queen's face. "Yes. It would be good to get her away from here for the next few days."

By the door Rider Jostan was already running into the yard, waving and shouting, trying to call back Silence before he and the princess launched into the air. He was too late. Semian watched the knight-marshal's face. She looked far from happy. But whatever her doubts, she bit them back and bowed again.

"Of course, Your Holiness. I would like to send an escort."

Shezira frowned. "We still have an encampment in the Spur. It's only a few hours away."

This time Nastria stood her ground. "Nonetheless."

"Very well." The queen sighed. "Two riders, no more. Make sure they are replaced from among the encampment."

Which wouldn't upset any of them, Semian thought ruefully. Since the day he'd been shot by the sell-sword, they hadn't found a trace of the white dragon, nor of the Scales who was with her. Almost certainly they were both long gone, and the search had become a complete waste of time. But no one had dared tell that to the queen, and so they carried on.

The queen wrinkled her nose. "What *is* that terrible smell?"

Lady Nastria blanched. "It's the cellars, Your Holiness. Something has rotted. It will be removed shortly."

"And the smell with it, I hope." Shezira strode on, starting up the sweep of spiral stairs that rose through the middle of the Tower of Dusk. "Someone tell my steward to prepare for guests this evening. And send an invitation. I think I should spend some time with my son-in-law and see what sort of impression Lystra has made on him. As soon as he is willing. Marshal, with me. You look like a peasant, and I'll be wanting you at your best. And since we're having guests, that smell had *better* be gone."

The queen vanished around the curve of the stairs. Lady Nastria followed, but before she did, she pressed something into Semian's hands. "Take this to Princess Jaslyn at the eyrie, and be quick about it."

Semian's mouth fell open. *She's a princess. How can I tell her what to do?*

"Take Rider Jostan with you. The princess has an eye for both of you." And then Knight-Marshal Nastria winked at him, which left him even more speechless.

On horseback he raced with Jostan to the Adamantine Eyrie, his leg getting steadily worse all the way. As they arrived, Princess Jaslyn swept out of the eyrie, heading toward one of the queen's carriages.

"Your Highness!" Semian jumped off his horse. In his haste, his leg almost buckled under him. Jaslyn gave him a cold look, certainly not the sort the knight-marshal had been talking about.

"Semian?" She didn't break stride.

"Your Highness, Her Holiness commands you to the stronghold of the alchemists."

Jaslyn threw back her head and barked a laugh. She opened the carriage door.

"Your Highness! Lady Nastria has executed Rider Tiachas for treason. He is implicated in a plot to poison the queen."

Jaslyn climbed into the carriage and made to close the door.

"Prince Jehal is also implicated."

That made her stop. Breathlessly, Semian explained what the queen had ordered them to do. Jaslyn's eyes narrowed.

"So Mother is sending me away, is she?" She spat, and storm clouds flashed in her eyes. "Will this be enough to bury Jehal, do you think, Rider Semian?"

Semian lowered his eyes. "I cannot say, Your Highness."

The princess snorted and slowly climbed back out of the carriage. "Why does she send me, Rider Semian? Why not you? Are you not competent to run errands?"

Semian stayed carefully silent.

"Or you, Jostan?" She barked out another harsh laugh.

"Rider Nastria would have gone herself, Your Highness," said Jostan quietly. "It was the queen who ordered otherwise."

"Of course." Jaslyn bared her teeth. Without another word, she strode back into the eyrie.

BY THE TIME THEY WERE flying again, the sun was already sinking toward the horizon. Dragons were nervous in the dark, but Jaslyn drove them on at a merciless speed. They'd all spent months among the valleys of the Purple Spur looking for the white dragon. Even blindfolded, Semian could have flown among them and been almost sure to reach his destination.

A dozen dragons and three times as many riders, together with several alchemists and scores of camp followers, were still camped out in the Worldspine. Over the months the tents had gone, replaced by a neat row of log cabins alongside the river. Sections of the forest were still being cleared, making way for cattle, driven up from the nearby valleys in King Valgar's realm.

A bonfire, lit at the highest end of the camp, guided them in. The dragons circled overhead, spitting blasts of fire to announce themselves, and then glided nervously down along the river, dipping the tips of their tails, feeling for the ground. As soon as they touched water, they tipped back, spread their wings and stopped dead in the air, dropping the last twenty feet onto the rocks of the riverbed. Rider Semian's dragon lurched sideways and almost toppled over. Semian screwed up his face and closed his eyes, but Matan-izkan found her balance and righted herself. By the time Semian dismounted, Princess Jaslyn had gone, vanished into the same cabin that she'd lived in for most of the last two months. Semian and Jostan looked at each other, shrugged and went to bed.

By first light they were in the air again, flying north through King Valgar's realm, skirting the edge of the World-spine. In the afternoon they reached an apparently make-shift eyrie that was little more than a field with a small fortified manor house. Semian took it to be the provincial home of some bumpkin baron at first, a convenient place to stop and then move on. It didn't take him long to realize that he was wrong. The house was run by the Order of the Scales and contained alchemists, several of them. There were soldiers here too, and not any soldiers, but Adaman-tine men. The speaker's soldiers.

He listened as Princess Jaslyn and the alchemists talked, and he slowly understood. Somewhere a few miles to the east was the start of an old hidden road that ran deep into the Worldspine. At its far end was the alchemists' hidden strong-hold, the source of their power—a day on dragonback, but a week or even more on foot or on the oxcarts that carried the barrels filled with the alchemists' potions. Every week, no matter the weather, a convoy left the stronghold, feeding the eyries of the realms. The secret of the alchemists' potions was a precious one, closely guarded by the order and shared only with the kings and queens of the realms. Semian knew better than to ask exactly what they did, but it was something to do with taming the dragons. Everyone knew *that*.

Princess Jaslyn still carried storm clouds on her shoul-ders, the alchemists were taciturn and suspicious, and when he left, Semian was glad to go. He was bored too. Flying beside the princess was something of an honor, and cer-tainly better than sharing a tower with a blood-mage, but after a while all the mountains looked the same. Back at the palace the tournaments and games would soon be starting. There was glory to be had, and gold too. Out here there was nothing. Nothing to do and nothing to see.

Nothing at all.

46

THE VALEFORD TRACK

Snow dived out of the sun. Stretched out along the mountain track were five wagons, a couple of men on horses at the front and perhaps a dozen soldiers at the back.

"Burn the soldiers first," screamed Kemir, trying to make himself heard over the wind. He had a saddle now, and he and Nadira rode on Snow's back instead of being carried in her claws.

"You don't need to shout," yelled Nadira in his ear. Kemir closed his eyes. He still hadn't grown used to Snow plucking the thoughts out of his head.

No.

Snow ignored the soldiers. Instead, the first burst of fire hit the riders at the front. They had felt the rush of wind, perhaps, because Kemir thought he saw one of them look up and behind him just as Snow let loose. A blast of hot air hit Kemir in the face and he hugged Snow's neck.

They heard you shout.

Kemir felt Snow land. The air smelled of burning. He sat back up and saw that they were straddling the mountain track, blocking the way. The first wagon was on fire. Either side of the track smoke rose from a swathe of smoldering heather and gorse. Snow dropped to all fours, exposing Kemir and Nadira. She sent a second blast of fire along the road across the remaining wagons and toward the soldiers. Then she snatched up one of the dead horses and bit it in two, swallowing the back end whole.

Somehow, one of the horsemen was still alive. Staggering to his feet among the ashes, he started to scream. His clothes were burned to his skin; every part of him was either blackened or raw and red. And he was obviously blind. Kemir put him down with an arrow.

The smoke and flames from Snow's flamestrike cleared. All the wagons were blazing now. The soldiers at the back were still there, though. They'd formed up behind a wall of interlocking shields, and as Kemir watched, the shields dropped for a moment. Behind the shields, the soldiers had a crossbow. A big one.

They were pointing it at *him*.

"Shit!" Kemir threw himself flat against Snow's neck, but what saved him was Snow herself. She lifted up her head as the crossbow fired. Instead of hitting Kemir, the bolt hit the dragon in the shoulder. Kemir felt the shock, the surprise, the unexpected pain. The bolt must have been as long as his arm, and the crossbow had enough power to puncture Snow's scales and drive the missile deep into her flesh.

Then came the rage. It rose up from somewhere deep inside, in a tight seething ball, and bloomed, filling Snow's thoughts; and as it filled the dragon, it filled Kemir too. He started to unbuckle his harness so that he could get at the soldiers with his knives, then stopped himself. Snow leapt forward. She smashed the five carts to pieces, hurling their burning wreckage far away across the valley as she went. The soldiers scattered, some of them struggling through the gorse on either side of the track, most running away down the trail. A few of them actually ran past Snow, dodging between her legs. The dragon flicked her tail back and forth over the track, and at the same time sent another spear of fire down the trail ahead. Kemir glanced over his shoulder. One soldier had been knocked flying. Another seemed to have dived into the gorse and was still alive. A third had somehow ducked under Snow's tail, but she caught him just as he was getting away, cracking the tip against the side of his head so hard that Kemir could actually see the man's neck snap.

Behind him Nadira unleashed a scream of banshee violence. Kemir's fingers were fumbling at the harness again, tearing at the straps that kept him on Snow's back. The anger was overwhelming. He *needed* to fight.

Snow reared onto her back legs and pounded along the track, picking up soldiers as she caught them. She crushed one, hurled the next high into the air and tossed the third into her mouth, biting down so hard that his armor shattered. Finally Kemir freed himself. He slithered down the back of Snow's wing and then down her leg. He landed hard, almost got himself trampled, had to dive out of the way of Snow's flailing tail, but none of that mattered. The dragon-rage had him and he couldn't feel anything else. He leapt up to his feet again and jumped into the gorse, chasing one of the fleeing soldiers. His bow was still tied to Snow's saddle, and that was fine. He didn't want to shoot these men in the back. He wanted the joy of driving his knives into their bones.

The gorse was dense and the soldiers were in heavy armor. The man he'd set his sights on stumbled; Kemir bellowed and threw himself on top of him, wrestling him, hacking at him with his knife. The soldier was wearing dragonscale plates, which would turn his knives no matter how hard he stabbed, but armor always had gaps. In the crotch, behind the knees and elbows, around the throat. The soldier half rose to his feet, raised an arm to ward Kemir off and reached for his sword with the other. Kemir's first knife found the soldier's armpit, driving up into his shoulder. The soldier opened his mouth in shock, and Kemir drove his other knife down the man's throat. He pulled both blades out as the soldier fell, howled in exultation and looked for someone else to kill. Snow was a few hundred yards down the track now. She'd stopped and was sweeping the bushes with flames.

He remembered the soldier who'd dived into the gorse to escape Snow's tail.

Alive. We need one alive. Although it was hard to remember that through the haze of murder in his head.

Nadira was off Snow's back as well. He saw her in the gorse, lifting up a heavy stone and smashing it down again.

He couldn't see what she was crushing. *Someone's head, most likely.*

He couldn't see any soldiers now. They were all gone, lost among the thorn bushes, most of them shattered or burned by Snow's wrath. If any of them were still alive, they were hiding. You couldn't outrun a dragon.

"She can hear your thoughts," he shouted. "You can't hide from her."

The dragon had finished burning soldiers. She came pounding back along the track, shaking the earth, past where Kemir was standing, back to the ruins of the burning wagons.

Alchemists. Where are they? She didn't make a sound, but the thought was so loud in Kemir's head that it made him wince. He started back toward the wagons as well. Snow was rummaging in the bushes, clawing out the half-burned bodies of the wagon drivers, the ordinary men who'd happened to be in the way. She gave each one a cursory glance and then tossed it into the air.

Dead.

When the bodies came down again, she caught them in her mouth and swallowed them whole.

Dead.

Nadira staggered out of the gorse onto the track. Her hands were bloody, her face a strange expression of exultant shock. She came toward Kemir. Her eyes were very wide.

Dead.

"I killed one!" She sounded amazed. "I never killed anyone before, but I did it. I smashed his head with a rock."

Dead.

The bloodlust was still there, still strong, but no longer overwhelming. Kemir took her hands in his. "Do you know who these soldiers were?" She shook her head. "These were Adamantine Guardsmen. The speaker's men. The best soldiers in the realms, or so they say. They train to fight dragons."

Dead.

He looked around at the carnage and laughed. So much for the Guard, but then what were they thinking? What was anyone thinking? How could a man fight a dragon? How could even an army of men fight a dragon?

Dead.

He left Nadira to search the corpses for anything worth stealing and went to look at the weapon they'd used to shoot at him. It was smashed, crushed under Snow's claws as she'd run past, but the remains told him enough. He'd been right—it *was* a crossbow, the biggest one he'd ever seen. It probably took two men to even carry it. The mechanism for cocking it was splintered beyond recognition, but Kemir guessed it was some sort of crank. It probably took three or four soldiers to use the weapon. Grudgingly he found himself impressed that the soldiers had been quick enough to use it at all.

Alive! Kemir, there is one alive. Ask it! Make it tell you where the alchemists are to be found!

A shriek echoed between the mountains. A dark shape swooped out of the sky toward them. Kemir's heart sank.

Shit. Ash.

47

✤

ASH

When he'd set out with Snow to find the alchemists, Kemir had soon realized that he didn't know where they lived after all. What he knew was that the blood-mages who had first conquered the dragons had lived somewhere in the north of the Worldspine, and that the alchemists had raised their stronghold in the same place. It had never occurred to him how vast the Worldspine was. They'd searched for days, and the mountains had stretched on forever in every direction they looked. The days had become weeks. All they ever found were bleak snow-covered peaks, lush forested valleys and, when they strayed close to the realms, occasional Outsider camps.

You lied to me. You do not know where the alchemists live.

All he could do was let Snow peer into his thoughts, let her see for herself that he'd never meant to fool her, that he'd always thought that his knowledge was enough. Sometimes, when she was angry with him, she was terrifying. It was hard to live with a creature that could extinguish him so easily, over which he had no power.

Because of your alchemists, it is my kind who have no power, she'd replied.

He'd gone into a couple of Outsider settlements with some of the weapons and money they'd stolen from Queen Shezira's dragon-knights. The first village had given him a cautious welcome and taken his gifts, but they hadn't known anymore about the alchemists. The second had taken him captive. They probably would have killed him if Snow hadn't crashed in first. She'd destroyed the village and any-one who wasn't quick enough to run away into the trees. She was pitiless. Man, woman or child, if it moved, if it thought, it burned. Some of them got away, and Kemir al-most had to beg her not to hunt them down. Snow had given him a curious look, an expression he'd come to recog-nize as a mixture of incomprehension and indifference. She'd let the survivors go in the end, but the memories made him shiver. They'd been Outsiders, which sort of made them his people. Snow didn't care. She'd squashed them with all the compassion of a child crushing ants.

They'd flown south again, deep into the Worldspine, still searching. There, Snow had spotted a lone dragon in the far distance. Kemir couldn't even see it at first but then made out a tiny black speck in the sky, miles away.

There is another dragon, Kemir. Alone.

"Where there's a dragon, there's a rider. Maybe *he* knows where the alchemists hide away."

Snow climbed higher and surged through the air. The dragon-knight saw them coming but didn't seem particu-larly bothered until Snow swooped down and almost landed on his dragon's back. She ripped the knight out of his saddle. The other dragon shrieked and did what they always did—it dived for the ground. Snow banked into a steep spiral, fol-lowing it down. This new one was shorter than Snow, but heavier, squat and compact. A war-dragon, Kemir decided. A poor one too, since its scales were a dull dark gray, almost black in places, and barely gleamed at all.

Alchemists! Where are the alchemists?

It took Kemir a moment to realize that Snow wasn't thinking to him, but to the rider she'd seized. The two drag-ons whirled toward the ground. Kemir's fingers gripped into Snow's scales. Riding behind him, Nadira's arms around his waist were like a vise, crushing the air out of him. The wind took his breath away. Nadira might have been screaming, but he didn't hear it so much as feel it reverberating through him.

Where?

His heart almost stopped as the ground hurtled toward him—he could almost believe that Snow was so set on having an answer to her question that she hadn't noticed—but, as always, at the last moment she spread her wings and he nearly fell off her back, and then they were suddenly down on the ground.

The near-black dragon was eyeing them mournfully. Snow hurled the rider at it. The beast sniffed the body and then curled up around it, head held erect and alert. It never blinked, Kemir noticed.

Your kind are too fragile, grumbled Snow.

"Did you get an answer?" Kemir was shaking and Nadira was sobbing. He badly wanted to get off Snow's back and feel the solid ground beneath his feet, but the sight of the other dragon made him stay where he was. For all he knew, Snow might simply fly off and leave him there.

I might, conceded Snow. *You have been little use to me.*

Kemir tried not to think about that. "Well, did he tell you anything or not?"

No. He was in pain and fear and then he died. I saw a place in his mind, very briefly. It is somewhere in the realm of one of your kind called Valgar.

"King Valgar."

You know this man?

Kemir couldn't help but laugh. "He's a king, dragon. He wouldn't spit on my corpse, much less know me. I know where to find him. It's north again. Where we've already looked."

Then we will look again.

He sighed, ready for Snow to take to the air straightaway expecting to find the alchemists before the sun set. And then when she didn't, she'd fly into a rage, and he and Nadira would cower and pray to whatever gods might hold sway over a vengeful dragon, and he'd wish that Sollos was here because somehow Sollos had always known what to do.

"I should run off and leave you," he muttered.

I would not let you, Kemir. Not now.

But Snow didn't take off; she cautiously stepped closer to the other dragon.

Get down and hide among the trees for a while. This one has a deeper rage than mine inside it.

They didn't fly away to continue the search that day, nor the next, nor the one after that. Instead, Snow stopped looking for the alchemists and stayed with the dark dragon for a month. Sometimes she ignored him for days at a time. She hunted alone and brought back food for the other dragon. Kemir, in his turn, hunted with his bow. He kept himself and Nadira alive. The mountain valleys were cold and wet and treacherous. Ordinary men died in places like this, but there was always food and water, and shelter as well, if you knew where to look for it.

Finally Kemir decided he'd had enough. He'd barely even seen Snow for four days, and the two dragons were flying together now.

"They don't need us anymore," he said to Nadira. "They've forgotten us. When they remember, they'll eat us."

They packed what little they had and left, striking west. He didn't know where they were, but the Worldspine ran from north to south, so heading west was bound to take them back into the realms sooner or later.

Snow caught them three days later. She landed as close as she could, while the other dragon circled over their heads.

There are two of us now. Her thoughts didn't seem angry, but Kemir felt the conviction behind them.

"Is that one of you for each of us?" he asked. He couldn't help himself.

There is one harness for your kind. It is of no consequence to me to wear it.

"And what if I don't want to ride you?"

Ash will burn you where you stand.

"Ash?" Kemir glanced up. From below, the war-dragon simply looked black.

Ash. That is the name your kind gave him, and now that he has awoken, he hungers for the same vengeance. So, Kemir, will you ride with us?

"Do I have a choice?"

You always have the choice to die.

Wearily, Kemir climbed up the ropes onto Snow's back. It took him a good part of the day to adjust Ash's harness so that it fitted her properly and didn't threaten to tip them out every time Snow launched herself into the air. They turned north once more, Ash flying alongside them. The black dragon made Kemir's skin crawl. Snow's indifference was bad enough—but to Ash, Kemir and Nadira simply didn't exist. His thoughts, when he spoke to Snow, were clear enough. Men and women were food, nothing more.

They resumed their search. One fruitless day passed and then another, and then, in the middle of the wilderness, Snow spied a cluster of wagons driving along a hidden track.

AMID THE BURNING WRECKAGE SNOW rose onto her hind legs. In her foreclaws she was holding a body. *Alive! Kemir, this one is alive. Ask it! Make it tell us where the alchemists are to be found!*

Kemir shouted, "Then put it down before you break it!" As he walked toward her, Ash swooped low over the track.

Hungry!

Snow looped her tail around one of the bodies and hurled it into the air. Ash caught it on the fly.

You should have waited, Ash thought reproachfully. *The smell of them burning has given me an appetite, yet you've left me nothing to sate it. At least, nothing still breathing that I can chase.*

Kemir shivered.

Soon. Snow cocked her head as Kemir came closer, and gently lowered the twitching soldier onto the ground in front of him.

"I said don't break him," Kemir growled. "When you want to know something, all you have to do is pick someone up and shout inside their head. When they've stopped screaming in terror, the next thing they'll do is tell you anything you want to know. Even if they lie to you, you'll know it. What you don't do is crush his rib cage while he's still shitting his trousers." He looked at the man and cursed. "You're as impatient as a two-year-old."

Snow snarled at him. *I am seven years hatched, Kemir.*

"You're as impatient as a *human* two-year-old. You have

to wait until whoever you've got can properly understand what's about to happen to them. *Then* ask your questions." He turned quickly away and kneeled beside the soldier. If Snow decided that now was finally the time to eat him, he didn't want to see it coming. "Have you got anymore? This one's probably past caring."

No. Make this one tell me what I want to know!

The soldier was coughing up frothing blood. Snow had caved in one side of his chest. It was a miracle the man was still alive.

"Soldier?" Kemir got down onto his hands and knees so he could talk into the man's ear. "Soldier? Can you hear me? What's your name?"

The soldier mumbled something that Kemir couldn't make out.

Iyan. He knows himself as Iyan of the house of Liahn.

Next to Snow, Ash came to watch. The war-dragon looked bemused. Then he seemed to sneer and turned his attention to the bolt still embedded in Snow's shoulder.

"Iyan? The dragons are their own masters here. They mean to burn the alchemists. Every one of them. They will stop the alchemists from making their potions. All the dragons will be free. They'll burn us all. Every man, woman and child, every last one of us. No matter what it costs us, we must not let these dragons know where the alchemists are. Do you understand? If you know where they are, you must not even think about which way they are to be—"

That was as far as he got before a claw came down, and Ash drove the crossbow bolt into the soldier's chest, pinning him to the ground. The soldier gasped and was still.

Clever, Little One. Very clever.

"Well, I hope he had a good think about all the things I told him not to tell you before you skewered him." Kemir backed away from the dead soldier. Ash had never even acknowledged him before.

When we have all we need from you, I will "skewer" you too. The dragon gestured with a wing along the track. *That way. I have seen a place in his mind.*

Ash didn't bother to wait, but that didn't matter since he was slower than Snow in the air.

As Kemir and Nadira strapped themselves into the harness on her back, Snow spoke in his head again. *When you spoke to the broken man and told him of the things that would come to pass, and that he should not tell us or help us, I could not tell whether you were speaking only to trick him, or whether you meant every word. Which is the truth, Kemir?*

Kemir grunted. "I don't know. I couldn't tell either."

48

❦

ALLIANCE AND BETRAYAL

"The trouble is," drawled Prince Jehal, "that I'm simply not important enough." He was lounging against the battlements on the top of the Tower of Dusk, quietly enjoying himself.

The night air was cool and fresh and clear. If he looked over the wall, he could pick out the night-watch patrols in the City of Dragons by the light of their lamps. Beyond the city the moon shimmered in the sky and in the Mirror Lakes below, and then the Purple Spur rose like a black wall, creeping up from the horizon into the sky, eating the stars as it went. Queen Shezira's feast had been sublime, far better than Speaker Hyram's. He felt sated, serene and relaxed. It helped his mood immensely to see that Queen Shezira was anything but. She paced back and forth across the top of the tower, face set in a deep frown.

He smiled. "Hyram is a bastard," he added. "Did you know he summoned me here about Queen Aliphera, and then when I dutifully came, he tortured me? I wasn't going to make anything of it when it looked like he was going to die very slowly and miserably. Didn't seem much more I could do than nature had already done. Now, though ..."

He shook his head and sighed. "What difference can *I* make? Hyram will oppose your challenge and so will his family. So will Zafir, and so will Narghon and Silvallan. So should I. A speaker from the south is overdue, and I've no reason to dislike Queen Zafir. As I said, the trouble is that I'm not important enough."

Queen Shezira stopped her pacing and looked at him directly. They were alone on the battlements by her insistence. No one, she said, was to hear what they had to say to each other. Even the rooms below the roof had been cleared, and the stairs were guarded by her most trusted rider. And one of his as well, so they could keep an eye on each other.

"You're important enough. I already have King Valgar and one other that I can count on. Valmeyan won't be here and so won't have a say. Neither do the Syuss. I only have one question for you. What do you want?"

Jehal's smile widened. "I told you, sweet Queen. The trouble is, I'm not *important* enough." He met her gaze. If she was too stupid to understand what he meant, she didn't deserve his help.

She wasn't stupid. Slowly, she nodded. "The Speaker's Ring. You want to succeed me when my years are up."

"That would be a most enticing prospect."

"And the most obvious demand. Yes."

"And will you make Lystra your heir? To take your crown when you take Hyram's ring. So she need not worry so much about my rabble of half-cousins sniffing after my father's throne?"

She pursed her lips. "Perhaps. If you'll give me your word to pass the Speaker's Ring on to Lystra when your time is done, and let Almiri become Queen of Sand and Stone in her place."

Jehal nodded, then made a show of looking concerned. "Wait. Begging your pardon, Your Holiness, but isn't all this the same assurance that Hyram gave to you? His word?"

"Are you calling me a liar, Jehal?"

He folded his arms. "Let's just say I'm still a little irked that you dismissed me from Hyram's table two nights ago. One might have the impression that you think Hyram is right, and that I *am* poisoning King Tyan. Perhaps I've been poisoning Hyram as well, who knows? But if you did think such a thing, I would have to wonder as to the worth of your promises. Your word given to a prince may bind you, but your word given to a poisoner? I don't think that means very much to you."

"If I had thought there was any truth to Hyram's suspicions, I would never have given you my daughter, Jehal."

A warm feeling spread out from somewhere deep inside him. Jehal smiled again. "Thank you, Your Holiness. I cannot describe how grateful I am to know that. You will declare me your successor when you make your challenge? In front of everyone?"

"Yes."

Jehal bowed. "Then King Tyan's vote will be yours, Your Holiness."

"Good. Our business is done. Return with me to the feast, if you will."

"Leave me here a while, Your Holiness. My mind is filled with ways to turn Silvallan and Narghon against Hyram and Zafir. Your victory would surely be even more pleasant if the two of them stood alone. I will rejoin you shortly, Your Holiness."

Shezira hesitated, then nodded. Jehal watched her go, sinking slowly down the stairs into the guts of the tower. As soon as he was alone, his eyes shifted. He looked across the Tower of Dusk into the palace beyond, to the tall and slender Tower of Air, which looked down on everything. He was smiling.

"Speaker. At last. So sorry, Zafir. Nothing personal."

Then he turned to look out to the mountains, leaning out over the stones, wondering what it would feel like to know that everything he could see was his.

He didn't look down. If he had, he might have seen a tiny pair of glittering ruby eyes.

49

THE EYRIE OF THE ALCHEMISTS

Princess Jaslyn was the first to see the smoke. It hung, a slight haze staining the air, a mile or two ahead of them. When she waved at him and pointed, Semian saw it too. As they got closer, he made out the remains of the wagons on the ground, and the gleam, here and there, of shattered swords and armor.

The three dragons split smoothly. Semian and Jostan dived low, one to the left and one to the right. Silence and Princess Jaslyn powered up. While she circled overhead, the two knights swooped over the battle site from opposite angles. They made a second pass and then climbed back to Princess Jaslyn.

"Wagons and soldiers. All dead," shouted Rider Semian at the top of his voice. "Dragon attack." He had no way of knowing whether Princess Jaslyn had heard him. There was a crude sign language that all dragon-riders learned, but it didn't cover things like this. The best he could do was: *Friends. Dead. Dragon spoor.*

He heard Jaslyn shout something back, but all her words were stolen by the wind. She signed: *How long?*

One hour. Two hours. "Recent. Not long ago."

Danger?

No. "Whoever did this, they've gone." Or at least he hoped so. There wasn't any sign of anything alive and moving on the ground, and whoever had burned these men could be miles away by now.

She told him to land and followed him down while Jostan circled overhead. They dismounted and picked their way through the wreckage. Parts of the wagons were recognizable—scorched axles and wheels. Most of the rest was charcoal and ashes, some of it still too hot to touch. There were a lot of bodies. *No. Bits of bodies. Soldiers.*

"These were the speaker's soldiers," said Princess Jaslyn. With a start Semian realized she was right. Adamantine Guardsmen. Most had been eaten, and all that was left were hands and arms and legs and pieces of crushed armor chewed and spat out. The few bodies still in one piece had been burned and crushed. There was one impaled to the ground by one of the Guards' own scorpion bolts.

"They're all dead, Princess," he said, and she nodded. "Do we search for who did this? They cannot have long gone. They may be resting their dragons or letting them hunt."

"Or they may be gone." Jaslyn shook her head. "We go on as we were. We'll tell the alchemists when we reach them. Once my mother is speaker, she'll put an end to these outrages." She walked back to Silence and climbed onto his back. "We fly at three levels now."

Semian nodded. Three levels meant that one of them would fly close to the ground and the other two much higher, separated by thousands of feet and impossible to surprise all at once. Which was Jaslyn's way of saying she thought they were in some danger. They took to the air once more. Jostan stayed high, so Semian flew low, with Princess Jaslyn somewhere between them. Flying in the middle put her in the safest part of the formation, but also meant that they were relying on her eyes to spot any danger. Semian tried not to think about that and concentrated on following the rutted track leading to the alchemists' stronghold. In a lot of places it was almost invisible. It vanished into wooded vales, twisted over flat slabs of rock and skulked under overhangs, almost as if it had been designed to be difficult to find and almost impossible to follow.

Late in the afternoon the track led Semian over a high pass and down into a lush green valley. A village lay spread out beneath him nestled against a rushing river and surrounded by fields and cattle. The track followed the river, past the village and through a stretch of woodland. The sides of the valley grew steeper and closer together until he was flying between two sheer walls of rock hundreds of yards apart. The cliffs were pitted with fissures stained with streaks of black and dark green. Tiny trickles of frothing water bubbled over the cliff edge and dissolved into clouds of spray. In every possible crack, stunted trees and bushes struggled to grow.

The cliffs came steadily closer together. Semian could feel Matanizkan's unease. She didn't like flying in such a confined place.

Abruptly, the cliffs closed completely. At the base where they joined, a loose collection of stone buildings hugged the rocks. Among them Semian could see the mouths of several caves, shafts of darkness disappearing into the earth. The river vanished into one of them; beside it was an eyrie, small but unmistakable. There were no dragons.

Matanizkan pulled up. There was nowhere left for her to fly. The walls of rock spun wildly as she pitched over. For a moment, Semian was hanging upside down; and then she'd turned and was diving toward the valley floor. Semian gritted his teeth and gripped his harness. Somehow she found the space to spread her wings and leveled out, her claws skimming the ground.

"Down," he told her, and she seemed almost grateful to land and catch her breath. He stayed in the saddle and walked her slowly back to the head of the valley, to the eyrie. By the time he got there, several alchemists were waiting for him. There were soldiers too, and several scorpions pointed in his direction. Cautiously he dismounted. He glanced up for Jostan and Princess Jaslyn but couldn't see either of them. Sandwiched between the walls of rock, he couldn't see much of the sky at all.

"Rider Semian in the service of Queen Shezira," he

called. The soldiers relaxed as he walked away from the dragon, and one of the alchemists approached.

"Keitos, senior alchemist." He bowed. "Apologies, Rider. We had no warning you were coming, and these are troubled times."

Semian wasn't sure what Keitos meant by that but kept his silence. They walked away from Matanizkan. "I'm riding escort to Princess Jaslyn. There is one other dragon-knight as well. Rider Jostan. They'll be arriving shortly." He forced a grin. "Interesting landing."

Keitos nodded gravely. "It was certainly an unusual approach. You haven't been here before, then. This place is difficult for dragons. That's one of the reasons it became a stronghold for us in the old times, before our order mastered them."

Back when you were blood-mages. But reminding the alchemist of his order's sordid origins would have been poor behavior for a guest, so Semian held his tongue. They waited at the edge of the eyrie as Matanizkan was lured out of the way. Eventually, he saw Jaslyn and Jostan flying down the valley toward them. They'd clearly seen him almost crash into the cliff and even Jaslyn was coming in low and slow. They landed gracefully, one behind the other, and dismounted. Keitos left Semian and went to greet them. When the alchemist returned with Jostan and Princess Jaslyn, he looked grim. Jaslyn was telling him what they'd passed on their way.

"Everyone was dead," she was saying, "and it was clearly a dragon attack." She looked at Semian. "Would you not agree?"

Semian nodded. Keitos bowed his head. "And the wagons, Your Highness?"

"Everything was destroyed. You know, I imagine, that several of my mother's knights were attacked some months ago."

"We are aware, Your Highness. One of your dragons was never found."

"A perfect white. We're still searching for her."

Keitos nodded vigorously. He led them into a crumbling stone longhouse. Semian noticed that the roof leaked. Everything here was damp.

"We don't have much by way of lodgings, Your Highness. There are a few rooms but . . ."

Jaslyn waved him away. "We won't be staying long, Master Keitos. I have something of a mystery to show you. When you can tell me what it is, we'll be on our way. I hope to leave at first light tomorrow."

"A mystery?" Keitos paused and his eyes lit up. "How unusual. I'm sure Your Highness will be most well received. Forgive me, Your Highness, but since many of our elder masters are now guests of the speaker for Queen Shezira's accession, might I ask why you came here? I'm sure their knowledge of potions would have sufficed."

"It's not a potion, Master Keitos. It is something more like liquid metal."

Keitos bowed. "We shall do our best, Your Highness."

"Good. And you will do it today, and then I will leave in the morning with all the proof I need to destroy Prince Jehal forever."

For the first time since they'd left the palace Semian saw something like a smile flicker across Princess Jaslyn's face.

50

THE DRAGON-PRIESTS

Hyram stood at the window of the Tower of Air. Over on the Tower of Dusk he could see two figures on the battlements and nothing more. Then Zafir wrapped the black strip of silk around his eyes and he was *there,* clinging to the stonework only a few feet from Jehal. He couldn't see much, until the end when Jehal leaned out and stared over at the City of Dragons. But that didn't matter. He heard it all. Every word. Even after Jehal had gone inside and there was nothing to see except the stars in the sky and nothing to hear but the wind, he stood there, silent and motionless. He felt as if his heart had been turned to stone. Very slowly he took off the silk.

"She's going to make the Viper speaker after her," he said. He still didn't quite believe his own ears. Shezira was almost a part of his family. It was unthinkable that she'd do such a thing, and yet he'd seen it. He'd *heard* it.

"I told you she would plot against you." Zafir's soft hands took his.

"But the *Viper.* How can she?" He shook his head in disbelief.

Zafir stood close behind him, close enough that he could

feel her heat. She was wearing a thin silken shift that clung to her in the breeze from the window. "Your family gave her their word that she would follow them. She's a proud and stubborn queen." Zafir shook her head. "And look at how much she's prepared to give him. She almost makes him king of her own realm while he waits."

"I would have had one of her daughters succeed you as speaker. She herself, if she was still sound of body and mind." Hyram wrung his hands. "Why? Why did she have to betray me like this? With the *Viper* . . ."

"It doesn't matter, my lover. Whatever you decide, I will be there for you, and surely you can rely on your own clan. What does Shezira have? King Valgar and King Tyan?" She snorted. "Not enough."

"Jehal will bring Silvallan and Narghon with him." He shook his head. If Zafir hadn't been holding him, he would have been pacing back and forth. He should have thought of this. Stupid to let Shezira see what was coming, and now he was going to pay for it.

"No." Zafir squeezed his shoulders and whispered in his ear, "I can promise you at least one, if not both."

"How?" Still, no decision was made. He could always name Shezira, as he'd first intended. He could still marry Zafir and live out his years as a king. Would that be so bad?

"Trust me, Speaker Hyram." Zafir slipped the black silk out of his hands. "I need to bring back my little spy." She wrapped the silk around her eyes and moved to stand right in front of him, facing the window, leaning very slightly into him. "Hold me," she breathed. "I lose myself sometimes when I do this. Don't let me fall."

"Yes, of course." One hard push and she'd fall out of the open window. The ground was a hundred feet below. She'd be smashed to pieces. *Just like Aliphera.*

No. He couldn't let Jehal win. He couldn't change his mind. Not now.

"Hold me tighter." Zafir was pushing herself into him, swaying slightly, gently grinding against his groin. She might have been doing it deliberately or she might not; either way, he felt himself respond. His arms reached around her, pulling her closer still. His fingers caressed her skin through the gauze of her shift. She was shivering.

"Are you cold?"

"No." She took one of his hands and moved it slowly over her until it reached her throat. She held it there. "If you thwart Prince Jehal in this, you'll be the center of his life. Everything he does will orbit around the hate he'll have for you."

Hyram nuzzled her ear and whispered, "Not for long. You'll hang him for the murderer that he is."

"Will I? I steal the potions that keep you a man from Jehal, but he's the one who knows what they are, and only he knows where they come from. Tell me, Speaker, what means more to you? Is it me? Is it Jehal? Or is it the potions? Would you give them up for all this? Would it be worth it?"

Hyram didn't answer. A decade ago he might have said it was Jehal and vengeance that mattered the most. Two decades and he would have said Zafir and the smell of her skin. Now, though . . . He closed his eyes. The potions. It was the potions.

Zafir gripped him tightly. "I know. I understand. Just remember that we might need Jehal for a little while longer, until we can find out where he gets them." As she spoke, a little golden dragon fluttered through the window on metal wings and settled on the bedpost. Zafir moved his hand down to her breasts. "Close the shutters. What's done is done. Queen Fyon is Jehal's aunt. She'll try to sway King Narghon behind Jehal. I can do something about that. You make sure of Silvallan and your cousin. That will be enough for us."

Hyram reached to untie the knot in the black silk around her face, but she turned deftly to face him and took his hands in hers.

"Let it stay there. I'd like to watch with the dragon's eyes."

She pulled him onto the bed, and as he pulled back her gown and pushed his way inside her, he forgot about Jehal and about the potions and there was only her. With the silk covering her eyes, it was easier to see Aliphera's face gasping beneath him.

He tried to slip out of her bed in the middle of the night, but she pulled him back and made him forget himself until the sun was creeping over the horizon once more. Then she slept, and Hyram lay wide-eyed and awake, staring at the

ceiling, and at the two pairs of ruby eyes that stared down
from the bedposts. Hadn't there been only one mechanical
dragon the night before? He tried to remember and found
that he couldn't. When he looked at his hands they were
shaking. Not a lot, but enough that he could see it. Fear
gripped him. Potions! He needed another draft already.

He dressed quickly and hurried away to his own rooms.
The potions were still where he'd left them, waiting for him.
He gulped down a mouthful and looked at what was left.
Slowly but surely they were running out. He was getting
through them faster than he had at the start.

Best not to think about that. Once all this was done, once
Zafir was the next speaker, he could concentrate his ener-
gies on the alchemists. Find out what these potions were
and where they came from. Make as much as he'd ever
need. Yes. That was the way it would be. And he'd have to
make Zafir speaker, because if he didn't, what then? To lose
her was to lose everything now.

The potion took hold of him. The shaking went away and
he felt strong again. He dressed himself properly and hurried to the Glass Cathedral, then stood at the altar and
waited. He tried not to remember being here months ago,
at his weakest, with Queen Shezira standing over him, cold
as ice and hard as stone.

"Lord Hyram." Out of the dark recesses of the church,
the dragon-priests filed toward the altar. They formed a circle around him and bowed as one. They never once spoke
of it, but he could feel their hunger for him, urging him to
go the way of the speakers of old, on a pyre lit by dragon
fire, his charred remains to be carted to the eyrie as fodder
for the beasts.

"High Priest Aruch." Hyram didn't bow. As speaker he
was bound to respect the traditions of the Glass Cathedral,
but as plain Lord Hyram he would treat them with the disdain they deserved. "I have not come to be reforged, if
that's what you're hoping."

Aruch didn't move. "Your Lordship was so close to the
ultimate mysteries," he whispered. "So close. Closer than
any speaker since the time of the Narammed. You are
fallen, Lord Hyram. Fallen by the hand of woman. So tragic.
You could have been one with us."

"Oh please, anything but that. Cut out my organs while

I'm still alive and take them to the eyrie. Even that would be preferable."

"Your words are meant to wound, but you cannot pierce our scales, Lord Hyram. We pity you, now and forever."

"You can do something else for me, Aruch, *if* you can spare the time. I intend to marry the woman you so despise."

"We know. We are prepared. And we do not despise Queen Zafir. We despise no one, and all are welcome within our walls. Always."

"Well, there will be a lot of us within your walls and sooner than you might have thought. The wedding is to come forward. Tomorrow, at dawn. Everyone is already here, so why not." Yes. It was an impulse, but it felt right. Bring it forward, if only by a day. Let everyone know. Let the battle lines be drawn. Let all his enemies array themselves out in the open where he could see them. Antros would have done the same, and Shezira too. So be it. Hyram turned and strode out of the circle of kneeling priests.

"Some even find comfort here, if you remember," murmured Aruch as he passed.

Hyram snorted.

"Some will, some won't. It will be interesting to see, don't you think?"

"Thy will be done, Lord Hyram. Thy will be done."

As he left, he felt the priests silently rising and returning to their shadows.

51

REBIRTH

They left the wagons still burning, the soldiers all dead and broken. Nadira watched as they shrank away into nothing, until even the pall of smoke was gone. She was a survivor; she prided herself on that. She'd had a husband, four children, the pox; she'd lost herself in Soul Dust and been attacked by dragons, raped by their riders and she'd survived it all. She thought about surviving for a long time as the dragons flew, and she thought about the soldier she'd killed, hammering his head with a stone until there was nothing left of his face. It had left her with a strange feeling, an empty floating sensation that she didn't understand.

She had no idea where they were anymore except somewhere in the Worldspine. The mountains she was used to were huge towering things that glowered at one another and kept their distance across deep wide valleys. Here, everything seemed all squashed together. The mountains were piled up right next to each other, sometimes on top of each other. The valleys were more like ravines. No one could live here. Or that's what she thought until she saw the village.

The dragons passed over it and then turned and soared away. She could feel their excitement. No thoughts came to her but she knew they'd found what they were looking for. They spent the rest of the day hunting, gorged themselves, and when they were done they curled up on a tiny plateau to sleep. Nadira sat resting her back lightly against Snow's scales. The air up here was bitterly cold, but in places the dragon was almost too hot to touch. Kemir stood up, strung his bow and went off. She understood men like Kemir. He was strong. He brought food. He kept her alive and made her feel safe, and in return she would stay close to him. If he asked, she would close her eyes and imagine herself somewhere far away and give herself to him. As far as Nadira knew, that was the way of the world for someone like her, as good as it could be. She should count herself lucky.

He came back an hour later empty-handed, looked at her and shrugged an apology, then walked off again. After a while she got up and followed him. He was standing at the edge of a precipice looking out at the mountains. Away from the dragons, the cold air quickly worked its way through her clothes to her skin. She shivered and huddled next to Kemir.

"There's no food up here," he said. "We go hungry tonight."

He didn't speak much, and usually she was glad of that. The dragons spoke even less. The white one said things to her sometimes. The black one only spoke as though she wasn't there. Hearing them inside her head had been a terror at first. Now, when they flew into a rage she flew into one too; apart from that, she barely noticed. They were all quiet company. She liked that, but not tonight.

"I've been hungry before. This is it, isn't it? They've found what they're looking for."

Kemir nodded.

"Good." It ought to frighten her, but it didn't. Instead, she felt a sharp stab of anticipation.

"Might be. Might not be." Kemir shrugged. "When they've done what they've come to do, I don't know what happens to us. They might leave us here. They might eat us."

"I don't think so. We'll find some way to be useful to them."

"We should run away again. They might not look for us this time."

Nadira put her arms around his shoulders. "Come back

to the dragons. I'm cold." When he talked at all, Kemir mostly talked about running away. She wasn't sure how much he meant it. They'd tried it the once, and that was all.

He shook her off, so she went back to the dragons on her own and curled up beside them to sleep. Kemir came back a few minutes later. He lay next to her, wide awake, staring at the stars.

"I was born in a settlement," he said. "I lived there until I was fifteen. Then the King of the Crags came. He was only a prince then. I wasn't there. I should have been, but I was off larking about with one of my cousins. When we came back, it was all gone. Nothing but ash. All we had was each other. On the day that you first saw me, they'd just killed him too. I can't run away. Not now. I want to see it all burn. They know that too, Snow and Ash. They know I'll stay."

Ash had started to snore. The sound was so deep that she didn't hear it so much as feel it gently shaking the mountainside.

"Riders came to my settlement too," she said quietly. "It was deep in the forest. Everyone thought we were safe. It was all trees. There was nowhere nearby for a dragon to land. Didn't help though. The trees weren't big enough. They found us and burned us through the leaves and branches, and then the dragons crashed into what was left and knocked it flat. The riders came after us, those they hadn't burned. Everyone was either killed or they took us as slaves. I wasn't good enough to be a slave. Too old, too ugly, too something. They took my boys though, the ones they didn't kill. I saw them." Her eyes glistened. That was the one memory she hung on to, watching her two boys, one eight years grown, one ten and almost a man, being dragged away. They'd been weeping and cowering, but it was a happy memory in a way, because at least they might still be alive, even if they were chained to the oars of a Taiytakei galley somewhere.

"They did what they always do," she said quietly. Kemir was still staring blankly at the sky, so she lay down next to him, forced herself to rest her head on his chest and run her fingers through his hair. "When they were done with us, they killed all the other women too old to be sold. But not me. They took me back to their castle and helped themselves whenever they wanted. After a few days I must have bored them. They took me back to where they'd found me and left me there in the cold ashes to die. The others were still there, their corpses already chewed to the bone. I suppose they thought that some snapper would find me before I could reach another settlement."

Kemir muttered something and draped an arm over her shoulder.

"The snappers must have eaten their fill. But it was all wrong after that." All wrong because she was useless. She was too old and no one wanted her. Among the settlements a woman on her own could mean only one thing. She'd moved from one place to the next, never staying long, selling herself to stay alive, stealing when she could, until she got caught and sold to a Dust gang. She didn't remember too much for a while after that, just doing everything they asked. Anything.

"Whatever it took to get more Dust," she breathed, and felt a pang of craving inside her. Even thinking about it, even after all this time . . . "And then they had enough too, and left me for the snappers again. Them or the cold." She laughed bitterly. "Snappers don't like me, I suppose. Too skinny. Not good eating. I thought I was seeing things. There was a huge white dragon. And then there was Kailin Scales. And then there was you, and then Kailin Scales went away, and I was still alive, and even the Soul Dust was gone, as much as it ever can be gone."

And she'd survived.

She felt the rise and fall of Kemir's chest. He was sleeping. She rolled away and lay next to him, watching the stars, feeling the heat from the slumbering dragon on the other side of her. She ran a hand over Snow's scales. They should have run away. They both knew it. They should have left when Snow found Ash. Right then, when the dragons were so distracted they might have got away. Instead they'd waited too long. Now the dragons would never let them go, but it didn't bother her; if anything it made her feel special. There were worse places to be.

Snow was deliciously warm. She could feel the sense of purpose that filled the dragons now, even while they were sleeping. It hadn't been there the day before. It was infectious. She wanted to *do* something. She had no idea what. She'd never had a purpose before, never had time for it. Not

starving, not being eaten, not dying of cold and exhaustion—
all that had been purpose enough. Suddenly she didn't have
to worry about those anymore.

Kemir had a purpose. The dragons had a purpose.

She'd thought about that all through the day, as the
mountains grew shorter and steeper and sharper and more
pressed together.

"I want to help kill the dragon-knights," she whispered.
She wasn't sure if she'd meant it for Kemir or for Snow, or
whether she was simply speaking to the wind. "Every one
of them," she added. "I want to kill them all." This surprised
her. It wasn't the purpose she'd expected. Maybe it wasn't
her purpose at all. Maybe the dragons had made her want
it, in the same way that when they grew angry she grew
angry too. Or maybe she'd caught it from Kemir. In the end
it didn't really matter, did it?

Nadira hunched her shoulders and closed her eyes. She
made herself small and snuggled next to Snow. The dragons
were dreaming, and from their dreams she knew exactly
what was coming.

Yes. There were far worse places to be.

RETURNING THE CINDERS

There is one last price a dragon-rider must pay.
When a dragon finally dies, it burns from the
inside so that all that remains beneath the scales
is charcoal and ashes. The scales survive.

They are light and strong, and above all fire and
heat will not penetrate them. Thus they are
much sought after as armor.

When a dragon dies and only the scales remain,
the rider must gather them and return them to
the eyrie and the dragon-king from whence they
came. Thus the dragon returns to the place of its
birth. Only from the cinders, say the alchemists,
can a new dragon be born.

52

✤

THE ALCHEMISTS

Jaslyn had come to see the alchemists once before. She'd been thirteen years old. Lystra was eleven, Almiri sixteen and very soon to be wed to King Valgar. They'd come with their mother and Lady Nastria on the backs of two dragons, both dead now. Jaslyn's memories were of huge dark caves and wizened old men and damp stone, and of Almiri being unbearable. Their mother had taken them down through endless tunnels to a place that had never seen the sun, lit only by a few lamps. The rush of some underground river had echoed everywhere they went. They'd come out into a huge cavern, and her mother had pointed at the purple stains on the walls.

"This is where our power comes from," she'd said. "These tiny little plants. The alchemists make them into potions. The Scales feed the potions to our dragons. The dragons do as we command them. Without these little plants we are nothing. Remember that, always."

Jaslyn had hated every minute of it, but what she had hated most was the thought that her dragons did as she asked of them because of some little plant. They were supposed to do it for *her*. For their love of *her*.

She was older and wiser now, but the feeling was still there, and it hit her in the pit of the stomach as soon as she landed. *I hate this place.* She looked at the cave mouths and trembled, and so it was a relief when Keitos led them through the jumble of stone houses instead. He bowed and nodded his head and mumbled platitudes, none of which she really heard, and took them into a squalid little hut where an old man sat at a bench squinting through a piece of colored glass at a leaf. They stood in the doorway and waited, but the old man didn't seem to notice them. He just looked at his leaf. He was deathly pale, and all that was left of his hair were a few white wisps.

Eventually Keitos coughed.

"I know you're there, Master Keitos." The old man didn't look up. "I know you have visitors too. Three dragon-riders. I felt them land. Whoever you are, you'll just have to wait."

"This is Princess Jaslyn, Master Feronos, daughter of Queen Shezira, our next speaker. Soon to be our mistress. With her, Rider Semian, also in Queen Shezira's service." Jostan had stayed at the eyrie to see their dragons were well cared for.

The old man sighed. He stared at his leaf for another few seconds and then put it down and looked at them. "Princess Jaslyn. Yes. You came once before with your mother. Five years ago, in the winter, when we were all covered in snow. Yes, yes. I remember." He didn't get up or bow, or do any of the things Jaslyn was used to. "Shouldn't you be at the palace?"

Jaslyn stared at him.

"Master Feronos is the wisest of us in the lore of stones and metals," said Keitos nervously. He shuffled his feet and took a step into the room. "Her Highness has brought something that she says is a mystery, Master. A liquid that is like metal."

"A liquid that is *like* metal or a liquid that *is* metal?"

"Prince Jehal may be poisoning Speaker Hyram or King Tyan with it. Maybe both. And someone has used it to try and poison my mother," snapped Jaslyn. She pushed Keitos out of the way and thrust the clay pot, still sealed with wax, in front of the ancient alchemist.

A gnarled, trembling hand reached out and took it from her. Feronos wasn't ready for how heavy it was. It tumbled from his fingers, and Jaslyn barely caught it before it smashed on the floor.

"Ahhh." The old man nodded. "I know this. It's been a long, long time since I've seen it. It doesn't surprise me that you don't know what this is. There aren't many that would. You have to be old like me to remember."

"You haven't opened it, old man." Jaslyn clenched her fists. "How can you know what it is when you haven't even opened it."

Silently, Feronos put the pot on his table and broke the seal. Very carefully he opened it. "A metal that gleams like silver and runs like water. Very heavy. Nothing quite like it. Very hard to find."

"I know *that*." Jaslyn stamped her foot. "Where does it come from? Who made it?"

"No one *made* it, girl. You cannot *make* this. As for where it comes from ..." He shrugged. "Not from within the realms we know, I can tell you that. We had some once. It came across the sea, I think." His brow furrowed. "Oh, now ... who was keeping it? Not here. Somewhere in the west. Old Irios had some in Shazal Dahn, but he's gone now. Long gone."

The old man seemed to drift away.

Keitos bit his lip. "Our stronghold in the western deserts," he said reluctantly. "We like to keep it a secret."

"But that's ..." Jaslyn's gaze shifted to Semian. "That's Speaker Hyram's realm!"

"It was a long time ago," whispered the old man.

Jaslyn rounded on him.

"But it's poison, yes? It *is* poison?"

He shrugged. "Drink enough of it and you'll sicken. Like a lot of things. Irios liked to work with it, but he went mad. They say the liquid metal did it to him. Sailors used to bring it to him. The alchemist's disease, they call it. Old age I say. Couldn't stop shaking. In the end he just walked out into the desert and never came back. Or that's what someone told me once, I think. Fumes in the air. But not a poison. Not unless you want to spend a decade waiting. No. Quicker to let age take its course, I would think."

Jaslyn gripped the table. The world seemed to spin and rush around her. "No. It *is* poison. Alchemist's disease. That's what Almiri called it too. And King Tyan, yes, he's been dying of it for nearly a decade, and Hyram, he's been ill for more than a year. Slowly getting worse. It *is* a poison. It *is* Jehal." She clenched her fists. "He's killing them so slowly that they don't know they're being murdered. Hyram has the right of it, and no one else believes him!"

Master Feronos carefully sealed up the pot and put it on the floor. He seemed slightly disappointed. Jaslyn strode back out of the hut and filled her lungs with fresh air.

"Highness!"

"Rider Jostan!" She looked at him in surprise. "You're supposed to be at the eyrie, seeing to it that Silence is cared for exactly as I requested."

"Highness, there are other dragons nearby. The white has been seen."

Jaslyn blinked. "What? Here? With the alchemists?"

"No. But two dragons were seen near the village a few hours before we came. A black war-dragon and a white hunter. It can only be ours. There *are* no other whites."

She snorted. "And who told you this, Rider Jostan? A peasant already in his cups? A farmer? Or was it the village idiot?"

"Your Highness, a captain of the Adamantine Guard. A legion of them protects the alchemists' redoubt."

"I've never heard of such a thing. Nor did I see any Guard as we flew in."

"They camp within the forest, under the cover of the trees."

Jaslyn shook her head. "No matter. We must return to the palace at once. Go back to the eyrie and have our dragons readied. Queen Shezira is on the point of making a pact with Prince Jehal. We must be back before the speaker is named. So we must leave *now*."

Jostan looked unhappy. "Your Highness, by the time the dragons are fed and readied the sun will be almost set. I beg you, please do not camp in the wilds of the mountains in the middle of the night while there are other dragons nearby. We do not know if they are friends or enemies or what their purpose is, but if one is the white . . . Remain here, Your Highness, in safety. We can leave at first light and still be back in time."

"Rider Jostan is right," said Semian from behind her.

"We will fly with you if we must and die to defend your life, but it is unwise to leave in such haste."

Jaslyn growled and clenched her fists, but they were right and she knew it. She stamped back into the hut and snatched up the pot of poison. *The Viper's venom.*

"Very well. First light. Not a moment later." She swept up her cloak and marched away, striding impatiently across the ground without knowing where she was going. *Nastria should have come. Too many mysteries. Wait, wait, wait; we should leave* now; *I should be with Mother. And what does Jehal get from poisoning her ten years from now? Why would he do that?*

And why is the white here?

53

❧

FIRST LIGHT

A low droning hum filled the Glass Cathedral. Hyram and Queen Zafir stood on either side of the altar. They wore jeweled dragon masks and long robes of gold and silver leaf that flowed and spilled across the floor. They were supposed to stand absolutely still, like statues, while the sun rose, until the first light of the day spilled in through the windows.

Shezira watched them carefully. She'd been through the same ordeal when she'd married Antros. She'd had to be still for nearly half an hour, and apart from giving birth to their daughters it remained the hardest thing she'd ever done. Antros, of course, had fidgeted constantly. Now Zafir was so still that she might have been made of stone. Hyram, she thought, was trembling very slightly.

The droning of the priests grew very slightly louder. The sun was nearly at the window. Shezira glanced over her shoulder. Jehal was sitting somewhere at the back with King Tyan. Tyan had gone into one of his moaning phases, and she could hear him even over the hum of the priests. If he was trying to say something, he'd long ago passed the point where anyone could understand him.

She'd made a point of going to see King Tyan and spending some time with him. He seemed to recognize her. He couldn't talk and hardly moved, and when he did, he trembled so violently that everything around him went flying. Yet she couldn't shake the feeling, when she looked into his eyes, that he was still in there somewhere, hopelessly alone and mad with despair. Afterward she'd found it hard to be angry with Hyram anymore. She'd even suggested to Jehal that he should give Hyram some of his secret potions himself, that they should make peace, but Jehal had only shaken his head.

"Never," he'd whispered. He was doing everything he could to discover how Queen Zafir had stolen them. It was all her doing. She had an iron wickedness inside her. A true dragon-queen.

Shezira looked at her, across the altar, trying to see it, but she could never get past how young Zafir was. *Too young to be a speaker.*

Finally, the first light spilled in and struck the altar. The priests stopped their moaning and closed in around Hyram and Zafir, waving their arms up and down, reaching for the sky and then the earth and then back to the sky. Whatever the symbolism of all these rituals, Shezira doubted that anyone but the priests understood it. No one cared about the dragon-priests anymore.

They backed away and fell to the floor, leaving Hyram and Queen Zafir standing alone in the orange dawn light. The masks were gone. They each reached out one hand toward the other, their fingers touched, and it was done. They were bound together, joined as one in the Cathedral of Glass, never to be split apart. Hyram was a king again.

Afterward, as the kings and queens walked amid a surfeit of petty princes toward the enormous breakfast feast that awaited them, Almiri fell in step beside Shezira.

"Is King Valgar well?" asked Shezira. They both knew she wasn't inquiring about his health.

"Resolute. King Tyan?"

"Bought."

"King Narghon?"

"Will do whatever Fyon tells him to, and Fyon has always doted on her nephew. Silvallan's going to be the hard one. He has reasons to be friendly to both Hyram and Zafir, but if Hyram's cousins turn against him, Silvallan will go with the tide. What have Sirion and his court got to say for themselves?"

Almiri pursed her lips. "They've said very little."

"Yes." Shezira glowered at Hyram's back, some yards ahead of them. "He's put them in a difficult position. He was their king before he became speaker, and acts as though he still is. But he's not the one who will suffer. If he gets his way and names Zafir, he'll stay at the palace. Sirion will remain on the throne and wear the crown, but Hyram's shadow will still be there. What does he do? He's an honorable man, I know that. Hyram's breaking a pact that their grandfather made. He needs to understand that I'll win without him and without Silvallan if need be. But it would be much better if the dragon-lords were united."

Almiri smiled. "Hyram's not quite himself. Ten years of peace and harmony shouldn't be ruined by one mistake of judgment. Let Zafir be the villainous witch that she is. Who can say what else she might put in the potions she feeds him? And she says she steals them from Prince Jehal, but does she?"

"King Tyan has hardly made a miraculous recovery, has he?" King Valgar was watching them. Shezira nudged Almiri away. "Go back to your husband."

"There is one thing, Mother."

"Yes?"

"Prince Dyalt needs a bride. I know Hyram asked after Lystra a year or more ago."

"Yes, and I told him that Lystra was already taken. I thought Dyalt was supposed to marry some Syuss princess."

"He was, but she died. Drowned in a lake. You know what the Syuss are like when they see water. Besides, Dyalt is the king's youngest son and so not far removed from the throne. His father thinks he ought to do better than one of the Syuss, and I think you should offer Jaslyn's hand for Dyalt."

Shezira snorted. "Would they have her? Just as well I sent her away."

"You bought Valgar with me and Jehal with Lystra. Jaslyn is your daughter and your most likely heir. Dyalt could be marrying himself to your throne, and if you do become speaker, they will wonder which one of us will succeed you."

"Will they?" Shezira tried not to laugh.

"They can always hope. Mother, they'll have her."

"Dyalt is fourteen; Jaslyn is too old for him."

Almiri laughed and shook her head. "Mother, how old is Hyram? How old is Zafir? Make the offer."

"No." Shezira shook her head. "No, I can't do that."

"Why, Mother? Why?"

"Because that would be far too direct and Hyram would be certain to learn of it." She grimaced. "*You* make the offer. I have made no decision as to who will succeed me, but by all means let them think it will be Jaslyn. For the peace of the realms. If they stand by the pact, and only if they stand by the pact."

Almiri's eyes sparkled. She smiled and turned away to walk at her husband's side. Shezira went on alone. She wondered about her daughters sometimes. Were they all they seemed to be, or did they manage to hide some part of themselves, even from her? Offering Jaslyn to Dyalt was a clever ploy. Jaslyn would probably never speak to either of them again, but Dyalt could hardly say no.

My most likely heir? She chuckled to herself. *You all have to get rid of* me *first.*

54

THE FIRE WITHIN

The dragons took off as soon as the sky was light enough to fly. The very tips of the mountains shone like they were on fire, while the slopes below were still dark with shadow. Snow and Ash knew exactly where they were going, which was more than Kemir did. He tried to spot the alchemists' valley, but the first he knew of it was when Snow flew between two mountains, over the top of a narrow cliff, and plunged vertically down.

Walls of rock raced past on either side. He tried to breathe, but the wind was icy; it ripped the breath out of his lungs and brought tears to his eyes. He could see the ground hurtling toward him, blurred shapes rushing at him, and then Snow shuddered and he closed his eyes as the wind suddenly stopped and the air became blistering. She shot over the ground, pouring fire over everything. Ramshackle buildings made of stone, trees, little yards, men running, screaming; to get away; the flames engulfed them all.

There were dragons on the ground. Snow banked sharply, heading toward them. Three figures hurled themselves flat as she flew over them, scorching the ground where they lay. As one, Snow and Ash spat fire at the three dragons below. The dragons shielded themselves with their wings.

"Do dragons burn?"

Only our eyes. Soon there will be three more of us that are free. Ash landed in the makeshift eyrie, smashing buildings with his tail and burning anything that came out of them. The three harnessed dragons all watched, alert and wary but otherwise still. Snow stayed in the air, circling back round.

I knew those dragons before I awoke. I remember them.

Kemir glanced down as Snow flew back over them. They were hunting-dragons, he could tell that much. Otherwise, they looked the same as any others: dark gray or black scales with occasional flashes of deep metallic blues and greens, all three of them. Just like the dragons from the camp in the mountains.

He started in surprise as his eyes shot to the three figures Snow had burned. Instead of lying still and smoldering in the dirt, they had gotten up and were running. One of them seemed to have a slight limp.

"It can't be . . ."

Snow strafed them once more, and again they threw themselves to the ground. This time Kemir got a better look at them. They were riders, all three of them. Dressed in their dragonscale armor, which explained why Snow's fire wasn't putting an end to them. Two of them had large shields which they held up to deflect the worst of the blast. Kemir kept his eyes on them as Snow passed. As soon as the dragon was overhead, the three riders got up and started to run again.

"Rider Rod!" Kemir felt breathless. "Luck *is* with me today. Let me down, Snow. Let me down! *Now!*"

No. She flew back over the buildings. Most of what would burn was already ablaze. Kemir tried to keep his eyes on the three riders. Among the wreckage, men were still running about, most of them dashing for the shelter of a few large caves. Snow landed amid the ruins and Kemir lost sight of the riders behind a cloud of smoke. It was hard to do more than simply hold on as Snow bucked and lunged and lashed her tail and burned whatever lay before her until finally everything was still.

"*Now* let me down."

The dragon ignored him. She trotted to the largest of the

caves, where a river poured out of the cliff. She stepped slowly inside, splashing through the water. The entrance was large enough, but it quickly shrank. She squeezed in as far as she could and gushed fire into the depths.

Minds. I sense minds in here. Many of them. Many have escaped. Many are still alive.

They must all burn. The ground shook as Ash ran in from the eyrie. The two dragons surveyed the caves, then, one by one, burned them out.

They are still there. I feel them. Ash pawed at the ground. *Let them taste our fire!*

I cannot reach them.

Then we will wait, and sooner or later they will starve.

"Let me down! I'll go in there and get them out for you." The last he'd seen of the three riders, they'd been heading for the cave closest to the eyrie. He couldn't see their bodies, which meant that they must have reached it. That or Ash had simply eaten them.

Snow stamped with frustration. She lowered herself onto all fours and let Kemir slide down to the ground. Nadira stayed where she was. She frowned at Kemir as if she disapproved. He ignored her and ran to the cave where he thought the riders must be, but then hesitated. Three of them and one of him. Poor odds.

He crept slowly in. The sun only reached the ground outside at its zenith; inside, the cave grew very dark very quickly. He touched the walls, feeling his way forward. They were warm and dry from Snow's breath. That would tell him how far her fire had reached. It would tell everyone inside as well. They'd know how deep they had to go.

About a hundred yards into the cave it became too narrow for a dragon. Another hundred yards and the walls weren't warm anymore. Everything was pitch black except the circle of daylight behind him, yet when he squinted he thought he could see lights ahead of him, faint pinpricks of white light that looked more like stars than like lamps or torches. He moved slowly, feeling for each step with his feet, creeping silently forward. The pinpricks became brighter. They were lights, definitely lights. Which made him wonder how many other people might be hiding in this cave.

In the nearest of the lights he caught a faint glimpse of a face. He raised his bow, but the figure wasn't wearing the armor of a dragon-knight. The face vanished; the light bobbed and moved away.

Kemir moved faster, fumbling silently through the darkness toward the light. Whoever he was following stopped by the next light and took that too. And the next and the next. Kemir was close enough to see that the lights were like little lamps, but their flame was a cold white and he didn't smell any smoke or oil. The man carrying them wasn't a soldier and didn't seem to be armed. Kemir drew a knife then sprinted the dozen yards between them. The man heard him at the last moment and turned around as Kemir bundled into him, knocking him down and sending the lamps flying. In an instant he had his knife at the man's throat.

"Please please please . . ." The man was weeping with fear. There was a bad smell.

"Three dragon-knights came this way, didn't they?"

"Yes. Yes. I don't know who they are. Please, please don't kill me."

"Where did they go?"

"I don't know." Kemir pressed the knife harder against the man's skin. The man squealed. "Deeper! I don't know. Into the gatehouse."

"Gatehouse?" Kemir felt a sudden coldness inside him. "How many other people are down here?"

"I don't know!"

"Then guess."

"I don't know, I don't know. I'm just a servant. Please . . ."

"One? Two? Ten? A hundred?"

"A hundred? More, I think. I don't know. Please."

A hundred? Kemir's eyes grew wide. He slowly withdrew his knife. "Soldiers?"

"Yes."

"How many?"

"I don't know. A century? A legion? I don't know!"

A legion? In these caves? That can't be right. Still, a dozen, even half a dozen, was quite enough. Kemir gripped the man by the throat and hauled him to his feet. "One of the dragon-knights is called Rider Semian. Tell him that Kemir, the sell-sword who ruined his leg, is outside waiting for him."

He let the man go, picked up one of the lamps so he could see where he was going, and started back toward the entrance to the cave. He didn't run. In fact a part of him wasn't sure he wanted to go back at all. The dragons weren't going to like this. If they meant to starve this lot out, they were likely to be in for a long wait. And so far they hadn't exactly impressed him with their patience.

55

❧

THE TWO SPEAKERS

In the middle of the ten-sided table lay the Speaker's Spear and Ring. Hyram was on his feet; everyone else was watching him, waiting for him to sit down. Some of the dragon-lords looked bored, some looked impatient, some were simply annoyed that he was taking so long. He was shaking again this morning. Only a little bit, but Shezira could see it. Either the potions that held his sickness in check were losing their effect, or he was running out.

Opposite Hyram sat Acting Grand Master Jeiros and High Priest Aruch. On each other side of the table sat a dragon-king or -queen and one other knight. That was all. Two sides were empty. The Syuss had few dragons and were invited to the palace only as a courtesy, and the King of the Crags had held himself aloof from the rest of them for over a generation.

Shezira couldn't help but stare at the ring. *Seven of us, then.* Her hands gripped the table. She'd been waiting for this day for a decade. She'd done everything right; even this foolishness with Queen Zafir seemed nothing more than a last test to see if she was worthy of that ring. Sitting at the table, staring at it, she could almost believe that Hyram was testing her, nothing more, that Zafir wasn't even real.

Hyram finally sat down. Jeiros stood up and made a speech. Aruch followed him. They were the same speeches that were made every ten years. Jeiros spoke of responsibilities and burdens. Shezira knew all the words, yet now they were meant for her she found herself soaking up every one of them. When it had been Hyram, a decade ago, they'd simply been dull; this time they made her skin tingle. When Aruch spoke of humility and the grace of the dragon-god, she didn't roll her eyes as Jeiros did beside him but found herself wondering: *Is it true? Could it be the priests who keep the dragons at bay? Do the potions only work because they will them to?* Stupid thoughts that she would have laughed at on any other day seemed suddenly profound.

She pinched herself. *You're the Queen of Sand and Stone, the Queen of the North, not an idiot princess seeing her first dragon.*

When it was Hyram's turn again, he spoke of everything he'd done in his time at the palace. He spoke of peace and prosperity, of the unsurpassed strength of the Adamantine Guard, of the value of continuity. Then, in the same voice he'd used to inventory the armory of the Guard, he named Queen Zafir as his declared successor and sat down. It took Shezira a second to realize what he'd just said, that he'd actually done it and broken their pact, that it wasn't a test after all.

Sirion will back me. Valgar too. And Jehal and King Narghon. Silvallan, if he knows Zafir's cause is lost. The silence lasted for a second, then another. Everyone was looking at her. Hyram's mouth was slightly open. Anticipation shone in his eyes. With a start she realized that she still hadn't said anything. At the end of the table Jeiros was staring at his feet. He had two rolled-up scrolls in front of him. He reached for one.

"No," she whispered. It took her another second to fully find her voice. When she did, she rose smoothly to her feet. There would be nothing hurried or angry about her. Her voice would be calm when she spoke. Almost gentle. As though she was chiding an errant child. Jeiros looked at her. He had the scroll in his hand now, the words to anoint the next speaker. She met his eye and shook her head.

With a sigh Jeiros put down the scroll in his hand and picked up the other one. Aruch rose beside him. They looked tired, Shezira thought. Almost bored. She suddenly realized that everyone had known this was going to happen. They might as well have rehearsed it. In a way, wasn't that what they'd all been doing for the last few days?

"Are there any other challenges?" asked Jeiros. When no one spoke, he went on. "Seven times the anointing of a speaker has been challenged. Three times the challenge failed. Of the four that succeeded, three threw the realms into turmoil. Queen Shezira, for the good of the realms, will you withdraw your challenge?"

"No, Grand Master, I will not."

"Then, Your Holiness, what is your challenge?"

"Hyram, there is a pact between our clans that was made generations ago. If you violate that, you sully us all. Wiser men and women than I decreed long ago that only a reigning king or queen may take the office of speaker. They decided this because they understood that to govern the nine realms a speaker must first prove themselves worthy. Queen Zafir does indeed sit on a throne and may make an excellent speaker—twenty years from now, when she has proved herself. I call on you to honor the pact between our clans and name me as your successor."

"And who would be *yours*, Shezira?" hissed Hyram, glaring at Prince Jehal.

Jehal smiled back at him. "Someone who is wise and able, Hyram, and who does more to earn the honor than spread their legs."

Hyram shot to his feet. "Viper!"

Shezira glared at them both. "Prince Jehal, this is a sacred time. Show some respect."

Jehal lolled his head. "For what?"

Hastily, in the moment of silence that followed, Jeiros unfurled the scroll and read the text aloud: "As was written in the time of Narammed, the word of the speaker has been challenged before the assembled Kings and Queens of the Nine Realms. This council will disperse and re-form one day from now, at dawn, when a new speaker shall be chosen, by the word of the speaker, or by the vote of the Kings and Queens of the Nine Realms should the challenge remain."

Jehal groaned and slumped across the table. Shezira

wondered for one startled moment whether he'd somehow been poisoned, but then he raised his head. "Do we have to? *Another* day of acting like startled rabbits? Not daring to eat anything, keeping away from high places, constantly being surrounded by our armored dragon-knights." He bowed at Shezira. "As you say, Your Holiness, this is a sacred time, and I apologize for my previous words. But let us end this now, while we are all here and unquestionably alive. No more childishness. We all know where we stand."

Shezira frowned. "I sympathize, but there is a proper way, Prince Jehal."

Lady Nastria leaned into her and whispered, "You should agree with him, Holiness."

Shezira looked at her. She cocked her head. *Why?*

Nastria drew closer. Her words were so quiet that Shezira could barely hear them. "Because Princess Jaslyn will return from the alchemists at any moment, and when she does, Prince Jehal is finished. Use him now, Your Holiness, and then throw him away."

"Are you sure of this?" she mouthed back.

"As sure as I am of anything, Holiness." Nastria straightened and turned back to the table.

Shezira did the same. *Perfect.* It was hard not to smile. She looked at Hyram and then at Jeiros. "I am agreeable."

Hyram smiled back at her. "No. I say we wait."

Jeiros was looking at Queen Zafir. And Zafir was nodding. Jeiros appeared uncomfortable. "Apologies, Lord Hyram, but this is a matter for the Kings and Queens of the Nine Realms. You no longer have a voice in this." He avoided Hyram's gaze. "Do any object?" When everyone was silent, he sighed. "Very well. Queen Shezira, Queen Zafir, one by one you shall each call a monarch to your cause. Whoever the kings and queens decree shall be speaker." As he finished, Shezira glanced at Zafir. *This is your last chance to end this, to avoid making a fool of yourself.* But Zafir's face was a mask. She met Shezira's eye for a moment and her expression didn't flicker at all. She walked slowly to stand in front of Hyram. Shezira took her place by the alchemist and the priest.

Jeiros bowed to her. "Queen Shezira, you have issued the challenge. Which king or queen do you call to your side?"

"I call King Valgar."

Valgar didn't bother to say anything. He simply got up and walked to stand with Shezira. Jeiros bowed across the table to Queen Zafir. "Which king or queen do you call to your side?"

Zafir stayed silent; it was Hyram who answered. "King Sirion. My cousin."

Sirion was standing right next to Hyram, which meant that Hyram couldn't see what Shezira could. He couldn't see the tautness in Sirion's face, the whiteness of his knuckles. When he didn't speak, Hyram turned slowly to look at him.

"I'm sorry, cousin. I've always felt this crown wasn't really mine, that I was taking care of it for you, waiting for this day. But a pact is a pact. I must declare for Queen Shezira."

The warmth of victory blossomed in the pit of Queen Shezira's stomach. Two out of two. Hyram looked aghast, his face frozen in horror. Even Jeiros looked stunned; in fact, the only one around the table who didn't seem surprised at all was Queen Zafir. *Thank you, Jaslyn. At last you've done something useful.*

"King Tyan," she said. As hard as she tried to avoid it, her voice held a tremor of victory.

Jeiros bowed to Prince Jehal. "As King Tyan's regent, you have the right to speak with his voice."

"Yes, I do." Jehal grinned. He stood up, leaned over the table and looked straight at Hyram. "Old man, you've slandered me, you've even tortured me. I'd like nothing more than to see everything you value turn to ash before your eyes." He glanced at Shezira. "Your Holiness, will you name someone to follow you in turn? Here and now? A pact, such as the one Hyram here seeks to break? For what they're worth."

Shezira nodded. "You, Prince Jehal. I name you as my chosen successor." It left a sour taste in her mouth. *But if Nastria is right, I can relieve myself of that obligation. When I go, Valgar can have it; Almiri will take his throne and Jaslyn and Lystra could yet be queens. Antros, if you're watching, I hope you're smiling.*

Jehal's smile, when he looked at Hyram, was so broad it almost split his face in two. "Does that please you? Without your treachery I would never have had this. You've betrayed your allies. Your own cousins have turned against you. What possible reason could *I* have to ally myself with you? Think about that for a moment. Because that is what I choose. I choose Queen Zafir."

Shezira didn't move a muscle. She couldn't; Jehal's words had frozen her solid. She heard King Silvallan declare for Zafir as well, and then King Narghon, but it all seemed so far away that she barely heard their words. She couldn't think. For a moment the world seemed to fade completely; when it finally returned, Jeiros was halfway through another speech. He'd opened the second of his two scrolls, and Zafir was the next Speaker of the Realms.

56

❖

UNDONE

When he was done, Jeiros took the ring from the center of the table. He bowed before Zafir and put it on her finger. One by one, the monarchs kneeled before her and kissed the ring.

Nastria watched as her queen kneeled and kissed like the rest of them. With calm and dignity, as a queen should. It was the most inspiring thing she'd ever seen. *To be so noble even in defeat.*

More noble than she could ever be.

There would be a reckoning for this, she decided. No matter what Queen Shezira ordered her to do, there would be a reckoning. If she'd been a man, with a man's strength, she might have tried to kill Prince Jehal with her bare hands there and then. As it was, it would have to be something more subtle.

She wondered briefly whether any of what she'd seen between Jehal and Hyram had been real, whether it had all been an elaborate charade designed for that one moment of treachery. Hard to believe, but whenever Hyram was around, everything always came back to King Antros and his unfortunate demise. Was that what was behind this? Was that why he'd betrayed the pact between their clans?

In the endless hours that followed, Queen Shezira let nothing show. Nastria wanted to take the queen and whisper in her ear: *It can be undone. Zafir is named, but she's not crowned! Until High Priest Aruch hands her the Adamantine Spear in the Glass Cathedral in front of the full assembly of dragon-knights, it can be undone.* But there was never a chance; they were never alone. So she watched Prince Jehal and she watched Queen Zafir. There were games and entertainments, a display of courage and skill from the Adamantine Guard, tournaments of horsemanship for the lesser knights and of flying skills for the dragon-riders. Queen Zafir watched them with the same blank mask she'd worn in the Hall of Speakers. Jehal, on the other hand, was animated, excited, intoxicated with his victory. The two of them never looked at each other. Not once.

Jaslyn. Princess Jaslyn had the key. When she came back from the alchemists with the flask of liquid silver. With damning words, signed and sealed by the master alchemists of the redoubt, naming it as poison. One of Jehal's knights had gone with Tiachas. She would find him and bring him back for Master Kithyr, and then they'd uncover the true depths of Jehal's villainy. The queen would have to believe her, and then so would all the rest of them.

And then she saw Jehal pass close to Queen Zafir and whisper something in her ear. For a moment Zafir's mask cracked, and something electric flashed in her eyes. It lasted an instant, and whatever Jehal said could only have been a word. But Nastria wasn't watching his mouth, she was watching his hands; and for that instant, in the press of knights and lords, Jehal's hand had alighted on Queen Zafir's thigh and stayed there for a blink of an eye longer than it should. And in that touch Nastria saw it all, and understood that Hyram was the biggest victim of all.

She grinned. She had four more days before the ceremony in the Glass Cathedral. Quite long enough. Still smiling, she set herself to following Prince Jehal.

57

❦

THE CAVES

Dawn at the bottom of the ravine came late, and when it came, rained fire. Jaslyn stood in stupefied disbelief as the redoubt erupted around her. She glimpsed two dragons, a near-black and a perfect white, *her* perfect white, and then Rider Semian threw her to the ground and lay on top of her as the very air burst into flames. All she could think of was the white dragon, and how long she'd been looking for it, then a blinding heat seared her face. Her dragonscale armor kept her alive, and when she opened her eyes again, she could still see. She could see the two dragons burning down the alchemists' eyrie. Swallowing the three other dragons there in clouds of fire.

Silence!

She wanted to run, to hurl herself between them and her precious Silence, for what good it would have done. Rider Semian, though, was already dragging her back.

"The caves," she heard herself shout. "We have to get to the caves!" She glanced back as she ran. Silence was still there, shielding his head with his wings, but otherwise immobile. While the attackers stayed in the air, that was all a trained dragon would do, and so she willed them down, willed them to bring it to teeth and claws and lashing tails. *Then* Silence would show them.

The white had a rider. No, two riders. Jaslyn squinted, trying to make them out. She frowned. The dark one didn't seem to have any at all. Which wasn't possible. She must have made a mistake.

They were coming back. This time Jaslyn didn't need any prompting to throw herself down, and this time she remembered to cover her face. For a second time fire washed over them. As soon as the dragons had passed, they were up and running again. They reached the nearest cave.

"Deeper," she gasped. "There will be markings on the wall when we're far enough to be safe. And lamps. Alchemist lamps." They stumbled on into the darkness, groping for the walls. The floor of the cave was uneven and treacherous, but at last they reached a point where the cave narrowed. A little farther on Jaslyn felt the marks on the wall that meant they were safe. Groping around on the floor she found a crate filled with lamps, and when she picked one up and gave it a hard shake, it slowly started to glow with a cold white light. She gave it to Semian, then took another for Jostan and another for herself.

"That was our white," she said once they'd got their bearings. "The white for Lystra's wedding. What's it doing here?" She looked expectantly at her two knights, but they were clearly bemused. "What about the other one? That wasn't one of ours. Whose was it?"

Still no answer.

"Who was riding them? Who was on the back of the black? I saw two riders on the white but none on the black. Who were they?"

Semian grunted. "Last anyone saw the white, she was with her Scales."

"A Scales would not attack his own order." Jaslyn held up her lamp and peered into the darkness. As she did so, the tunnel back to the cave entrance lit up with an orange glow and a blast of hot wind slammed into them. "We need to go back out. We need to get to Silence and Matanizkan and Levanter. There are three of us and only two of them. We'll kill the riders and force them down."

"Your Highness, it would be death to go back out there." Jostan's voice was flat.

"Coward!" Jaslyn took an angry step toward him.

"Rider Jostan has the right of it." At least Semian had the grace to avert his eyes from her. "The alchemists have their own defenses. If we go out there alone, the dragons will kill us before we can reach our own mounts."

"They were attacking Silence!"

"They were burning the saddles and harnesses so that we couldn't ride them, Your Highness. Silence will not have been harmed. She is too precious."

For a long time Jaslyn stared back toward the cave entrance. She could hear noises from outside now, but they seemed very far away, as though the dragons were occupied elsewhere. Surely there was a chance? She tried to think about how far they'd have to run to get from the cave to the eyrie. Even in dragonscale it could be done, couldn't it?

But not if their saddles and harnesses were destroyed, and Semian was probably right about that. She would have done the same if it had been her riding the attack. She breathed a long sigh and turned around.

"Very well. We continue. The caves all come together. We'll find the alchemists and the soldiers they keep here." *Prince Jehal has done this. He must know why I'm here. He knows I've found out about his poisons. Well, I'll let the whole world know what he's been doing, and then no one will stand with him. Mother will be made speaker. She'll destroy him, and then Lystra will come home again.*

WALKING THROUGH THE CAVES WAS slow and tedious. The lamps gave off barely enough light for them to see their own feet, and though the floor and the walls were smooth, the tunnels sloped steeply up in places. At times the cave became almost a chimney, rising vertically. Metal rungs had been hammered into the rock, but in dragonscale, climbing them was almost impossible. Jostan dropped his lamp, which smashed to pieces on the floor. Then they reached a place so narrow that they had to abandon most of their armor. Jaslyn tried not to think how she must look, still in her gauntlets and helm and boots, the rest of her in plain doeskin, a bright red stripe across her face where the flamestrike had penetrated her visor.

It seemed like they spent half a day wandering through the cave, but at last, stopping to listen, they heard the rush of water somewhere ahead and she knew they were close. A few bends later they saw light, the sound of the water grew louder, and the next thing she knew she almost pitched over the edge of a chasm. Semian's hand on her shoulder caught her just in time.

The alchemists had built their tunnels along the underground river, she knew that much. She got down onto her hands and knees and felt over the lip of the chasm until her fingers found what she was looking for: a ladder secured into the stone. The water was more than a hundred feet below, and the cleft in the rock so narrow that her back sometimes touched the other side as she climbed down the ladder.

At the bottom a walkway of wooden boards hung over the swirling river. Little niches were cut into the walls, and after ten minutes of walking, the niches had lamps in them, filling the chasm with their ghostly white light. Rider Jostan stopped at the first lit niche and took the lamp.

"Someone must have come this way to light these," he said. "We must be close." Then he wrinkled his nose. "Does anyone else smell something?"

Jaslyn and Semian paused and sniffed the air. "Smoke," they both said. Jaslyn wasn't sure what to make of that. Smoke meant fire, and her first thought was dragons, but after all this walking they couldn't be so close to the entrances to the caves, could they?

The second thing she thought of was a kitchen firepit. She was hungry.

At a narrow point in the chasm, a little farther on, they found the alchemists. The lamps stopped, the wooden walkway ended abruptly, and a voice from the darkness above challenged them.

"Who are you?"

"Rider Semian, Rider Jostan and Her Highness Princess Jaslyn, in the service of Queen Shezira," shouted Semian. His voice echoed around the caves.

"Hold the lamps up so we can see your faces."

Jaslyn hoisted her lamp. Her tongue twitched, prepared to lash out at these idiots who were getting in her way, but she stilled it. She was tired, hungry, covered in bruises and scrapes from countless stumbles and falls, and the burn across her face was hurting.

The smell of smoke was stronger.

After a second, lights appeared above them and she could see a cluster of armored soldiers on a wooden platform. They threw down a rope ladder. When Jaslyn reached the top, she saw that they weren't just any soldiers; they were Adamantine Guardsmen.

"Your Highness." Their captain bowed. "I'll send a man ahead of you so there are no more mistakes." So that everyone knew she was coming, he meant.

"How many of the Guard are here?" she asked.

The captain bowed again. "Before the attack there were close to a hundred of us, Your Highness. Now I'm not so sure."

"A *hundred*? Then why are you here and not outside seeing off these dragons? There were only two of them!"

"Your Highness, we did fight, but the rider of the white dragon was too clever, and the black dragon . . ." He took a deep breath. "Your Highness, there was no rider on the war-dragon. We formed shield walls against their fire, but they didn't stay in the air. The black one came down and smashed our walls. It was killing with tooth and claw and that murderous tail. We lost between a third and a half our number."

"I had three dragons out there."

The captain shook his head. He didn't say anything, but his eyes said that the dragons were lost to her now.

"What is it, Captain?"

The soldier sighed. "Your Highness, your dragons are with the others now. They're trying to smoke us out."

58

❖

TURNING THE KNIFE

Sometimes Jehal felt he would burst. Sometimes his own cleverness seemed overwhelming. Hyram, Shezira, he'd played them both, and they still didn't even know how.

He dressed himself carefully. Two layers. On the outside he looked like an Adamantine Guardsman, with his heavy quilted coat and his colors and his helmet. If he took all that off, he might pass, in the dark, as a potboy. Potboys often ran errands at night. He knew; he'd sent Kazah off on enough of them, after all.

The moon was setting. He didn't know how late it was, except that he'd waited for more than half the night, and if he waited much longer he wouldn't have time to do what he wanted to do and be back before dawn.

He wrapped the white silk across his eyes for one last time and looked at Zafir, sleeping, through the tiny ruby eyes of his Taiytakei dragon. She was alone. Good enough.

No. He stared at her and then slowly undressed again. *Too dangerous. Not until after tomorrow. Not until all the other kings and queens have gone.* He didn't take the silk off, even once he was naked. Instead, he made the little metal dragon flutter across Zafir's room and settle beside

her head. It pecked gently at her face until she stirred.
When she saw the dragon, she smiled.

"It's the middle of the night."

The dragon nodded. As Zafir reached under her pillow
for her own strip of silk, Jehal looked over his shoulder. Two
ruby eyes glowed at him in the dark.

"You're naked," she whispered.

"I wish you were."

"I wish I could touch you."

Jehal sighed. "Soon, lover. When Hyram's out of the
way."

The smile faded from her face. "The potions are already
losing their effect."

"That's not right. There should have been enough to
keep him going for another month."

"Yes. You gave him too much, so I've been stealing them
and watering them down."

"What?"

Zafir rolled her eyes. "I want it done and over, Jehal."

Jehal growled. He started to pace the room. "Why did
you do that? He wasn't supposed to get sick again until this
was all long done."

"You ask me why?" Zafir sounded scornful. "Do you
have any idea how dirty all of this makes me feel? Sometimes, after he's finished with me and goes back to his own
bed, I make myself sick to force the nausea away."

"But now you're speaker—unless you fuck it up in the
next couple of days. Isn't that what you wanted?"

"No, Jehal, it's what *you* wanted. What I wanted was you.
Hyram disgusts me. I have to writhe and groan and call him
the king of my bed when all I want to do is break his neck.
And he knows something now. I don't know how, but he
knows something." She frowned. "Something he didn't
know this morning. He was asking questions."

"Questions?"

"About you. Someone's put it into his head that we
might be lovers, Jehal. Of course he doesn't believe it, but
he won't quite let go of it either. He's put men on my door.
He was enough of a bore before; now he's intolerable. Get
rid of him, my prince. I've had enough. You've got what you
wanted, so now give me what *I* want."

Jehal leered at the little ruby eyes that watched him

from the corner of his bed. "I would like nothing more, lover. Nothing more at all. Even thinking about it . . ." He glanced down. "Well, you can see for yourself."

"Don't you want to be here? Next to me, feeling my skin?"

"I'd like to feel more than your skin."

"Sliding under silken sheets together?"

"You know I would."

"Then *come*! Now!" She pushed back the covers of her bed, slowly revealing herself to him. When they were at her feet, she lay back and ran one hand slowly from her neck down to the soft hair between her legs. "Do I have to show you what to do?" she breathed, and then laughed as Jehal's Taiytakei dragon fluttered up into the air and flew erratically around in circles for a better view.

"We have to wait, lover. Wait until it's safe."

"No." Zafir suddenly sat up and snatched Jehal's mechanical dragon out of the air. She blew Jehal a kiss and then everything went dark and muffled.

"What are you doing?"

"If I can't have you, you can't have me. I'm done with this. I'm tying your little toy up and putting him under my pillow. Then I'm going to take this silk off my eyes and go back to sleep, and if you want to see any of this again, you get rid of Hyram and your stupid starling-wife. And you do it soon, lover, or I'll do it myself."

Jehal waited for a while, but all he heard was Zafir's breathing. After another minute he pulled the silk away from his eyes and took a deep breath. His heart was racing and his head spinning, and he wasn't sure whether it came more from lust or fury.

Get rid of Hyram. *She's too impatient.*

Could it be done? *If she does it herself, she'll botch it and everything will be for nothing.*

Could it be done?

He climbed back into bed and tried to sleep, but his head wouldn't stop. Thoughts blossomed and died faster than he could keep count of them. *Could* it be done?

And then it came to him, and he realized that yes, it could; and moments later he was asleep.

59

PATIENCE

Kemir sat slowly whittling a stick into an arrow shaft. Somewhere nearby Nadira was pacing impatiently. Even from here he could feel the dragons' determination. Their focus on what they were doing was frightening.

When the alchemists had scuttled away into their caves, the dragons had been furious for a while, raging up and down outside, smashing the few buildings that remained intact, flying around the cliff face, searching for other ways in. Then they'd calmed down. Now they'd built enormous pyres at the mouth of each cave, set them alight, and were methodically blowing the smoke down into the tunnels. The frightening bit was that they'd been at it for two days, all five of them, without a pause for breath. Two of the new dragons moved from fire to fire, blowing the smoke. The other three went to and from the woods, tearing down trees to burn. Every few hours Snow soared up out of the valley. Sometimes Kemir and Nadira went with her. They flew above and beyond the ravine, looking for wisps of smoke leaking up through cracks in the ground. Whenever she found one, Snow sealed it shut, and then she'd circle for hours, looking for more. Kemir understood exactly what she was doing. He'd done it himself, except his victims had been rats and rabbits.

Ash lumbered past, dragging a fifty-foot tree toward the caves with his tail. The dragon looked at him greedily. *Kemir, I am hungry. Which one of you has more meat on you?*

"Me." Kemir didn't bother to look up.

There's nothing left in the village, Kemir, and we need to eat.

"Then go and hunt." When the dragons weren't tending to the fires, they were eating. In the first two days they'd eaten all the animals from the eyrie and the bodies of the men they'd killed. Today they'd gone back to the village at the mouth of the ravine. It seemed to surprise them that they'd found it deserted. The villagers couldn't have gotten far, but they had clearly had the sense to run and hide, and had even taken most of their animals with them.

"Hey, Ash," shouted Kemir. "You know, I'm hungry too. What does dragon taste like?"

The dragon paused in his labors and turned to look at Kemir. It was impossible to read anything from a dragon's face, but Kemir got the impression he was laughing.

Suddenly, the dragon froze. He dropped the tree and rose onto his back legs, staring intently toward the caves.

Kemir stood up as well, but he couldn't see anything through the rubble and the smoke. "What?"

Ash began to run. *The smoke has worked. They're coming out!*

60

THE ASSASSIN

Side by side, two dragons shot across the Mirror Lakes. They barged and snapped at each other, looking for an advantage. Three more came after them, strung out in a line. Jehal squinted as they hurtled toward him, trying to work out which was which. Now and then he glanced sideways. Hyram was watching the dragons; so was Queen Zafir. In fact almost everyone was watching. The race was going all the way to the finish.

One person, though, wasn't watching the dragons. Among a group of messenger boys standing at the back among the guards, one wasn't jumping up and down and cheering. He was more interested in Zafir, and in him. Jehal smiled to himself. He wasn't sure who the boy was spying for, Hyram or Shezira. Both of them perhaps. In the end it didn't really matter. What mattered was who the boy really was.

The dragons were getting closer. An hour ago they'd launched themselves from the top of the Diamond Cascade. Ten immense wooden frames, each one a hundred feet high and a hundred feet wide, lay strung across the Hungry Mountain plains and around the lakes. Ten frames, one for each of the Kings and Queens of the Realms, and the last one for the speaker and her guests. Jehal was supposed to be out in the plains, at King Tyan's frame, but he'd quietly slipped away to be here instead. He'd made some effort not to be seen, but the boy had followed him here anyway.

Around him everyone was shouting. He peered over the water, trying to see whether there were anymore dragons on their way, but there weren't. The point of the race was to fly through all ten frames. From the ground they seemed enormous; on the back of a speeding dragon they became suddenly small. Accidents happened. Sometimes a dragon would be lost, but more often a rider. Losing four, though . . . Jehal felt briefly wistful. He'd ridden in these races and knew exactly how the riders fought for position. It must have been a particularly good battle over the plains, and for a moment he wished he'd been there to see it.

He shook himself. The two dragons fighting for the lead were still neck and neck heading for the last frame. They'd reach the finish in less than a minute. Time for him to go. He slipped away while everyone was watching the finish, and almost no one noticed him leave.

Almost. As he scurried away into the woods Jehal heard the roar of the crowd reach a peak and then a crash as one or both of the dragons hit the frame. He felt a flash of irritation. They'd be talking about this race for years, and he'd missed it.

He peered around among the trees. As he did, two figures began to rise from the undergrowth; hastily Jehal motioned to them to stay hidden. "Another minute," he whispered as he walked past them. "Dressed as a messenger boy." He stopped for a moment and held the white silk up to his eyes. Zafir was already on her way, walking quickly with a pair of her riders at her heels. Doing her best to seem furtive. He put the silk away and crouched down amid the ferns and brambles.

"Have you got it?" he asked. One of the men handed him a large sack. He thought about reminding them all how dangerous their quarry was, but he could already hear Zafir coming along the forest path. She passed barely a yard from where Jehal was hiding. He held his breath and waited.

And waited.

He was on the point of reaching for the silk again when

the messenger boy finally appeared, creeping silently down the path. Jehal tensed, ready to spring.

The boy must have had a sixth sense. As Jehal and his men launched themselves, he was already spinning around, jumping away with a knife in his hand. He lashed out and one of Jehal's men grunted and staggered. Then Jehal had the sack over the boy's head.

"It's a woman!"

"I know *that.* Pin her *down!* " Jehal hissed. She was deadly quick but no match for three strong men. "Get her hands. And get that bloody knife off her!" For a few seconds the four of them wrestled in grim silence, and then Jehal punched at where he guessed the woman's face would be and the struggling stopped. Together they wrapped another sack around her waist, pinning her arms.

"Shit." The wounded man was looking at himself, at his hands. His shirt was soaked in blood. He stood for another second and then slumped to the earth, lost among the bracken.

"Stay here," growled Jehal. "Deal with him."

"He's dead, Your Highness."

"Yes. Unfortunate. And he's a rider of Furymouth. We can hardly leave his body here, can we? Deal with him and then come back to me." He searched the woman carefully for more knives, made sure her arms were properly pinned and tied a rope around her neck. Then he dragged her away through the trees. Whenever she seemed to be coming to her senses, he pulled on the rope and made her fall. *I don't need you looking pretty, not that you ever were. Just alive and able to run, that's all.*

He'd come to the woods the day before, looking to see how far he'd have to go. There was a long-abandoned forge not far from where the dragon race ended. With a cellar. At the time it had seemed perfect. It had also seemed a lot closer to the place he'd chosen for the ambush.

Finally, after it seemed he'd been dragging the woman for an hour or more, he reached it. He pulled her inside and threw her down the stairs to the cellar, then closed the door behind them. Finally he pulled the sack off her head and threw a bucket of water over her. He smiled and gave a little ironic bow.

"Lady Nastria. Queen Shezira's knight-marshal. What a

pleasure to have your company at last. Shame about the circumstances."

She looked at him. Her lips were broken, her face bloody and bruised. One of her eyes was already so swollen she could barely open it. She spat out a tooth and opened her mouth.

"Scream if you want, but no one will hear you. That's what all women do in the end, isn't it? Scream for help?"

Nastria closed her mouth. "Traitor," she slurred.

"Traitor? Me? Because I gave your queen my word and then didn't keep it? Just like Hyram, eh?" He laughed. "Traitor? You don't know me, Knight-Marshal. Not at all. No, no treachery here. All I'm doing is righting a very old wrong." He shook his head and sighed. "I've been watching you. Would you like to see how?" Without waiting for an answer he took out the white silk and pressed it to her eyes. "Look. Look hard. A little bit of sorcery that someone gave me. And don't pretend to be shocked. Does Queen Shezira know about your blood-mage?" He took the silk away. "You understand, don't you, that I wouldn't have shown you that unless I was going to kill you?"

She looked at him, defiant and sullen at once. "What do you want, Jehal?"

"Here." He held out a cup of water. "Water. I thought you might be a bit of a mess by the time I got you back. You know you killed one of my riders back there."

Nastria looked at the cup and turned her face away.

"Lady, you and I both know that good poison is expensive and nowhere near as easy to come by as others may think. When I kill you, it'll be with steel." He picked up a sword from the corner of the cellar and drew it from its scabbard. "This was my father's, back when he could hold it."

"Then get on and use it, Jehal. Your fate is already sealed and you can't change it."

"I'd sooner destroy the palace itself than murder an artist such as yourself. But as I cannot have you following me . . . A lady knight-marshal. I've often wondered what it must be like for you, surrounded by riders who are all so much stronger. In full armor I imagine you can barely stand up. But you're quick, I'll give you that. And you can do something that almost no other rider could ever do: dress like a serving boy and slip through the palace, and no one gives you a second glance. Sometimes you're Lady Nastria, knight-marshal. Sometimes you're a potboy, a scullion, a maid. I admire you, I really do. You and I are alike." He smiled. "If you want to be sure that something is done properly, there's nothing like doing it yourself."

"How long?"

"How long what?"

"You and Zafir."

Jehal laughed. "A long time, Knight-Marshal. Long enough that we glance at each other in a way that only lovers do, no matter how much we try not to. It pleases me that you're the one to see through it. I suppose you've already told Hyram."

Nastria shrugged.

"Well I'm going to feel very silly if you haven't." He held out the cup again. "Please."

She spat and looked at him with scorn.

"No, you *have* told Hyram, and I know you have. 'Your wife and the Viper, Lord Hyram. Watch them closely.' That's what you said. He didn't take it very well. It's all falling apart for him, isn't it? He's ill again. The potions aren't working anymore. Zafir is young and he's old. And then there was the vote. I wish, I really do, that I could have read his mind just that once. Just to know what went through it right then."

"I know things, Prince Jehal. Things about the Taiytakei. Things you don't. They're not the friends you think they are."

Jehal laughed. "Poor Knight-Marshal." He held out the cup one more time. "Are you going to drink this or not?"

"Not."

He nodded. "It would have been a disappointment if you had. I don't suppose there's anything I could offer you that would make you betray your queen and bow your knee to me. To have someone of your abilities I would give a great deal. I'd have to know you meant it of course."

Nastria simply stared at him. He knew that look. It was hatred.

He sighed. It would have to be the hard way then, and

yet, in a way, that made him feel better. As he forced open her mouth and tipped the cup down her throat, he knew that he'd have felt dissatisfied somehow, if she'd crumbled.

She fought and spat, but she couldn't stop herself swallowing at least a little of the water, and slowly her struggles subsided. Her head lolled onto her chest. Jehal waited until she started to snore, and then tipped the rest of the cup on the floor and put his father's sword away.

"I told you it wasn't poison, Knight-Marshal. Although you're going to wish it was."

61

THE EMBERS

Tears streamed down Jaslyn's face. However much she wiped her eyes, it never helped because the smoke was always there. Semian had shown her how to breathe through a damp cloth like the others, and yet she was still constantly coughing. Even in the vast space of the central cavern, the air was becoming unbearable. Unpleasantly warm too, despite the river of ice-cold water running through the caves. Sooner or later the dragons were going to work out how to foul that as well.

"Turn back, Your Highness," rasped Rider Jostan. "There really is no need for this. Go back to the higher caves. Stay there with the alchemists. This is soldiers' work."

She knew he was right. She didn't even have most of her armor anymore. Yet, watching the figures moving through the smoke around her, she knew she had to go. "Do you want to die slowly in this smoke, Rider Jostan? I, if I *must* die, will do so quickly and with clean air in my lungs."

"The Embers will defeat the dragons, Your Highness," said Semian quietly. "One way or another." That's what they called themselves, these soldiers of the Adamantine Guard. Jaslyn had never heard of them before, but she recognized their weapons. No swords or axes or daggers, only huge shields as tall as a man and giant crossbows that fired bolts as long as her leg and needed three soldiers at a time to move them through the caves. Scorpions.

"How many soldiers *are* there, Rider Semian?"

"I don't know, Your Highness."

"Then guess. Sixty? Seventy?" As they stumbled along, the smoke grew thicker and the air hotter. Jaslyn had no idea where she was going. They were simply following the soldiers, and if they got lost they'd probably never find their way out. It wasn't a cheering thought.

"Around that number, yes."

"Against five dragons. So twelve soldiers for each one. Do you think twelve men could ever defeat a dragon, Rider Semian? Never mind that there were a hundred of them and only two dragons in the first place, and they achieved very little then." After their first meeting in the caves Jaslyn hadn't been allowed near the Guardsmen. They were a special legion, the alchemists said. The best of the best, trained from birth solely to defend the redoubt. They couldn't have a woman, even a princess, in their midst, she was told. And however much she insisted, the alchemists always found a way to stop her from talking to them. They never flatly refused, of course, but they might as well have done.

However special they are, they aren't going to win. Jaslyn's only hope was that she might be able to slip away in the confusion. Or get close enough for Silence to hear her voice.

"I suppose it *is* unlikely, Your Highness," said Rider Semian reluctantly.

"They're not going to fight the dragons, Your Highness," said Rider Jostan. "They will kill the riders."

Jaslyn shook her head. Rider Jostan hadn't quite understood what everyone else now knew, what the alchemists had explained with careful patience so there could be no confusion. That the dragons were acting on their own. That there were no rogue riders commanding Silence and Matanizkan and Levanter, but rogue dragons instead. Despite everything he'd been told, Jostan still firmly believed there were men outside, and all he had to do was kill those men and everything would be sorted out.

"One rider will do," growled Semian. He understood

perfectly; Jaslyn had seen his face when the message came to him. Someone *was* out there, and Semian clearly knew the man. Just a sell-sword, he said. One of the knight-marshal's more foolish ideas. He'd waved it away as unimportant, but his eyes were fierce.

They reached the river. The soldiers, apparently, were following it to get to the outside. As they left the vast space of the cavern and entered the river tunnel, the smoke grew even thicker and the air became scorching. Jaslyn could feel the hot wind on her face, steadily blowing in from the outside. Before long they were wading up to their waists in the freezing water and splashing it over their arms and faces simply to keep from burning. They didn't need their lamps anymore; the caves and the smoke here were lit up by a flickering orange glow.

"They've lit a fire at the cave mouth, haven't they?" The thought hadn't occurred to her before. "How are we going to get out?"

"The river, Your Highness," said Rider Semian.

"They're going to swim? In full dragonscale?" Despite herself she started to laugh, but her guffaws turned into a coughing fit as the smoke choked her.

"Highness, they're not wearing dragonscale."

"What?" She sat down at the edge of the river and splashed water in her face and down her throat until the coughing stopped. When she looked up, they'd lost sight of the soldiers in the gloom. Not that they needed any help to find their way out now they had the river to guide them.

"They are not wearing their armor, Your Highness."

"Then they'll be killed before they even climb out of the river! This is futile! Madness." Jaslyn punched the water. They'd come all this way, gone through all this pain, and now they'd have to make their way back through the smoke. They'd probably get lost in the main cavern, and even if they didn't, the smoke would get them in the end. Without armor the soldiers wouldn't last long enough for *anyone* to slip away.

"Perhaps not as futile as you think." Rider Semian started to strip off his armor. "Your Highness, it seems we will have to swim."

"Swim *where*, Semian?"

"Past the fire at the cave mouth, Your Highness."

"And then? Perhaps you think we could float down the river without the dragons noticing us?"

"That's exactly what I think," said Semian. He picked up his shield and poked two fingers through a hole that had been cut through it. Then he showed Jaslyn the two straps around it. "When the time comes, lie on your back in the water, Your Highness. Hold the straps and press your mouth to the hole. The shield will float, and you will be able to breathe. Don't swim, just drift. Let the water carry you away."

"When the time comes?"

Semian finished taking off his armor and waded deeper into the water. "If the Embers somehow fail, I will try to distract the dragons. If I can get close enough that Matanizkan hears my voice, maybe she'll still obey me. You'll know if I've succeeded. That's when you should go."

"They'll catch you." Jaslyn peered at Semian. She could only make out the shape of him in the haze now, head and shoulders still clear of the water. He was doing this for her, she realized. This wasn't some plan the alchemists had devised, this was *his* plan. He was doing it to save her. The revelation left her feeling strange inside. She half rose to order him not to go and then stopped. Either way they were most likely all going to die.

"Better to die on my terms than someone else's," he said. Those had been her own words when she'd insisted on coming down with the soldiers and somehow trying to escape. He was almost naked, armed only with a sword around his waist, a bottle of something on a string around his neck and a shield the size of a door. Jaslyn watched speechless as he lay back in the water and pulled the shield over him.

Madness. She bit her lip and watched him go dutifully to his death.

62

DISINTEGRATION

Climbing the stairs to the top of the Tower of Air was harder than it had been a week ago. Halfway up, Hyram paused to catch his breath. He looked at his hands. They were trembling. He could feel it in his legs too, and it was starting to affect his speech again.

Is it harder because of the sickness, or because of what I know?

No, that wasn't right. He didn't *know* anything. He only suspected.

No, that wasn't right either. He *knew* that Prince Jehal had given him his support. He *knew* that Jehal had betrayed his pact with Shezira and made Zafir speaker. And he *knew* what Jehal had said, there in the Hall of Speakers, as he did it.

He knew too what had been whispered in his ear, that Jehal and Zafir were lovers. At first he had simply refused to believe it. Then he'd sought the source of this whisper. He couldn't be sure who'd started it, but it seemed to originate from the Tower of Dusk, which meant it came from Shezira. Sour grapes then, besmirching Zafir in a last des-

perate attempt to overturn the decision of the kings and
queens? It wouldn't work. Silvallan wouldn't care and
Narghon would probably be pleased to hear it.

*It's too late, Shezira. I couldn't change it now even if I
wanted to.*

He started on the stairs again and eventually reached
the top. Usually the tower was loud and busy with servants
running up and down between the levels, but today it was
quiet and almost empty. The doors to the two topmost
floors were guarded. The soldiers hurried to let him pass
but they weren't usually here. *I have to keep an eye on her.
I have to know where she goes. I have to know what she does,
who she sees.*

"My lord."

He stopped. He'd been so lost in his thoughts that he
hadn't seen Zafir. She was sitting in the little anteroom that
separated her private rooms from the stairs.

"W-What are you doing out here?"

Zafir stood up. She lowered her eyes demurely and
showed him what she had in her hands. "Embroidery, my
lord."

"Embroidery?" Hyram shook his head. "And I-I don't
have to be your l-lord." She'd taken to calling him that as
soon as the wedding was over. He'd liked it at first, but now
it seemed to make her into a servant. It was almost as
though she was using it to build a wall between them.

"Isn't that what you want? Aren't I supposed to sit quietly in my nice airy tower, doing nothing very much while
you rule the realms?"

"One of those r-realms is yours, Zafir. You don't have to
relinquish it."

"The other kings and queens will expect it from me. It is
what the speaker is supposed to do, after all."

"Y-You could be d-different—" He stopped himself. This
was nonsense. This wasn't why he'd climbed the tower.
"Y-You sent word to me, my queen. A-About the
potions?"

"Yes." Zafir smiled and beckoned him into her rooms.
Past the anteroom was another staircase that led to the very
top of the tower, to the queen's dressing room. Beyond that,
most of the rest of the level was one large open audience
room. Or bedroom, as it had lately become. Zafir snapped

her fingers. A man came running with a pair of goblets. He seemed rather large and ungainly for a servant, Hyram thought, and the face was unfamiliar.

"Your manservant is n-new."

"He's hardly a manservant, my lord. He arrived very recently and brought a gift for you." She took the goblets and offered one to Hyram, then sat down and picked up her needlework again.

"A g-gift? I know of no riders r-reaching my eyrie in the night."

"*Your* eyrie, my lord? And I did not say he came on the back of a dragon."

Hyram sniffed the goblet that Zafir had given him. His eyes widened. "S-So you *do* have more."

"Yes, my lord. Drink. There's plenty more now. I have reached an arrangement with Prince Jehal." She glanced up at Hyram from time to time as she spoke, but mostly her eyes were fixed on what her fingers were doing, on the stab and thrust of the needle through the cloth.

"The Viper." Even hearing his name was like being stabbed. "W-What arrangement have y-you reached, my lady?"

"One that suits me, my lord."

"There have been w-w-whispers, Zafir."

"Whispers, my lord?" She stopped and looked up at him, as innocent as a child. For a moment Hyram wondered what he was doing. He had everything, didn't he? Everything he wanted. Why sully it with baseless suspicion?

But it was the Viper, and so he had to know, even if it ruined everything. "Yes, my lady. Whispers. About you and J-Jehal."

"The Jehal who murdered my mother?" Her eyes held him fast.

"I-I had not forgotten, my lady."

"Drink your potion, my lord. Recover your strength a little." She smiled, stood up and came toward him. "It is true I have an arrangement with Jehal. If you want to know, I will tell you everything about it." She briefly touched his hand, then went to stand behind him and put her hands on his shoulders. Hyram sighed and drank deeply as her fingers kneaded his muscles. "You must be exhausted."

"Yes." Hyram put the cup to his lips and drained it. He

could feel the potion coursing through him almost at once, hot and fierce.

"So here is the arrangement I have with Jehal. There will be no more potions for you. Not ever." Her hands stayed at their work. "Your sickness will take its course, just like King Tyan's has. I will be speaker; Jehal will be my lover. In time he will follow me. And you, my lord, will be kept perfectly alive, trapped in the prison of your own body, to watch it all unfold."

A numbness filled Hyram's head. He had to run the words through his mind two or three times before he understood that there hadn't been a mistake, and that she'd meant every word. He lurched out of his chair and staggered forward. Something was desperately wrong. The room was spinning. He could hardly feel his arms and legs. As though . . . He reached for her and she sprang away from him, snarling and spitting like an angry cat.

"Don't touch me! Never touch me!"

"T-The s-sickness . . ."

"Is getting worse, is it? Yes, my lord, this potion is a little different. It'll happen much more quickly now. I pray that the Ancestors leave you as useless as King Tyan, and quickly."

He had a dagger on his belt. Somewhere. He had to reach for it three times before his hands closed on the hilt. "Y-You . . . y-you . . ." he gasped, "vile . . . w-wicked . . ." There was a chair between them, but he had the dagger in his hand now. A huge pressure was building in his head.

"Me? And what about you, my lord?" she hissed and darted away behind a table. "You betrayed Queen Shezira, the most powerful friend you had. You've broken your clan's pact. And for what? Who do you think I am? You take me in my own bed and then you moan my mother's name in your sleep. I was never anything more to you than some *thing* to keep your memories burning. Oh, and the potions, let's not forget the potions."

Hyram stumbled around the table and lunged. Zafir jumped nimbly out of the way. "I-I . . . l-loved—"

She sneered at him, dripping scorn: "You loved yourself, my lord."

"I l-loved A-A-Aliphera." He felt obscenely drunk and his head was about to explode. Zafir's face swam in and out of focus. He wanted to reach out and grab it and destroy it, to smash her into bloody pulp, but his arms and legs felt as though they were made of lead. Sometimes it didn't seem to be Zafir's face at all that he saw, but Jehal's, laughing at him. He took another few steps and slashed the air with the dagger; Zafir was too quick for him.

"Well, she never loved you, my lord. She despised you. You made her sick." She darted forward and spat in his face at the same moment as he launched himself at her. He felt the dagger snag on her clothes and she gave a little yelp. He staggered a few steps forward as Zafir twisted away. She cursed and he heard the crash of something falling over. The pressure inside his head was crushing. The world was slowly losing its color. He turned around. Zafir was scrabbling on the floor, trying to get up, clutching her side.

"You cut me," she hissed.

"I'll do . . . more th-than c-cut you, y-you w-whore." He was made of stone, but inside was pure fire. His vision seemed to compress as he stepped over her, until all he could see was her face and everything else had dissolved away. He was splitting, falling away into elemental pieces. He raised the dagger to plunge into her flesh and brought it down, and then something crashed into him and everything went dark. He couldn't move and he couldn't see, but for some reason he could hear voices. He could hear Zafir shouting for her guards. And he could hear the Viper.

63

RIVER TREASURE

K emir watched from a distance. Men were emerging
from the river, clutching their enormous shields and
struggling to pull their ridiculous crossbows from the water.
They weren't wearing any armor. In fact, when he squinted
he could see they weren't wearing anything at all. They
were painted, however, covered in swirling patterns that
had somehow resisted the water.

He frowned and idly strung his bow. They were mad. He
wondered, for a second or two, whether the patterns painted
onto them were some kind of blood-magic so that dragon
fire wouldn't hurt them. Only for a second or two, though,
before Snow felled a dozen of them with a single blast.

Then Ash was among them, and Snow backed away and
left him to it. The other three dragons, the ones they'd found
at the eyrie, stopped what they were doing and watched.
Even as Ash was finishing off the soldiers one of them scuttled forward and snatched one of the bodies, gulping it
down. Ash turned and roared. For a moment the last few
Guardsmen were forgotten as the dragons squared up.
Then the other dragon lowered its head and backed away.

In the space of a minute the soldiers all died. They didn't

manage to erect a single one of their crossbows; Kemir wasn't even sure they'd tried. It was almost as though they knew they were doomed, and preferred to die quickly in battle than slowly choke to death. He stretched and ambled toward the aftermath in case any of them had had anything worth looting. Not likely, since they were all naked, but there might be a ring or a talisman on a chain. Pointless really, robbing the dead out here. Even if he did find anything, then what? He stared at the river, as bodies and shields floated past. *So futile . . .*

One of the shields moved. At first Kemir thought his eyes had played a trick on him, but when he stopped and watched carefully, he could see feet sticking out from underneath. They were kicking.

Slowly he pulled an arrow from his quiver and drew back his bowstring. He fired the arrow into the middle of the shield. Even at such a short range, it didn't go in very far, but it went in far enough. The water thrashed and splashed, and suddenly there was a man scrambling to his feet on the far bank. Kemir drew out another arrow and then stared in amazement.

"You! Murderer!"

Rider Semian stared back at him. He was naked, apart from a long thick shirt that reached to his knees and a sword belt. He still held his shield and had a bottle hanging around his neck on a piece of string. Kemir held an arrow in one hand and his bow in the other. Semian was only a few yards away but the river was too wide to jump. Kemir grinned.

"You're a dead man." Without looking away, he put the arrow to his bowstring. "You can't reach me, and you need to be a lot farther away before I'm going to miss. So what's the matter with you? Too much of a coward to die like the rest? Or is that what they were for? Were they all supposed to die, all the *little* soldiers, so that you, a *rider,* could live?" He drew back the bowstring.

Semian didn't move except to shift behind his shield so that Kemir could only see his head. "Who are you working for, sell-sword? Who bought you?"

"No one." Kemir laughed. "For the first time in far too many years. Just settling an old score." He might have gone on—tried to explain to the rider why he was helping Snow, how dragon-riders had destroyed his family, his friends and everyone he knew. There was a courtesy to killing a man, and part of that was making sure that he understood why he was marked to die.

Then again Semian hardly deserved any courtesy, so Kemir just released the arrow.

Semian yanked up his shield, which quivered as the arrow hit it exactly in front of his face.

Kemir's arm shot back for another arrow. At the same time Semian took a huge leap into the middle of the river. In midair he flipped his absurd shield sideways and hurled it at Kemir. As Kemir nocked his second arrow, he ducked and twisted sideways, but the shield was so big it caught the top of his bow, almost tearing it out of his hands. He dropped the arrow and nearly fell over.

By the time he'd regained his balance, Semian was scrambling up the near bank of the river.

"You'll have to do better than that, sell-sword."

Kemir hesitated. *Knives or arrows?* Arrows were more certain, but Semian was maybe too close.

He went for another arrow anyway. *No shield to hide behind this time.* Semian drew his sword. He sprang the last few yards between them and swung. As Kemir let the arrow go, the tip of the sword clipped his bow. The arrow went wide, and then the rider was on him. Kemir launched himself at Semian and the two of them tumbled to the ground, arms locked around each other, rolling back toward the river. Kemir had one hand around Semian's wrist, pinning his sword. His other hand went to the rider's throat. Semian let the sword go and punched Kemir in the face, hard enough to make his vision swim. They rolled apart. Kemir sprang to his feet and drew out his knives. Semian was up too. Unarmed. His sword lay between them.

"Last time you were the one surrounded by allies and dragons. Now it's me." Kemir tipped back his head and roared, "Hey, Snow!" then bared his teeth at Semian. "Show me which dragon is yours, so I can feed you to him after I've killed you."

"I don't see you surrounded by allies," said Semian. He took a step back. He still had the bottle on a string around his neck; now he lifted that over his head. "I see only you."

"This time, *I* have the dragons."

Semian kept his eyes on Kemir as he flicked the stopper out of the bottle. Kemir lunged forward. Semian skittered backward.

Kemir shook his head.

"Ah ah! No special potions from your friends the alchemists. You should have drunk those before you came out." Semian was even farther from his sword now.

"This is poison, sell-sword." He slowly put the bottle to his lips and tipped it back.

"Is it slow and painful?"

"I believe so, yes."

"So I could still carve you up and watch you bleed slowly?"

"Oh, you misunderstand." Semian glanced back toward the caves. "It doesn't kill *humans.*" He dropped into a fighting stance. "I'm unarmed. Are you going to try your luck with those knives of yours, sell-sword? Or do you have something else you should be doing?"

64

FANGS OF THE VIPER

Cold air brushed Hyram's face. He opened his eyes. He was flat on his back and Jehal was crouching over him. They were outside in the open air somewhere. It was night, and he was alive, barely. When he tried to throw out an arm to grab the Viper by his throat, he could barely move. His limbs tingled. They weren't really awake yet.

"You're shivering, old man." Jehal spoke softly and quietly, as though someone was sleeping nearby. "Are you cold? Or are you sick? Which is it, do you think?"

"I-I have n-nothing to s-say to you, V-Viper."

Jehal smiled. "That *is* a relief. If you'd got it in your head to make a long speech about what a terrible person I am, I might just have thrown myself off the balcony here. Anything to make it end."

"Y-Y-You'll . . ." He couldn't make his mouth work properly. His face was turning numb.

"Never get away with it? Is that what you were going to say? You must be losing your mind, old man. I already have. Do you know where we are? We're in your palace, old man. You're surrounded by your own guards." Jehal frowned and shook his head. "'There goes our lord, so drunk he can't stand straight again.' That's how easy it is." He laughed. "Of course we're friends ever since I backed your speaker, aren't we? I wonder if any of the soldiers I've just walked past were the same ones you had with you down under the Glass Cathedral when you tortured me." Jehal reached down and picked up something from the shadows beside him. "You've been wanting to know this for a long time." He held up a small round bottle made of thick smoky glass. Then he pulled a sack out of the shadows as well. When he tipped the bottle over the sack, a glittering silver liquid dripped out. "Yes, I *have* been poisoning you. You've got two very fine poisons in you already, in fact. A little Nightwatchman in your drink to start. Then a little prick from a needle dipped in Frogsback." Jehal held a needle in front of Hyram's face. "Gave you that just a couple of minutes ago, when you started to stir. It should be working by now. If you stop breathing, that means I've got the dose wrong, and I'm going to feel quite foolish. If you don't, well, then you should recover from it in a few hours. I do like Frogsback. This though . . ." Jehal stroked the bottle of silver liquid. "This is special. It's the vapors. Even in tiny doses they slowly destroy your mind. Very, very slowly. Of course in bigger doses they act rather more quickly."

With that, the Viper straddled Hyram and forced the sack over his head. Hyram tried to struggle, but he was so weak that he might as well not have bothered. He also tried not to breathe in, which was equally futile.

"You can't smell them," said the Viper. Hyram felt the rest of the bottle being tipped over his head. "A little pot of this in your bedroom for a year, that's all it took. That and someone to stir it up from time to time. A sort of scum forms on the top after a while which keeps the vapors from forming. Otherwise it's perfect, don't you think?

"Didn't you start to have a problem with your potboys about a year ago?" Hyram could tell that Jehal was grinning, simply from the sound of his voice. "Kept disappearing, didn't they? I don't suppose you thought anything of it. A different one every few months. Did you even notice? No? Shame on you, old man. You should always pay attention to your potboys. They're almost invisible yet they know all your secrets. They know who you take to your bed; they know who you talk to in the middle of the night. They sleep in the same rooms as us. They know every nook and cranny and corner of our sleeping lives. They breathe the same air." The Viper chuckled. "So you had to keep having new ones, before the vapors could affect them. Don't worry, they've all been well looked after. Oh, but then you probably don't care, do you, because you didn't even notice them. No, you're probably too worried about your own predicament just now. I suppose I can understand that."

The Viper's voice receded, as though he was standing up.

"Don't bother trying to move or shout out, old man. I hope you've learned by now that a Viper's bite is poison." He laughed. "But you had one little victory. I assume it was you who stole Queen Shezira's white dragon. Since it wasn't me, and it wasn't Zafir, and I sincerely doubt that King Valgar would dare do such a thing. But you . . . What was it? You couldn't bear the thought that I should own such a prize? And now Shezira's never going to know. Pity." He patted Hyram on the shoulder. "Good night, old man, and good-bye. I'm going to leave you now, surrounded by your Adamantine Guard. In a little while Zafir will come and take your hood off, and then she'll call in some of your loyal men, the ones you set to guard her door. They'll carry you back to your bed to sleep off the stink of wine that's on you. Sleep in peace. By tomorrow morning, when you see me again, you won't even know who I am."

The Viper walked away. Hyram heard his footsteps fade to nothing. Inside the sack he tried to turn his head, twisting it as far as he could from the fumes that he couldn't even smell. When he tried to pull off the sack, it was like slapping himself with slabs of dead meat. His arms flailed with a will of their own. They wouldn't do what he wanted them to. He couldn't move his fingers at all. He tried shouting but all he could do was rasp. Out here on the balcony, no one would hear him.

Frogsback. He's paralyzed me.

He kicked with his feet. He could do that at least. Hopelessly uncoordinated, but he could move them. After a few minutes he'd managed to push himself a few inches. Exhausted, he gave up. If anything, the numbness was getting worse, and the more he struggled, the more fumes he breathed.

Shezira. Time and space became a blur. He wasn't sure

where he was anymore. At some point he thought he felt strong arms take hold of him. They must have taken the sack off too, because he could see stars again. And faces.

Shezira. She was the only one left he could trust. The only one who could make it all go away. Even after everything they'd done to each other, after everything he'd done to her, she'd do the right thing. She'd have the strength that he lacked.

He tried to struggle, but the thoughts never got further than his mind, while the rest of his body slumbered in peaceful stupor.

"Shezira . . ."

65

❧

SMOKE AND POISON

Kemir turned and ran, sprinting toward the caves and the dragons. "Don't!" he screamed. "Stop! Don't eat the bodies!"

He was too late. Of course he was too late. Rider Rod wouldn't have told him if there was any danger he might stop it. All of the dragons had bloody muzzles. There were still a few corpses littered around the river, but there had clearly been a lot more. He clenched his fists in furious frustration. *No armor, no sword, I should have carved him up.*

And that was the point. That was *why* Rider Rod had told him. *Because I had him. Because for a moment there, with no sword in his hand, he was mine for the taking. Because this time I could have carved him up. And now I'm too late and I let him go. Shit!* The realization made him clench his fists again and scream.

"They're poisoned," he shouted when Snow and Ash both stopped and peered down at him. The other three dragons didn't understand. They still did what they were told, whether it was by a rider on their back or another dragon in their head.

Snow spat out half a knight. *How are they poisoned?*

"I don't know." Kemir pointed back down the river. "There was a rider. He got past you in the river. He told me."

Ash lifted his head and snorted fire at the heavens. *Perhaps he lied.*

"Perhaps he did!" Kemir shrugged. "Wait and find out if you like. Or go and find him and ask him. Last time I saw him he was a few hundred yards that way, behind those rocks and heading for the forest. He can't have got far." *He murdered Sollos.*

The dragons didn't say anything else. Ash stamped a clawed foot, shaking the earth, then the whole valley trembled as he and Snow pounded away toward the trees. The other three dragons went back to the cave-mouth fires. Kemir cast a nervous glance at the cliffs towering over them, wondering if they were about to come crashing down. As soon as he convinced himself that they weren't, he ran after Snow. *That's what they should have done. Not fire but stone. Shake the whole mountainside down and bury the place. Could they have done that?*

He reached the place where he'd found Semian and picked up his bow. He left it strung, just in case. Ash and Snow were at the edge of the trees and launching themselves into the air.

He is in there. Not far. I can feel his thoughts. He is cold, very cold, that is all I can sense.

Where?

Distant. Exactly where I cannot be sure.

Then burn it. Burn it all.

Burn it all.

"The river," shouted Kemir. Semian's shield was gone. "He'll be in the river." Except the river was so shrouded by trees that the dragons probably couldn't even see it from above. Kemir stood at the edge of the wood and watched. A part of him wanted to give chase himself. *Let Sollos rest in peace at last.*

"You want him alive, remember!" he shouted as the first lance of fire stabbed down into the trees. Semian would have his sword again and Kemir might not even see the knight until they stumbled into each other. And did he really want to hunt down a desperate rider while two dragons were raining fire down from above? No, probably not.

He took a deep breath. If Rider Rod had been telling the truth about the poison, and *if* all the dragons had eaten it, and *if* they all died, then what? Stuck in a valley full of angry soldiers and alchemists hadn't seemed too bad with two murderous dragons on his side. Stuck there without them he'd be the hunted one.

"Bugger." He growled. "Another day, Rider Rod. One day, if the dragons don't get you, I'll still be waiting for you in those shadows." He sat down to watch as Snow and Ash burned the forest. They'd give up soon enough. That was the trouble with the pair of them. No patience. Were all dragons like that?

Ash suddenly lurched in the air. He turned sharply, flew almost straight toward Kemir and landed heavily next to the river. Before he'd even come to a halt, he had rolled over into the water. *Hot! Too hot! I am burning inside!* Ash pressed his head into the ice-cold water, took a long swallow and then splashed more water over his back. A second later he was gently steaming.

Kemir backed away.

"It's the poison, you stupid greedy dragon. That's how dragons die. They burn from the inside." He wrung his hands in frustration and looked around for Nadira. It was hardly a surprise that Ash was the first, since he'd probably eaten more than the rest of the dragons put together. But he hadn't thought it would happen so quickly. How long had it been? Ten minutes? The alchemists in the caves, though, they'd know exactly how long the poison would take. Exactly when to come rushing out to finish off anyone stupid enough to remain.

He jumped up onto a rock and glanced around the valley. "Nadira!" he shouted. He couldn't see her. "Snow!"

Ash. Here, I will cool you. Snow landed to squat beside Ash, pouring river water over him. Over by the cave mouths the other three dragons didn't seem troubled. Yet.

"Snow! Did you eat the bodies of the dead?"

Yes.

"How many?"

I did not count mouthfuls, Kemir. Does it matter? Their poison is in me.

"Not as many as Ash, though."

Far, far fewer.

"Then perhaps not enough to do to you whatever it's done to him." Kemir looked around the valley for Nadira again. This time he saw her, not far away, sitting with her back to a tree, brushing her hair. He wondered, for an instant, where she'd found the brush. "Nadira!"

Ash! You must stay awake! Kemir could feel frustration in Snow's thoughts, and a deep sadness with it. Strangely little anger, though. *Kemir, I begin to feel it too. I must destroy the alchemists quickly now, while I still have the strength.*

"No! You should fly away, while you still can." He waved Nadira toward him. By the caves, one of the dragons had gone to lie down in the water as well.

I cannot leave Ash. He is sinking into torpor. It is our way of stopping the heat inside when it grows too strong. If they find him alone like this, they will feed him their potions again and he will be lost.

"Or they might get both of you. Or you might die from the poison. You don't know what it does. You don't know anything. We have to go."

I understand your fear, Little One, but I will not leave. There is too much undone.

"Then stay here and die! Or be enslaved again. For myself, I wish for neither." Kemir got up. He trotted to Nadira and took her hand. "Come on! We need to go. And quickly."

The poison is in me, Kemir, and it will do what it will do. If I am to die, I will die in battle against my enemies. I am a dragon, and that is my nature.

"In battle?" Kemir threw up his head to the heavens. "They're not going to come out and fight you, you stupid creature. They're going to wait and watch as you fail. They'll hide in their caves and come out when you're too weak to lift yourself off the ground. Is that battle?" He was shouting now, filled with a bitter sense of loss that he didn't understand. "Fly up into the mountains! Find a lake by a glacier and immerse yourself in it! If that doesn't keep you cold, nothing will. If you want to fight, fight the poison."

No, Kemir. I will stay with Ash.

Kemir stamped his foot. "If the poison doesn't kill you, you can come back and try again! You can free Ash, free them all. If you die, you're dead, and everything you want dies with you."

Snow stared at him. For a second he thought she was going to eat him. He could feel the thoughts in her head, the rivers of anger and desire, the knotting indecision. Then, slowly, she nodded.

It is not our nature to flee, Little One Kemir, and I do not understand why you would betray your own kind. But yes, then. Let us leave. She lowered her head and shoulders to the ground. Kemir scrambled onto her back and hauled Nadira after him.

66

THE NIGHT OF THE KNIVES

Almiri tiptoed across the floor. She was shaking, still sweating from running up the stairs. And from what had gone on before. She held a single candle, and the flame flickered restlessly, casting dancing shadows across the walls. Her hands were trembling. She approached her mother's bed and felt like a young girl again, a child looking for a comfort she rarely received.

Shezira tossed and turned. Almiri knew those dreams. She'd had her own dreams, of being at home in the far-off north. Of someone tapping on her window, of the tapping growing louder, and then the rooms shaking and swaying. Of pictures falling off the walls, candles tipping over, ceilings cracking, beams breaking. *Of castles falling and of the earth splitting open.*

She kneeled by the bed and gave her mother a gentle nudge. "Your Holiness . . ."

Shezira twisted violently away. *Someone in her bed-chamber. In the middle of the night. Ill deeds . . .*

Almiri tried again. "Mother!" This time Shezira heard her. She sat up, wild-eyed.

"Almiri?"

"Yes. Mother, you have to wake up."

Shouts outside. Swords clashing. Men screaming. Hiding . . .

Shezira rubbed her eyes and squinted at her daughter, shielding her eyes from the candlelight. "Almiri," she said again. "What are you doing here?"

"Mother, someone has tried to kill the speaker."

"Hyram's dead?"

"No, Mother." Almiri tried to keep her voice steady, but she couldn't hide the tension. "Queen Zafir. Someone has tried to kill Queen Zafir."

Lying on the floor in the dark, trying not to breathe. Armored feet in front of her eyes. Vicious words and bared, bloody swords . . .

"I don't suppose they succeeded?"

"No, Mother. She was wounded but not killed."

Shezira chuckled. "Pity."

"Mother! This is not a joke." Almiri's voice sounded shrill to herself. She wanted to scream.

"Who did it?"

"They say it was a rider disguised as a messenger boy. They say it was your knight-marshal." She could see the coldness blossom inside her mother and sweep across her face. *How long has it been since you were afraid, Mother?*

Her own husband, a king, dragged from his bed and thrown to the floor with a sword to his neck.

"Nastria?"

"Yes, Mother."

"No!" Shezira threw off her blankets and got up. "No, Nastria would never do such a thing. Not without my order."

"Yes, Mother. They say that too."

"Servants!" Shezira peered at her. "I ordered no such thing. You look frightened, daughter. Why?"

"Because . . ."

The sword is lifted up . . .

Because I am. Because I'm terrified. Petrified. Paralyzed. But she could never say that. Not to her mother. Shezira couldn't begin to understand. She wouldn't even try.

"Because the Adamantine Guard have seized our tower, Mother. Valgar's riders are either dead or taken. They dragged my husband out of his bed." *. . . but never comes* *down. The feet march away and take him with them and she is alone in the dark, still silent and unbreathing.* "When he fought, they beat him like a common criminal. I hid under the bed. I heard them talking. They didn't see me in the dark."

Servants were coming in now, sluggishly, rubbing the sleep from their eyes. Shezira scowled at them. "Dress me," she snapped. "Awake my riders. Awake everyone. Daughter, you're not making much sense. Why would Hyram's guards do such a thing?"

Almiri sat on the bed and held her head in her hands. No matter how hard she tried, she couldn't keep it all clenched up inside her for much longer. "They're Zafir's Guard now, Mother. Your knight-marshal tried to kill her. They *saw* her. She fled, and they saw her come to our tower. But she's not there, Mother. When they don't find her, they'll come here."

"I'm quite sure you're right, especially if they saw *you* come here too."

"What was I supposed to do, Mother? It was dark. I wasn't asleep. I saw them take Valgar and so I ran. They killed our riders!"

Shezira held out her arms to be dressed. "Yes, so you said."

"Where *is* Lady Nastria, Mother?"

"Missing."

What's that, Mother? A touch of fear? It is, isn't it? So you do remember what it feels like from all those years ago.

"Missing," Shezira said again. She frowned.

"Would she—"

"No, daughter, she would not. She would never be so mindlessly stupid."

Someone ran into the room and groveled at Shezira's feet.

"Your Holiness—"

"What?"

"The speaker's soldiers are hammering on the door, Your Holiness. They demand—"

Shezira waved him away. "Tell them that I am dressing and that when I am ready they may enter. Tell them that the person they're looking for is not here, but I shall be happy to allow them to see that for themselves. Tell them that my riders shall not be the first to bare their swords. And remind them that I have a good few more than King Valgar did."

Another servant approached. "Your armor, Holiness?"

"Are we at war? Don't be foolish." She waved that one away too.

"Mother—"

"*Enough,* Almiri. The Guard may take their orders from Queen Zafir today, but for the last ten years they've answered to Hyram, and old habits are not so easily forgotten. Does he think I plan to go to war with them? That would be absurd. I will speak to Hyram in person, and if he intends to imprison everyone who disagrees with his foolishness then he can do it himself. No, daughter, something else is afoot here. Hyram will release King Valgar and Zafir will pay compensation to the families of his dead riders. I will see to it." Finally she was dressed. She shooed all her servants away and marched out and down into the body of the Tower of Dusk. She swept down the stairs into the great hall with Almiri on her heels. A dozen riders were already there, some of them armored, some of them still in their nightclothes, but all armed. Most of them were pressed against the doors to the outside. A heavy bar was braced across both doors, and the riders were shouting at the soldiers outside, such a cacophony of cursing that Almiri couldn't make out a single word. When the queen reached the bottom of the stairs, she snatched a spear and banged it on the floor. "Open the doors," she shouted. "Let them in."

"Mother, don't go outside." Almiri almost snatched at Shezira's sleeve, but that would have earned her nothing but contempt.

The riders fell silent. Shezira glared at them. "What are you waiting for?" She pointed at the nearest two knights, who'd managed to scramble into their armor. "You come with me. The rest of you—"

"*Mother!*" Almiri almost screamed. It was a mistake to shout at a queen, but she couldn't help herself anymore.

Shezira rounded on her. "Queen Almiri is our guest," she said very clearly. "See to it that the Adamantine Guardsmen understand that. And we are not King Valgar, but the Queen of the North, the Queen of Sand and Stone, with twelve score dragons at our beck and call. See they understand that too." She swept her cloak around her and marched toward the door. "Why is this door still closed? Must I open it myself?"

She would have lifted the bar with her own hands if some of her riders hadn't hastily removed it. The doors swung open. Outside, dozens of Adamantine men stood waiting, fully armored and with bared steel in their hands. They paused and then parted as Shezira strode toward them, and after all the shouting an eerie silence fell. Almiri watched her go into the gloom of the night. Tears stung her eyes.

You're wrong. Mother, this time you're wrong.

She kept her thoughts to herself, though, and as Shezira vanished into the darkness, she quietly slipped away.

67

❧

JOSTAN

For a time that felt like forever, the smoke was unbearable. In the caverns Jaslyn sat by the river, a wet cloth wrapped across her mouth, and tried not to cough herself to death. Not coughing was almost impossible, and whenever she succumbed, she inevitably took in lungfuls of hot smoke and that made it a hundred times worse. Jostan sat beside her. The first time she fell to coughing, he had wrapped his arms around her ribs and then pressed his lips to hers. She tried to fight, pushing him away, thinking he'd lost his mind, but he wasn't trying to kiss her. He blew air out of his lungs and into hers and then drew away. His air still reeked with smoke, but at least it was cool and moist, not bitter and dry. When she'd regained her composure, he had kneeled at her feet.

"Forgive me," he whispered.

"I should have your head," she rasped. But the coughing fit had gone, and anyway the only person who could have defended her honor was Semian, and he was gone too.

The second time she began to cough, he did it again, and she realized that a part of her liked the closeness of it. Instead of fighting him off, she found herself wanting to pull him to her, to have someone to hold on to at last, if only for the last hours of her life. Eventually she pushed him away, firmly but gently this time. After that she made sure that she didn't cough anymore. In the end she lay beside the river, eyes closed, listlessly splashing her face whenever they started to sting again. The water tasted delicious. She tried to pretend that Jostan wasn't there and think only about that.

"Princess! There is a breeze," he said at last. "Do you feel it?"

She lifted her head. He was right. A gentle wind whispered along the river from the depths of the caves.

"What does it mean?" she asked.

"It means that the fires are drawing air out of the caves. It means that the dragons are no longer tending them, Your Highness." He could barely contain himself. "The Embers have won!"

Jaslyn wanted to cry. Coming down here had been stupidity. *Her* stupidity. "I'm sorry, Jostan. I know we should have stayed with the alchemists." The Embers were dead. She hadn't seen it with her own eyes, but the shouts and the screams and the roars of the dragons had echoed far into the tunnels.

"No, Princess. This means the dragons are gone. The Embers have won."

"The Embers are dead, Jostan." Speaking was a trial. Her throat was raw and burning, and every word was a battle against the smoke.

"Yes." He was smiling, she realized. "And the dragons ate them."

She was missing something. She struggled upright. "Why is that a cause for happiness, Rider Jostan?"

He frowned and peered at her. Twice he opened his mouth to speak and then closed it again. At the third attempt words finally came out. "I'm sorry, Your Highness. I thought you knew."

"Knew what, Rider?"

"That the Embers . . ." He wouldn't look at her. "Highness, the Embers took poison. The bottle that Rider Semian had around his neck, that was poison too. Dragon poison."

"What are you talking about?" *Dragon poison? No such thing. I would have known.*

"The Embers, Your Highness, they went out there to die. They knew what awaited them."

"Poison?" *Would she have known?*

He bowed his head.

And then it hit her—far, far later than it should have. "Silence!"

Jostan stared at the ground. "And Matanizkan and Levanter. I am sorry, Your Highness."

"Sorry?" For a moment even the smoke didn't matter. *Sorry? What use is sorry? My Silence! You've poisoned my Silence. Graceful, elegant, beautiful, perfect—*

And trying to kill us, she reminded herself. *Or was.* No, best not to think about it. Would she ever have sacrificed Silence to save her own life? No. To save Jostan? Semian? No. To save anyone at all? She didn't know.

"I have to see!" She was already getting to her feet.

"No, Your Highness. Wait. It's not safe."

She screamed at him. "You've poisoned my Silence! I want to see him."

"We have to wait."

"Wait for what?"

"Wait for Rider Semian, Your Highness. He went out to watch. When they're all dead, he will come back and tell us."

"When they're dead?!" She was rigid with fury. If she'd had claws, she would have torn Jostan to pieces. "So they're still alive?" She pressed her face up close to his. "There must be something to take this poison out of them. Poison the white if that's the only way, but not Silence. Not my Silence!" But there wasn't something. The alchemists wouldn't have an antidote. Why would they? And even if they did, it would take hours to walk back to where they were hiding, and hours more to get back to the mouth of the caves.

She turned and ran toward the entrance, heedless of the smoke, but Jostan pulled her down. "Your Highness!"

"Silence!" She screamed and fought and tore at him. "My Silence! Don't eat them! Don't!" But Jostan was strong, much too strong, and he wouldn't let her go. She ordered him, cursed him, berated him as best she could before the next coughing fit seized her, but his arms stayed wrapped around her and all her struggles were useless. "Silence," she whispered. Tears streamed down her face. Jostan still held her, but his arms were gentle now, and suddenly welcome. She rested her head on his chest and wept. Here in the murderous choking dark she didn't want to be a princess anymore.

They crept down the river until they could see the massive pyre at the cave mouth, and there they waited for an hour, maybe longer, before she decided she couldn't bear anymore. She was careful this time, waiting until Jostan was distracted before she ran, sprinting along the riverbank and then diving into the water when the heat from the fire was too much. She heard Jostan shouting after her, but she didn't look back. By the time he finally caught her, they were already outside, thrashing in the river alongside the fires.

"Keep your head down!" shouted Jostan, and then they were past, and the air was suddenly cold and crisp and deliriously fresh. It felt so gloriously clean that she wanted to gulp it down as fast as she could. For a second she almost forgot about Silence.

And then she saw him. A hundred yards from the river, flat on his belly, eyes closed. Still.

"Your Highness! Wait!" But she didn't, and this time Jostan didn't try to stop her. She hauled herself out of the freezing river and ran as fast as she could, collapsing to the ground by the dragon's head. Silence was gone. She could already feel the heat burning him from the inside.

Jostan came toward her, then saw the look on her face and stopped dead in his tracks.

"Is he . . ."

Jaslyn shook her head. She couldn't speak.

"I . . . I should look for the others, Your Highness. Please be careful. The others . . . They might not . . ."

He should have taken her back into the cave, and they both knew it. She should have stayed there until all the other dragons had been found. He should never have let her escape in the first place, and her mother would probably have his head for being so careless. But for a moment Jaslyn loved him more than anyone in the world simply for leaving her alone.

68

THE BALCONY

Jehal watched through the eyes of one of the Taiytakei dragons. He saw the doors of the Tower of Dusk open and watched Shezira storm toward Hyram's keep. He grimaced. *Like an arrow from the bow of a master archer,* he mused. *Straight and deadly and utterly predictable. And when Hyram cannot be roused, what then, mighty Queen?* He took off one strip of silk and put on the other, to see through the eyes of the little dragon that he'd left watching over Hyram's bed. The Adamantine Guardsmen had taken Hyram from Zafir's rooms back to his own and put him to bed, just as their new mistress had ordered them. He should be snoring nicely by now. Everyone would assume he was drunk.

The bed was empty.

It took Jehal a couple of seconds and a close inspection to believe what he was seeing, but Hyram was gone. Despite all the poisons, somehow Hyram had woken up and got out of bed. The dragon found him a few minutes later, out on his balcony, leaning over the parapet. His face was slack and vacant and he was shaking; it was all Jehal could do not to laugh. Hyram could have ended up anywhere. As it was, it was a miracle that he hadn't simply tipped over the parapet and dashed himself to pieces on the ground below.

Now there's a thought.

He tore off the silk and fumbled for his boots. "Kazah! Help me get dressed." If Shezira got to Hyram and Hyram could actually string a sentence together, there was just a chance that everything might unravel. He ought to feel afraid, he supposed. Or at least annoyed, alarmed, worried— something like that. Exhilarated though? *Not good.*

Which only made the feeling stronger. He grinned at Kazah. However this ended, he was definitely going to miss it once it was all over.

SHEZIRA REACHED HYRAM'S KEEP EXPECTING to have to take the place by storm and quite prepared to do so, single-handed if she had to. Instead, the doors were flung open for her, which made her pause. But Hyram was not a murderer. Whatever else he might do, despite all his betrayals, he wasn't a killer.

Nonetheless. She whispered to the two riders she'd brought with her, "Stay close to me."

Inside, an old man was waiting for her, so withered and bent he made even Isentine look young. She took a moment to recognize him.

"Wordmaster Herlian?"

He bowed, as best he could. "Your Holiness."

"I am here to see Hyram." She could demand that now. Of course, the Guard might not see it that way.

"He's . . . Your Holiness, he's not himself."

Shezira snorted. "He's not the speaker and he's not a king. I can march straight into his bedchamber whenever it pleases me, Wordmaster. Whoever he is."

Herlian bowed again. "Your Holiness, I wouldn't dream of trying to stop you. He's been asking for you. Or at least he's said your name. But he's not well, Holiness. His mind has wandered. He talks of you and of Antros and of Aliphera and of dragons, and makes little sense."

"He'd better make sense when I ask why his soldiers are hammering on my doors."

Herlian shrugged. "I will take you to him, Your Holiness."

* * *

HYRAM WAS FLYING. HE WAS on the back of a dragon high in the sky with the wind streaming past his face. He didn't know the name of his dragon. It belonged to someone else; he wasn't sure who. His brother, perhaps. Antros. The giant of his life, always casting him into shadow.

Maybe it was the wind that was making him weep, or maybe not, for hadn't Aliphera ripped out his heart and torn it to pieces in front of his very eyes, flaunting herself with that dashing prince from the south, Tyan? She'd wanted Antros, but Antros wasn't for having. She should have wanted him instead, but no, no, she didn't, and now she'd left him with nothing, just an empty shell, devoid of feeling.

No, that wasn't right either. There hadn't been any feeling for a long time, but now it was back, all of it, decades and decades of pain, all at once.

"Hyram."

The dragon was talking to him. That must be it. There couldn't be anyone else with him, up here in the sky. Except suddenly there *was* another dragon, flying alongside him, with that frightened young slip of a girl from the north that Antros was off to marry. Not much to look at, but they had dragons, lots of dragons.

"Are you drunk?"

That made him laugh. If only he *was* drunk. Now there was a way to take all that pain, round it up and throw it back into the box from where it had escaped. *Back where you belong. No business being out here after all this time.*

"You are, aren't you? Drunk again."

"No!" he screamed at the stupid girl on her dragon, wishing she'd leave him alone. "Go away!"

"I'll go away when you explain to me why your Adamantine Guard have taken Valgar, have killed his riders, and why they were hammering on my door."

"Guards?" He didn't know anything about that. "Ask the speaker. He must know. They're his men." He grinned. "My brother's going to be the speaker one day." Then he looked away. That was a stupid thing to say. The girl was about to marry Antros. Of course she knew about the pact.

The dragon underneath him suddenly banked and sank through the air. Hyram swayed and clutched at the harness.

For some reason he hadn't strapped himself in. He had no idea why he'd forget a thing like that. That was the sort of thing Antros would do, except Antros didn't forget; he did stupid things on purpose and then mocked Hyram for being a coward. And he always got away with it too.

The girl grabbed hold of him. He couldn't even remember her name, but she must have jumped off her own dragon and landed on the back of his, and now she was pulling at him.

HYRAM LURCHED VIOLENTLY AND STUMBLED toward the parapet of the balcony. Shezira caught him, stopped him from falling to the ground, and then let go as he fought her away.

"If it's not you, then who's doing this?" But she could see in his eyes that he was somewhere else, somewhere far, far away.

"Get off my dragon," he shouted at her. "Get off it! Stay on your own!" She backed away from him. "Yes, that's right. Back where you belong. Stay away!"

The hairs on the back of her neck rose. She'd seen Hyram drunk often enough. This was something else. "Hyram? If you didn't send the Guard, then who did? Zafir?"

"Zafir?" he looked at her blankly, as though he'd never heard the name. "Prince Tyan, that's who did this to me. And that little bitch Aliphera, with her flashing eyes and her stone-cold heart. She did this. And Antros, always blocking out the sun, wherever I stand. You're welcome to him. Take him away and leave me be, all of you." He lurched again.

"Aliphera's dead, Hyram. Tyan's mad. Antros has been gone for fifteen years. What are you talking about?"

"Death." For a moment his eyes focused on her. "Death, Shezira. Life is like a wheel rolling through time, and sometimes little pieces stick to it. They stick to it all the way round and come back again when you least expect them. I'm sorry I betrayed you to them. Aliphera and Tyan." He reached out to her, and then his eyes went wide and she could see him fall away back to whatever place held him. A door closed behind his face. He wasn't coming back.

Shezira shook her head and pursed her lips. "You mean Jehal and Zafir, don't you? I'm sorry too, Hyram. Sorry for you, but I don't have time for this. Whatever they're—" Hyram's face had gone rigid with terror. He was looking past her.

"Get away! Get away!"

Something fluttered past her and flew at Hyram. In the darkness she couldn't see what it was. Some sort of bird perhaps, but it glittered like gold and made a strange sound as it flew, more a clattering of metal than the fluttering of feathers. It buzzed at Hyram's head.

"Get away!" He flailed at it, stumbling toward the parapet.

Shezira took a step toward him. Somewhere inside the keep a commotion had started. It was rapidly getting closer.

"Get away! Get off my dragon!"

He was going to fall.

"Hyram!" She lunged at him, trying to grab his arm. He shrieked and hurled himself away from her, straight into the parapet. His head and arms kept going, tipping over into the emptiness beyond. His legs flew up. It all seemed to happen very slowly, so slowly that Shezira couldn't understand why she couldn't do anything about it. And then he was gone. He didn't scream at all, but she heard the thud, a few seconds later, as he hit the ground.

There were people running into Hyram's bedchamber behind her.

"Murder!" shouted a woman's voice. It was Queen Zafir. "She's murdered my husband!"

For the first time in many years Shezira didn't know what to do. She stood staring over the edge. Behind her she could hear her riders trying to defend her. There were only two of them, though, and Zafir had come in force. It didn't last long.

JEHAL UNWRAPPED THE SILK FROM his eyes. Then he lay back on his bed while Kazah pulled his boots off again. He stared at the ceiling filled with immeasurable satisfaction.

I win.

69

 ❧

THE GLACIER

She was getting hotter. Kemir felt it. They hadn't gone very far before Snow's back grew first uncomfortable, then painful and finally almost unbearable. He'd made a mistake, he thought. She *was* dying, and there wasn't much to be done about it.

At least we'll be far from the alchemists when they finally come out of their caves. We can just die slowly from cold and hunger instead.

He could live with that, he decided. Better to die out here, fighting to survive in these harsh lands, than rot in some dungeon. Nadira probably wouldn't see it that way, but there wasn't much she could do about it now. They'd tried, him and Snow. They'd tried and they'd failed, and that felt so much better than not having tried at all. He could die happy with that.

Snow flew higher and higher, arrowing deep into the Worldspine. The mountains and valleys grew more wild and broken, the peaks higher, until they arched into a narrow valley filled with an azure lake. Snow dropped through the air until she was skimming the water. Her flying had become erratic. She was aiming for the end of the lake, where a glacier stretched down from the mountainside and immense chunks of gray ice drifted lazily in the brilliant blue water. As she reached it, she crash-landed close to the shore. Even as Kemir and Nadira were struggling out of the freezing water, Snow was backing away into the deeper parts of the lake, toward the ice cliff of the glacier. There was madness in her thoughts now, mixed in with the fury. She wasn't afraid, though. She was sure she was dying, but she wasn't afraid.

Good-bye, Little One Kemir.

Kemir spat and shook as much water as he could from his clothes. The air up here was so cold the wet furs were already starting to freeze. "Live, dragon," he hissed. "If you live, you can free as many dragons as you want. But if you're gone, who else will do it?" *Never mind that there's little chance of us surviving on our own up here.*

She was sinking beneath the freezing water. When she finally lifted her head and looked up, she was instantly wreathed in steam. She must have read his thoughts, though, for with one last gasp, she spat a stream of fire at the trees nearby, setting them ablaze. Giving him warmth and fire and a chance, at least, to survive. Then she gave Kemir a look and cocked her head. Her thoughts felt distant and vague, and also a little confused, as if the answer to his question was obvious. *You, Kemir. You will do it.*

Kemir laughed. "I don't think so, dragon."

He pulled Nadira after him into the forest and didn't look back. Behind him, the dragon sank with barely a ripple and was gone.

EPILOGUE—THE PERFECT WHITE

"Where is she?" Almiri had barely landed. She wore full armor and had nearly fifty dragons with her: Shezira's from the encampment in the Purple Spur, and a detachment of Valgar's riders. She started to take the armor off. The weight of it left her almost unable to walk.

Rider Jostan glanced toward the caves and bowed. "She's still with the body, Your Holiness."

Almiri wrinkled her nose. The valley still stank of smoke. The alchemists were out of the caves now. Some of them had left; most had stayed to rebuild the ruins of their homes.

"Did you find all the others?"

"No." Jostan sounded solemn. "We found four dragons. The fifth is missing. The white."

"The four you found, were all of them dead?"

"Yes, Your Holiness." Then he smiled a little. "We even found Rider Semian. Or he found us. Naked and half-dead from the cold, but he recovered quickly enough. It was hardly a problem to get him warm."

"So one more to find. And the riders? The ones that brought the dragons here in the first place?"

Jostan shrugged. "Left on the back of the white. Semian saw them go, heading into the deepest parts of the World-spine. He says there were two of them. A man and a woman. The man used to work for—" He didn't finish, but Almiri knew what he had been going to say: Queen Shezira's knight-marshal. For the assassin who'd tried to murder Speaker Zafir, who'd died rather than be taken when she failed, and who might just have started a war.

Jostan bit his lip. "I'm afraid Semian took the Ember poison, Your Holiness. His mind is—"

"I need to speak to her."

Jostan looked uncomfortable. "Yes, Your Holiness."

He left her presence and headed for the caves.

Almiri took her time with her armor. They couldn't stay long; the alchemists' eyrie was tiny, and all the cattle they'd kept to feed visiting dragons were gone. She wasn't entirely sure what to say to her sister. She'd waited for a couple of days, hoping that Jaslyn would come to her, but she hadn't.

Eventually she couldn't put it off any longer. She walked toward the cave mouths and the dead dragons that lay there. The ground around them was already blackened from the heat. She could still recognize Matanizkan, Levanter and Silence, all three hatched and raised in Outwatch. Jaslyn was sitting, legs crossed, beside the river, as close to Silence as she could without being scorched. She was soaking wet. Sweat, Almiri thought, until she saw Jaslyn scoop handfuls of water from the river and splash it over herself.

She sat beside her sister. The air was burning hot and hard to breathe. There wasn't any wind.

"This is as close as I can get," said Jaslyn quietly.

Almiri felt herself begin to cook under her flying clothes. "You have to leave him," she said uncomfortably. "He's gone. We can make sure you get his scales."

"I want to take them myself, when he's cooled enough."

"I . . ." Almiri stood up. The heat was intolerable. "Can we go back to the eyrie?"

"Have some water from the river." Jaslyn splashed some over her own face. She made no move to stand. Almiri sighed and sat down again.

"We fought our way out of the Adamantine Palace, Jaslyn. After they took Mother and Valgar. Out of a hundred riders, twenty of us reached the eyrie and our dragons. We took as many as we could. I have Mistral. They say our mother murdered Hyram, and that our knight-marshal tried to kill the speaker. They mean to put Mother and Valgar on trial. They'll be executed. They won't even be given the Dragon's Fall."

Jaslyn didn't move.

"Our mother is imprisoned, Jaslyn. King Valgar too. Valgar had less than a hundred dragons, but you—"

"You're the eldest. Mother's realm is yours."

"No." Almiri shook her head. It was hard, sometimes, not to be bitter. "No, Mother has made you her heir, and she has given you away. To Prince Dyalt, King Sirion's youngest. You have to use him. You and Sirion have five hundred dragons between you. You can fight them. Make them give Mother back to us. The realms need you, Jaslyn. Mother needs you."

"Mother never needed anyone."

Almiri bit her lip. "Then I need you, sister."

For a long time Jaslyn didn't say anything. Then she took a deep breath. "The dragons weren't dead when we found them. Did anyone tell you that?"

Almiri shook her head.

"They were still alive. In torpor. And you know what? Just before he died my Silence woke up. Somehow, he woke out of his torpor. He was nearly gone, and he woke up, and he spoke to me. He spoke to me, Almiri. I heard his thoughts in my head."

"Dragons don't speak, Jaslyn."

"Yes, they do. When we don't poison them. He spoke as though he'd plucked the words out of my head. He told me a lot of things that I didn't know. About our dragons. He was beautiful before all this, but when he spoke . . . I would have saved him if I could. I would have done almost anything. *Even if there was something to take this poison away, I would not go back to what I was.* That's what he said."

"You've seen what one rogue dragon can do. Look around you. We have to do what we do, Jaslyn."

"You know, don't you? You know all about it. What we do to them. Why didn't anyone tell me?"

Almiri shuffled her feet. "You're not a queen, Jaslyn.

Only a princess. And there are secrets even queens do not hear."

"He asked me why I was so sad. 'Because you're dying,' I said to him. And he lifted his head with what little strength he had and looked at me. *And you will follow me,* he said. *One day. The difference between us is that I will die today and be reborn tomorrow. You will not.* That was all. An hour later he was gone. Do you suppose that's true? Are dragons reborn when they die? Or is that another secret too dire for a princess?"

"If it is, then it's too dire for this queen as well." Almiri chewed her lip. "I don't know, sister, but if they do come back, then one day there will be another Silence."

"That's what I thought at first, when he died. Perhaps, at that moment, another dragon was born in some eyrie." Jaslyn slowly got to her feet. "But will he remember me, Almiri? I don't think so." They walked away side by side, as sisters should.

"I don't want a war, Jaslyn. None of us wants that. But they can't do this."

Jaslyn wasn't listening. "If it's true, then the white will remember me. She will remember us all."

VERY SLOWLY, THEY WERE DYING. Nadira couldn't see it yet and Kemir didn't have the heart to tell her, but it was true. He'd kept them alive for five days now, since Snow had vanished beneath the frozen waters of the lake, but it couldn't last. The weather had been kind to them, but wind and rain were always fickle in the Worldspine. One day he'd run out of arrows, or his bowstring would break. Or one of them would get hurt or fall ill. He wasn't catching enough food, and they didn't have the clothes or the shelter to stay properly warm. A hundred things could go wrong, and sooner or later one of them would.

They had to move. He tried to break it to Nadira, to make her understand that Snow wasn't coming back, that their only chance was to leave and head for lower ground. A boat, he thought. Or at least a raft. Water always found the quickest way down the mountains.

She screamed in his face. Shrieked at him that Snow *was* coming back. He backed away. One more day, he promised himself. One more day and then he'd leave, with or without her. He could force her to come, he knew, but he'd let her choose. She could stay and die if she wanted. That's what Sollos would have done.

As that last day began to fade he made his weary way back to the lake, carrying with him what little food he'd been able to hunt or gather. The forests here were harsh and hostile, and yielded little. He was hungry. They were both hungry. They'd eat and they'd still be hungry.

He reached what passed for their camp at the edge of the lake, and the hairs on the back of his neck bristled. He couldn't see Nadira. The forest was silent except for the wind and the ever-present creaking and groaning of the glacier. He stared out across the lake. And suddenly he felt the fire and iron of her presence, a moment before the water began to churn.

Little One Kemir, I am hungry.

Look for

THE KING OF THE CRAGS

Book Two in the Memory of Flames Trilogy
Available now in hardcover for Roc.

ALSO AVAILABLE FROM

Stephen Deas

THE KING OF
THE CRAGS

THE MEMORY OF FLAMES, BOOK II

In *The Adamantine Palace*, Stephen Deas "restored [dragons] to all their scaly fire-breathing glory" (*Daily Telegraph*). Now, as the Realms teeter on the brink of war, the fate of humanity rests in the survival of one majestic white dragon.

Prince Jehal has had his way—now his lover Zafir sits atop the Realms with hundreds of dragons and their riders at her beck and call. But Jehal's plots are far from over, for he isn't content to sit back and watch Zafir command the earth and sky. He wants that glory for himself—no matter who he must sacrifice to get it. The one thing Jehal fears is that the white dragon still lives—and if that is so, then blood will flow, on all sides...

**Available wherever books are sold or at
penguin.com**

E. E. KNIGHT

DRAGON CHAMPION

Book One of the Age of Fire

After escaping those who killed his siblings, Young Auron, a rare, defenseless gray dragon, fears he might be the last of his breed. Armed with nothing but his claws and a boundless determination to survive, he sets off in search of his kind. But to find other dragons—or, at least, find out who's killing them off—Auron will have to search a world of mercenary elves, vicious humans, and dangers of all kinds. Finding allies in the strangest places—and himself along the way— Auron is on the trek of a lifetime.

Also Available
Dragon Avenger
Dragon Outcast
Dragon Strike
Dragon Rule
Dragon Fate

R0063

THE ULTIMATE IN
SCIENCE FICTION AND FANTASY!

From magical tales of distant worlds to stories of
technological advances beyond the grasp of man, Penguin has
everything you need to stretch your imagination to its limits.

penguin.com

ACE

Get the latest information on favorites like
William Gibson, Ilona Andrews, Jack Campbell,
Ursula K. Le Guin, Sharon Shinn, Charlaine Harris,
Patricia Briggs, and Marjorie M. Liu,
as well as updates on the best new authors.

ROC

Escape with Jim Butcher, Harry Turtledove, Anne Bishop,
S.M. Stirling, Simon R. Green, E.E. Knight, Kat Richardson,
Rachel Caine, and many others—plus news on the
latest and hottest in science fiction and fantasy.

DAW

Patrick Rothfuss, Seanan McGuire, Mercedes Lackey,
Kristen Britain, Tanya Huff, Tad Williams, C.J. Cherryh,
and many more—DAW has something to satisfy the
cravings of any science fiction and fantasy lover.
Also visit dawbooks.com.

*Get the best of science fiction and fantasy
at your fingertips!*